# Professional CSS

# Professional CSS

# Cascading Style Sheets for Web Design

## Second Edition

Christopher Schmitt
Todd Dominey
Cindy Li
Ethan Marcotte
Dunstan Orchard
Mark Trammell

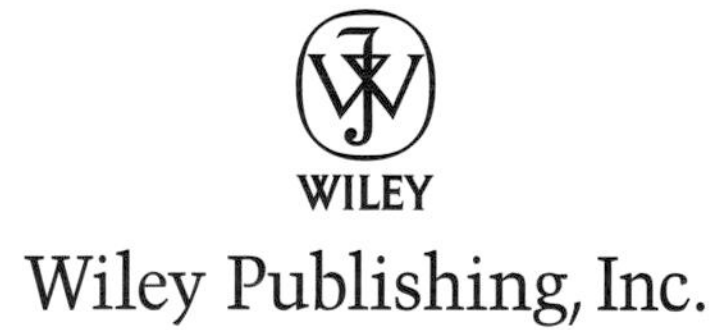


Wiley Publishing, Inc.

# Professional CSS: Cascading Style Sheets for Web Design, Second Edition

Published by
**Wiley Publishing, Inc.**
10475 Crosspoint Boulevard
Indianapolis, IN 46256
www.wiley.com



Published simultaneously in Canada

ISBN: 978-0-470-17708-2

Manufactured in the United States of America

10 9 8 7 6 5 4 3 2 1

Library of Congress Cataloging-in-Publication Data is available from the publisher.



For general information on our other products and services please contact our Customer Care Department within the United States at (800) 762-2974, outside the United States at (317) 572-3993 or fax (317) 572-4002.



Wiley also publishes its books in a variety of electronic formats. Some content that appears in print may not be available in electronic books.

# About the Authors

**Christopher Schmitt** is the creative director of Heatvision.com, Inc., a small new media publishing and design firm based in Cincinnati, Ohio.

An award-winning Web designer who has been working with the Web since 1993, Christopher interned for both David Siegel and Lynda Weinman in the mid '90s while he was an undergraduate at Florida State University working on a fine arts degree with an emphasis on graphic design. Afterward, he earned a master's degree in Communication for Interactive and New Communication Technologies while obtaining a graduate certificate in Project Management from FSU's College of Communication. In 2000, he led a team to victory in the Cool Site in a Day competition, where he and five other talented developers built a fully functional, well-designed Web site for a nonprofit organization in eight hours.

He is the author of *CSS Cookbook*, which has been translated into several languages and was named Best Web Design Book of 2006, and one of the first books that looked at CSS-enabled designs, *Designing CSS Web Pages* (New Riders). He is also the coauthor of *Photoshop in 10 Steps or Less* (Wiley) and *Dreamweaver Design Projects* (glasshaus) and contributed four chapters to *XML, HTML, and XHTML Magic* (New Riders). Christopher has also written for *New Architect Magazine*, *A List Apart*, *Digital Web*, and *Web Reference*.

At conferences and workshops such as Train the Trainer and SXSW, Christopher has given talks demonstrating the use and benefits of practical standards-based designs. He is the list moderator for Babble (`www.babblelist.com`), a mailing list community devoted to advanced Web design and development topics.

On his personal Web site, `www.christopherschmitt.com`, Christopher shows his true colors and most recent activities. He is 6'7" and doesn't play professional basketball but wouldn't mind a good game of chess.

**Todd Dominey** of Atlanta founded Dominey Design (`domineydesign.com`), an interactive Web development and design studio that has produced original work for Budweiser, *The Washington Post*, Google, Winterfresh Gum, and others. He is also a senior interactive designer at Turner Sports Interactive, designing and developing Web destinations for major PGA tournaments (including the PGA Championship and The Ryder Cup).

**Cindy Li** is a graphic/Web designer living in San Francisco. Born in Taiwan, she earned a bachelor of fine arts degree in Graphic Design from the University of Florida. Her own site can be found at `cindyli.com`.

**Ethan Marcotte** of Boston works at Airbag, `airbagindustries.com`, a Web design shop. A steering committee member of the Web Standards Project, he is a leading industry voice on standards-based Web design. Ethan is also the curator of `unstoppablerobotninja.com`, a popular Web log that is equal parts design, coding, and blather.

**Dunstan Orchard** of Dorset, UK, and San Francisco is senior UI engineer at Apple's online store. He is a member of The Web Standards Project, a silent developer for the popular Open Source blogging platform Wordpress, and an occasional contributor to his own site at `http://1976design.com`.

**Mark Trammell** of San Francsico directed Web presence at the University of Florida before joining Digg (`digg.com`) as its user experience architect.

# Credits

**Acquisitions Editor**
Jenny Watson

**Development Editors**
Maryann Steinhart
Sydney Jones

**Technical Editors**
Benjamin Schupak
Kynn Bartlett

**Contributor**
Robert Shimonski

**Production Editor**
Debra Banninger

**Copy Editor**
Foxxe Editorial Services

**Editorial Manager**
Mary Beth Wakefield

**Production Manager**
Tim Tate

**Vice President and Executive Group Publisher**
Richard Swadley

**Vice President and Executive Publisher**
Joseph B. Wikert

**Project Coordinator, Cover**
Lynsey Stanford

**Compositor**
Laurie Stewart, Happenstance Type-O-Rama

**Proofreader**
Publication Services, Inc.

**Indexer**
Jack Lewis

# Acknowledgments

I thank the Wiley team for helping me to shepherd the book you are now reading. Also, special thanks to Carole Jelen McClendon at Waterside for her guidance and support on this project.

With the support of my coauthors Cindy, Todd, Ethan, Dunstan, and Mark, the book became better and bolder than my original vision. I thank you all for your hard work.

Special thanks to my family and friends. Their continued support while I was busy managing and writing another book was immeasurable, even those who nodded politely while I ranted about Internet Explorer for Windows.

Also, if I don't give special thanks to my sister, Tiffany, specifically in one of my books, I believe she will disown me. So, might as well do it with this one. Here goes: "Hi, Tiffany! Thanks for being my best sister ever! Couldn't have done this without you!"

*— Christopher Schmitt*

First and foremost, my thanks to everyone at Turner Sports Interactive in Atlanta — notably Phil Sharpe, Michael Adamson, and John Buzzell — for giving me the opportunity to work not just on the PGA Championship but also The Ryder Cup and numerous other PGA online projects. My participation in this book would not have been possible without their trust and support.

Additional thanks to those in the Web development community who early in my professional career provided an immeasurable amount of inspiration and instruction: people like Jeffrey Zeldman, whose tireless promotion of Web standards and well-formed code changed my approach to Web design, and CSS gurus Douglas Bowman, Dan Cederholm, and Dave Shea not only for their continued exploration and experimentation with CSS but also for freely offering their knowledge and code for the rest of the world to benefit from.

Last, but certainly not least, I thank my wife, Heather, and our entire family for their support.

*— Todd Dominey*

To Veerle, Geert, and my family and friends for always believing in me and always watching out for me. XOXO

*— Cindy Li*

# Acknowledgments

There is always a short list of people who need to be thanked when one has written a book such as this, and mine is no different. While Jeffrey Zeldman, Doug Bowman, Dave Shea, and Dan Cederholm are all recognized CSS pioneers, I don't think they receive enough acknowledgment as the talented, inspiring writers they are. I'd like to do so now.

I'd like to thank my parents for talking me down from several ledges during this whole writing business. Richard Ohlsten did the same and deserves tons of high fives as a result. And while I've not spoken to her in some time, Marion Wells renewed my faith in my writing when I needed it most.

Were it not for Garret Keizer, I wouldn't have the words.

And finally, as I worked through this process, there was one person who was infinitely patient, supportive, and kind. She knows who she is, and there isn't ink enough to thank her properly.

— *Ethan Marcotte*

I acknowledge the help of Douglas Bowman, Mike Davidson, Molly Holzschlag, and my fellow authors.

— *Dunstan Orchard*

Many thanks to Al, Daniel, Taylor, Joe, Malik, Chuck, Gail, Steve, and Christian for their trust and sage advice. I am truly blessed to serve alongside people who love what they do and why they do it.

Christopher, Dunstan, Ethan, and Todd are among the Web's most talented developers and thoughtful commentators today. I feel privileged and humbled to have worked on this project with them.

— *Mark Trammell*

# Contents

# Introduction

Designers are traditionally creative types, tending to favor the right brain. Programmers examine the details of technology more clearly, preferring a left-brain mode of thinking.

So when faced with the challenge of designing for the Web, designers have what on the surface appears to be an oxymoron, a *design technology* named Cascading Style Sheets (CSS).

CSS is a Web markup standard set by the Worldwide Web Consortium (W3C) to define consistent styles in Web pages and to apply the template to multiple pages. By its nature, CSS is a technology that, for the most part, must be written out manually to create compelling work. The problem with that is that most designers have a hard time committing to writing lines of code to get their work done.

You don't find designers raving about writing PostScript by hand. But you do find designers letting Adobe Illustrator provide the visual authoring environment and hide the coding in the background to make PostScript files.

While WYSIWYG Web page editors are getting closer and closer to a complete visual authoring experience, those software applications aren't true professional CSS design tools in the way PostScript is for Illustrator.

There's another hurdle with CSS, though, that PostScript doesn't have: browsers. Browser vendors have slowly incorporated the technology into their browsers over time. While CSS support is getting better (especially with the leap in CSS support in Internet Explorer 7 for Windows), designers still run into problems when trying to shore up their designs in older or outdated browsers. That means diving into the guts of CSS and coding hacks and workarounds.

The bottom line is that this means more time spent writing and revising code, and less time spent working in WYSIWYG tools.

Even if you know the basics of CSS (the properties, the acceptable values, the selectors, and so on), putting the technology to effective use can be difficult to downright frustrating. CSS stymies the best of us — even those who actually understand the W3C specifications as opposed to those who can only skim them in awe.

In the right hands, however, CSS is *the* tool.

Once designers have mastered the basics of the technology, understand its purpose, and have obtained a certain amount of experience with the technology, almost any design idea sketched on a cocktail napkin or doctored in Adobe Photoshop becomes possible.

To help you get to that point, keep *Professional CSS* nearby.

*Professional CSS* is one of the few books on the market today that addresses designing standards-based CSS on large, multi-page, well-designed, real-world sites using CSS in an integrated fashion. Focusing on the best-practices aspect of Web development and using examples from real-world Web sites, this book uniquely offers applied, CSS-enabled solutions to design problems.

Christopher Schmitt
`ChristopherSchmitt.com`
Cincinnati, OH
January 2007

# Whom This Book Is For

Those designers who understand CSS at an intermediate to advanced level, but who are not clear on how to effectively develop CSS-enabled designs at a professional level, will benefit tremendously from the information in this book. In particular, the following readers will find this book most useful:

- **Intermediate to experienced HTML users new to CSS** — Any professional Web developer who has been exposed to CSS but needs a better understanding of how to put the pieces together to create professional-level Web sites.
- **Professional designers** — Professional Web developers learning CSS (without any knowledge of traditional, 1990s-era design practices) and wanting to understand the best practices for utilizing the technology.

# How This Book Is Structured

Each core chapter of this book focuses on one designer and a Web site that designer worked on. Each chapter provides easily digestible demonstrations of CSS tips and techniques used for the site. Additionally, designers provide greater insight into their process by talking about what they would have done differently.

Following is a brief overview of how this book is organized and which co-authors have contributed their insights:

- **Chapter 1, "Best Practices for XHTML and CSS"** — Ethan Marcotte, a steering committee member of the Web Standards Project and a recognized leader of the standards-based Web design movement, shares some insights on using Extended HTML (XHTML) with CSS.
- **Chapter 2, "Google's Blogger.com: Rollovers and Design Touches"** — Dunstan Orchard, also a member of the Web Standards Project, delves into the behind-the-scenes development of a new look and feel for blogger.com (a Google Web log site). Orchard's interview with one of the principals in the project, Douglas Bowman (an influential designer whose highly publicized and hugely successful redesigns of several Web sites have pushed him to the forefront of standards-compliant Web design), provides some extremely valuable insight.
- **Chapter 3, "The Classic U.S. PGA Championship Web Site"** — As a senior interactive designer at Turner Sports Interactive, Todd Dominey has been designing and developing Web destinations

for major Professional Golf Association (PGA) tournaments, including the PGA Championship and The Ryder Cup. In this chapter, Dominey provides a first-hand perspective on the ins and outs of designing a site relied upon by millions of sports fans all over the world. Key issues addressed in this chapter include drop shadows, drop-down menus, and embedding Flash content into a Web site.

- **Chapter 4, "The University of Florida's UFL.edu"** — Mark Trammell, who is in charge of directing the Web presence at one of the country's leading universities, discusses how the University of Florida developed a Web site to benefit both students and faculty. Key issues addressed in this chapter include tackling browser compatibility issues as well as developing functional navigational structures.
- **Chapter 5, "Stuff and Nonsense: Strategies for CSS Switching"** — In addition to an interview with Andy Clarke (creative director for Stuff and Nonsense), Ethan Marcotte explores how to improve Web site accessibility for all users to further ensure universal access. In this chapter, Marcotte delves into CSS switching and ways to overcome pesky browser compatibility problems. The innovations displayed at the Stuff and Nonsense site provide excellent examples of these techniques.
- **Chapter 6, "Adventures of CindyLi.com: Blog Modifications"** — Cindy Li talks about how she customized her own Web site through her illustrations and CSS coding.
- **Chapter 7, "AIGA Cincinnati: HTML Email Templates"** — Christopher Schmitt runs through the process of creating HTML email templates and, while he steps back in time to create a basic HTML table layout, he shows how CSS plays a key role.
- **Chapter 8, "Professional CSS Book Site: Using Transparent PNGs"** — Christopher Schmitt discusses how he used PNGs to create the book Web site while getting around Internet Explorer 6's lack of native support for PNGs' alpha-transparency.
- **Chapter 9, "Building CSS Layouts"** — Christopher Schmitt discusses the importance of grids and layouts in design, and Ethan Marcotte explores how to create a stable framework for a three-column layout.

Additionally, the appendices in this book provide handy reference material for HTML 4.01 elements, rules for HTML-to-XHTML conversions, properties of CSS 2.1, and even a troubleshooting guide to help with common problems.

# Conventions

A number of conventions are used throughout the book to help you get the most from the text and keep track of what's happening.

> **Boxes like this one hold important, not-to-be forgotten information that is directly relevant to the surrounding text.**

*Tips, hints, tricks, and asides to the current discussion are offset and placed in italics like this.*

As for styles in the text:

- New terms and important words are *highlighted* when introduced.
- Keyboard strokes look like this: Ctrl+A.
- File names, URLs, and code within the text looks like this: `persistence.properties`.

## Source Code

As you work through the examples in this book, you may choose either to type in all the code manually or to use the source code files that accompany the book. All of the source code used in this book is available for download at `www.wrox.com`. Once at the site, simply locate the book's title (either by using the Search box or by using one of the title lists), and click the Download Code link on the book's detail page to obtain all the source code for the book.

*Because many books have similar titles, you may find it easiest to search by ISBN; this book's ISBN is 978-0-470-17708-2.*

Once you have downloaded the code, just decompress it with your favorite compression tool. Alternatively, you can go to the main Wrox code download page at `www.wrox.com/dynamic/books/download.aspx` to see the code available for this book and all other Wrox books.

## Errata

Every effort is made to ensure that there are no errors in the text or in the code. However, no one is perfect, and mistakes do occur. If you find an error such as a spelling mistake or faulty piece of code in one of our books, Wrox would be grateful for your feedback. By sending in errata, you may save another reader hours of frustration, and at the same time you will be helping us provide even higher-quality information.

To find the errata page for this book, go to `www.wrox.com` and locate the title using the Search box or one of the title lists. Then, on the book details page, click the Book Errata link. On this page, you can view all errata that has been submitted for this book and posted by Wrox editors. A complete book list, including links to each book's errata, is also available at `www.wrox.com/misc-pages/booklist.shtml`.

If you don't spot "your" error on the Book Errata page, go to `www.wrox.com/contact/techsupport.shtml` and complete the form there to send us the error you have found. We'll check the information and, if appropriate, post a message to the book's errata page and fix the problem in subsequent editions of the book.

## p2p.wrox.com

For author and peer discussion, join the P2P forums at `p2p.wrox.com`. The forums are a Web-based system for you to post messages relating to Wrox books and related technologies and interact with other readers and technology users. The forums offer a subscription feature to email you topics of interest of your choosing when new posts are made to the forums. Wrox authors, editors, other industry experts, and your fellow readers are present on these forums.

At `http://p2p.wrox.com` you will find a number of different forums that will help you not only as you read this book but also as you develop your own applications. To join the forums, just follow these steps:

1. Go to `p2p.wrox.com` and click the Register link.
2. Read the terms of use, and then click Agree.
3. Complete the required information to join as well as any optional information you wish to provide, and then click Submit.
4. You will receive an email with information describing how to verify your account and complete the joining process.

*You can read messages in the forums without joining P2P, but to post your own messages, you must join.*

Once you join, you can post new messages and respond to messages other users post. You can read messages at any time on the Web. If you would like to have new messages from a particular forum emailed to you, click the "Subscribe to this Forum" icon by the forum name in the forum listing.

For more information about how to use the Wrox P2P, be sure to read the P2P FAQs for answers to questions about how the forum software works as well as many common questions specific to P2P and Wrox books. To read the FAQs, click the FAQ link on any P2P page.

# 1

# Best Practices for XHTML and CSS

*Great works are performed, not by strength, but by perseverance.*
*— Samuel Johnson*

In its early years, the Web wasn't exactly the most attractive thing on the planet. Created by and for nuclear physicists, hypertext was simply a means by which content-heavy documents could be shared over an open, distributed network. Needless to say, high-caliber design wasn't a top priority for the Web's earliest authors. In fact, HTML's much-used (and, as will be discussed, oft-abused) `table` element was created with one purpose in mind: the display of tabular data.

By the heyday of late-1990s' Web design, the "L" in HTML was often ignored. Many professionals felt that the code used to build Web pages wasn't a language per se and, thus, wasn't subject to the rules and restrictions of a real programming language. Besides, clients weren't paying for "compliant," "accessible," or "future-proof" code. In fact, many sites were produced with the requirement that they be "backward compatible." That was a misnomer if ever there was one because it simply required a consistent display in version 4.0 browsers or higher.

Browsers of that time were temperamental, to say the least. With poor support for the specifications written by the World Wide Web Consortium (W3C) — `www.w3.org` — you could count on a page rendering differently in Browser A than in Browser B. So, while many programmers were dimly aware of the "standards" the W3C produced, the browsers they had to support were less than tolerant of standards-compliant markup. In this sense, the divide between the science and the reality of the Web was far too great. Programmers deliberately invalidated HTML with proprietary, browser-specific markup to ensure that things "looked good" in target browsers. And for a time, all was good. Programmers had narrow specifications, they had deadlines, they probably weren't paid by the hour, and as you can see, they had excuses.

Of course, designers learned early on that by zeroing out a table's cellpadding, spacing, and border, they could create complex grid-based layouts and bring a new level of aesthetic appeal to their sites. Granted, given browsers' poor support for Cascading Style Sheets (CSS) in those days, they had no alternative but to weigh pages down with presentational cruft. The result was a Web that is bogged down by the weight of its own markup, saturated with kilobyte-heavy pages that are hard to maintain, costly to redesign, and unkind to users' bandwidth.

Thankfully, there is a way out. Extensible Hypertext Markup Language (XHTML) and CSS are two standard technologies that will enable you to clear away the clutter in your pages, facilitating the construction of pages that are significantly lighter, more accessible, and easier to maintain. Of course, these two tools are only as effective as your ability to wield them. This chapter examines the need for XHTML and CSS and introduces some practical strategies for applying them intelligently to your design.

# Shoehorning Structure and Presentation Together

Now, take a deep breath, and be honest with yourself: Does this HTML snippet look familiar?

```
<body marginwidth="0" marginheight="0" leftmargin="0" topmargin="0">
```

In the heyday of early Web design, this was *the* way to place your pages' content flush against the browser window. Without these four attributes, the designs would be surrounded by a margin of 10 or so pixels — and yes, some were sufficiently finicky that something like that would keep them up at night.

This approach highlights the extent to which an emphasis upon "looking right" pervaded early Web design. Despite HTML's origins as a well-structured language, pages evolved into a kind of "tag soup" — a not-so-tasty goulash of structural and presentational markup. Because contemporary browsers had nonexistent or imperfect support for cascading style sheets, programmers relied on transparent spacer graphics, `font` elements, and deeply nested tables to control sites' designs. The attribute-heavy `body` element perfectly illustrates this mismatch of structure and style in the markup. While the `body` element itself performs an important structural purpose (it contains a Web page's content), the small army of attributes crammed into its opening tag is there only to make that structure *look* a certain way.

Granted, the little `body` element might not seem all that egregious — is it really worth wringing your hands over one little line of markup? For a concrete example of the problems with presentation-rich markup, take a look at the Harvard University home page (`www.harvard.edu`). The site's design (see Figure 1-1) admirably reflects the university's well-established brand: a conservative, earth-toned color palette accentuates the distinctive Harvard crimson, while the centered two-column layout emphasizes content over flash, delivery over glitz. By all accounts, it's a successful site design — and one that garners more than a little traffic each day.

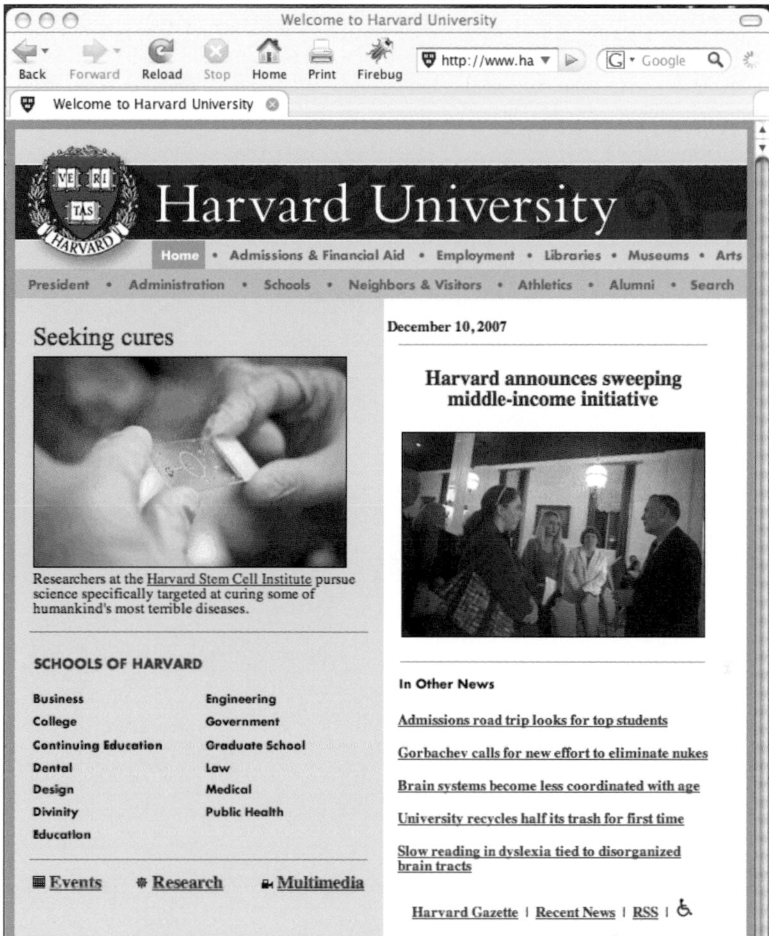


**Figure 1-1: The Harvard University home page.**

Clearly, this is an effective, straightforward design. But if you "turn on" borders for all table elements in the HTML, the site reveals something much less straightforward under the hood (see Figure 1-2).

*There are a number of browser utilities that you can install to quickly affect the display of a page, as has been done here. For Mozilla browsers, the Web Developer Toolbar (*`http://chrispederick.com/work/firefox/webdeveloper`*) is one such tool, and an excellent one at that. It's an invaluable part of the CSS toolkit, allowing designers to turn on borders of different page elements, quickly edit a page's CSS, and easily access various online code validators. For Web developers on the Mac platform, take a look at plug-ins and add-ons written up at* `http://hicksdesign.co.uk/journal/web-development-with-safari`.

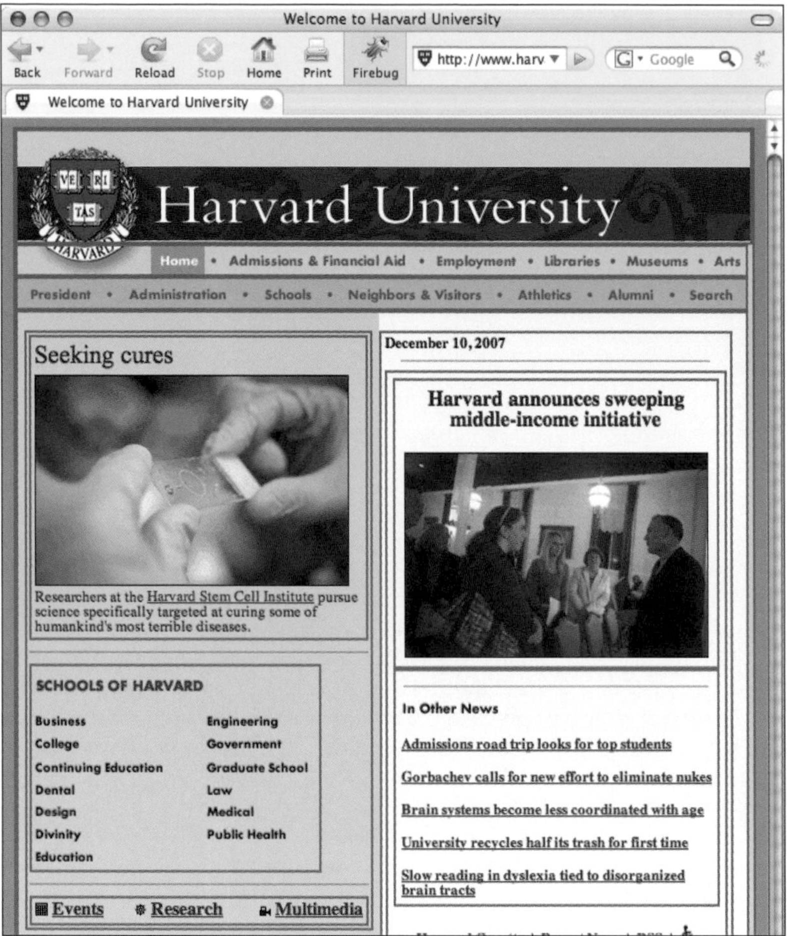


**Figure 1-2:** The Harvard home page again, with table borders activated.

Quite a change, isn't it? There's a lot of markup vested in such a simple layout: tables are pristinely nested five levels deep, logo graphics are split with pixel precision into multiple files and strewn across multiple table rows. Even looking at the code for the primary navigation bar is a bit dizzying:

```
<table bgcolor="#cdd397" border="0" cellpadding="0" cellspacing="0" width="650">
<tbody><tr>
<td valign="top"><img src="images/shield3.gif" alt="Harvard University shield"
border="0" height="25" width="117"></td>
<td valign="top"><a href="http://www.harvard.edu/"><img src="images/home2.gif"
alt="Home" name="nav01" border="0" height="25" width="47"></a></td>
```

```
<td><img src="images/nav_bullet.gif" border="0" height="25" width="14"></td>
<td><a href="http://www.harvard.edu/admissions/" onmouseover="imgOn('nav02')" ;=""
onmouseout="navOff('nav02')"><img src="images/admissions.gif" alt="Admissions"
name="nav02" border="0" height="25" width="166"></a></td>
<td><img src="images/nav_bullet.gif" border="0" height="25" width="14"></td>
<td><a href="http://atwork.harvard.edu/" onmouseover="imgOn('nav03')" ;=""
onmouseout="navOff('nav03')"><img src="images/employment.gif" alt="Employment"
name="nav03" border="0" height="25" width="80"></a></td>
<td><img src="images/nav_bullet.gif" border="0" height="25" width="14"></td>
<td><a href="http://lib.harvard.edu/" onmouseover="imgOn('nav04')" ;=""
onmouseout="navOff('nav04')"><img src="images/libraries.gif" alt="Libraries"
name="nav04" border="0" height="25" width="59"></a></td>
<td><img src="images/nav_bullet.gif" border="0" height="25" width="14"></td>
<td><a href="http://www.harvard.edu/museums/" onmouseover="imgOn('nav05')" ;=""
onmouseout="navOff('nav05')"><img src="images/museums.gif" alt="Museums"
name="nav05" border="0" height="25" width="64"></a></td>
<td><img src="images/nav_bullet.gif" border="0" height="25" width="14"></td>
<td><a href="http://www.harvard.edu/arts/" onmouseover="imgOn('nav06')" ;=""
onmouseout="navOff('nav06')"><img src="images/arts.gif" alt="Arts" name="nav06"
border="0" height="25" width="33"></a></td>
</tr>
</tbody></table>
```

The table begins by setting the background color for the first navigation row (`#cdd397`, a light, desaturated green) and by zeroing out the table's border, as well as the padding within and spacing between each of its cells. Once that's completed, the site's author is left with an invisible grid, upon which graphics can be placed with pixel-perfect precision. Every other table cell contains `nav_bullet.gif`, the bullet graphic that abuts each navigation item. The remaining cells contain the navigation graphics themselves, each of which is surrounded by an anchor upon which `onmouseover` and `onmouseout` attributes are placed to control the graphics' rollover effects.

Remember, this is simply the markup for one of the navigation bars. The rest of the page follows this same layout model: Zero out a table's default attributes; place content, graphics, and additional markup therein; repeat as needed. After a while, reading through this page begins to feel something like running down the rabbit hole. Just when you think you've reached the end of one table, another presents itself, and you're reminded how much effort goes into seeking that Holy Grail of "looking right" — a truly consistent, bulletproof display across all target browsers.

Of course, that Holy Grail is a bit of a tin cup. Until recently, designers have been concerned solely with the visual display of sites on graphical desktop browsers. There are other devices and other users whose needs should be taken into account. If you view the Harvard University home page in an environment that can't render the carefully arrayed graphics, what happens then?

A screenshot of a text-only browser's view of the site holds the answer (see Figure 1-3). Without the aid of color or headings, it's certainly more difficult to navigate through this environment than in the context of the site's design. If it's difficult for sighted users, consider the problems that visually impaired users must encounter.

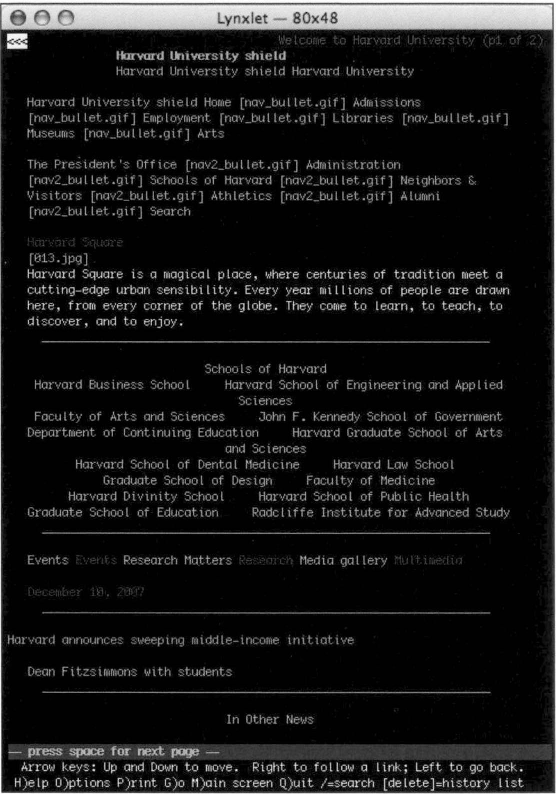


**Figure 1-3: View of** `www.harvard.edu` **in Lynx, a text-only browser.**

For example, a number of the graphics on the page are missing `alt` attributes, an important accessibility requirement as well as needed for valid XHTML. Creating valid markup allows CSS to more easily be applied to a Web document.

Also, if a blind user were using a screen reader to read the Web pages' content aloud, the filenames of these `alt`-deprived graphics would be read out loud. To that user, the navigation menu might sound like "link Home nav underscore bullet dot gif link Admissions nav underscore bullet dot gif link Employment nav underscore bullet dot gif link Libraries," and so forth.

First and foremost, this is not an indictment of the Harvard home page; in years past, hundreds of pages have been built with these exact same tactics. Rather, it is a reminder of the reality of the Web that, until only recently, *all* were forced to work in. With such shoddy support for CSS, `table`-based layouts were a matter of course. Designers were devoted to ensuring an excellent display in all graphic browsers, at the expense of bandwidth-heavy markup and inaccessible site designs. Of course, this prompts the question: What do you do about it?

By now, if you're thinking that there must be a better way, you're right — there most certainly is. Today's browsers have become much more intelligent, and you should, too. With greater support for cascading style sheets across the board, you no longer have to rely upon bandwidth-hogging markup to realize a site's design. You can instead focus on abstracting presentational cruft out of your markup and move it into your cascading style sheets.

The promise of separating structure from style is at the heart of standards-based Web design, and it makes for one of the most compelling arguments for creating page layouts with CSS. By drawing a line in the sand between Web pages' content and their presentation, those pages will not only be drastically lighter but far easier to maintain as well.

# Learning to Love Your Markup

Let's revisit that lonely little `body` element one more time:

```
<body marginwidth="0" marginheight="0" leftmargin="0" topmargin="0">
```

It is worth remembering that none of these attributes was in any HTML specifications (`www.w3.org/MarkUp`). `marginwidth` and `marginheight` were Netscape-only attributes and would work only in that browser. On the other hand, while the `leftmargin` and `topmargin` attributes had the same margin-trimming effect, they would work only in Internet Explorer. Valid or not, that didn't keep programmers from placing this proprietary markup on their sites. They were dealing with browsers offering nonstandard (and often contradictory) implementations of HTML, and they did so with smiles on their faces — as well as with every snippet of invalid, proprietary code in the site builder's arsenal.

And, because they served up the same invalid, proprietary HTML to *all* browsers that visited their pages, this one line of HTML demonstrates just how tolerant browsers were (and continue to be) of flawed markup. And that's by design. If you neglect to include a closing tag (such as `</tr>` or `</div>`) or introduce a proprietary element into the markup to work around a layout bug (as in the preceding `body` element), your Web browser has a recovery strategy in place. It has had to "repair" your markup while parsing it, rendering the page despite any imperfect code found therein.

But the real headaches arise because each browser has its own internal logic for interpreting invalid code, which invariably leads to unpredictable results when doing cross-browser testing. One browser might recover gracefully from a missing angle bracket, while another might break the entire layout because of it. These inconsistent rendering strategies make one thing certain: Invalid code means spending more time coding and testing to ensure that a site displays correctly across all target browsers. Rather than focusing on improving a site's design and content, designers are forced to spend far too much time nursing broken markup. It's true. The early reliance on malformed, proprietary, or otherwise invalid markup allowed designs to be consistently displayed on old-school browsers. But in availing themselves of markup hacks, designers created a dependency in every page of a site. They placed code in documents that targets a specific browser's idiosyncrasies. When today's browsers finally slip over the upgrade horizon and the next generation appears, each of those hacks is a potential landmine. Will newer browsers be as tolerant of the code, bloated as it is with such nonstandard markup? Or will the next version of Internet Explorer ship with a bug that refuses to render a page when it encounters the `marginheight` attribute on a `body` element?

Yes, this is the kind of stuff you worry about. But the simple truth is that invalid markup creates a long-term liability that you can't afford to ignore. Rather than fretting about how markup hacks will perform (or won't) in another year or eight, perhaps it's finally time to pay attention to the "L" in HTML.

## *XHTML: The New Hotness*

XHTML is described by the W3C as "bring[ing] the rigor of XML to Web pages" (`www.w3.org/MarkUp/#xhtml1`). In short, XHTML was created so that site owners would have a cleaner upgrade path between HTML and a stricter document syntax, Extensible Markup Language (XML). Compare this snippet of HTML to its XHTML equivalent:

```
<!DOCTYPE HTML PUBLIC "-//W3C//DTD HTML 4.01//EN"
"http://www.w3.org/TR/html4/strict.dtd">
<html>
 <head>
  <title>My sample page</title>
  <meta http-equiv="Content-Type" content="text/html; charset=utf-8">
 </head>
 <body>
 <ul>
  <li>Here's a sample list item,
  <li>And yet another.
 </ul>
 <p>I like big blocks,<br>and I cannot lie.
 <p>You other coders can't deny.
 </body>
</html>
```

And now, look at the XHTML:

```
<!DOCTYPE html PUBLIC "-//W3C//DTD XHTML 1.0 Transitional//EN"
"http://www.w3.org/TR/xhtml1/DTD/xhtml1-transitional.dtd">
<html xmlns="http://www.w3.org/1999/xhtml">
 <head>
  <title>My sample page</title>
  <meta http-equiv="Content-Type" content="text/html; charset=utf-8" />
 </head>
 <body>
  <ul>
   <li>Here's a sample list item,</li>
   <li>And yet another.</li>
  </ul>
  <p>I like big blocks,<br />and I cannot lie.</p>
  <p>You other coders can't deny.</p>
 </body>
</html>
```

Don't feel bad if you didn't spot any changes — there are more similarities here than differences. And, in fact, both of these pages render the same in any browser. Your end users won't be able to tell the difference between the two languages. While the similarities in syntax do outweigh the differences between XHTML and its predecessor, those few differences are quite significant.

## Beginning with the DOCTYPE Declaration

The first item in the two sample pages is a `DOCTYPE` (geek-speak for "document type") declaration. Point your browser to the URL in the `DOCTYPE` element like this one:

```
http://www.w3.org/TR/xhtml1/DTD/xhtml1-transitional.dtd
```

Depending on your browser and how your computer handles `.dtd` file extensions, you might be prompted to download the file or it might appear in your browser window as plain text. Once you view the file either in the browser or in a text editor, you'll be presented with a long, complex text document known as the Document Type Definition, or DTD. The DTD outlines the rules of the language to which the ensuing markup is supposed to conform. Declaring this DTD at the beginning of your markup signals what language is used on the page to "user agents," a blanket term for *any* device or program that can access your page. It's not just about graphical desktop browsers anymore. Printers, cellular telephones, and screen readers are all examples of user agents, and each benefits from knowing what markup language they will encounter on the rest of the page.

Online validation tools are another example of user agents, and they (above all others) benefit from your opening `DOCTYPE` declaration. This allows them to assess how effectively your code conforms to the DTD — in effect, whether it's valid or not.

## Keeping Your Markup Well Formed

"Well formed" is essentially a new name for an old rule. It simply means that your elements must be nested properly. Consider this example:

```
<p>Here's <em>my <strong>opening</em></strong> paragraph!</p>
  <title>My sample page</title>
```

Here, the `em` is opened first, and the `strong` opened second. However, markup follows a "first opened, last closed" rule. Because the `em` is opened before the `strong`, it must be closed *after* the `strong`'s final tag. If you revise the markup so that it's well formed, the elements' nesting order makes a bit more sense:

```
<p>Here's <em>my <strong>opening</strong></em> paragraph!</p>
  <title>My sample page</title>
```

As you've no doubt noticed, this concept of proper nesting is an old one. While it's never been valid to write incorrectly nested markup, it is still quite common in many pages built today. As a result, browsers have become far too tolerant of the tag soup you feed them. Any given browser will have a different strategy in place for how to "fix" this incorrectly nested markup, which can often yield differing results once the page is rendered. XHTML is a language that explicitly demands structural soundness. By requiring your markup to be well formed, this stricter document syntax enables you to combat structural inconsistencies in your own code.

Of course, it's important to remember that "well formed" does not equal "valid." Consider this example:

```
<a id="content">
 <em>
  <div class="item">
   <p>I'm not exactly sure what this means.</p>
   <p>...but at least it's well-formed.</p>
```

```
      </div>
    </em>
  </a>
```

This code is immaculately nested, but it's far from valid. HTML differentiates between *block-level elements* (div, p, table, and the like) and *inline elements* (such as a, em, strong). Inline elements can never contain the block-level elements, making the previous markup invalid. While browsers will be able to read this code correctly, it's almost certain to cause display errors when the CSS is applied. Depending on the browser, styles applied to the anchor element may or may not cascade down to the text contained in the div. It certainly would be an unpleasant surprise if all of your content suddenly gained the link's signature underline, or visibly changed when you hovered over it with your mouse.

This is yet another example of the importance of validation. By beginning your document with a DOCTYPE declaration and validating frequently, you can proactively squash layout bugs before they arise. This translates into less debugging time for you, which in turn translates into more time you can spend focusing on your site's design.

## Closing Every Element

When you opened an element in HTML, you weren't always required to supply the corresponding closing element. In fact, the HTML 4.01 specification differentiates between elements whose ending elements are optional (such as the paragraph element: www.w3.org/TR/REC-html40/struct/text.html#h-9.3.1), required (phrase elements such as em or strong: www.w3.org/TR/REC-html40/struct/text.html#h-9.2.1), and, in some cases, outright forbidden (the good ol' br: www.w3.org/TR/REC-html40/struct/text.html#h-9.3.2).

Thankfully, this ambiguity has been removed from XHTML, largely because of XHTML's insistence that your markup be well formed. If you open an element, a closing element is required — simple as that. The following is valid markup in HTML 4:

```
<ul>
  <li>Here's a sample list item,
  <li>And yet another.
</ul>
<p>I like big blocks,<br>and I cannot lie.
<p>You other coders can't deny.
```

However, the XHTML looks slightly different (the changes are shown here in bold):

```
<ul>
  <li>Here's a sample list item,</li>
  <li>And yet another.</li>
</ul>
<p>I like big blocks,<br />and I cannot lie.</p>
<p>You other coders can't deny.</p>
```

Because you're working in XHTML, you don't have the option of leaving your list items (<li></li>) and paragraphs (<p>) open. Before starting a new element, you need to close each with </li> and </p>, respectively. However, the sharp-eyed readers may be wondering why a forward slash (/) is added to br.

No, no one has gone slash-happy. Elements such as br, img, meta, and hr are considered "empty" elements because they don't contain any text content — which isn't the case for p, li, td, and, in fact, most elements in the HTML specification. But while empty elements traditionally have *not* had a closing element, XHTML doesn't play any favorites when it comes to keeping your document well formed. So, by ending an empty element with />, you can effectively close it. Structural consistency is a strong requirement for your new markup, and XHTML certainly delivers that consistency.

> *See the space between <br and /> in the previous example? This space ensures that legacy browsers (those developed before the XHTML spec) can still access your content.*

### Setting Elements and Attributes to Lowercase

The HTML specification never mandated a particular letter case for your pages' markup elements. As a result, developers have become accustomed to writing elements and their attributes in any case at all:

```
<P CLASS=Warning>Alert!</P>
  <title>My sample page</title>
```

In XHTML, all elements and their attributes must be written in lowercase. This is because XML is quite case-sensitive. For example, <body>, <Body>, and <BODY> would be considered three different elements. Because of this, the authors of the XHTML specification standardized on lowercase:

```
<p class="Warning">Alert!</p>
  <title>My sample page</title>
```

You may notice that the value of Warning has been kept intact for the `class` attribute. This is perfectly acceptable in XHTML because attribute values may be in mixed case (for example, pointing the `href` of a link to a case-sensitive server). However, they *must* be quoted.

### Requiring a Value for Every Attribute

Additionally, there were attributes in HTML that previously didn't require a value:

```
<input type="checkbox" checked>
<dl compact>
```

Both `checked` and `compact` are examples of "minimized" attributes. Because they didn't require a value; it was simply enough to declare the attribute and then carry on. However, XHTML mandates that a value must be supplied for all attributes which are used. For "minimized" attributes, they can be easily expanded like this:

```
<input type="checkbox" checked="checked">
<dl compact="compact">
  <title>My sample page</title>
```

This is a small distinction but one that's integral to ensuring that your code remains valid.

## Abstracting Style from Structure

Many standards advocates tout "the separation of style from structure" as the primary benefit of adopting CSS in your site's design — and I agree, with a slight qualification. As you'll see in the coming pages, there never is a true divorce between your markup and your style sheets. Change the structure of the former, and dozens of rules in the latter might become obsolete.

Because your markup and your CSS are quite interrelated, you can think of style as *abstracted from* structure. Your markup primarily exists to describe your content, that's true — however, it will always contain some level of presentational information. The degree, however, is entirely up to you. If you so choose, you could easily offload the presentational work onto the XHTML — replete with `font` elements, `tables`, and spacer GIFs.

On the other hand, our style sheet can contain rules that determine all aspects of our pages' design: colors, typography, images, and even layout. And if these rules reside in an external style sheet file to which your site's pages link, you can control the visual display of *hundreds or thousands* of HTML documents on your site — not only an appealing prospect for day-to-day site updates but also one that will pay off in spades during that next sitewide redesign initiative. Simply by editing a few dozen lines in a centralized style sheet, you can gain unprecedented control over your markup's presentation.

This should make you and your marketing department very happy.

Because your CSS can reside in that separate file, your users could ostensibly cache your entire site's user interface after they visit the first page therein. This is quite a departure from the tag soup days of Web design, where users would be forced to redownload bloated markup on each page of a site: nested `<table>` elements, spacer GIFs, `<font>` elements, `bgcolor` declarations, and the like for every single Web page to keep the same design style. Now, they simply digest your site's look-and-feel once, and then browse quickly through lightweight markup on the rest of your pages.

This should make your users very happy.

And finally, the most obvious benefit is how very simple your markup has become. This will further positively impact your users' bandwidth, allowing them to download your pages even more quickly. And, of course, this lighter markup will benefit your site in any search engine optimization initiatives you might undertake. If you think it's easy for *you* to sift through five lines of an unordered list, just think of how much more search engine robots will love indexing the content in your now-lightweight markup.

This should — oh, you get the point. Happy yet?

## *Avoiding Divitis and Classitis*

When abandoning tables for more lightweight markup, it's not uncommon for beginning developers to rely heavily on `class` attributes to replace their beloved `font` elements. So, you might have dealt with a navigation bar table that looked like this:

```
<!-- outer table -->
<table bgcolor="#000000" border="0" cellspacing="0" cellpadding="0">
<tbody>
<tr>
<td>
<!-- inner table -->
<table border="0" cellspacing="1" cellpadding="3">
<tbody>
<tr>
<td bgcolor="#DDDDDD"><font face="Verdana, Geneva, Helvetica, sans-serif"
size="2"><a href="home.html">Home</a></font></td>
<td bgcolor="#DDDDDD"><font face="Verdana, Geneva, Helvetica, sans-serif"
size="2"><a href="about.html">About Us</a></font></td>
```

```
<td bgcolor="#DDDDDD"><font face="Verdana, Geneva, Helvetica, sans-serif"
size="2"><a href="products.html">Our Products</a></font></td>
</tr>
</tbody>
</table>
<!-- END inner table -->
</td>
</tr>
</tbody>
</table>
<!-- END outer table -->
```

This version isn't much better:

```
<!-- outer table -->
<table class="bg-black" border="0" cellspacing="0" cellpadding="0">
<tbody>
<tr>
<td>
<!-- inner table -->
<table border="0" cellspacing="1" cellpadding="3">
<tbody>
<tr>
<td class="bg-gray"><a href="home.html" class="innerlink">Home</a></td>
<td class="bg-gray"><a href="about.html" class="innerlink">About Us</a></td>
<td class="bg-gray"><a href="products.html" class="innerlink">Our Products</a></td>
</tr>
</tbody>
</table>
<!-- END inner table -->
</td>
</tr>
</tbody>
</table>
<!-- END outer table -->
```

This is known as *classitis,* a term coined by designer Jeffrey Zeldman (`www.zeldman.com`) to describe markup bloat from overuse of the `class` attribute. The monkey on your back has been exchanged for another. Rather than spelling out presentational goals explicitly in the markup, this example uses the `class` attribute to achieve the same end. All that's been changed is that the values of the `bgcolor` attributes and `font` elements have been moved to an external style sheet — a fine start, but the markup is still unnecessarily heavy.

Even worse, it's far too easy to succumb to *divitis,* taking otherwise sensible markup and turning it into soup loaded with `div` elements:

```
<div id="outer-table">
 <div id="inner-table">
  <div class="innerlink"><span class="link"><a href="home.html"
class="innerlink">Home</a></span></div>
  <div class="innerlink"><span class="link"><a href="about.html"
class="innerlink">About Us</a></span></div>
```

```
    <div class="innerlink"><span class="link"><a href="products.html"
  class="innerlink">Our Products</a></span></div>
   </div>
  </div>
```

If that made any sense to you, perhaps you'd be kind enough to call us up and explain it to us. There's no obvious attempt here to write well-structured markup. While `div` and `span` are excellent markup tools, an overreliance upon them can lead to code bloat and hard-to-read markup. And not just hard for *you* to read but for your users as well. Remember the earlier text-only screenshot (refer to Figure 1-3)? If someone has style sheets turned off, using generic markup will make it difficult for those in a nongraphical environment to understand the context of your content.

## Moving toward Well-Meaning Markup

Alternatively, you can use markup elements as they were intended — using `div`s and `span`s to fill in the gaps where no other elements are available. In this section, we discuss some strategies for stripping your pages' markup to a well-structured, well-*meaning* minimum, getting it (and you) ready for the CSS tips and strategies contained throughout the remainder of this book.

In the following sections, you revisit some of the HTML used in the Harvard Web site (refer to Figure 1-1). You'll apply some more well-structured thinking to the old-school markup and see if you can produce something a bit sleeker.

## Familiarizing Yourself with Other Markup Elements

Here, you're in the process of *describing* content, not designing it. Therefore, the more well versed you are in the XHTML specification, the more adept you'll be at accurately depicting your site's structure with it.

### Better Know Headers

Take a look at the markup for one of the news items in the right column:

```
<b>'Illuminating the beauty of life'</b>
<br>Yannatos starts 41st year conducting Harvard-Radcliffe Orchestra
<a href="http://www.news.harvard.edu/gazette/"><font size="-
1"><b>More</b></font></a><font size="-1"><br></font>
</td>
<td width="120">
<a href="http://www.news.harvard.edu/gazetta/"><img src="images/041029a.jpg:
alt="James Yannatos" border="0" height="120" width="120"></a><br><br>
```

In this news item, the content leads with a header displaying the title of the featured story. However, you wouldn't know it was a header from the markup:

```
<b>'Illuminating the beauty of life'</b>
```

Rather than using markup to describe how the element should look to sighted users on desktop browsers, why not use a header element?

```
<h4>'Illuminating the beauty of life'</h4>
```

This code uses an h4, which would be appropriate if there were three levels of headers above this one in the document's hierarchy. Now, any user agent reading this page will recognize the text as a header and render it in the most effective way it can.

*When building your well-meaning markup, it's helpful to think of your document as conforming to a kind of outline — the most important header sits at the top in an* h1*, beneath it are a number of* h2s*, beneath each of which is an* h3 *or two, and so on down to* h6*. How you envision your document's outline is entirely up to you. Settle on a model that makes sense to you, and keep it consistent throughout your site's markup.*

## Better Know Paragraphs

After the news story's headline, a paragraph-long excerpt follows it — but, again, the markup belies the content's intent:

```
<br>Yannatos starts 41st year conducting Harvard-Radcliffe Orchestra
<a href="http://www.news.harvard.edu/gazette/"><font size="-
1"><b>More</b></font></a><font size="-1"><br></font>
```

If this is a paragraph, you should mark it up as such, and not just rely on break elements (<br>) to visually set it apart from the content surrounding it:

```
<p>Yannatos starts 41st year conducting Harvard-Radcliffe Orchestra <a
title="Harvard Gazette: &quot;Illuminating the beauty of life&quot;"
href="http://www.news.harvard.edu/gazette/">More</a></p>
```

Here, you can see that the More link is within the paragraph — as you'll see later in the chapter, you could easily use CSS to move the anchor down to the next line. So, while keeping the anchor inside the paragraph is intentional, you may opt to take a different approach.

## Better Know Unordered Lists

As for the menus at the top of the page, what is a site's navigation but a list of links? You can replace the table-heavy navigation menus with unordered lists, each list item element containing a link to a different part of your site as in this example:

```
<ul>
 <li><a href="home.html">Home</a></li>
 <li><a href="about.html">About Us</a></li>
 <li><a href="products.html">Our Products</a></li>
</ul>
```

*With a little bit of JavaScript magic, nested unordered lists can be quickly and easily converted into dynamic drop-down menus. One of the most popular examples of this is the "Son of Suckerfish" (SoS) menu script (*www.htmldog.com/articles/suckerfish/dropdowns*) developed by designers Patrick Griffiths and Dan Webb. The SoS menu is a perfect example of how behavior (JavaScript) and style (CSS) can be layered atop a foundation of well-structured markup, all the while degrading gracefully to non-CSS or non–JS-aware Internet devices.*

## Take Stock of Your Content, Not Your Graphics

First and foremost, you should perform an inventory of your page's content areas. Taking another look at the Harvard University home page (see Figure 1-4), you can see that the site's layout quickly breaks down into the following outline:

- Header
- Navigation
  - Primary
  - Secondary
- Content
  - Main Content
  - Additional Content
- Footer Navigation
- Copyright Information

Figure 1-4: The entire Harvard University home page.

Within the two columns, you can further describe the various blocks of content therein — which is exactly what's been done in Figure 1-5. Within the Main Content column, there is a featured story, a list of school links, and a list of miscellaneous other links. The second column is devoted primarily to news stories, with the first content block containing the news features you examined earlier, and the second containing news items of lesser importance.

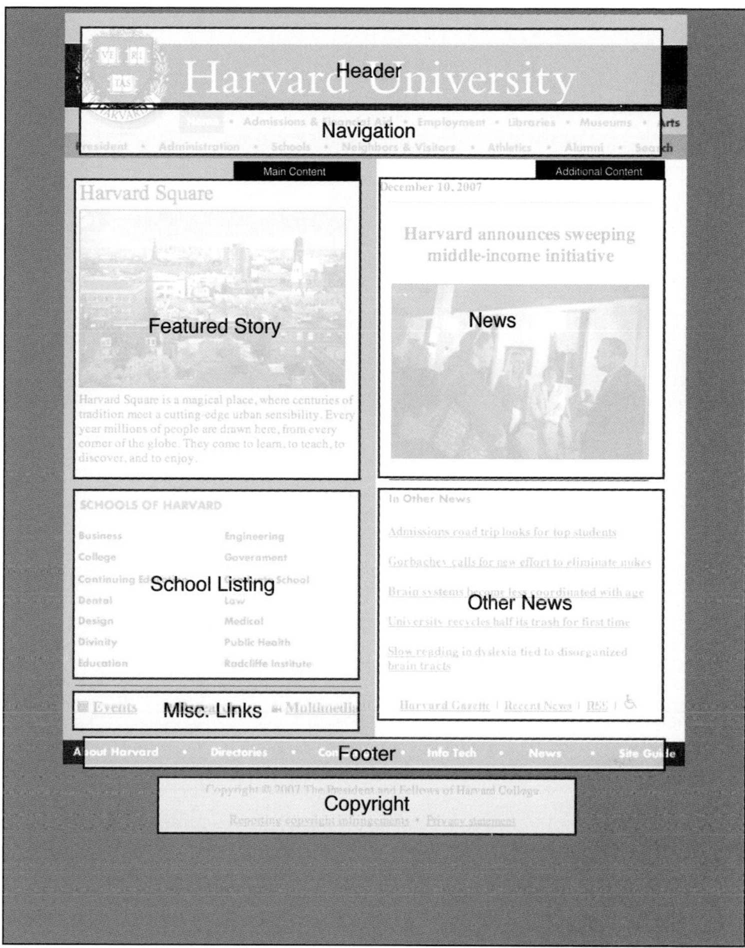


**Figure 1-5: Identifying the areas of content on the Harvard home page.**

From this mental map of the page's content, you can then describe it through markup. Each one of the content areas can be described by a `div` with a unique `id`, and — in the case of the two content columns — nested child content blocks in `div`s as necessary. Once you do so, you have an XHTML document that looks something like Figure 1-6. Every content area is marked up with a descriptively `id`'d `div`, with the nesting order reflecting the relationships outlined in the content inventory (refer to Figure 1-5).

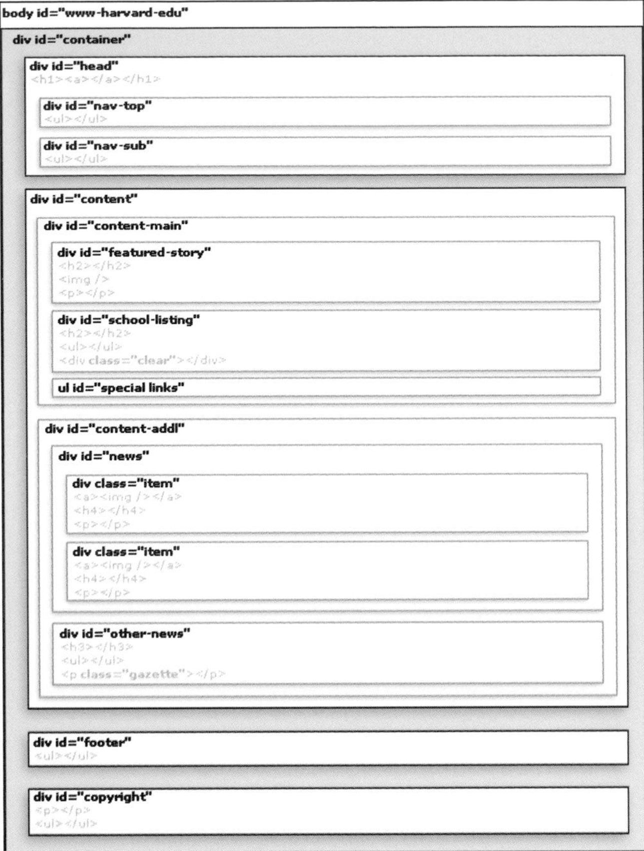


**Figure 1-6: The outline for the new XHTML template.**

At this point, the markup is basically a blank slate, upon which you can layer style. Users unable to see styles are left with a well-structured, easy-to-follow markup structure (see Figure 1-7). In the rest of this chapter and throughout this book, you'll be examining strategies for how to best add this presentation layer on top of this foundation of valid markup.

# CSS: Adding a Layer of Style

As with any other language, getting your bearings in CSS is contingent upon your understanding of its syntax. Doing so will not only improve your own fluency in writing style sheets but also increase your understanding of how the browser interprets the rules you write.

## Better Know Selectors

Your CSS comprises style *rules* that are interpreted by the browser and then applied to the corresponding elements in your document. For example, consider Figure 1-8.

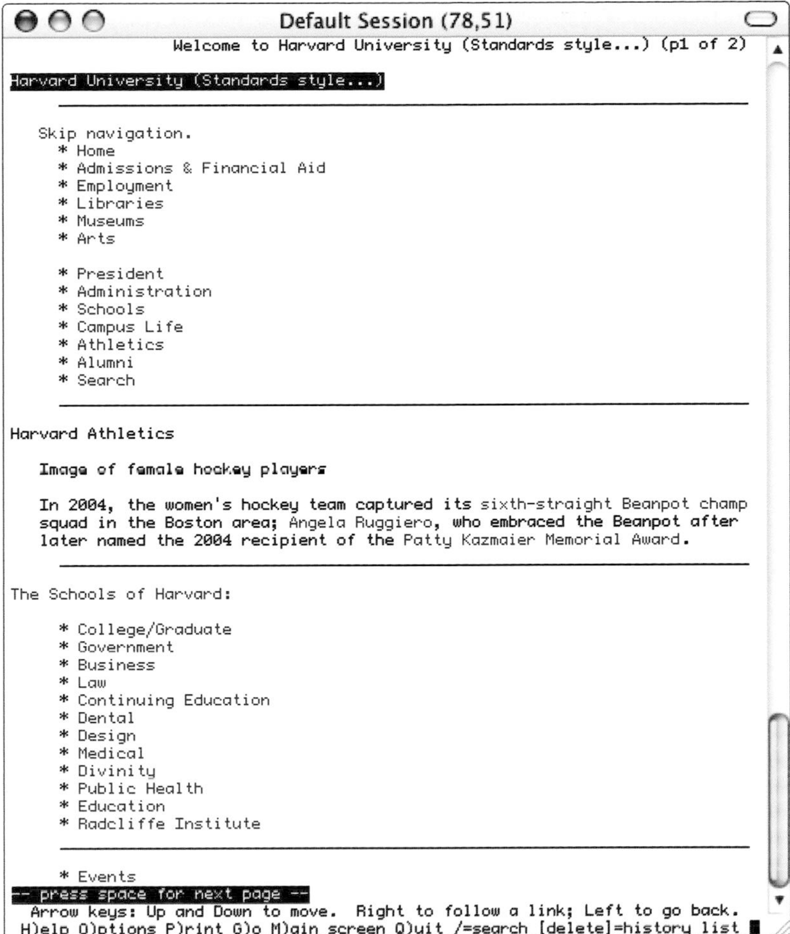

**Figure 1-7: Lynx view of the revised Harvard XHTML.**

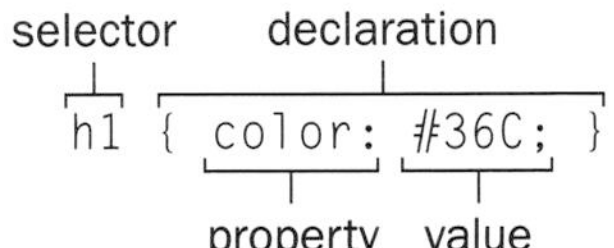

**Figure 1-8: A simple sample style rule. Say that five times fast.**

Every CSS rule comprises these two parts: a *selector*, which tells the browser which element(s) will be affected by the rule; and a *declaration block*, which determines which *properties* of the element will be modified. In Figure 1-8, you can see that the selector comprises everything up to, but not including, the first curly brace (`{`).

The braces encompass the *declaration block*, which is the real meat of the rule. It consists of one or more *declarations*, as well as a *property/value* pair that decides how the elements in the selector will be styled. In Figure 1-8, `color` is the property, and `#36C` is its declared value.

If you think this sounds simple, it certainly is. Commonsense logic pervades through the syntax of CSS. But this is just the beginning. You can use these very simple principles to build increasingly complex rules and gain even more control over your sites' presentation.

## Type Selectors

Let's revisit the simple `h1` rule:

```
h1 {
color: #36C;
)
```

This is what's known as a *type selector* because it instructs the browser to select all elements of a certain type (here, all `h1`s found in our markup) and render them in a lovely blue.

In case you were wondering, that sound you just heard was a few thousand `font` elements taking their last gasping breath.

> *Wondering about that odd-looking `#36C` color value? That's a shorthand way of notating hex colors. You can abbreviate your RGB triplets in this way if each of the hex pairs is the same. So, rather than typing `#3366CC`, you can instead write `#36C` because the red (33), green (66), and blue (CC) hex pairs all contain duplicate characters. You could similarly shorten `#FFFF00` to `#FF0`, `#000000` to `#000`, `#CC3300` to `#C30`, and so forth.*

## The Universal Selector

Another selector with far-reaching authority, the *universal selector*, has a much broader scope than the type selector. Rather than selecting elements of a specific type, the universal selector quite simply matches the name of *any* element type. Aptly enough, its notation is the asterisk, or wildcard symbol, as shown here:

```
* {
color: #000;
)
```

This rule renders the content of every element in your document in black. This is simple enough, right? You might not encounter a rule like this too frequently because use of the universal selector is limited a bit by its intimidating scope. Furthermore, there are a few support issues with it that might warrant testing. However, you'll later explore some specific uses for this selector, which sometimes leaves its mark by not showing up at all.

## Descendant Selectors

Suppose for a moment that you were faced with the following markup:

```
<p>I just <em>love</em> emphasis!</p>
<ul>
 <li>Don't <em>you</em>?!</li>
```

```
  <li>Oh, certainly.
   <ol>
    <li>I <em>still</em> love it!</li>
   </ol>
  </li>
 </ul>
```

By default, most browsers render em elements in italics — nothing new there. But what if you're feeling a bit arbitrary? Let's say that you want all em elements in your uls to be displayed in uppercase. Using what you've learned up to this point, you could write a rule that uses a type selector and matches on all em elements:

```
em {
 text-transform: uppercase;
}
```

However, you want to match only the ems within the ul — in other words, any ems in the opening paragraph should be unaffected by our rule. Simply using the em in your selector will match on *all* ems from your document, so you have to be a bit more specific:

```
ul em {
 text-transform: uppercase;
}
```

This rule begins with a *descendant selector* and tells the browser to "select all em elements that are descendants of ul elements." Just as you're a child of your parents, you're a *descendant* of your grandparents and your great-grandparents. In this way, em elements at every level of the unordered list would have the style applied — even those contained within the ordered list. Most importantly, your rule won't select the em element in the opening p, just as you intended.

Granted, there aren't too many occasions when you'll need to style your poor little ems in this way. Instead, bear in mind that these kinds of selectors can afford you a highly granular level of control over your pages' design. Should you ever need to exempt certain sections of your content from otherwise global style rules, you now possess the means to do so.

### Class Selectors

Looking for even finer-grained control? Style sheets can hook into even more aspects of your markup. Remember the class attribute used in the Harvard University makeover? It was used to denote an "item" category of divs. Well, it's not just auspicious timing that brings us to the *class selector*:

```
input.box {
 border: 1px solid #C00;
}
```

This selector allows CSS authors to select elements whose class attribute contains the value specified after the period (.). In this example, the rule would select all input elements whose class attribute contained the word "text," like so:

```
<form id="sample" action="blah.html" method="post">
 <fieldset>
```

```
<p>
 <label for="box-one">Box #1:</label>
 <input type="text" id="box-one" size="15" class="text" />
</p>
<p>
 <label for="box-two">Box #2:</label>
 <input type="text" id="box-two" size="15" class="text" />
</p>
<input type="submit" id="submit" value="Submit!" />
</fieldset>
</form>
```

The submit button at the end of the sample form is unaffected, and the rule is applied to the two text fields — classed, aptly enough, as "text."

If you want your `class` selector to be even more generic, you can simply omit the "input" like this:

```
.text {
 border: 1px solid #C00;
}
```

Though you might not recognize it, the universal selector is making an appearance here; if you wanted to, you could write this rule:

```
*.box {
 border: 1px solid #C00;
}
```

Both selectors achieve the same goal: both will select *all* elements whose `class` attribute contains the word "text."

## *id Selectors*

Similarly to `class` selectors, `id` selectors enable you to select an element based on the `id` attribute:

```
h1#page-title {
 text-align: right;
}
```

Whereas the `class` selector used a period (.), the `id` selector relies on a hash (#). In this rule, you selected the `h1` element that has an `id` attribute whose value matches the text after the hash (namely, "page-title"). As with class selectors, you could again rely on the implicit universal selector here, leaving the `h1` out of the picture altogether:

```
#page-title {
 text-align: right;
}
```

How are you able to do this? Well, the value of an element's `id` attribute is unique, within the context of a valid XHTML document — no other element in our markup may share the "page-title" `id` with our `h1`. Therefore, you know that both rules match only one element in your markup, making the results of the two rules equivalent.

Nothing especially exciting, you say? You ain't seen nothing yet.

The true power of `id` selectors is apparent when they're used as the foundation for descendant selectors, like this:

```
#content h2 {
 text-transform: uppercase;
}
```

Rules such as this are the foundation of complex layouts. As a CSS designer, this allows you to create style rules that are incredibly context-aware. For example, this rule will select all `h2` elements that are descendants of the element with an `id` of "content," and *only* those `h2`s. All other second-level heading elements in the document will be unaffected by this rule.

## Other Selectors

In this section, you examine some of the other selectors available to you in the specification.

*As of this writing, Microsoft Internet Explorer 6 for Windows (MSIE 6/Win) does not support these selectors. While other modern browsers enjoy rich support for them (including Internet Explorer 7 (MSIE 7/Win), Firefox, Opera, and Safari), many of these selectors are new as of CSS2. MSIE 6/Win's implementation of that specification is nascent at best.*

*While MSIE 7/Win is enjoying a hearty adoption rate and will eventually eliminate the need to support its predecessor, be sure to check the log files for your site to see if support for MSIE 6/Win or other legacy browsers is needed before implementing these selectors into your CSS-enabled designs.*

### Child Selectors

Earlier you discovered that you could write rules that instantly affect all elements beneath another element. Let's assume that you want to style all the paragraphs in the body of your document:

```
<body>
 <p>I am the very model...</p>
 <div class="news">
  <p>Of a modern markup general.</p>
 </div>
 <p>I use every attribute, be it vegetable or mineral.</p>
</body>
```

To have all paragraphs displayed in bold, you could write either of the following:

```
p {
 font-weight: bold;
}
```

or

```
body p {
 font-weight: bold;
}
```

Both would have the same effect. As discussed previously, they would select all paragraphs contained within the document's `body` element, at any level.

But, what if you wanted to restrain the scope of your match a bit and just select the paragraphs immediately beneath the `body` element in your document's hierarchy?

Enter *child selectors*:

```
body>p {
 font-weight: bold;
}
```

The greater-than sign (>) instructs the user agent to select all *child* `p` elements, not all *descendants*. Therefore, the paragraphs contained by the `div` would not be affected because they are children of that element — not the `body`. However, the paragraphs immediately before and after the `div` would be affected because they both share the `body` as their parent element.

## Attribute Selectors

Rather than peppering your form with `class` attributes, the CSS specification has defined *attribute selectors*. These selectors enable you to match not only on a given element's `class` but also on any other attribute it possesses. Denoted by a set of square brackets, attribute selectors can match in any of the four ways shown in the following table.

| Attribute Selector Syntax | Result |
|---|---|
| [*x*] | Matches when the element has the specified *x* attribute, regardless of the value of that attribute. |
| [*x*=*y*] | Matches when the element's *x* attribute has a value that is exactly *y*. |
| [*x*~=*y*] | Matches when the value of the element's *x* attribute is a space-delimited list of words, one of which is exactly *y*. |
| [*x*\|=*y*] | Matches when the value of the element's *x* attribute is a hyphen-separated list of words beginning with *y*. |

Seem a bit confusing? A few concrete examples of attribute selectors, and the elements they would select, are shown in the following table.

| Selector | What It Means | What It Selects | What It Won't Select |
|---|---|---|---|
| `p[lang]` | Selects all paragraph elements with a `lang` attribute. | `<p lang="eng">`<br>`<p lang="five">` | `<p class="lang">`<br>`<p>` |

| Selector | What It Means | What It Selects | What It Won't Select |
|---|---|---|---|
| `p[lang="fr"]` | Selects all paragraph elements whose `lang` attribute has a value of exactly `"fr."` | `<p lang="fr">`<br>`<p class="gazette" lang="fr">` | `<p lang="fr-Canada">`<br>`<p lang="french">` |
| `p[lang~="fr"]` | Selects all paragraph elements whose `lang` attribute contains the word `"fr."` | `<p lang="fr">`<br>`<p lang="en fr">`<br>`<p lang="la sp fr">` | `<p lang="fr-Canada">`<br>`<p lang="french">` |
| `p[lang\|="en"]` | Selects all paragraph elements whose `lang` attributes contain values that are exactly `"en"` or begin with `"en-."` | `<p lang="en">`<br>`<p lang="en-US">`<br>`<p lang="en-cockney">` | `<p lang="US-en">`<br>`<p lang="eng">` |

The potential application for these selectors is exciting, to say the least. Revisiting the form from before, the work gets a lot easier:

```
<form id="sample" action="blah.html" method="post">
 <fieldset>
  <p>
   <label for="text-one">Box #1:</label>
   <input type="text" id="text-one" size="15" />
  </p>
  <p>
   <label for="text-two">Box #2:</label>
   <input type="text" id="text-two" size="15" />
  </p>
  <input type="submit" id="submit" value="Submit!" />
 </fieldset>
</form>
```

Using an attribute selector, it would be very easy for you to hone in on all `input` elements whose type attribute exactly matched "text":

```
input[type="text"] {
 border: 1px solid #C00;
}
```

The advantage to this method is that the `<input type="submit" />` element is unaffected, and the border is applied only to the desired text fields. No longer do you need to pepper your markup with presentational class attributes. Instead, you can use XHTML itself as a kind of API for your style sheets, writing selectors that "hook" into the very structure of your document.

*Lest I be accused of turning my nose up at class selectors, let me reassure you that I'm not guilty of semantic grandstanding. At the end of the day, the selectors you're able to use — that is, those compatible with Microsoft's Internet Explorer — are excellent tools, if perhaps not the ideal ones. While using classes in a form might not be the most "semantically pure" solution, they afford a great deal of flexibility and structural control in designs today.*

## Combining Multiple Declarations

Now, all of the style rules you've looked at so far have had only one declaration — thankfully, this doesn't have to be the case. Imagine how verbose your CSS would be if you had to restrict yourself to this sort of syntax:

```
h1 { color: #36C; }
h1 { font-weight: normal; }
h1 { letter-spacing: .4em; }
h1 { margin-bottom: 1em; }
h1 ( text-transform: lowercase; )
```

Were your browser to read your style sheet aloud to you, this snippet would be an incredible cure for insomnia. It might sound something like, "Select all `h1` elements, and apply a color of `#36C`. Select all `h1` elements, and weight the type normally. Select all `h1` elements, and space the letters by point-four ems. Select all `h1` elements, and apply a bottom margin of one em. Select all `h1` elements, and transform the text to lowercase." Not exactly a gripping read, is it? Rest assured, it'll knock your kids out faster than *Goodnight Moon* ever could.

Thankfully, there's a way out of this oververbose mess. Multiple declarations for the same selector can be compressed into one semicolon-delimited, easy-to-carry rule. With that, let's revisit the multiple `h1` rules:

```
h1 {
 color: #36C;
 font-weight: normal;
 letter-spacing: .4em;
 margin-bottom: 1em;
 text-transform: lowercase;
}
```

This is much better. As this example shows, you can style multiple properties of your `h1` elements in one rule. This enables you to keep your style sheets clutter-free and the cost of managing them way, way down. After all, brevity *is* the soul of style.

*When writing a rule with multiple declarations, the semicolon is technically considered a delimiter — something to separate the end of one declaration with the start of another. As such, it's perfectly valid for you to omit the semicolon from the final rule in a style block because there isn't another subsequent declaration. For consistency's sake, it is recommended that you end every declaration with a semicolon. That way, if you need to change a declaration's position in a rule or globally edit a property's value, you won't need to worry about whether or not a semicolon is present.*

## Grouping Selectors

But what if you want to apply the style of your h1 rule to other elements in your document? If you wanted to have all h2 and h3 elements share the same style as your h1s, you could, of course, be quite explicit about it:

```
h1 {
 color: #36C;
 font-weight: normal;
 letter-spacing: .4em;
 margin-bottom: 1em;
 text-transform: lowercase;
}
h2 {
 color: #36C;
 font-weight: normal;
 letter-spacing: .4em;
 margin bottom: 1em;
 text-transform: lowercase;
}
h3 {
 color: #36C;
 font-weight: normal;
 letter-spacing: .4em;
 margin-bottom: 1em;
 text-transform: lowercase;
}
```

No small amount of code, you say? Right you are. But once again, the specification has provided with another way to keep your CSS lean and bandwidth-friendly. Namely, when several rules share the same declarations, the selectors can be "grouped" into one comma-delimited list. For example, you can write your three header rules into one all-encompassing rule:

```
h1, h2, h3 {
 color: #36C;
 font-weight: normal;
 letter-spacing: .4em;
 margin-bottom: 1em;
 text-transform: lowercase;
}
```

The order of the list is irrelevant. All the elements in the selector will have the corresponding declarations applied to them.

Of course, you can be even more intelligent about consolidating shared properties. If rules share only certain properties but not others, it's simple enough to create a grouped rule with the common values and then leave the more unique properties in separate rules, as shown here:

```
#content {
 border: 1px solid #C00;
 padding: 10px;
```

```
  width: 500px;
}
#footer {
  padding: 10px;
  width: 500px;
}
#supplement {
  border: 1px solid #C00;
  padding: 10px;
  position: absolute;
  left: 510px;
  width: 200px;
}
```

You can see that all the previous rules share a padding of 10 pixels. The `#content` and `#footer` rules share the same width. `#content` and `#supplement` have a 1 pixel–thin red border applied to the matching elements. With these similarities in mind, you can consolidate like-valued properties into grouped selectors, like this:

```
#content, #footer, #supplement {
  padding: 10px;
}
#content, #footer {
  width: 500px;
}
#content, #supplement {
  border: 1px solid #C00;
}
#supplement {
  position: absolute;
  left: 510px;
  width: 200px;
}
```

It may not look like you've gained all that much — you're now left with 14 lines compared to the previous example's 16, and you've even gained an extra rule to keep track of. But the advantage to this intelligent grouping is cumulative and will become more apparent once you begin writing more complex style rules. When you consolidate shared style declarations, you need edit only *one* style rule to change the border color of the `#content` and `#supplement` elements, or to increase the width of the `#content` and `#footer` elements. Once your style sheets become not a few dozen rules long but a few *hundred*, this grouping can be a real timesaver when it comes time to edit shared values.

## Indulging in Inheritance

When writing CSS rules, it bears remembering that some properties (and the values you assign to them) will be inherited by descendant elements. In fact, it helps to envision inheritance much in the same way you'd think of traits that you inherit from your family. A Web page isn't all that dissimilar, in fact. There are parent-child relationships, in which elements inherit style properties from the elements that contain them. In fact, you can almost draw a family tree of your page's elements, as shown in Figure 1-9.

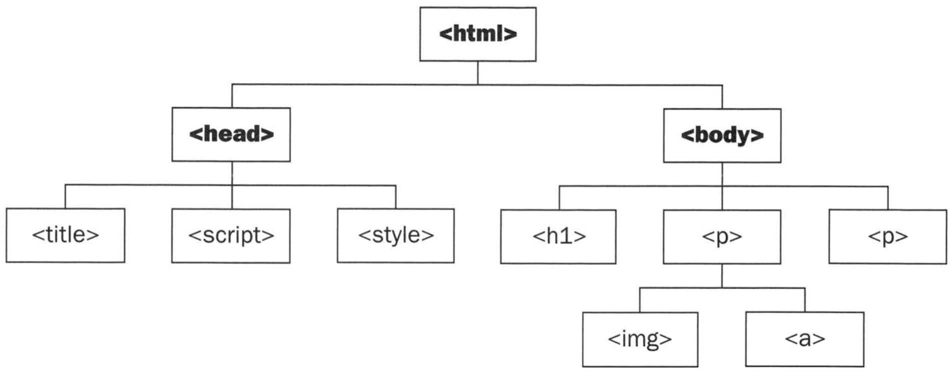


**Figure 1-9: Your markup document tree.**

## Examining Element Hierarchy

The `html` element is the root element of your page, and as such, is at the base of your "document tree." It is the *parent* of its *child* elements — namely, the `head` and `body` elements, which have their own children, which in turn have their own children, and so on down the line. Elements that share the same parent are called *siblings*. Tags placed more than one level down the tree from a given point are considered *descendants*. Conversely, elements near the top of the tree can be considered *ancestors* to those that are nearer the bottom. There you have it, all the neatly arranged hierarchy of a family tree, without such niceties as your Uncle Eustace's habit of telling off-color jokes during Thanksgiving dinner. (I'm much better at writing Web design books than I am at making jokes about genealogy. Honest.)

When thinking of your markup in this hierarchical manner, it's much easier to envision exactly how styles will propagate down the various branches. Consider the following example:

```
body {
 color: #000;
 font-family: Georgia, "Times New Roman", serif;
 font-size: 12px;
}
```

According to the syntax rules already covered, you know that this rule tells the user agent to select all `body` elements and apply a serif typeface (looking on the client's machine for Georgia, Times New Roman, or a generic sans-serif font, in that order), sized at 12 pixels and colored in black (`#000`).

Now, applying the rules of inheritance to your document, these three properties will be handed down to all elements contained within the `body` of your document — or, to use the language of your document's family tree, to all elements that are *descendants* of the `body`. Already you've seen why CSS is such a powerful presentation engine. The four lines of a single style rule do the work of a small army of `font` elements.

While inheritance is perhaps the most powerful aspect of CSS, it can at times also be one of the more confusing. Keep in mind that *not all properties are inherited*. Margin and padding are two such examples. Those properties are applied solely to an element, and they are not inherited by its descendants.

For a reference of what properties are passed along to an element's descendants, you're best served by the specification itself (`www.w3.org/TR/CSS21/about.html#property-defs`).

### Overriding Inheritance

What if you don't want a specific section of your document to inherit some of its ancestors' traits? Consider the following example:

```
<body>
 <p>I still like big blocks.</p>
 <ul>
  <li>...but lists are even cooler.</li>
 </ul>
</body>
```

If the earlier CSS rule for the `body` element were applied here, then all of the text within the `p` and `li` would inherit the values declared therein. But when your client walks in and demands that all list items should be in a red (his wife's favorite color) sans-serif typeface? Simply write a rule to select the descendant elements you're worried about, like this:

```
body {
 color: #000;
 font-family: Georgia, "Times New Roman", serif;
 font-size: 10px;
}
li {
 color: #C00;
 font-family: Verdana, sans-serif;
}
```

This is your first glimpse at how the *cascade* part of "cascading style sheets" works. Because the list items are descendants of the `body` element, the second rule effectively breaks the chain of inheritance and applies the declared styles to the selected elements — here, the `li`. However, because you've not declared a new font size for the list items, they'll still inherit that property's value (`10px`) from their ancestor, the `body`. The end result is that your users will see the list items rendered in the requested red, sans-serif font, while all other elements on the page will inherit the rules from the `body`. Let's hope you, your client, and your client's wife are happy with the result.

## Putting It All into Action

Let's take another look at an example of some overworked markup. Consider the rather bare-bones navigation bar shown in Figure 1-10.

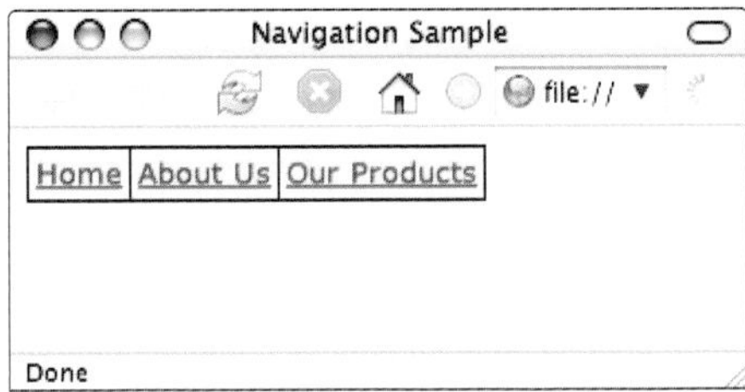


**Figure 1-10: A simple navigation bar.**

Notice the three links in a light-gray, horizontal row, each surrounded by a 1 pixel–thin black border. This seems rather unassuming, until you consider the traditional markup method for creating it:

```
<!-- outer table -->
<table bgcolor="#000000" border="0" cellspacing="0" cellpadding="0">
<tbody>
<tr>
<td>
<!-- inner table -->
<table border="0" cellspacing="1" cellpadding="3">
<tbody>
<tr>
<td bgcolor="#DDDDDD"><font face="Verdana, Geneva, Helvetica, sans-serif"
size="2"><a href="home.html">Home</a></font></td>
<td bgcolor="#DDDDDD"><font face="Verdana, Geneva, Helvetica, sans-serif"
size="2"><a href="about.html">About Us</a></font></td>
<td bgcolor="#DDDDDD"><font face="Verdana, Geneva, Helvetica, sans-serif"
size="2"><a href="products.html">Our Products</a></font></td>
</tr>
</tbody>
</table>
<!-- END inner table -->
</td>
</tr>
</tbody>
</table>
<!-- END outer table -->
```

There are two tables involved in creating this simple navigation bar. The first, outer table has a black background applied to it (`bgcolor="#000000"`). The inner table has no background color of its own, but has a `cellspacing` of 1 pixel. This allows the parent table's black background to bleed through, creating the "border" effect around each of the navigation items. It also includes 3 pixels of `cellpadding` on the inner table, so that there's some breathing room between the text of each link and the table cell (`<td>`) that contains it. Finally, the gray background color (`bgcolor="#DDDDDD"`) is applied to each cell of the inner table, as well as a `<font>` element denoting the appropriate typeface and size.

Twenty-four lines of code — about 1KB of data — might seem rather innocuous when contained to one code snippet in a Web design book, but consider that the code spread across 20 pages of your site — or perhaps a hundred, even a thousand. What happens when you're asked to modify this code? Perhaps your marketing department needs the gray background universally changed to a light green, or it has since standardized on Arial as the corporate typeface. In either event, you'll need to edit, test, and redeploy the markup used on each of those 20, 100, or 1,000 pages to meet those requirements.

Suffice it to say that this isn't exactly an appealing prospect. Thankfully, you can use what you've learned about XHTML and CSS to improve this navigation bar, as well as make your life easier. First, start with some fresh markup. Rather than relying on the bloated, `font`-heavy table from before, let's take a different approach.

```
<ul id="nav">
 <lia href="home.html">Home</a></li>
 <li><a href="about.html">About Us</a></li>
 <li><a href="products.html">Our Products</a></li>
</ul>
```

That's right, this is a simple unordered list. As mentioned earlier in the chapter, you don't need to worry about presentation at this level. You just need to ensure that you're marking up your content in a sensible way, which is exactly what the previous markup does. It produces the humble beginnings shown in Figure 1-11.

First, get rid of that unseemly bulleted look — that's so 1996.

```
ul#nav, ul#nav li {
 list-style: none;
 margin: 0;
 padding: 0;
}
```

Figure 1-12 shows the result.

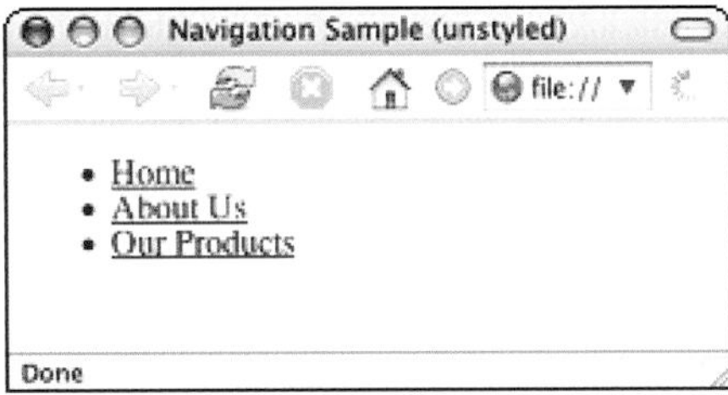


**Figure 1-11:** A simple unordered list.

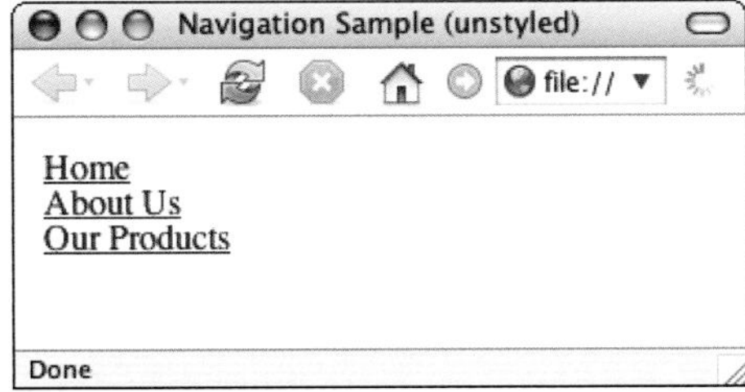


**Figure 1-12:** An unordered list sans bullets.

As you can see, ID selectors are used quite liberally here. By specifying `ul#nav` in your rules, you'll be able to style your navigation list (and the elements within it) independently of the rest of the markup on your page. And by grouping the `ul#nav` and `ul#nav li` rules into one comma-delimited selector, you can simultaneously remove the bullets from the list items (`list-style: none;`) *and* remove superfluous margin and padding at the same time (`margin: 0; padding: 0;`).

Of course, the original navigation table was horizontal, and the list currently isn't anything remotely resembling that. However, that's easily fixed.

```
ul#nav, ul#nav li {
 float: left;
 list-style: none;
 margin: 0;
 padding: 0;
}
```

Figure 1-13 shows the result.

Adding the `float` property to your rule gets the list back in line, literally. Each list item floats to the left of the one after it, pulling them out of their vertical stacking order and into the horizontal line shown here.

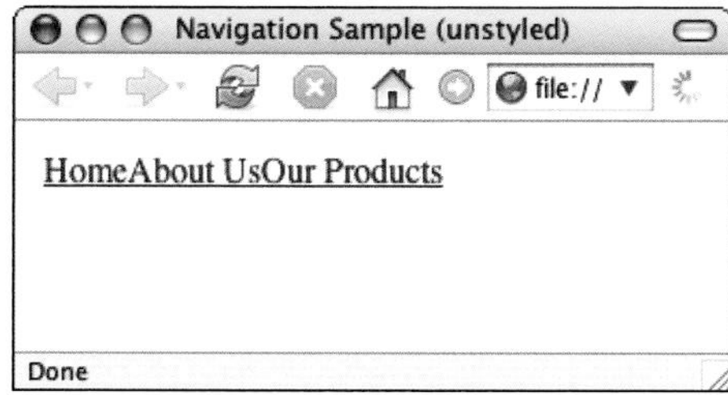


**Figure 1-13: Using floats to get the list in order.**

*The float model is a powerful CSS construct and is, in fact, the basis for many CSS-based layouts. Eric Meyer's article "Containing Floats" (*`www.complexspiral.com/publications/containing-floats`*) explains floats in more detail and clears up some common misconceptions about this remarkably handy layout tool.*

*For an interesting angle on using floats to center list items, see David Hopkins' article "When Is a Float Not a Float?" (*`www.search-this.com/2007/09/19/when-is-a-float-not-a-float`*).*

With the basic layout established, you can begin adding a few more of the visual components. Make the black border and gray background your next priority:

```
ul#nav {
 font-family: Verdana, Geneva, Helvetica, sans-serif;
 font-size: .82em;
 background-color: #DDD;
}

ul#nav li a {
 border: 1px solid #000;
 display: block;
 float: left;
 padding: 3px;
}
```

Figure 1-14 shows the result.

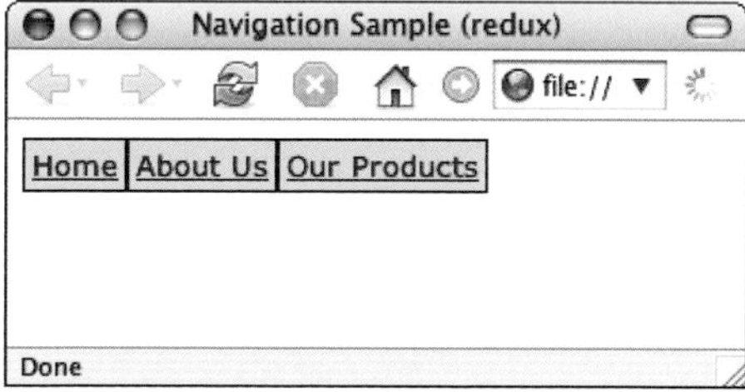


**Figure 1-14: Applying borders and color to the navigation list.**

As you can see, the gray background color is directly applied to the unordered list. And by setting the font attributes on the list as well, you can use inheritance to apply a sans-serif font to all elements therein. By default, anchors are rendered as inline elements. This presents a slight problem, because any padding you apply to them will affect only their horizontal edges. Because you want 3 pixels of padding on each side of your navigation links, you must turn your links into block-level items with `display: block;`.

However, things aren't quite right. You'll notice that the border is too thick between the Home and About Us links, and again between About Us and Our Products. This is because the border on each item abuts its siblings, creating a doubled-up effect when two of the links touch. So, you have to rethink your style slightly:

```
ul#nav li a {
 border-color: #000;
 border-width: 1px 1px 1px 0;
 border-style: solid;
 display: block;
 float: left;
 padding: 3px;
}
```

Figure 1-15 shows the result.

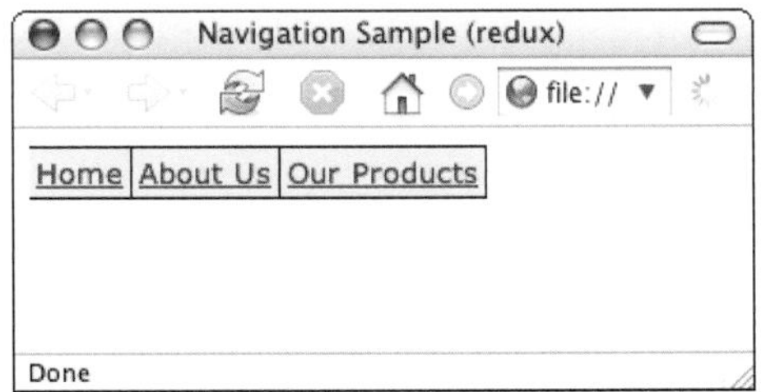


**Figure 1-15: Rethinking the borders.**

That's more like it. The more verbose border declarations (`border-color`, `border-width`, *and* `border-style`) achieve the same effect as the earlier `border: 1px solid #000;`, but the final 0 in the `border-width` declaration instructs the browser to leave off the left-hand border from each list item, whereas the top, right, and bottom edges each get a 1px-wide border applied. Now, you simply need to restore the border to the first list item, and *only* the first list item — you don't need that double-border effect again, thank you very much. To do that, apply a `class` attribute to the first list item in your markup:

```
<ul id="nav">
 <li class="first"><a href="home.html">Home</a></li>
 <li><a href="about.html">About Us</a></li>
 <li><a href="products.html">Our Products</a></li>
</ul>
```

Now that you have supplied that "hook" into your document's structure, it should be pretty straightforward to write a style rule that applies a border to that element, and that element alone:

```
ul#nav li.first a {
 border-width: 1px;
}
```

Figure 1-16 shows the result.

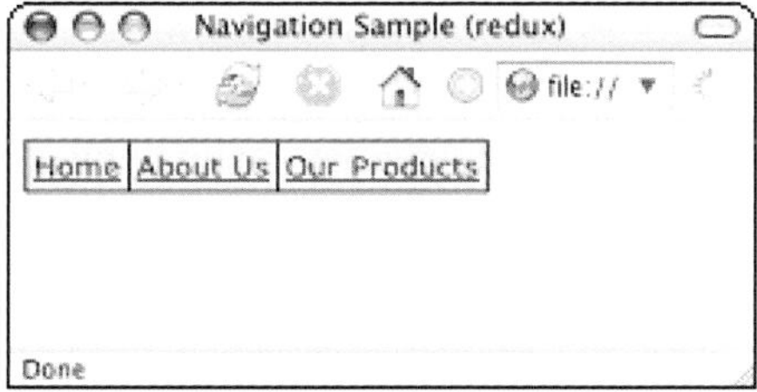


**Figure 1-16: The final list.**

And that's done it! Here's the entire set of rules you've written:

```
ul#nav, ul#nav li {
 float: left;
 list-style: none;
 margin: 0;
 padding: 0;
}

ul#nav {
 font-family: Verdana, Geneva, Helvetica, sans-serif;
 font-size: .82em;
 background-color: #DDD;
}

ul#nav li a {
 border-color: #000;
 border-width: 1px 1px 1px 0;
 border-style: solid;
 display: block;
 float: left;
 padding: 3px;
}

ul#nav li.first a {
 border-width: 1px;
}
```

You've successfully combined grouping, ID, class selectors, and some well-placed inheritance to turn a humble navigation list into a horizontal navigation menu. Instead of resting on your laurels (comfy though they are), consider the benefits of this approach. Is this really any better than building this in a `table`?

Absolutely. Granted, the number of lines of code hasn't changed all that much, when you tally up the XHTML and the CSS together. However, this achieved a measure of abstraction of the content's style from its structure. Rather than muddying your markup with presentational cruft, you can let cascading style sheets do all the heavy lifting in your user interface. Now, if you need to add another link to your menu, you simply add another `li` to the end of your navigation list, and the CSS handles the rest of the presentation.

# Understanding the Cascade

Now that you've examined the basics of CSS syntax, let's take a closer look at the mechanics behind it, to determine how it is that a user agent determines what styles are delivered to users.

## *Discovering Style's Origin*

To do so, you must first identify the appropriate rules because the origin of the style rule determines how much "influence" it has in the cascade. Following are the three areas from which style sheets may originate:

- **User agent** — To fully conform to the CSS specification (`www.w3.org/TR/CSS21/conform.html#conformance`), a user agent must apply a default style sheet to a document before any other style rules are applied. This internal set of CSS rules establishes the default display rules for every HTML element. This is how your browser knows to display an `h1` in a garishly huge serif font or to put a bullet before every unordered list item.
- **The user** — Yes, that's right — your users can write CSS, too. User style sheets were introduced in the CSS2 specification and conceived as a means of allowing users to override an author's chosen fonts and colors for any given page. While some designers might blanch at the thought, this is a very important accessibility initiative. Under certain design conditions, some users might be unable to perceive your site. Writing custom CSS enables users to increase font sizes that may be illegible, or avoid certain color/contrast combinations that are otherwise invisible to them.
- **Author** — This means you. These are the style sheets you include in your markup and are the primary focus of this book.

When a user agent is faced with evaluating style rules from these three distinct sources, it must figure out which style sheet's rules should be presented to the end user. To do so, it assigns a certain degree of importance (or "weight") to each. The listing of the origins is ordered in an increasing level of importance (that is to say, the browser's default style rules are considered less important than the user's, which are in turn less important than the rules you specify in the CSS files that reside on your site's server).

However, both the author and the user can define `!important` rules:

```
h2 {
 font-size: 2em !important;
 color: #C00 !important;
}
```

According to the CSS specification (`www.w3.org/TR/CSS21/cascade.html#important-rules`), the `!important` rules "create a balance of power between author and user style sheets." As already mentioned, rules contained in a user style sheet are typically weighted less than those in the author's CSS. However, the presence of an `!important` rule turns this relationship on its head; a user's `!important` declarations are always weighted *more* than the author's, as shown in **Figure 1-17**.

How does this affect your CSS? Let's say that a browser is trying to determine the style for a basic paragraph element (`p`). After parsing all available style sheets — browser, user, and author — all relevant styles are evaluated, as shown in **Listings 1-1, 1-2, and 1-3**.

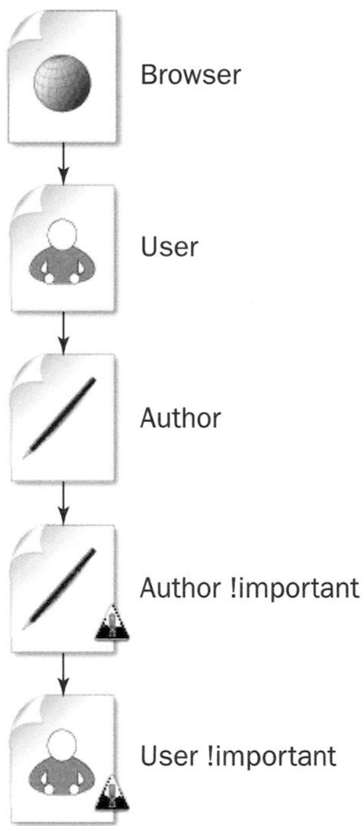


**Figure 1-17:** Style origin and the cascade, from least to most important.

**Listing 1-1: The Browser's Style Sheet**

```
p {
 color: #000;
 font-size: 1em;
 margin: .9em;
}
```

**Listing 1-2: The User's Style Sheet**

```
p {
 color: #060 !important;
}
```

**Listing 1-3: The Author's Style Sheet**

```
p {
 color: #300;
 font-size: 1.2em;
```

*Continued*

**Listing 1-3** *(continued)*

```
    line-height: 1.6em;
    padding: 10px;
  }
```

Let's set aside the user's style sheet for a moment. Therefore, for general users, paragraphs will be styled according to this final, calculated rule:

```
p {
  color: #300;           /* author overwrites browser rule */
  font-size: 1.2em;      /* author overwrites browser rule */
  line-height: 1.6em;    /* specified only by author */
  margin: .9em;          /* specified only by browser */
  padding: 10px;         /* specified only by author */
}
```

*Note the use of CSS comments in the preceding code. Using a pair of slashes and asterisks, you can hide notes within the CSS rules.*

Now, if someone views your page with the user style sheet from Listing 1-2, the final result is changed somewhat:

```
p {
  color: #060;/* user !important rule overwrites author rule */
  font-size: 1.2em;      /* author overwrites browser rule */
  line-height: 1.6em;    /* specified only by author */
  margin: .9em;          /* specified only by browser */
  padding: 10px;         /* specified only by author */
}
```

## Sorting by Specificity

Every selector is given a *specificity rating*, which is yet another qualitative assessment of a selector's importance in the cascade (`www.w3.org/TR/CSS21/cascade.html#specificity`). The higher a rule's specificity, the more influence it is granted when your browser sifts through all the rules in the cascade. For example, `id`-based selectors are inherently more specific than class-driven selectors, as the `id`, by design, occurs once in each document.

Specificity is calculated by the selector's syntax itself and is weighted according to four separate factors.

- **A.** Whether the selector is the HTML `style` attribute of an element, rather than a true selector.
- **B.** The number of `id` attributes in the selector.
- **C.** The number of other attribute (for example, `[lang]`, `[rel]`, `[href]`) and pseudo-class (for example, `:hover`, `:visited`, `:first-child`) names in the selector. Remember that class selectors (such as `li.active`) are a type of attribute selector and are tallied up in this category.
- **D.** The number of element (for example, `a`, `li`, `p`, and so on) and pseudo-element (for example, `:before`, `:after`, and so on) names in the selector.

With these four components in hand, it's rather easy to calculate a given selector's importance in the cascade. The following table shows a list of selectors, from least to most specific (columns A–D).

| Selector | A | B | C | D | Specificity |
|---|---|---|---|---|---|
| `a` | 0 | 0 | 0 | 1 | 0,0,0,1 |
| `h3 a` | 0 | 0 | 0 | 2 | 0,0,0,2 |
| `ul ol+li` | 0 | 0 | 0 | 3 | 0,0,0,3 |
| `ul ol li.red` | 0 | 0 | 1 | 3 | 0,0,1,3 |
| `li.red.level` | 0 | 0 | 2 | 1 | 0,0,2,1 |
| `#other-news` | 0 | 1 | 0 | 0 | 0,1,0,0 |
| `style="..."` | 1 | 0 | 0 | 0 | 1,0,0,0 |

With this information in hand, let's return to the humble paragraph styles from before and calculate their specificity, as shown in Listings 1-4, 1-5, and 1-6.

**Listing 1-4: The Browser's Style Sheet**

```
p { color: #000; font-size: 1em; margin: .9em; }
/* A:0, B:0, C:1, D:1  = specificity of 0,0,0,1 */
```

**Listing 1-5: The User's Style Sheet**

```
p { color: #060 !important; }
/* A:0, B:0, C:1, D:1  = specificity of 0,0,0,1 */
```

**Listing 1-6: The Author's Style Sheet**

```
p { color: #300; font-size: 1.2em; line-height: 1.6em; padding: 10px; }
/* A:0, B:0, C:1, D:1  = specificity of 0,0,0,1 */
p.gazette { color: #0C0; }
/* A:0, B:0, C:1, D:1 = specificity of 0,0,1,1 */
p#footer { color: #FFF; }
/* A:0, B:1, C:0, D:1  = specificity of 0,1,0,1 */
```

Because there are multiple rules assigned for the color property, the browser will need to use the specificity rules to calculate which color to make a paragraph that has an ID of p`#footer` and a class of `p.gazette`.

You can see from this that `p#footer` has the highest specificity, with `p.gazette` coming in second.

Assuming that your site's visitor doesn't have a user style sheet (and is, therefore, unaffected by the `!important` rule):

1. The paragraph element with an `id` of `footer` will be displayed in white (`#FFF`).
2. Those paragraphs with a class of `gazette` will be displayed in green (`#0C0`).
3. All others will be displayed in a dark red (`#300`).

All paragraphs in the document obey the property values declared in the original `p` rule: a font size of 1em, line height of 1.6ems, and 10 pixels of padding. However, the browser's default margin of .9em still reaches the user's display because the author's CSS didn't override it.

### Sorting by Order

Let's assume that an author style sheet has declared two rules, one after the other. This is considered to be multiple rules for the same element. The second rule on color will win (and thus be used). In this case, 000 would be the color chosen, which is the hex code for the color black.

```
p { color: #C00; }
p { color: #000; }
```

When multiple rules have the same specificity, weight, and origin, origin always wins. According to this rule, all paragraphs will be rendered in black. Of course, you could change the weight and then make the first statement the one selected:

```
p { color: #C00 !important; }
p { color: #000; }
```

The rules are no longer equivalent because `!important` author rules are weighted more heavily than regular author rules — therefore, all paragraphs will be rendered in red.

## Putting Theory into Practice

Of course, talking at length about the CSS specification gets us only so far (and does wonders for your attention span, I'm sure). Integrating the standards to practice into your daily workflow is another matter entirely. To do so, let's examine two critical items in a modern Web designer's toolkit — and no, neither of them has a magic wand tool or a layers palette in sight.

### Building to a Reliable Browser

If you build a site when testing in a broken browser, you're building code that relies upon broken rendering. It's as though you're building a house on a foundation of sand. Once you begin testing on other browsers or platforms, the flaws in your work will become far too apparent. Instead, start with a modern browser with an acknowledged level of standards-compliance. As you'll see later in this chapter, you can write hacks into your code that will address lesser browsers' rendering quirks.

This isn't a browser snob's apology, nor is it an attempt to switch your favorite browser. Rather, this approach will save you time and resources when building your site. If you begin building to a flawed browser's bugs, you will spend far more time debugging when you test in a more standards-compliant one. As of this writing, this means one of three options: Opera, Safari, or a Gecko-based browser such as Camino, Mozilla, or Firefox.

You'll note that Internet Explorer doesn't appear in this list, and that's unfortunately intentional. While its standards implementation has increased dramatically over recent years, the Windows version of Internet Explorer is universally regarded as lagging behind other modern browsers with regard to support for standards like CSS and XHTML.

Regardless, we're not yet at the point where clients ask by name for better Firefox support or improved Opera layouts. While each is an excellent browser in its own right, they have some work to do before capturing the hearts, minds, and — let's face it — the market share of your clients.

# Rationalizing the Need for Hacks

Of course, issues are bound to arise when working with CSS-based layouts. While browser implementations have vastly improved over the past few years, the playing field still isn't level. Unless you're supporting just one browser on just one platform, you'll most certainly run into bugs when testing across different browser/platform combinations. Proponents of `table`-layout techniques might interpret these issues as weaknesses in cascading style sheets as a viable layout method. However, the fault lies with the browsers, rather than the CSS specification itself.

But while every browser has its own rendering issues, you're in a rather enviable position. Most of these issues — and their causes — have been well documented and, in many cases, solved outright. What follows is an example of one of the most widespread browser bugs. It's not the only one you'll encounter, but it's a fine example of some of the workarounds available to you. When the chips are down and the browsers aren't behaving, there's almost always a way out.

## The Bug

According to the CSS specification (`www.w3.org/TR/CSS21/box.html`), every element in your document tree has a content area; this could be text, an image, or so forth. Additionally, padding, border, and margin areas may surround that content area, as shown in Figure 1-18.

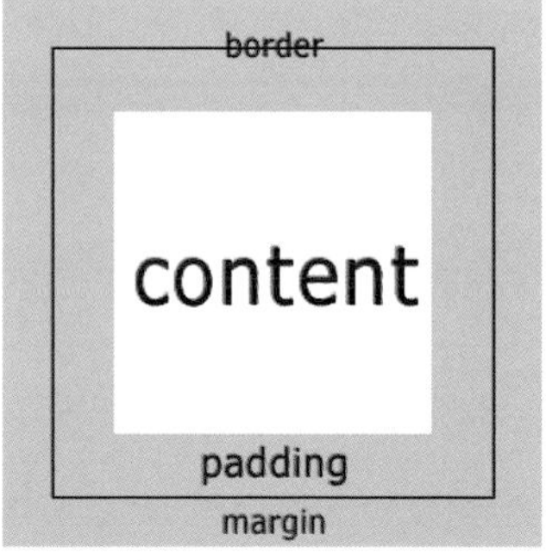


**Figure 1-18: The box model.**

*If seeing the box model in resplendent black-and-white leaves you scratching your head, Web designer Jon Hicks has built a full-color, three-dimensional diagram that might be worth checking out as well* (`www.hicksdesign.co.uk/journal/483/3d_css_box_model`).

Now, the dimensions of those three "extra" areas — padding, border, and margin — add to the total calculated width and height of the content area. Let's look at a style rule that demonstrates this in action:

```
p#hack {
 border: 20px solid #C00;
 padding: 30px;
 width: 400px;
}
```

The `width` property declares that the content within the paragraphs will not exceed 400 pixels. On top of that, are 10 pixels of padding and a 10 pixels–thick red border *to each side of the box* — top, right, bottom, and left. So, if you're trying to figure out the full, calculated width of the paragraphs, you move from left to right across the box's properties and tally the final width:

```
Left Border:        20
Left Padding:      +30
Content:          +400
Right Padding:     +30
Right Border:      +20
TOTAL WIDTH:     = 500 PIXELS
```

In short, the padding and border are outside the declared width of the content area, as the specification requires.

However, there are older versions of Internet Explorer on Windows that have an incorrect (or more specifically, a "nonstandard") implementation of the box model, and instead put the border and padding *inside* the declared width. Version 6 of that browser is the first to get the calculations right, but only if the browser is in standards-compliant mode — that is, if there's a `DOCTYPE` at the top of your markup. Otherwise, these browsers incorrectly see the declared 400 pixels as the space into which all of the box's properties — content width, padding, and border — must be placed. So, the calculation in one of these browsers would look something like this:

```
Declared Width:     400
Left Border:        -20
Left Padding:       -30
Right Padding:      -30
Right Border:       -20
CONTENT WIDTH:    = 300 PIXELS
```

When you're trying to ensure a consistent design across all browsers, a difference of even 1 pixel is unacceptable — a few hundred are enough to make you want to run back to your trusty `tables`. Thankfully, there's way out.

*It's worth noting that this rendering bug happens only when an element has a declared width and either padding or borders, or both. Another strategy to avoid all this CSS hackery is to apply the padding to an element's parent and leave the width on the child — or vice versa. Understanding the cause of a rendering bug is, at times, more important than knowing the hack or fix and can help you more strategically plan your style sheet's architecture.*

## The Solution

CSS hacks provide a workaround for browser inconsistencies such as this IE bug and ensure that you can have your layout looking sharp across the board. Typically, these hacks exploit a parsing bug in a browser's CSS implementation, allowing you to hide or display sections of your CSS to that browser. In effect, this allows you to serve up the "correct" value to more CSS-compliant browsers, while delivering the "incorrect" value to the ones with the poor math skills.

To work around the little IE bug, let's resort to using some hacks to ensure that display is looking sharp across all target browsers:

```
p#hack {
 border: 20px solid #C00;
 padding: 30px;
 width: 400px;
}

* html p#hack {
 width: 500px;
 w\idth: 400px;
}
```

You've turned a single CSS rule into two. The first rule contains the `border` and `padding` information to be applied to the paragraph, as well as the desired width of 400 pixels.

The second rule (beginning with the universal selector, `*`) contains the hackery. If you were to read the `* html p#hack` rule in plain English, it would tell you to "Select all `p` elements with an `id` attribute of `'hack'` that are descendants of an `html` element *that is itself a descendant of any element.*" The last part of the rule is emphasized because that's where the hack lies. Because `html` is the root of HTML and XHTML documents, it can't be a descendant of any other element. So, if this second rule shouldn't match any element, why include it?

Actually, this rule returns a valid match in all versions of Internet Explorer (Windows and Macintosh), which erroneously disregard the universal selector and interpret the rule as `html p#hack`. As a result, this rule is seen *only* by Internet Explorer and is disregarded by all other browsers. The first property declares an "incorrect" width of 500 pixels, ensuring that the buggy browsers leave sufficient space for your content. Because they put the padding and border *inside* the declared width, you must send them a pixel width that matches a correct browser's interpretation of the spec. And because the `html p#hack` selector is more specific than the last, this new width value overrides the previous value of 400 pixels.

But you can't rest on your laurels yet because there is one last hack to perform. Internet Explorer 6 on Windows and Internet Explorer 5.*x* on the Mac implement the box model correctly, so the previous fix just fed two good browsers that "incorrect" value of 500px. To remedy this, the second width property contains the proper value of 400px. However, by escaping the "i" with a backslash (`w\idth`), you can exploit a bug in older versions of Internet Explorer and hide this rule from that browser. And with this hack-within-a-hack approach, the bug is fixed!

> *If your head's spinning a bit, I feel your pain. Thankfully, there are some excellent resources available to help you better understand this and other CSS hacks. I recommend reading through the CSS-Discuss Wiki (discussed in greater detail in the next section), which has an in-depth analysis of the box model hack used here, as well as other approaches* (`http://css-discuss.incutio.com/?page=BoxModelHack`). *Its near-exhaustive list of other style sheet hacks is worth poring over* (`http://css-discuss.incutio.com/?page=CssHack`), *as are its tips for avoiding needless hacks* (`http://css-discuss.incutio.com/?page=AvoidingHacks`).

## The Road Is Long

As you've seen, the number of idiosyncratic browsers to which you build makes testing CSS a necessary part of a site's development cycle. While browser support for the standard is excellent (especially when compared with that of a few years ago), you're bound to encounter some of these browser bugs in your own code. But don't worry: it's a natural part of the site-development process.

Every CSS designer hits a roadblock at some point. If someone tells you that every site they've built went off without a hitch, feel free to back away slowly — they're either lying or just downright talkin' crazy-talk. When your own debugging fails to fix the problem (you *did* validate your code, right?), there are some excellent sites to which you can and should turn.

If you're facing an inexplicable bug in your layout, knowing the resources available to you is often more important than immediately knowing the solution. If nothing else, it should lend you some security as that deadline approaches. The chances are excellent that, at some point, someone's encountered the same issue that you are facing.

### CSS-Discuss

The CSS-Discuss mailing list (`www.css-discuss.org`) was founded in early 2002 and is currently administered by Eric Meyer, CSS guru and former Netscape standards evangelist. According to the site's manifesto, the mailing list is "intended to be a place for authors to discuss real-world uses of CSS." As such, the list is an incredible success; a small army of helpful, CSS-aware Web designers and developers are subscribed to the list. Each is willing and eager to help other Web professionals work through the trials of CSS, so that they might better understand the joys of working with it.

Just as valuable as the list itself is the CSS-Discuss Wiki (`http://css-discuss.incutio.com`), a community-authored and -edited site containing information regarding font sizing (`http://css-discuss.incutio.com/?page=FontSize`), layout strategies (`http://css-discuss.incutio.com/?page=CssLayouts`), CSS editors (`http://css-discuss.incutio.com/?page=CssEditors`), and of course, CSS hacks (`http://css-discuss.incutio.com/?page=CssHacks`). The Wiki is a site worth poring over and, once you're ready, adding your own contributions.

### Position Is Everything

The Position Is Everything (PIE) site (`www.positioniseverything.net`) is an exhaustive CSS resource, and one to which you should refer whenever you're stumped by a browser issue. Maintained by John Gallant and Holly Bergevin (two extremely capable CSS developers), PIE contains a dizzying number of browser quirks, workarounds, and unresolved bugs — all written up in the clear, easy-to-understand style for which John and Holly have become known.

## The Problem with Hacks

Of course, it's perfectly acceptable to write hacks directly into your CSS: Find a bug in Internet Explorer 5 on Macintosh OS X, isolate the problematic rule, add a hack, move on to the next issue. This "as-you-go" approach is one that most style sheet developers take, and it *does* afford you great flexibility in dealing with browser inconsistencies. Besides, there is a certain level of security in writing the workaround directly into your code, anyway: Write it, test it, and move on. Simple, right?

Actually, while quite effective, this improvisational approach to hack management does pose some problems for the long-term viability of your code. First and foremost, it's all too easy for your code to become weighed down with an unseemly number of hacks, like this:

```
#album-thumbs {
 float: left;
 list-style-image: none;
 list-style: none;
 margin: 0;
 padding: 0;
}

/* hide from MacIE5 \*/
* html #album-thumbs {
 display: inline;
 height: 1%;
 width: auto !important;
 width /**/: 90%;
}
/* hide from MacIE5 */

#album-thumbs a {
 display: block;
 float: left;
 padding: 6px;
 margin: 5px;
 width: 70px;
}

#album-thumbs a {
 \width: 60px;
 \width: 50px;
}
```

Does this look like gibberish? It's not too far from it. Granted, this style sheet's author left us with nearly no comments to lead us through this goulash of style rules. The backslash in the first comment (`/* ... \*/`) will cause the Macintosh version of Internet Explorer to stop parsing the CSS until reaching a properly formed comment (`/* ... */`). Only the 5.*x* versions of Internet Explorer will read the declaration with the backslash before the "w" in `\width`, and so forth down the daisy-chain of broken CSS implementations.

What if you had to look at code like this, day in and day out? If this code is difficult for you to sift through, you can bet it's going to be difficult for someone else to maintain. Team members, coworkers, interns, stray dogs — if anyone else is ever going to be responsible for editing your CSS, this approach to hack management isn't a viable one. But putting code readability (or the lack thereof) aside for a moment, these rules *are* valid CSS, and they *do* serve their purpose — they fix bugs in different browser/platform combinations, and they do it well. So what's the problem?

Well, imagine that your CSS is littered with code like this. What happens when you need to render obsolete a given hack? Perhaps one of the problematic browsers passes over the upgrade horizon, or the next version of Internet Explorer will stop reading your style sheet when it encounters a hack for the Opera browser. At some point, you might need to edit your CSS and remove some of the hacks you introduced. But what if these hacks aren't spread over 30 lines of CSS, but over 3,000? What then?

## Hacking Artfully for Fun and Profit

Rather than muddying your style sheet with browser-specific hacks, you're much better served by placing your workarounds into browser-specific style sheets. While this kind of "hack quarantine" isn't strictly necessary, it does have the benefit of keeping your "clean" CSS distinct from the hacks required to get it working in less-compliant browsers. Consider Figure 1-19.

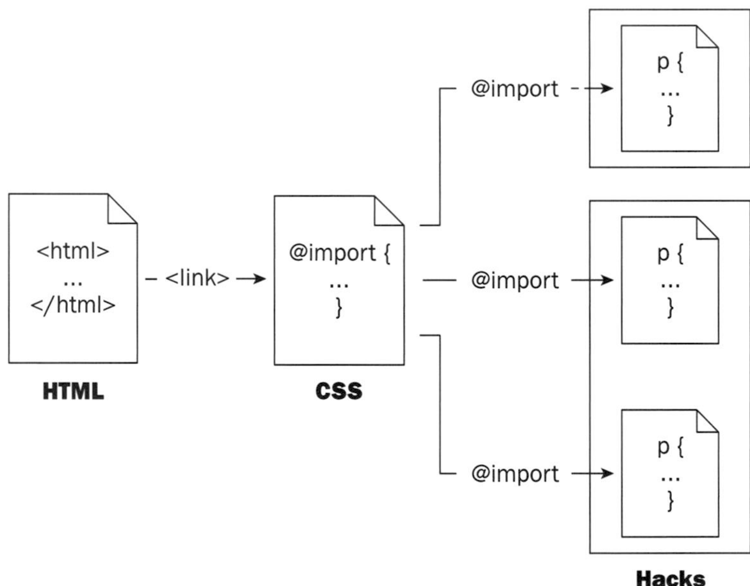


**Figure 1-19: A more scalable hack management system.**

In this model, there's a `link` to the style sheet — nothing unusual there. But this first style sheet simply acts as a gateway to multiple other style sheets, which are invoked through the `@import` rule. The first imported style sheet is the one that contains the site's presentation, clean and hack-free. Thereafter, you can simply import browser-specific style sheets that contain the hacks necessary to ensure that your site displays consistently across all target browsers.

*There are other ways to manage your hacks, of course. Web developer Mark Pilgrim describes how he uses user agent detection on his Web server to deliver up browser-specific CSS hacks* (`http://diveintomark.org/archives/2003/01/16/the_one_ive_never_tried`). *This kind of server-side content negotiation is excellent, although it requires knowledge of, and an ability to configure, the Apache Web Server and its* `mod_rewrite` *component. So while the technical bar's set a bit higher than the solution offered here, this sort of server-side solution is an excellent alternative.*

For the first line of the gateway CSS file, you call in your core style sheet:

```
@import url("core.css");
```

There is nothing surprising there. A simple `@import` rule pulls in `core.css`, which has been well tested in the more reliable CSS-aware browsers.

Now, were you simply to use `@import` to include additional files, there's nothing to prevent all browsers from parsing them. Instead, you need a way to serve these CSS files up selectively, so that only the problem user agents digest the rules there. If possible, the "good" browsers should remain blissfully unaware of little hacks. How do you do this, you ask? Well, fire *is* the best way to fight fire. You use CSS hacks to hack more intelligently.

First, let's deal with Internet Explorer 5.*x* on Windows. Its implementation of the CSS box model is notoriously problematic, and it is bound to cause some issues for your layout. So, rather than adding workarounds to the core style sheet, you can make use of a wonderful technique known as the Mid Pass Filter:

```
/* Import IE5x/Win hacks */
@media tty {
 i{content:"\";/*" "*/}} @import 'hacks.win.ie5.css'; /*";}
}/* */
```

Developed by CSS pioneer and Web developer Tantek Çelik, the Mid Pass Filter allows you to deliver a style sheet to the 5.*x* versions of Internet Explorer on Windows, and to those browsers alone. All other user agents skip right over this rule because they don't fall prey to the same parsing bug as IE5.*x*/Win.

While the Macintosh version of Internet Explorer 5 is considered to have CSS support that's far superior to its Windows-based cousins, it's not without its bugs. Development on the browser ended in mid-2003, leaving you to deal with its occasional layout quirks. Thankfully, you have another filter at your disposal, the IE5/Mac Band Pass Filter:

```
/* Import IE5/Mac hacks */
/*\*//*/
@import url("hacks.mac.ie5.css");
/**/
```

Also developed by Tantek Çelik and popularized by Web designer Doug Bowman, the IE5/Mac Band Pass Filter serves up only the imported CSS to — you guessed it — Internet Explorer 5 on the Mac OS. Still, the effect is the same as the Mid Pass Filter. Other browsers disregard the style sheet that's targeted at one browser's quirks.

*For a discussion of other CSS filters and hack-management techniques, read Molly Holzschlag's article "Integrated Web Design: Strategies for Long-Term CSS Hack Management"* (`www.informit.com/articles/article.asp?p=170511`). *This section owes much to her excellent essay, in which Molly discusses additional filters not mentioned here.*

You might be asking yourself why these parsing bugs are the best way to manage other hacks. I'm not trying to be needlessly abstract, honest. By isolating browser-specific hacks into one CSS file and keeping the core style sheet relatively pure, you gain two rather tangible benefits. First and foremost, these work-arounds are easier for other folks to locate, maintain, and modify. Second, you resolve the issue of hack obsolescence. Now, if you need to stop supporting a browser, you simply delete a few lines from your core style sheet and move forward.

# Summary

In coming chapters, you'll learn real-world, professional strategies for getting the most out of your style sheets. This chapter provides some of the foundations for high-octane XHTML/CSS design, ideas, and goals that you can bring forward into the more applied chapters that await. By beginning with a base of valid, well-structured markup, you can use CSS to layer your pages' presentation thereupon. This lightens your pages' weight, lowers the cost of maintenance and future redesigns, and increases your sites' accessibility.

In the next chapter, you take an in-depth look at the first of several companies to be profiled in this book, Google. Taking to heart some of these benefits, their recent redesign of the Blogger site makes for a compelling case study and demonstrates that it's an exciting time indeed to be pursuing CSS-driven design.

# 2

# Google's Blogger.com: Rollovers and Design Touches

*Designers can create normalcy out of chaos; they can clearly communicate ideas through the organizing and manipulating of words and pictures.*

*— Jeffery Veen*

In August 1999, a small company known as Pyra Labs released a new product called Blogger to the Web. Not only would it go on to earn that team fame and fortune, it would also kick-start the blogging revolution.

Blogger lets people such as you, your friends, and really anyone publish a Web site, or more specifically, a blog. It makes this process simple, fast, and really very friendly indeed. It's also free, which is a bit of a bonus on the Web, where no one wants to pay for anything.

In February 2003, a company called Google (you *might* have heard of it) whipped out its checkbook and acquired Pyra Labs, bringing Blogger into the Google fold. Along with the contracts and funding came something rather nice as far as the Blogger Team was concerned: the appearance of a BlogThis! button on the Google Toolbar. The overwhelming number of people using the Google Toolbar each day has enabled blogger.com to experience a huge surge in traffic. Signups should have gone through the roof. But they didn't. What was going on?

A few phone calls later and user-experience experts Adaptive Path were on the case. With them came designer and CSS maestro Douglas Bowman of Stopdesign. Together they would examine the behavior of visitors to Blogger.com and realize that something fundamental was stopping the conversion of these new visitors into new customers: the design of the site itself.

Plans were drawn up, ideas bandied about, and eventually, after 6 months of development, a new design was released. Blogger.com had a new face, and with it would come a mass of new customers. Since then, Blogger.com and other providers have become a large part of how many people communicate over the Internet, and the number of their customers has skyrocketed.

Bowman's redesign of Blogger.com involved a number of subtle yet effective design touches. This chapter discusses some of these design touches and looks at how to re-create them using the cleanest XHTML and the cleverest CSS around today. It also touches upon issues these solutions have with Internet Explorer (IE), and provide workarounds (where possible) for this troublesome browser.

This chapter provides some understanding of what is possible if your first thought is not, "Does this work in Internet Explorer?" but rather, "What is the cleanest, most forward-looking way I can build this?"

The solutions provided here might not be suitable for you to push into production today (that decision is up to you), but they provide a starting point in the whole development process. Kick off with an ideal solution, and then work your way back until you reach a practical solution. For many developers, those two points may be one and the same, in which case the techniques described here can be slotted in to the next site they build. For others, there may be some distance between those two points, with more weight being given to ensuring a design works 100 percent on IE and less weight being given to the cleanliness of the solution.

So, read the chapter, take in the lessons, and decide, project by project, Web site by Web site, to what extent you want to compromise your ideal solution.

# Interviewing the Designer

*Douglas Bowman is an influential designer whose highly publicized and hugely successful redesigns of sites such as Blogger, Wired News, and Adaptive Path have pushed him to the forefront of standards-compliant Web design. Some time after working on this project, Douglas Bowman accepted an offer to work for Google as its visual design lead, a newly opened position.*

**Q:** *First off, are you pleased with how things have turned out?*

**A:** I'm quite pleased with results of the entire project. The first measure of success in any project for me is whether or not it met or exceeded the client's goals. Usually, if the client is happy, I'm happy. In this case, one of the project's goals was to increase user sign-ups. Another goal was to increase use (by its existing user base) of Blogger in general. I can't be specific about numbers, but I can say that end results far exceeded Google's expectations.

This project had multiple facets to it; all of them contributed to the ultimate success of the Blogger redesign. Adaptive Path and Stopdesign worked with Google to redesign and simplify Blogger's home page and registration system. In addition to this site redesign, Stopdesign contracted five other designers to help create over 30 new user templates. Adding to the impact, Google worked really hard to up the ante by expanding Blogger's feature set and capabilities. User profiles, commenting, new ad-free hosted blog pages on BlogSpot, and blog search were just some of the new features that were added at or around the same time as the redesign.

**Q:** *Which bit of the design is the internal team most pleased with? And which part are the site's visitors most pleased with?*

**A:** I think this probably depends on whom you ask on the team. From talking with the developers and engineers at Google, I think they're most pleased with the design system, and how easy it is to expand and tweak the pages. The design is simple and straightforward. Obviously, it uses very simple HTML and an all-CSS layout. Google ended up taking the XHTML templates and CSS we provided for the home page and registration pages and used them as a base to redesign the entire application. In addition to the required page types Google needed from us, we also provided some generic templates that they're able to quickly grab and repurpose for new sections of the site.

If you were to ask a product manager, they might say they like the simplified design the best. Especially in regard to how much better the new home page helps communicate what a blog is, and the benefits of starting one immediately by using Blogger.

Blogger's visitors probably don't notice the site's design as much. In fact, if we did our job right, users might have a small affinity to the look of Blogger, but they wouldn't really pay as much attention to the design. They should be able to immediately grasp the benefits, and see a clear path to publishing their own blog in as a short amount of time as possible.

Users immediately noticed the huge increase in number of available templates from which they could choose for their own blog. When it comes to customization, an abundance of prefabbed choices gives them lots of options with which to express their voice and personality.

**Q:** *Later on in this chapter, we look at the code behind the rounded corners on Blogger.com but present a different solution to the one you used on the site. Our method requires no additional* `divs` *but sacrifices some cross-browser performance, with IE receiving no corner styling. If you were doing the project again would you consider such an approach, or, as a designer, do you demand that each and every element of the design be adhered to?*

**A:** If the choice were strictly up to me, and I was the only one working with the code, I'd go for the leaner, no-additional-`divs` option. I have the benefit of understanding exactly what the benefits and tradeoffs are, and exactly how the more advanced CSS operates. Leaner, simpler HTML is always a plus, especially if HTML can be removed that was inserted specifically for the purpose of style hooks. Page module code would not only be simpler, but more stable and less reliable on a precise number of classed `divs`.

I've made several choices with recent personal projects to give IE only a base set of styling, and then give other more CSS-capable browsers additional advanced styles. The term for this approach is "Progressive Enhancement," coined by Steven Champeon, in an article he wrote for *Webmonkey* a couple of years ago. Give some browsers an acceptable base design that functions well, give more capable browsers a more and more advanced design that builds on the base.

But the choice isn't only mine to make. In this case, the rounded corners throughout the site design were pretty big players in helping to give Blogger a simple, friendly feeling. A large number (possibly the majority) of Blogger users are still using IE as their default browser. If we had gone with the progressive enhancement approach, those IE users would see a page design that didn't quite mesh with the new Blogger "appearance."

With other projects, getting all the design details in IE correct may not have been important. But because Google was specifically targeting a wider, less-techy audience with this Blogger redesign — one that is also more likely to be using IE as their browser — compromising on this design aesthetic in IE browsers for the sake of leaner HTML wouldn't necessarily have been a good choice.

**Q:** *Has Blogger noticed any benefits from the redesign, either financial or just in the number of customers they're attracting?*

**A:** As stated previously, I can't be specific with numbers. But I can say that the number of new user registrations Blogger receives went up dramatically after the redesign of the home page and registration system. The revamped home page drove more users into the registration system. The simpler registration system had fewer pages than the previous system. And it was designed to guide the user all the way through as quickly and as effortlessly as possible, allowing them to set up a blog and be posting to it in less than 5 minutes. Those changes basically guaranteed success. But not even Google knew how big the success would be.

**Q:** *Would you have done anything differently, looking back?*

**A:** With each major redesign I complete, I usually discover a better way to do something within a week or two of completing that redesign. A light bulb that turns on. A tweak to the design that could have made coding it so much easier. A CSS selector that I never tried to use before suddenly makes sense and I can see all its various uses.

Specifically, with Blogger's CSS, there are lots of floats used that I wish didn't need to be there. Some were used solely to fix bugs in one or two browsers. Others were used for more legitimate purposes, like containing other nested floated elements.

I also wish I could have been involved in more of the latter aspects of the project. The team at Google did a great job at expanding the designs and templates we provided. But I wish I could have helped or overseen some of that expansion in order to maintain the consistency and quality of the design approach. Budget is always a limiting factor in this regard, and there simply wasn't enough of it to have Stopdesign or Adaptive Path involved at every major step of the project.

**Q:** *How much interest has the Blogger redesign produced for you, personally? Are other large companies looking at the finished product and wanting to go the same route?*

**A:** The Blogger redesign was a great project all around. Collaborating with Adaptive Path is always a fun learning experience; working with the Blogger team produced good results because they naturally "get it." Having the opportunity to execute successfully on a big project for Google brought lots of attention to both Adaptive Path and Stopdesign. Both companies have picked up a few projects as a result of people really noticing the Blogger redesign, and with the help of a few referrals from Google.

I think the Blogger redesign is just one more solid example, added to the heaps of others, that helps convince large companies that standards-based design is really the only way to go now. Pair all the benefits of standards together with the strengths and talents of a couple design consultancies. Then add on top of that the fact that the project was done for a high-profile client with a product that tons of people use and write about on a daily basis. No doubt there has been, and will be, a lot of attention given to the Blogger redesign. It stands out as a good example of the importance of effective design and a sound implementation of that design. Let's hope that Blogger bolsters another developer's case, and gives one more reason for a designer's plea to value properly executed design.

**Q:** *Two of Blogger's three "competitors" have been using standards-based design for some time now. Do you think this was the main driving force behind Blogger's adoption of standards, or was it just a natural progression to commission the site in this way?*

**A:** I don't necessarily think Google was thinking, "Uh-oh, our competitors are all using standards-based design, we need to get on the ball and do the same." When they came to us, they had a few simple objectives in mind. They probably hadn't thought out exactly how those objectives were to be achieved, but they knew we were capable of helping them solve their problems and greatly improve the user experience. Both Google and Adaptive Path also knew, by default,

Stopdesign's philosophy when it comes to implementing its designs, so I think a standards-based solution was probably assumed by default.

Sometimes, clients are remotely aware of the benefits of standards. But they really start to understand and get excited about a standards-based approach once they start working with one for their own site. The benefits are logical on paper, but they're tactical once the benefits are experienced.

No matter what CMS or scripting language is used to output code, simpler leaner HTML is always appreciated. It's just easier and faster to work with, and it's usually immediately parsable without needing to dissect multiple tables and rows and cells. Once the basic design was approved and fairly stable, the fact that Google's engineers and developers were able to continue making changes to the underlying code base, while we hosted the CSS files and continued making small changes to the design proved a convenient method of simultaneous iteration from both sides.

# CSS-Enabled Rollovers

If there's one thing that CSS has helped to simplify on the Web, it's the humble rollover — the act of swapping one image (or color) for another when the user moves the mouse over a section of the page. Until about 2001, the only reliable way to achieve such an effect was by breaking out JavaScript and writing something like this:

```
<html>
 <head>
  <title></title>
<script type="text/javascript">
<!--
function SwapOut()
     {
     document.getElementById('picture').src = 'picture-rollover.jpg';
     return true;
     }

function SwapBack()
     {
     document.getElementById('picture').src = 'picture.jpg';
     return true;
     }
-->
</script>
 </head>
 <body>
  <p><a href="" onmouseover="SwapOut()" onmouseout="SwapBack()"><img id="picture"
src="picture.jpg" width="100" height="150" /></a></p>
 </body>
</html>
```

CSS, thank heavens, has given us a number of different ways to achieve the same goal, and they're all delightfully simple. Let's take a look at them.

## Changing the Color and Background Color of Links (Simple)

This is the simplest (and most common) of all CSS rollover techniques. It is used to alert the user that the mouse is placed over a hyperlink. Figure 2-1 shows some examples of the rollover in action.

To see a great example of a rollover in action, visit the following links:

- `http://pootato.org/examples/rollover.html`
- `http://pootato.org/tutorials/css/css-rollovers/`

Let's look at that last example and see how it might be copied.

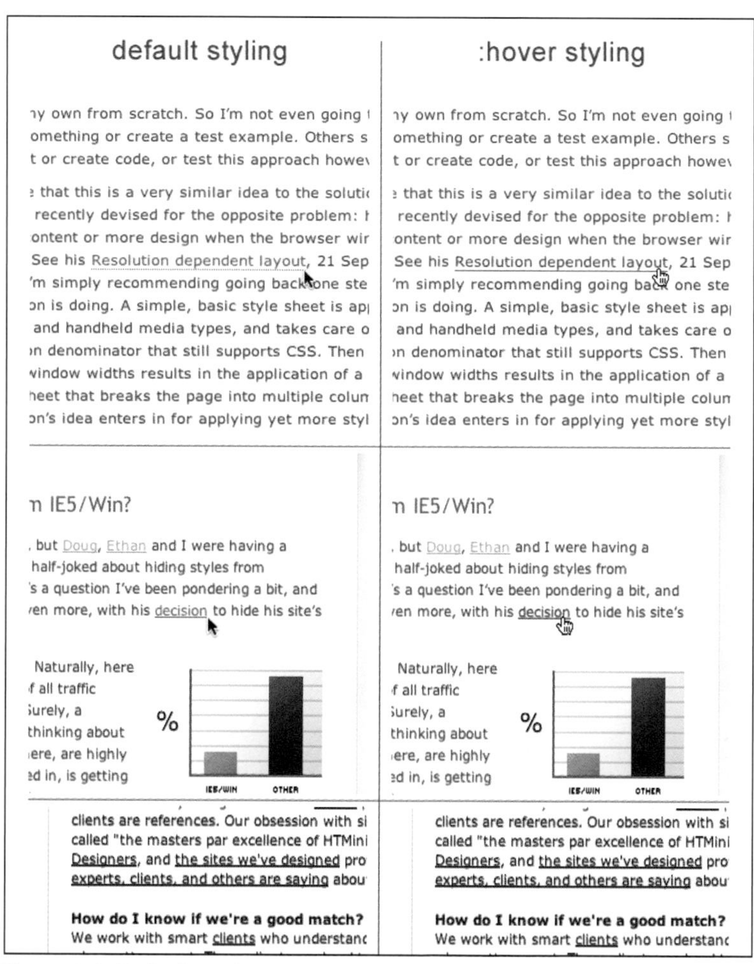


**Figure 2-1: Default and `:hover` link styling from various sites.**

### The XHTML

Following is the XHTML:

```
<p>If you're interested then <a href="">bung me an email</a> and we can talk about
what you want </p>
```

So, all that's needed is a simple a tag. How about the CSS?

### The CSS

Here's the CSS:

```
a {
 border-bottom: 1px solid #eee;
 color: #d17e62;
 text-decoration: none;
}
a:visited {
 border-bottom: 1px solid #eee;
 color: #9d604c;
 text-decoration: none;
}
a:hover {
 background-color: #ffffda;
 border-bottom: 1px solid #ddd;
 color: #c30;
 text-decoration: none;
}
```

It's important to note the order in which those rules are written. The first rule, `a {}`, affects all links. The second rule, `a:visited {}`, affects those links that the user has already visited (this is determined by the browser's cache). The third rule, `a:hover {}`, affects those links that the mouse is currently hovering over.

Following the logic of the CSS Cascade (`www.htmlhelp.com/reference/css/structure.html#cascade`), each of those rules has precedence over the one before it. So, a normal link will have its styles overwritten by a visited link, and a visited link will have its styles overwritten when the user hovers over it. Simple, really, but you'd be surprised how many people get those in the wrong order.

## Changing the Color and Background Color of Links (Complex)

This is a great trick for fast, low-bandwidth rollovers, and it's something Bowman has used on the front page of Blogger. It involves nothing more than altering the background color of an element while keeping the image on top of that background (be it an inline image or a CSS background image) the same.

To see it in action, Figure 2-2 shows four links on the front page of blogger.com.

Figure 2-3 shows what happens when you move the mouse over one of those links.

**Figure 2-2: Four links on the front page of Blogger.com. (The rest of the page has been dimmed so you can clearly identify the links.)**

You'll see that the background color has changed color and the word "thoughts" has become black. The actual button image, however, hasn't changed at all.

How has this been achieved? Well, first, let's look at the XHTML, CSS, and images that make up this section.

## *The XHTML*

Here's the XHTML:

```
<li id="wpub"><a href="https://www.blogger.com/tour_pub.g"><strong>Publish</strong>
thoughts</a></li>
 <li id="wcon"><a href="https://www.blogger.com/tour_con.g"><strong>Get</strong>
feedback</a></li>
 <li id="wshr"><a href="https://www.blogger.com/tour_shr.g"><strong>Post</strong>
photos</a></li>
 <li id="wpst"><a href="https://www.blogger.com/tour_pst.g"><strong>Go</strong>
mobile</a>
</li>
```

Figure 2-3: One of the rollover links in action.

## The CSS

Following is the CSS:

```
ul {
 list-style: none;
 margin: 0;
 padding: 0;
}

ul li {
 float: left;
 margin: 0;
 padding: 0;
}

ul li a {
 color: #777;
 display: block;
 padding: 80px 10px 5px;
```

```
  text-align: center;
  text-decoration: none;
  width: 75px;
}

ul li#wpub a {
  background: transparent url(icon_wpub.gif) no-repeat top center;
}

ul li#wcon a {
  background: transparent url(icon_wcon.gif) no-repeat top center;
}

ul li#wshr a {
  background: transparent url(icon_wshr.gif) no-repeat top center;
}

ul li#wpst a {
  background: transparent url(icon_wpst.gif) no-repeat top center;
}

ul li a strong {
  color: #000;
  font-size: larger;
}

ul li a strong {
  color: #000;
  display: block;
  font-size: larger;
}

ul li#wpub a:hover,
ul li#wcon a:hover,
ul li#wshr a:hover,
ul li#wpst a:hover {
  background-color: #f8f2eb;
}

ul li a:hover {
  color: #000;
}
```

### The Images

For this to work, the images being used must have transparent sections that let the background color of the image (or of the parent element) show through. In each case, the images shown in Figure 2-4 have had their transparent sections replaced with a checkered pattern, so you can see which bits are see-through, and which aren't.

**Figure 2-4: The checkered pattern indicates transparent areas.**

## *What Does It All Mean?*

Figure 2-5 shows the starting display.

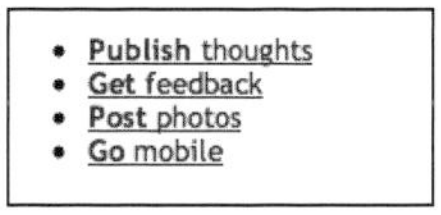

**Figure 2-5: The unstyled display.**

Now, let's go through the CSS line by line and see what effect each part has. First, remove the bullets (dots) that precede each list item, as shown in Figure 2-6:

```
ul {
 list-style: none;
}
```

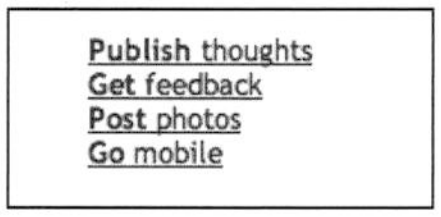

**Figure 2-6: Removing the bullets.**

Then remove any margin and padding the unordered list might have, as shown in Figure 2-7:

```
ul {
 list-style: none;
 margin: 0;
 padding: 0;
}
```

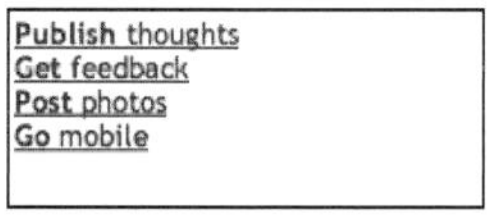

**Figure 2-7: Removing margins and padding.**

You do this so that when you come to position the finished list in the page, you're not fighting against the default browser settings for padding and margin on unordered lists.

Next, style the list items. First, float each item left, so that they are no longer displayed vertically and instead line up next to each other, horizontally, as shown in Figure 2-8. You also remove the margin and padding of each list item.

```
ul li {
 float: left;
 margin: 0;
 padding: 0;
}
```

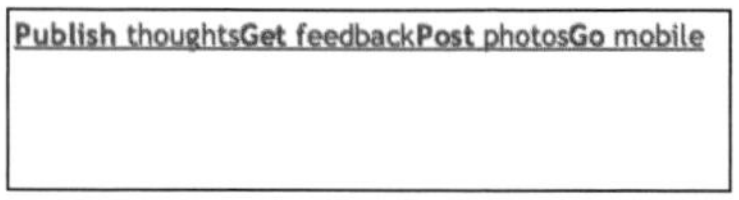

Publish thoughtsGet feedbackPost photosGo mobile

Figure 2-8: Floating each item in the list.

Now to style the links. First set a font color (see Figure 2-9):

```
ul li a {
 color: #777;
}
```

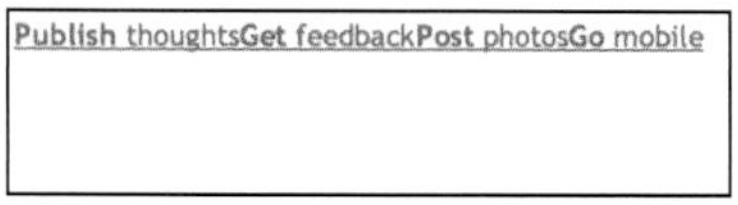

Publish thoughtsGet feedbackPost photosGo mobile

Figure 2-9: Setting a font color.

Next, set the links to `display: block`, and apply a `width` of `75px`, as shown in Figure 2-10 (this is equivalent to the width of the images you'll be using):

```
ul li a {
 color: #777;
 display: block;
 width: 75px;
}
```

Publish
thoughts
Get
feedback
Post photos
Go mobile

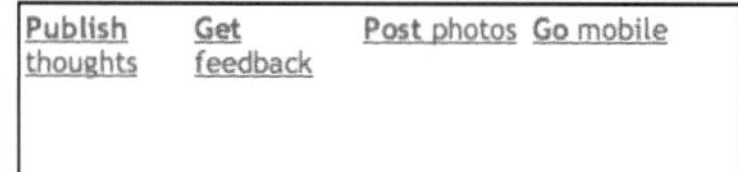

Figure 2-10: Blocking the elements.

Now you must insert some white space so that the images (which you'll be adding in a short while) will have somewhere to sit, as shown in Figure 2-11. Do this by adding in 80px of padding at the top (75px for the image and 5px to make a gap between the image and the text).

```
ul li a {
 color: #777;
 display: block;
 padding: 80px 0 0 0;
 width: 75px;
}
```

Publish
thoughts
Get
feedback
Post photos
Go mobile

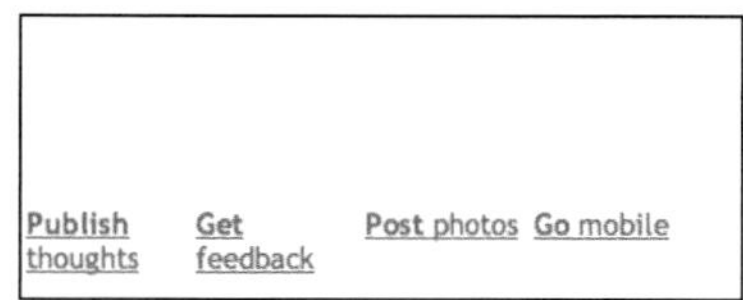

Figure 2-11: Inserting white space for placement of the images.

Next add in 10px of padding on the left and on the right, and 5px of padding on the bottom (see Figure 2-12):

```
ul li a {
 color: #777;
 display: block;
 padding: 80px 10px 5px;
 width: 75px;
}
```

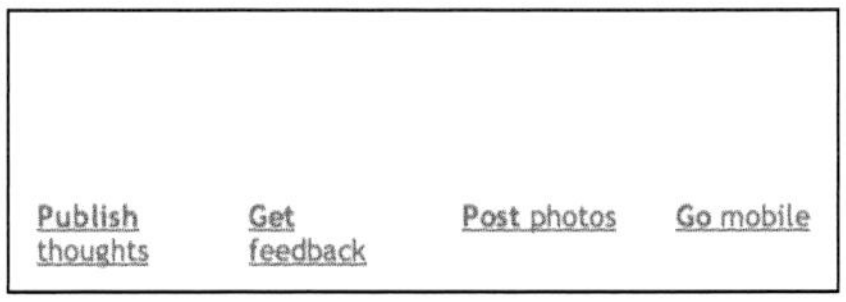

Publish thoughts Get feedback Post photos Go mobile

Figure 2-12: Adding padding.

And, to finish off the generic link styling, center-align the link text and remove its underline (see Figure 2-13):

```
ul li a {
 color: #777;
 display: block;
 padding: 80px 10px 5px;
 text-align: center;
 text-decoration: none;
 width: 75px;
}
```

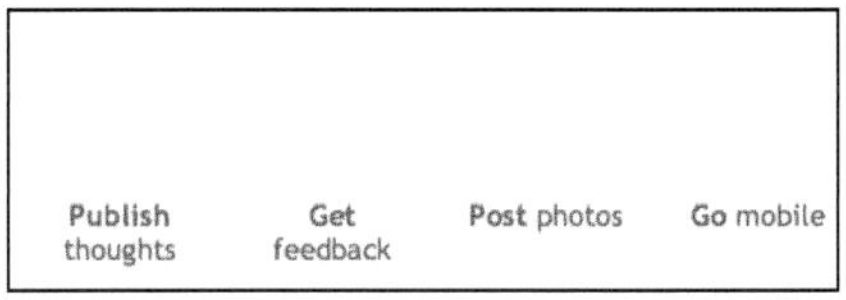

Publish thoughts Get feedback Post photos Go mobile

Figure 2-13: Centering text and removing underlining.

Now it's time to add in the background images for each of the links, as shown in Figure 2-14:

```
ul li#wpub a {
 background: transparent url(icon_wpub.gif) no-repeat top center;
}

ul li#wcon a {
 background: transparent url(icon_wcon.gif) no-repeat top center;
}

ul li#wshr a {
 background: transparent url(icon_wshr.gif) no-repeat top center;
}

ul li#wpst a {
 background: transparent url(icon_wpst.gif) no-repeat top center;
}
```

**Figure 2-14: Adding background images.**

Things are coming together nicely. Next, make the first word of each link darker and larger, as shown in Figure 2-15:

```
ul li a strong {
 color: #000;
 font-size: larger;
}
```

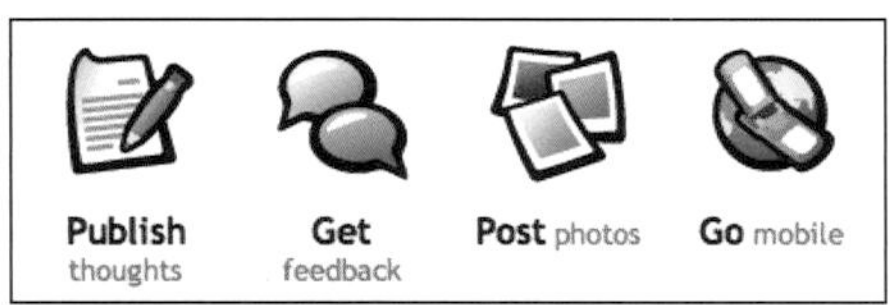


**Figure 2-15: Making the first word of the links darker and larger.**

To ensure that the second word of each link is forced onto a new line (see Figure 2-16), add a rule:

```
ul li a strong {
 color: #000;
 display: block;
 font-size: larger;
}
```

**Figure 2-16: Forcing the second word of the link to a new line.**

That's all looking very nice, so let's add in the CSS that will make the rollovers work.

The following rule alters the background color of each link as the user hovers the mouse over it (see Figure 2-17):

```
ul li#wpub a:hover,
ul li#wcon a:hover,
ul li#wshr a:hover,
ul li#wpst a:hover {
 background-color: #f8f2eb;
}
```

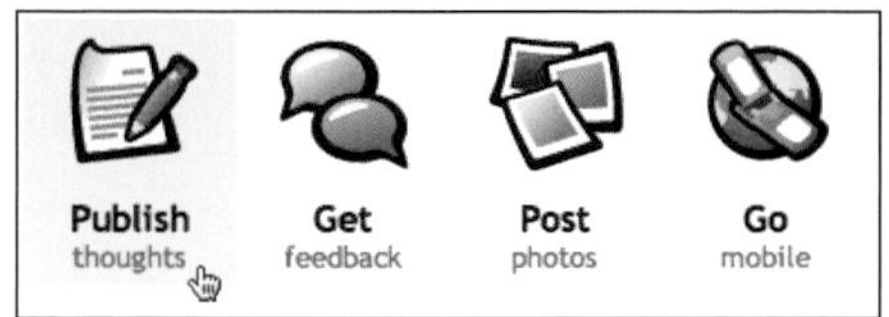


Figure 2-17: Altering the background color.

To finish things off, here's a little rule that will alter the color of the text on `:hover` so that it changes from gray to black, as shown in Figure 2-18:

```
ul li a:hover {
 color: #000;
}
```

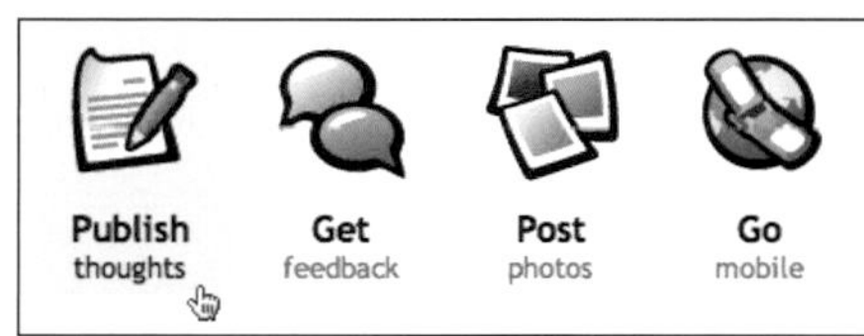


Figure 2-18: The finished product in action.

And you're done!

## Changing the Background Color of Table Rows

The use of alternating row colors in tables has become a well-recognized design touch (think of iTunes), providing structure to long tables and letting the eye scan easily across a row of information.

If this is combined with a hover effect to highlight the row under the mouse pointer, it can produce an attractive and functional look, as shown in Figure 2-19.

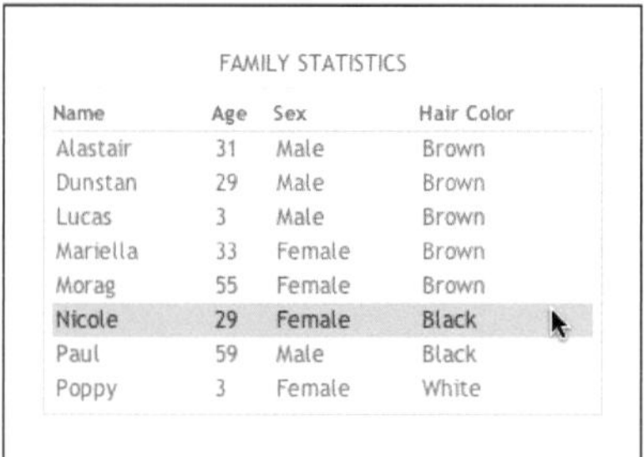

FAMILY STATISTICS

| Name | Age | Sex | Hair Color |
|---|---|---|---|
| Alastair | 31 | Male | Brown |
| Dunstan | 29 | Male | Brown |
| Lucas | 3 | Male | Brown |
| Mariella | 33 | Female | Brown |
| Morag | 55 | Female | Brown |
| Nicole | 29 | Female | Black |
| Paul | 59 | Male | Black |
| Poppy | 3 | Female | White |

Figure 2-19: An example of alternate row coloring and row highlighting.

The code for this hover effect couldn't be simpler. Using the previous example, here's the XHTML and the CSS needed to style the table rows.

## The XHTML

Following is the XHTML:

```
<table cellpadding="5" cellspacing="0" border="1">
 <caption>Family Statistics</caption>

 <thead>
  <tr>
   <th>Name</th>
   <th>Age</th>
   <th>Sex</th>
   <th>Hair Color</th>
 </tr>
 </thead>

 <tbody>
  <tr class="odd">
   <td>Alastair</td>
   <td>31</td>
   <td>Male</td>
   <td>Brown</td>
  </tr>
  <tr class="even">
   <td>Dunstan</td>
   <td>29</td>
   <td>Male</td>
   <td>Brown</td>
  </tr>
  <tr class="odd">
   <td>Lucas</td>
   <td>3</td>
   <td>Male</td>
   <td>Brown</td>
  </tr>
  <tr class="even">
   <td>Mariella</td>
   <td>33</td>
   <td>Female</td>
   <td>Brown</td>
  </tr>
  <tr class="odd">
   <td>Morag</td>
   <td>55</td>
   <td>Female</td>
   <td>Brown</td>
  </tr>
  <tr class="even">
   <td>Nicole</td>
   <td>29</td>
   <td>Female</td>
   <td>Black</td>
  </tr>
  <tr class="odd">
```

```
    <td>Paul</td>
    <td>59</td>
    <td>Male</td>
    <td>Black</td>
   </tr>
   <tr class="even">
    <td>Poppy</td>
    <td>3</td>
    <td>Female</td>
    <td>White</td>
   </tr>
  </tbody>
</table>
```

## The CSS

Most of the following CSS is needed to style the table. The rules that actually do the hover effect have been boldfaced for you.

```
table {
 background-color: #fff;
 border: 1px solid #ddd;
 empty-cells: show;
 font-size: 90%;
 margin: 0 0 20px 0;
 padding: 4px;
 text-align: left;
 width: 300px;
}

table caption {
 color: #777;
 margin: 0 0 5px 0;
 padding: 0;
 text-align: center;
 text-transform: uppercase;
}

table thead th {
 border: 0;
 border-bottom: 1px solid #ddd;
 color: #777;
 font-size: 90%;
 padding: 3px 0;
 margin: 0 0 5px 0;
 text-align: left;
}

table tbody tr.odd {
 background-color: #f7f7f7;
}

table tbody tr.even {
 background-color: #fff;
```

```
}

table tbody tr:hover {
 background-color: #ffe08e;
}

table tbody td {
 color: #888;
 padding: 2px;
 border: 0;
}

table tbody tr:hover td {
 color: #444;
}
```

## What Does It All Mean?

We're not going to go through each and every line of that CSS because it's not all relevant to this rollover section. However, let's look at the last few rules in detail.

The first thing to note is that you've given each of the two row classes (`.odd` and `.even`) a background color:

```
table tbody tr.odd {
 background-color: #f7f7f7;
}

table tbody tr.even {
 background-color: #fff;
}
```

That lets you create the alternating row-color effect.

Next, you set a rule that changes the background color of a row when the user's mouse hovers over it:

```
table tbody tr:hover {
 background-color: #ffe08e;
}
```

And finally, you change the color of the text contained within the row that is being hovered over, making it darker to stand out against its new background color:

```
table tbody tr:hover td {
 color: #444;
}
```

It really is wonderfully simple stuff.

## Changing the Color of Text

The final hover application you're going to look at in this section is highlighting text (be it plain text or linked text) when a user hovers over a `div` or similar element.

Why might this be useful? Imagine a site that contains many links. Developers usually style their links so that they're a bright color, making them stand out from the surrounding text. That's all very well when you have a few links per page, but what happens if your site contains hundreds of links per page? The eyes of the users will be assaulted by a mass of bright color as hundreds of links vie for their attention. How can you expect to view the subtleties of your design if all you can see is a sea of color?

The solution (or one of them) is simple. If you hide the bright colors of these links until the user hovers the mouse over the relevant section of the page, then you can present users, at first glance, with a much calmer site. You make the links obvious only when the user is indicating that he or she is interested in that section of the page by moving the mouse over it.

That's pretty effective. Let's see how that might be re-created.

### The XHTML

Following is the XHTML:

```
<div id="links">
 <h3>Blogmarks</h3>

 <p>A collection of miscellaneous links that don't merit a main blog posting, but
which are interesting none-the-less.</p>

 <ul>
  <li><a href="">What WordPress is currently doing to combat comment spam</a>.</li>
  <li><a href="">Mobile web tools</a>, from <a href="">Pukupi</a>.</li>
  <li><a href="">The photography of E.J. Peiker</a>.</li>
  <li><a href="">Some handy tips for advanced Google use</a>.</li>
  <li><a href="">Make your own church signs</a>, or <a href="">view some real
ones</a>.</li>
  <li><a href="">Michael Heilemann</a> is doing a great job with his new <a
href="">WordPress</a> theme, <a href="">Kubrick</a>.</li>
  <li>I'm late to the party, but <a href="">Dan</a> has a <a href="">book
out</a>.</li>
  <li><a href="">A crazy concept for laying our housing estates</a>.</li>
  <li><a href="">Spiderman reviews crayons</a>.</li>
  <li>Some <a href="">beautiful images</a> from photographer <a href="">Greg
Downing</a>.</li>
  <li><a href="">Lots of links from the Link Bunnies</a>.</li>
  <li>Nice <a href="">&#8220;when I was a child&#8221;</a> sort of post frin
Stuart.</li>
  <li><a href="">How much does SafariSorter cost?</a></li>
  <li>Some handy <a href="">maintenance tips for Mac owners</a>.</li>
  <li><a href="">Ming Jung</a>, <a href="">Anil Dash</a>, and I get <a
href="">interviewed for HBO's Real Sex</a>.</li>
 </ul>
</div>
```

### The CSS

And here's the CSS:

```
div#links {
 color: #333;
 border: 2px solid #ddd;
 padding: 10px;
 width: 240px;
}

html > body div#links {
 width: 220px;
}

div#links ul {
 margin: 0 0 0 19px;
 padding: 0;
}

div#links ul li {
 list-style-image: url('list-dot.gif');
 margin: 0 0 .5em 0;
}

html > body div#links ul li a {
 color: #333;
 text-decoration: none;
}

div#links:hover ul li a {
 color: #0000ff;
 text-decoration: underline;
}

div#links ul li a:hover {
 background-color: #ffff66;
 color: #000;
 text-decoration: none;
}
```

## Images

All you're using is a little "dot" image to replace the browser's default "list dot" (or bullet), as shown in Figure 2-20.

**Figure 2-20: A replacement list dot (or bullet).**

## What Does It All Mean?

Again, we won't look at every little bit of that CSS code because it's not all relevant to the rollover technique being discussed. However, here are a few bits that are worth examining.

First, you set the default text color for everything in the `div`. You choose a shade of gray because gray is a nice calm color, and that's one of the things you're trying to achieve here — calm.

```
div#links {
 color: #333;
}
```

Next, style the links so that they fit in with the gray text, removing anything that would make them stand out from their surroundings:

```
html > body div#links ul li a {
 color: #333;
 text-decoration: none;
}
```

Use the child selector (>) to style the links so that IE (which doesn't interpret rules containing the child selector) won't apply the rule. For a full explanation of why you do this, see the following section, "Dealing with Internet Explorer."

Now come two `:hover` rules. The first will be activated when the user moves the mouse over the `div`. It will cause the links to change from gray to blue and to show their underline text decoration.

```
div#links:hover ul li a {
 color: #0000ff;
 text-decoration: underline;
}
```

The second `:hover` rule activates when the user moves the mouse directly over a link. It changes the text color to black, removes the underline, and makes the background of the link bright yellow.

```
div#links ul li a:hover {
 background-color: #ffff66;
 color: #000;
 text-decoration: none;
}
```

And that's all there is to it.

## Dealing with Internet Explorer

IE6 doesn't understand the `:hover` selector on elements other than links. So, Firefox, Opera, Safari, and IE all understand this:

```
a:hover {
 color: red;
}
```

But only Firefox, Opera, and Safari understand these:

```
div:hover {
 color: yellow;
}


div:hover a {
 color: green;
}
```

Why is that relevant? Well, it affects what's just been done in this demonstration. Imagine that you're using Firefox to browse a Web site. The page loads, and CSS turns all the text and links gray to mellow things out for you. You zero in on a section that interests you. You move your mouse over it and, ah! The links turn bright blue. You can now see what's a link and what's plain text.

Now, imagine that you're browsing the same site using IE. The page loads, and CSS turns all the text and links gray. You zero in on a section that interests you. You move your mouse over it and nothing. No links pop out at you, and you're just left with a sea of unresponsive gray text. Why? Because IE doesn't understand that you're hovering over a `div`, and so it can't apply a different, brighter style to the links. Disaster!

So, you can see why you have to stop the links being turned gray right at the start in IE. There's no point turning them gray if the browser can't turn them back to blue at the appropriate moment. Hence, you use the child selector.

Now, here's the bugger of using a child selector to hide styles from IE: IE for the PC doesn't understand the child selector (great!), but IE5 for the Mac does! So, any time you use > to block IE, you must remember you're blocking only IE for the PC, not IE for the Mac.

# Changing the Background Position on Links

The second approach to CSS-based rollovers is one that focuses on swapping not just background color but images as well, and it does so using the increasingly important method of background positioning.

If you've never heard of this idea, don't worry; it's easy as pie, but it does require a little explanation.

## Making Rollovers from Embedded Images

Let's say you've been given the page layout shown in Figure 2-21 and have been asked to jazz up the photo a bit — add in a rollover, maybe a bit of a drop shadow, something a bit more interesting.

You can do that, right? Well, what if you were told that you have to make those changes without touching the XHTML? Could you still do it? Let's tale a look at some code:

```
<div id="sidebar">
 <div class="box">
  <h2>Lucas says...</h2>
```

```
    <div id="photo-lucas">
     <img src="lucas.jpg" width="150" height="100" alt="Portrait of small boy" />
    </div>

    <p>Hello there, my name is Lucas. I am 3-years old and the bi-lingual monkey-
  child of an English man and an Italian woman.</p>

    <p>I like cars and trucks and buses and trains and almost anything that moves.
  I'm not so keen on sprouts or the Welsh.</p>

    <p>My Grandma has a dog, called Poppy. She's small and cute and she widdles when
  she gets excited.</p>

    <p>When I grow up I want to be like my Uncle... what a guy he is...</p>
   </div>
  </div>
```

**Figure 2-21: Can you replace this photo using CSS?**

Well, if you're fortunate, and you're working with well thought-out XHTML, then this sort of thing is a breeze to do. It may sound daunting, but with a bit of Adobe Photoshop magic and some CSS, you can very quickly have a layout that not only inserts a new image and repositions it but also makes that image function as a rollover whenever the user moves the mouse into the "Lucas says..." box.

Figure 2-22 shows the finished result. It's shown twice so that you can see the page in its normal state (on the left) and in its "rolled-over" state (on the right).

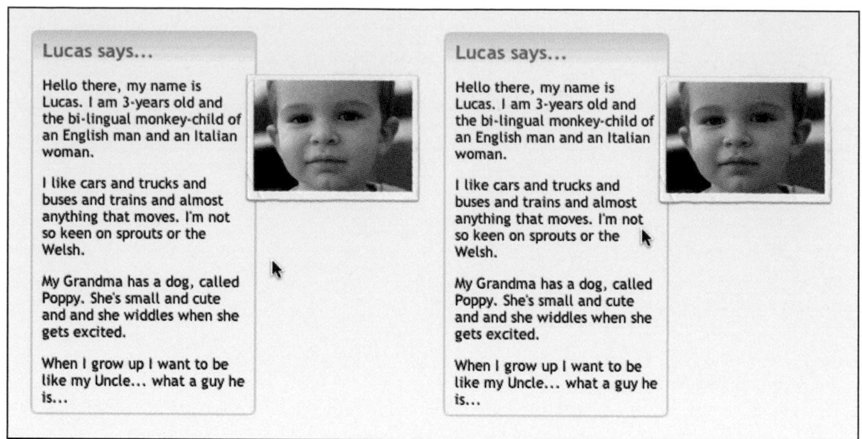


**Figure 2-22: The finished layout and rollover in action. Mousing over the text causes the rollover to trigger and the color image to be revealed.**

Let's see how that was achieved.

## *The XHTML*

Let's focus on the photo section of the code, which has been boldfaced for you:

```
<div id="sidebar">
 <div class="box">
  <h2>Lucas says...</h2>

  <div id="photo-lucas">
   <img src="lucas.jpg" width="150" height="100" alt="Portrait of small boy" />
  </div>

  <p>Hello there, my name is Lucas. I am 3-years old and the bi-lingual monkey-
child of an English man and an Italian woman.</p>

  <p>I like cars and trucks and buses and trains and almost anything that moves.
I'm not so keen on sprouts or the Welsh.</p>

  <p>My Grandma has a dog, called Poppy. She's small and cute and she widdles when
she gets excited.</p>

  <p>When I grow up I want to be like my Uncle... what a guy he is...</p>
 </div>
</div>
```

## The CSS

Let's look at the CSS. What's going is that you're removing the original image and replacing it with a completely different one, and you are using a single image to create a mouseover effect:

```
.box {
 position: relative;
}

html > body div#photo-lucas img {
 left: -5000px;
 position: absolute;
}

html > body div#photo-lucas {
 background: transparent url(lucas-rollover.png) no-repeat top left;
 height: 124px;
 left: 185px;
 position: absolute;
 width: 160px;
}

div.box:hover div#photo-lucas {
 background-position: top right;
}
```

## The Images

Figure 2-23 shows the original JPG image referenced in the XHTML.

**Figure 2-23: The original image, referenced in the XHTML (lucas.jpg at 150 × 100px).**

Figure 2-24 shows a PNG file you're going to use as the replacement image. You use a PNG file because you want to have a realistic, semi-transparent drop shadow, and neither JPG nor GIF files can do that.

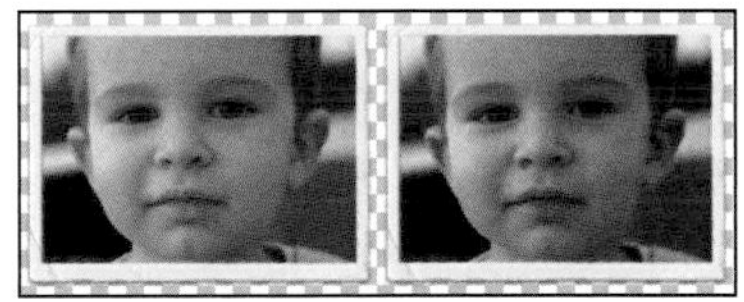

**Figure 2-24: The image used for the rollover (Lucas-rollover.png 320 × 124px). Transparent sections are denoted by the checkered pattern.**

## What Does It All Mean?

The XHTML isn't worth examining in any more detail, but let's have a look at what the CSS does.

Figure 2-25 shows the starting point.

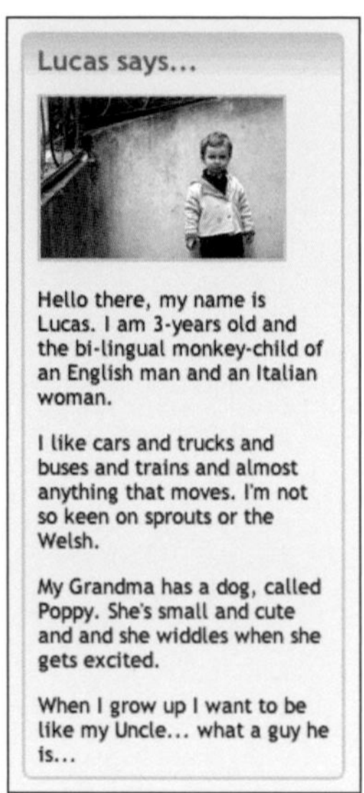


**Figure 2-25: Starting point.**

First, you must remove the original `lucas.jpg` image. There are a number of ways to do this using CSS, but the best all-around method is to set its position to absolute and then fling it as far off the edge of the screen as possible (see Figure 2-26):

```
html > body div#photo-lucas img {
 left: -5000px;
 position: absolute;
}
```

You use `position: absolute` and not `position: relative` because absolutely positioning an object removes it completely from the document flow. In this case, it causes its parent element (`div#photo-lucas`) to collapse and lets the text below it move up and reflow to fill the now-blank space.

Having cleared out the old image, it's time to insert the new one. You're going to insert it as a background image to `div#photo-lucas`, the `div` that contained the original image (see Figure 2-27):

```
html > body div#photo-lucas {
 background: transparent url(lucas-rollover.png) no-repeat top left;
}
```

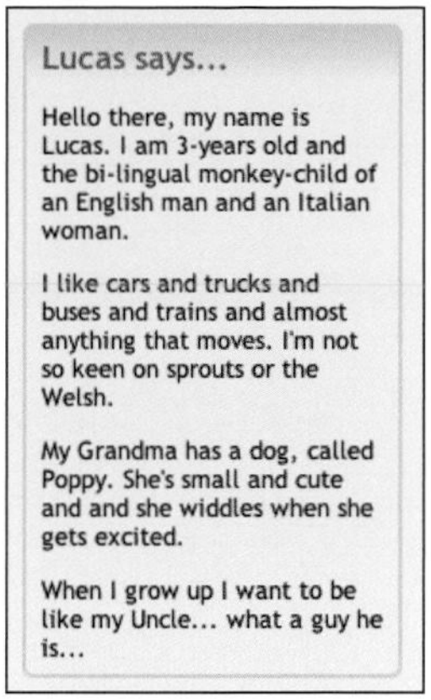

Lucas says...

Hello there, my name is Lucas. I am 3-years old and the bi-lingual monkey-child of an English man and an Italian woman.

I like cars and trucks and buses and trains and almost anything that moves. I'm not so keen on sprouts or the Welsh.

My Grandma has a dog, called Poppy. She's small and cute and and she widdles when she gets excited.

When I grow up I want to be like my Uncle... what a guy he is...

**Figure 2-26: Removing the image.**

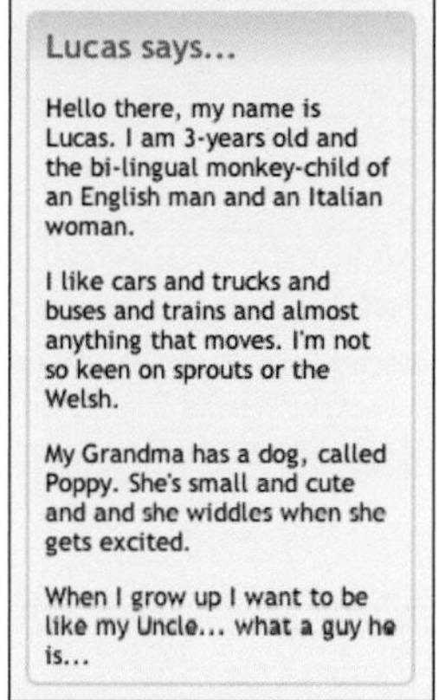


**Figure 2-27: Inserting the new image.**

Hmm... you've inserted it, so where is it?

Well, remember that this is a background image to `div#photo-lucas`, the element that contained the original photo. But because you threw the original photo off the edge of the screen, `div#photo-lucas` has no content, and no content means no dimensions. So, yes, the new background image is there, but you must give `div#photo-lucas` a width and a height to be able to see it, as shown in Figure 2-28:

```
html > body div#photo-lucas {
 background: transparent url(lucas-rollover.png) no-repeat top left;
 height: 124px;
 width: 160px;
}
```

**Figure 2-28:** Revealing the hidden image.

Ah! There it is; very nice. Notice that the height you set corresponds to the height of the new rollover image (`lucas-rollover.png`), and the width is exactly half that image's width. This way you see only one-half of `lucas-rollover.png` at a time, which is just what you want.

With the new image onscreen, reposition it off to the right. To do that, once again use `position: absolute` (see Figure 2-29):

```
html > body div#photo-lucas {
 background: transparent url(lucas-rollover.png) no-repeat top left;
 height: 124px;
 position: absolute;
 width: 160px;
}
```

Now, don't worry, it hasn't gone wrong. All that's happened is that `div#photo-lucas` has been removed from the document flow, meaning that it no longer interacts with anything around it. Instead, it floats above everything else (or underneath if you want to start using `z-index`) and can be positioned anywhere onscreen.

Because that's the case, move it to its new position on the right of the box. The first thing to do is to alter a bit of that original box CSS and insert the following rule:

```
.box {
 position: relative;
}
```

**Figure 2-29: Repositioning the image.**

This means that whatever XY coordinates you give to `div#photo-lucas`, you will be positioning it relative to its containing element, the box (`.box`). The `top left` will be the top-left corner of the box, `bottom right` will be the bottom-right corner of the box, and so on.

Now that your reference point is established, move the image. First of all, set the left position, as shown in Figure 2-30:

```
html > body div#photo-lucas {
 background: transparent url(lucas-rollover.png) no-repeat top left;
 height: 124px;
 left: 185px;
 position: absolute;
 width: 160px;
}
```

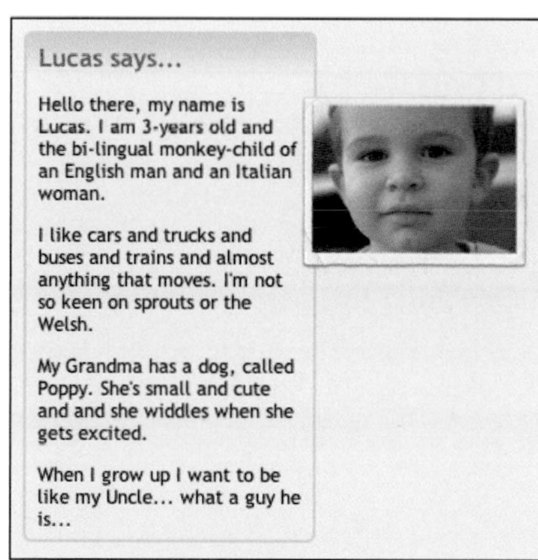


**Figure 2-30: Setting the left position.**

Perfect. And in fact, you don't need to set a top position because it's already in the right place. Now all that's left to do is activate the main point of this demonstration: the rollover, as shown in Figure 2-31. Hopefully you're starting to understand just how easy this final step always is:

```
div.box:hover div#photo-lucas {
 background-position: top right;
}
```

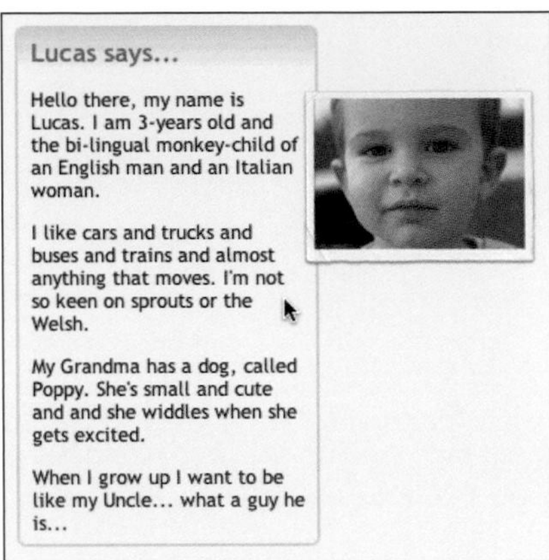


Figure 2-31: Activating the rollover.

## Dealing with Internet Explorer

IE gets rather short shrift here. Not only does it not interpret `:hover` on `div`s, but it also doesn't handle semi-transparent PNGs. As a consequence, it's blocked from implementing any of these changes by using the child selector, as described earlier in this chapter.

There are certainly instances where you could use an Internet Explorer for Windows 6 (IE6)-friendly version of this technique. You could use a regular JPG, instead of a PNG. (You wouldn't get the drop shadow, but that's not always a bad thing.) As long as your original image sat inside a link the rollover would work as well (in a limited way).

You may be thinking, "Stop showing me demos that don't work in IE!" However, what you should be taking away from this is an idea of what's possible with today's best browsers. Once you realize what's possible, you can start to adjust these demos until you reach a happy balance — a balance between CSS and cross-browser functionality; between lean, mean XHTML, and making the site work on your client's machine.

But okay, let's make this demo work in IE6. Changes to the code have been boldfaced in the following example. All you are doing is inserting one image for IE6 (a JPG), and then replacing that image for Firefox, Opera, and Safari. As always, you're using the child-combinator selector to do this.

```
.box {
 position: relative;
}

div#photo img {
 left: -5000px;
 position: absolute;
}

body div#photo-lucas {
 background: transparent url(lucas-ie.png) no-repeat top left;
 border: 2px solid #e1d4c0;
 height: 113px;
 left: 175px;
 position: absolute;
 width: 156px;
}

html > body div#photo-lucas {
 background: transparent url(lucas-rollover.png) no-repeat top left;
 border: none;
 height: 124px;
 left: 185px;
 position: absolute;
 width: 160px;
}

div.box:hover div#photo-lucas {
 background-position: top right;
}
```

Figure 2-32 shows the new, IE-only image.

**Figure 2-32: The lucas-ie.jpg file at 156 × 113px.**

And how does all that look in IE? Figure 2-33 shows how the complete package looks.

**Figure 2-33: The finished IE product.**

Not bad.

# Summary

This chapter looked at rollovers that manipulate text color and background color, and you saw rollovers that manipulate the position of background images. You noted that Internet Explorer lets you down with its incomplete support of `:hover`.

This chapter should provide you with an understanding of the underlying principles of the techniques discussed and not leave you blindly copying code examples. If you find that you can't put these ideas to work on your client's site, at least you can play with them and try to duplicate your work using these techniques. You'll be amazed at how simple it can be, and you'll also be amazed at how easy it is to cut and paste one set of code to get it working.

In the next chapter, you'll explore the inner workings of a successful event-driven site: The PGA Championship.

# 3

# The Classic U.S. PGA Championship Web Site

*I know I am getting better at golf because I'm hitting fewer spectators.*

*— Gerald Ford*

The PGA Championship is one of the world's premier sporting events. Presented in the late summer each year by the PGA of America, the tournament is the final major event of the golf season, features the best players in professional golf, and is followed by millions of fans around the world.

Turner Sports Interactive, a division of Time Warner, was responsible for the site development and editorial content during the event. The technological goal was to create a dynamic, rich, standards-compliant site, using CSS for all layout and presentation, and easily digestible Extensible Hypertext Markup Language (XHTML) markup, and Flash for special features. The creative goal was for a Web presence that was visually unique, sophisticated, and most of all, without any of the typical golf design clichés. A palette of desaturated, warm neutral tones was chosen, plus white and black to emphasize original photography and place as much attention on the textual content as possible.

Soon after its launch in July 2004, the PGA Championship site received overwhelmingly positive feedback from golf fans and the Web development community for its unique presentation, adherence to Web standards, and overall design. Traffic exploded on the first day of competition, as the PGA.com editorial team delivered a steady stream of news, scores, and multimedia content to millions of users per hour.

It's been a few years since the launch of this version of the PGA Championship Web site, and the PGA has launched variations of the design in years since then. However, it's the 2004 version of the Web site that captures our attention. It is a classic, thanks to the combination of lightweight CSS/XHTML markup, solid design, and gorgeous photography of the golf courses.

This chapter provides detailed walkthroughs of some of the techniques used for a few of the site's original features. Included in this discussion are general CSS/XHTML tips and tricks, as well as real-world caveats to watch out for in your own projects. The topics discussed in this chapter include the following:

- How to create the layered, drop-shadow effect using CSS and Photoshop
- A powerful, ultra-light method for adding CSS-powered drop-down menus
- Embedding Flash content without breaking standards compliance

# Developing the Drop-Shadow Effect

One of the more eye-catching features of the PGA Championship site was the nearly three-dimensional (3D), layered separation of content. The effect was subtle, but if you look closely at the home page (`www.pga.com/pgachampionship/2004/index.html`) shown in Figure 3-1, the left column appears to hover above its surrounding content. This wasn't just a cool visual trick but served an editorial purpose. The left column contained the most up-to-date Championship news and features. By giving the area a subtle (but noticeable) sense of visual lift, end users could quickly discern where the freshest Championship content was published.

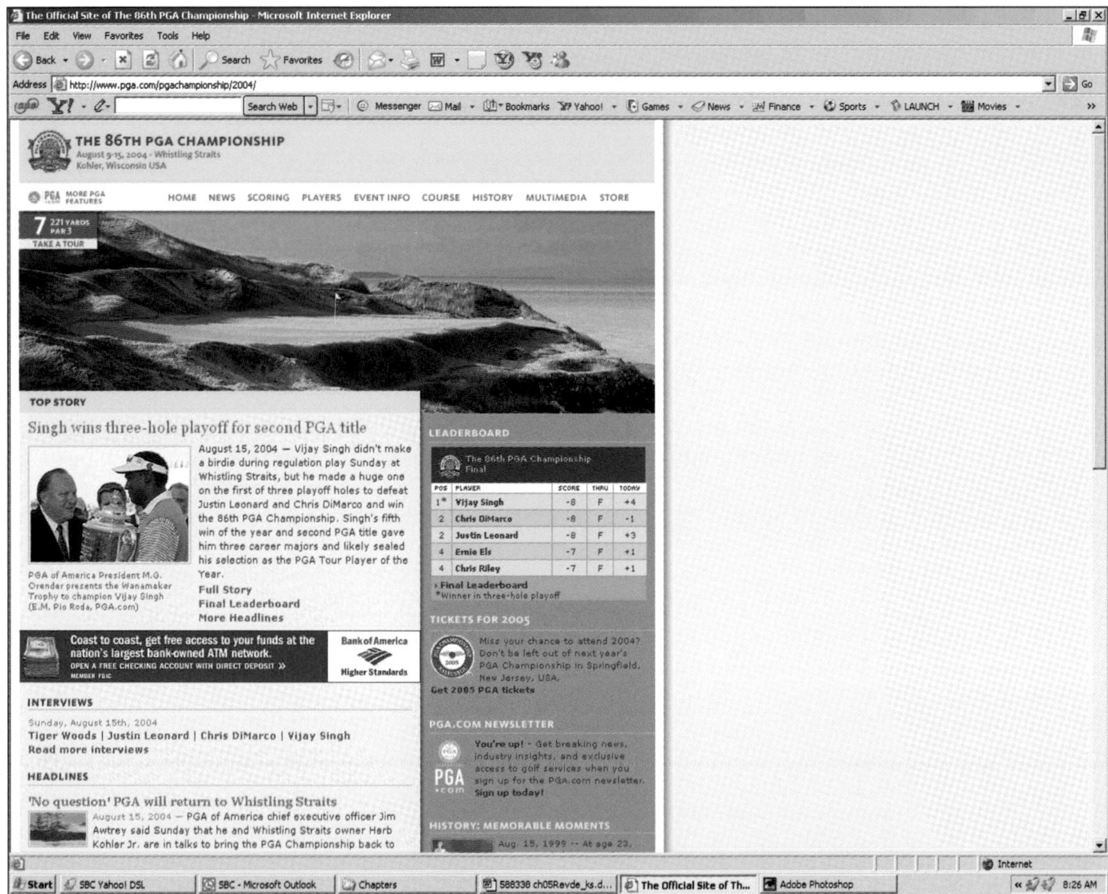


Figure 3-1: The PGA Championship home page.

The left column couldn't simply be "higher" than its neighbors but needed to partially obscure the content so that the space appeared to realistically float above the page. This was the idea behind the "Top Story" header at the top of the left column. Because it appeared to be connected to the left column and provided the right edge for the beginning of a drop shadow running down the page, it *seemed* to be part of the XHTML and to be sitting on top of the Flash movie. But the illusion was just that.

The total effect may look complex and bandwidth-intensive, but it was actually very light in byte size and code and fairly straightforward to create with a little advance planning. This section examines the effect by using Photoshop, Flash, CSS, and XHTML and offers an extra tip for pushing the effect to an even greater height.

## Creating the Illusion

Before you begin with the nuts and bolts, back up for a moment and revisit the goal — to visually meld the Flash movie at the top of the page with the content below, and to create the appearance that the left column is on a higher layer than its surrounding content by running a drop shadow down the length of the document. It's tricky because if the shadow in either the Flash movie or the XHTML were 1 pixel off, the effect would be ruined. But, thanks to the preciseness of both CSS and XHTML, it was possible.

Flash movies, like any embedded content, are always square. It's impossible for a Flash object to have an irregular shape. To "break the bounding box" and create the illusion of layers, part of the left column's design was placed inside the bottom of the Flash movie. It was positioned (to the pixel) so that, when the Flash and XHTML content were placed next to each other, they snapped together to complete the illusion.

To start, a new document was created in Photoshop and filled with the hex color used by both the Flash movie and the column running down the right side of the page. A new layer (named "bar") was created. Next, a space the same width as the left column was selected (using the Rectangular Marquee tool) and then filled the area with the color of choice. A Drop Shadow layer effect was applied to "bar," and the shadow options were set to produce a look that wasn't too pronounced or heavy but was sufficient to provide a subtle sense of separation.

When completed, the document looked like Figure 3-2.

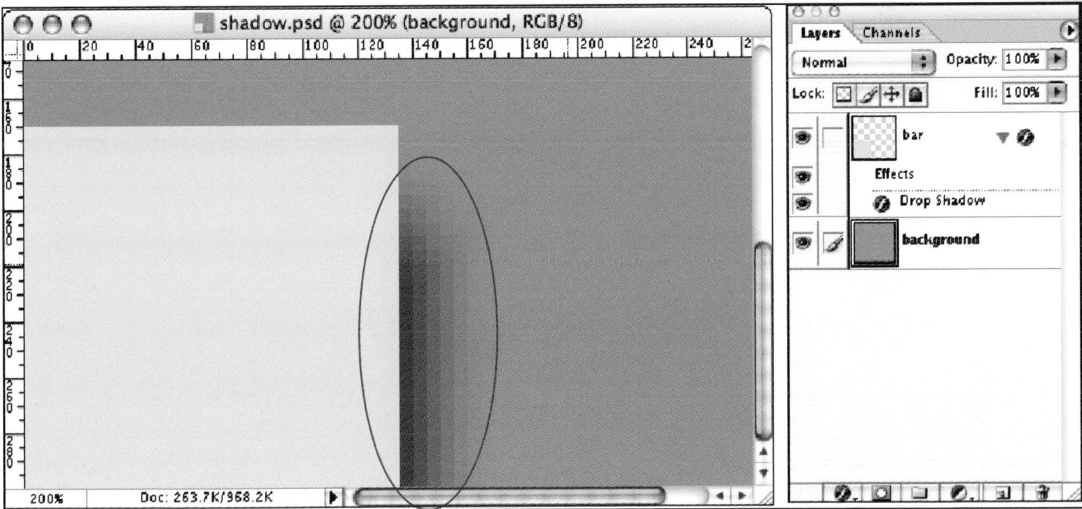


**Figure 3-2: Original Photoshop document magnified 200 percent for a closer look at the shadow.**

Once the shadow looked about right, the visibility of the background layer was turned off, and the Rectangular Marquee Tool was used to select the shadow itself (see Figure 3-3). The shadow was copied to the clipboard (Edit ➪ Copy Merged), a new Photoshop document with a transparent background was created, and the shadow was pasted inside. The graphic was saved as a PNG file and placed in the Flash movie (where a vector shape the same width and height of the "bar" from the Photoshop document already existed).

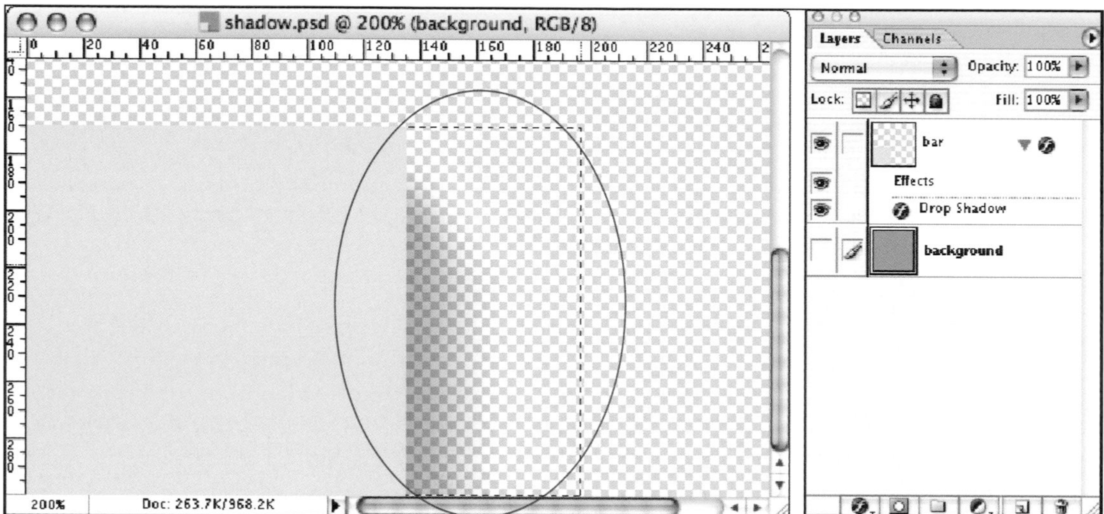


**Figure 3-3: Shadow area selected using the Rectangular Marquee tool.**

You may be wondering why the graphic was saved as a PNG instead of the more commonplace GIF or JPEG file types. PNG is the preferred format to use when importing bitmaps into Flash. Why? Because the PNG file format offers alpha channels with 256 levels of transparency. This enables you to export highly detailed images from your favorite bitmap editor (Photoshop, Fireworks, and so on), import them into Flash, and publish movies that retain their transparent data, while simultaneously applying lossy JPEG compression. It's literally the best of both worlds — the visual quality of the PNG file format with the small file size of a JPEG.

With the Flash movie done, next up was replicating the shadow using CSS/XHTML. Because the shadow would run all the way down the length of the page, and the browser had to automatically repeat the shadow effect for as long as there was content, a "replicable" section of the graphic was needed. This required a graphic that could be vertically tiled (with copies of the image repeated one after another after another) without gaps, seams, or anomalies. So, as shown in Figure 3-4, an area 1 pixel high was selected, making sure to include some of the background color for a smooth blend.

Once the area was copied, a new document was created (which Photoshop automatically set to the exact width and height of the clipboard) and the selection was pasted inside, as shown in Figure 3-5.

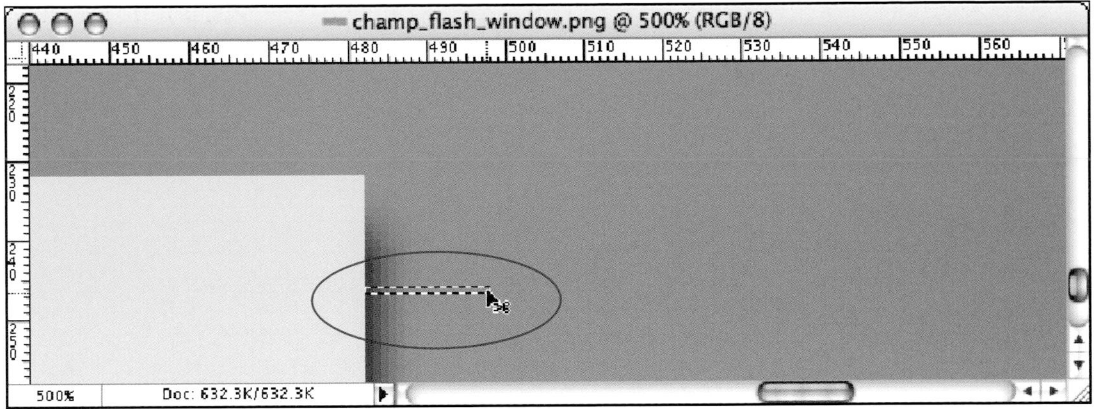


**Figure 3-4: Using the Rectangular Marquee tool, a repeatable area 1 pixel high, including the shadow and a little of the background, was selected and copied to the Clipboard.**

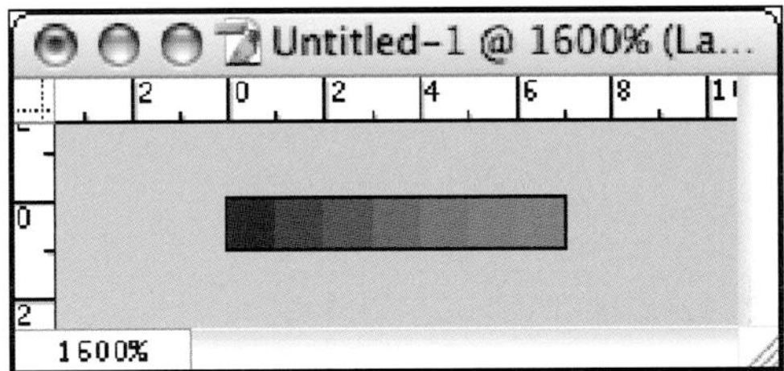


**Figure 3-5: The Clipboard's contents pasted into a new document and magnified to show details.**

That took care of the shadow itself, but the lighter gray background that ran under the left column had to be addressed. To do that, the canvas size of the graphic was increased to the pixel width required, with the shadow aligned to the right. As shown in Figure 3-6, the transparent area was filled with the left column's hex color, and the whole graphic was saved as a GIF file.

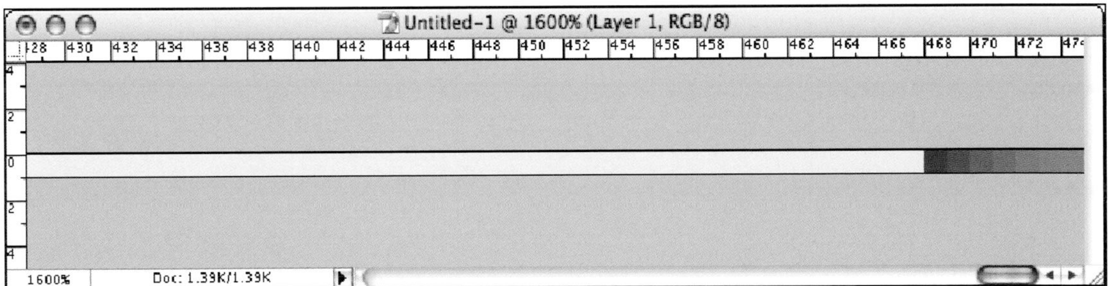


**Figure 3-6: Final background image containing the left column's background color and a drop shadow.**

Let's back up a moment and discuss image file formats again. Why was GIF used here, but not PNG as discussed earlier? The culprit is Internet Explorer (IE) and its infamously poor support of PNG. Nearly eight years ago, Microsoft touted in a white paper that version 4.0 of its browser would "provide native support" for PNG, unlike "other browser manufactures [who] include PNG support as a third-party option." Well, 4.0 didn't fulfill its claim, and it wasn't until version 7 — more than nine years later — that it came through. While Internet Explorer 7 for Windows supports PNG, IE6 is still used by a large share of the audience, so reliance on a PNG-only solution isn't feasible for this project.

So, for now, GIF solution offers cross-browser acceptance and the lossless compression the nonphotographic content required.

Now, let's look at the CSS magic. In the style sheet, a "container" was created with a `div` — an invisible block that would provide an outer framework for positioning groups of content (which, in this case, were the left and right columns). As the content inside either column grew vertically, the outer container would expand accordingly. This is precisely why the background image was applied to the container and not to the columns — the image would be repeated regardless of the interior content's length. To set this up in CSS, the following was created in the style sheet:

```
#colwrap {
 width:740px;
 background:#96968C
url(http://i.pga.com/pga/images/pgachampionship/img/bg_home_content.gif) repeat-y;
}
```

A specific pixel width was set with `div`, followed by the background attribute (which is where all the action took place). We use a hex value that is the same as the background of the Flash movie and the right column, a `url` to the desired image, plus an instruction to the browser to repeat the image vertically (`repeat-y`) for the complete length of the `div`.

Without `repeat-y`, the browser (by default) would have tiled the graphic not only vertically but *horizontally* as well. This would have caused the left edge of the graphic to appear again after the right edge of the shadow. This obviously wouldn't have worked with the design, so `repeat-y` was used to tile the image in only one direction (down). If your design requires a horizontally tiled graphic, you could use `repeat-x`.

Because CSS allows you to apply a hex color *and* an image to a single element, you can (with a little planning) shave a few bytes from your file size by using CSS to draw areas of consistent color (known as "spot" colors in the print world). This is the reason that the container's background image was cropped at the edge of the drop shadow. The remainder of the background (the dark gray area the shadow bled into) was drawn by the browser using the stipulated color value. While this method was not required (all of it could have been included in the background GIF file), a few bytes were saved by doing so. As we all know, every little bit helps.

When completed, the `div` appeared as shown in Figure 3-7.

With the `div` background completed, the Flash movie was placed above the container `div`, and the two pieces snapped together perfectly, as shown in Figure 3-8.

**Figure 3-7: The container** `div` **with background graphic applied and viewed in a Web browser. Notation is added to illustrate which area is an image and which is drawn by the browser.**

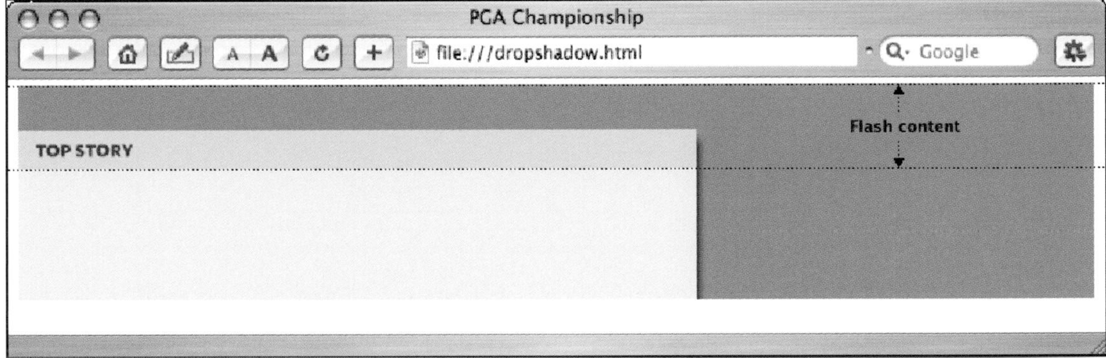


**Figure 3-8: Flash movie placed above container** `div` **from Figure 3-7.**

Before moving on, here's a tip to consider. Ensure that your design is nailed down ahead of time, preferably on a grid with elements snapped to the pixel. An effect like this requires you to know the exact placement of content beforehand. If you get ahead of yourself and try to apply effects such as these while layout considerations are still taking place, you'll have to retrace your steps more than once. Think of effects such as these as a "sweetening" stage of your design workflow. A little patience and planning will save you many headaches and a significant amount of time down the road.

## Adding Extra Realism

This is a good spot to include a bonus tip that can add extra visual definition and realism to the drop-shadow effect built thus far.

In reality (yes, that place outside your monitor), the opacity of a shadow changes according to appearance of the surface it falls across. If the surface is white, the drop shadow appears in gradations of light gray. If the surface is dark, the shadow appears even darker. This all may be rather obvious, but in the flat world of computer screens, it isn't so straightforward.

So, with the PGA Championship site, the concept was pushed further by manipulating the drop shadow's appearance whenever it came in contact with areas of a different background color. Most of the content in the right column had a transparent background and thus used the existing color underneath, but the news links presented a unique problem. Without some sense of visual separation, it was hard for users to tell them apart. So, the background of every other news item was darkened (like alternating row colors in a table), then the drop shadow was manipulated wherever necessary.

To do this, the original Photoshop document used to create the drop shadow was reopened, and the background color was changed to a slightly darker value (#828279) that would harmonize well with the overall layout. An area 1 pixel high in the middle of the shadow was selected (as was done earlier for the main area shadow) and copied into a new document. As shown in Figure 3-9, the finished graphic looked just like the first one, but a little darker.

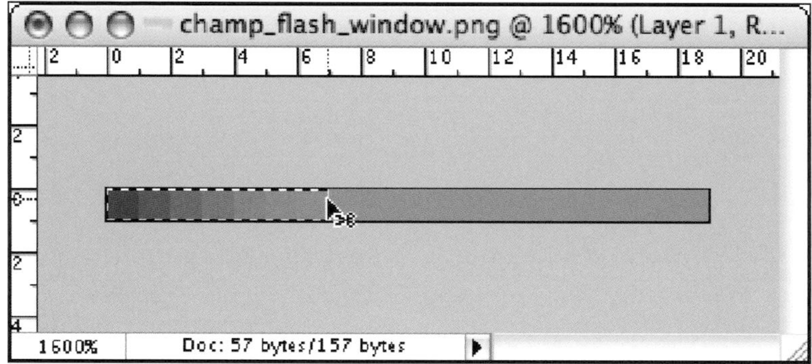


**Figure 3-9: Shadow sitting on top of a slightly darker background and selected with the Rectangular Marquee tool.**

For the XHTML, an unordered list was created to mark up the content. Semantically, list elements are perfect for wrapping grocery-list bits of data (and navigation, as you'll see a little later in this chapter). When paired with a style sheet, they provide all kinds of presentational opportunities.

So, in the right column of the XHTML template, an unordered list of news items was created, like this:

```
<ul class="stories">
 <li>DiMarco and Riley play their way into Ryder Cup</li>
 <li>'No question' PGA will return to Whistling Straits</li>
 <li>Sullivan lowest club professional at PGA since 1969</li>
 <li>PGA of America adjusts Sunday yardages at Whistling Straits</li>
</ul>
```

The class assigned to the unordered list element, `stories`, was then added to the style sheet:

```
ul.stories {
 margin:0;
 padding:0;
 color:#E9E9DF;
}
```

First, `stories` was assigned as a subclass of the `unordered-list` element. The default properties Web browsers would automatically apply to the `unordered-list` elements were then reset. This was accomplished by setting both the margin and the padding to zero. A color property was then added, which affected all text inside the list.

*Technically, you could leave out the* `ul` *and create a standalone class named* `stories`. *However, assigning classes directly to HTML elements is not just good form but also makes your style sheets much easier to read. Think of elements as inline comments that describe their function at a glance so that whether you're returning to a style sheet months later to make an edit, or your style sheet is shared among multiple developers, it's easy to see which classes belong to which elements. A little organization up front pays off big time down the road.*

After taking care of the `unordered-list` object, it was time to tackle each of the list elements inside:

```
ul.stories li {
 list-style:none;
 margin-bottom:2px;
 padding:4px 4px 4px 10px;
}
```

Let's walk through this line by line. First, the `list-style` property was set to `none`, which killed the browser's default behavior of attaching a rounded bullet to the list item. From there, a smidgen of `margin` was added to push the list items a little further apart vertically, plus `padding` (4 pixels to the top, right, and bottom, as well as 10 pixels to the left).

By default, each list item generated inside the `stories` unordered list received these values. At this stage, they all had the same background (using the color underneath), but here's where the extra effect came into play:

```
ul.stories li.odd {
 background:#828279
url(http://i.pga.com/pga/images/pgachampionship/img/bg_stories_shadow.gif) repeat-y;
}
```

Through the beauty of inheritance, this `odd` class came preloaded with all the attributes assigned previously, leaving only what was necessary to produce the change — the `background`. The darker background color's hex value was applied, then the `url` for the shadow graphic was provided, and the browser was instructed to repeat the background vertically, but not horizontally.

The unordered list code was added to the XHTML, and the `odd` class was applied (manually, although this could also be done programmatically with JavaScript, PHP, and so on) to every other list item:

```
<ul class="stories">
 <li class="odd">DiMarco and Riley play their way into Ryder Cup</li>
 <li>'No question' PGA will return to Whistling Straits</li>
 <li class="odd">Sullivan lowest club professional at PGA since 1969</li>
 <li>PGA of America adjusts Sunday yardages at Whistling Straits</li>
</ul>
```

All together, the unordered list appears to be part of the right column and located underneath the main content area's drop shadow, but it actually sits *above* the background created earlier (see Figure 3-10). The trick was to position the right column (which contained the unordered list) directly up against the right edge of the left column. This creates the illusion that the list item's darker background color is a part of the existing drop shadow on the page, when actually it is layered on top of it.

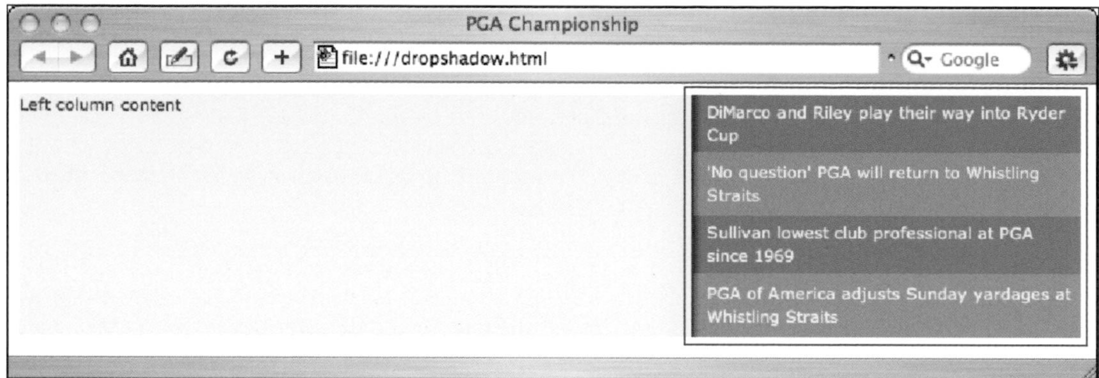


**Figure 3-10: List items with darker shadow background placed in the XHTML container** `div`**.**

Here's the CSS for the left and right columns:

```
#lcol {
 width:468px;
 float:left;
}
#rcol {
 width:271px;
 float:right;
}
```

The basic XHTML necessary to create the effect is:

```
<div id="colwrap">
 <div id="lcol">
  <!—Left column content —>
 </div>
 <div id="rcol">
  <ul class="stories">
   <li class="odd">DiMarco and Riley play their way into Ryder Cup</li>
   <li>'No question' PGA will return to Whistling Straits</li>
   <li class="odd">Sullivan lowest club professional at PGA since 1969</li>
   <li>PGA of America adjusts Sunday yardages at Whistling Straits</li>
  </ul>
 </div>
</div>
```

And with that, the extra drop shadow effect is complete.

If you take one idea away from this exercise, remember this. By leveraging the Web browser's capability to automatically repeat background images and also apply color to the same element, there are countless creative opportunities to add visual depth and richness to an otherwise flat, static layout with barely any effect on overall document weight. All it takes is a little patience, planning, and experimentation.

# Creating CSS Drop-Down Menus

In the dot-com gold rush of the late 1990s, the hallmark of a sophisticated, cutting-edge site was often signaled by the inclusion of fancy drop-down navigational menus. They may have been pleasing to the eye, but behind their glitzy façade was often a hornet's nest of JavaScript, bloated HTML, or even worse, proprietary browser API methods. For all a site's intent on making the user experience more fluid and straightforward, early drop-down solutions more often than not added levels of frustration (especially when they failed to operate) and unnecessary bloat.

Then along came CSS and the magical `:hover` pseudo-class selector. Gurus like Eric Meyer and Christopher Schmitt published tutorials on how to tap into the capabilities of an anchor tag's `:hover` attribute, which when used with regular ol' unordered lists, could create drop-down menus similar in appearance to, yet a fraction of the weight and complexity of, those created with conventional methods.

But for all the promise of pure CSS menus, there was one huge problem: Internet Explorer for Windows. By far the most popular browser accessing the Web, the browser had limited support for the `:hover` attribute (and CSS in general, but that's another story), and thus it couldn't render the drop-downs. As a result, CSS menus were relegated to being a hobbyist tool at best.

But that started to change in November 2003, when Patrick Griffiths and Dan Webb set the CSS community on fire with *Suckerfish Dropdowns* (`www.alistapart.com/articles/dropdowns`), a lightweight, CSS-powered, drop-down system that worked in nearly every browser available, including Internet Explorer for Windows. Suckerfish was a revelation not just in file weight but also in cross-browser compatibility, compliance to Web standards, semantic richness, and accessibility.

Suckerfish drop-down menus were also incredibly easy to build. If you knew how to create an unordered list in XHTML, you were halfway home. All of the presentation and functionality was controlled with a small set of style properties.

A few months after the initial release of Suckerfish, Griffiths and Webb upped the ante with *Son of Suckerfish Dropdowns*, an even lighter version of the original with greater compatibility and multiple drop-down menus to boot. It was the "Son" flavor of Suckerfish that the PGA Championship site used, but this discussion won't delve into the basic structure (which you can download examples of for free at `www.htmldog.com/articles/suckerfish`). This section discusses the customizations made, potential caveats, and a few general usage tips.

## Customizing the Positioning of Drop-Down Menus

The first issue encountered when modifying Suckerfish for the PGA Championship site's navigation involved positioning the drop-down menus. By default, the nested drop-down menus appeared directly below their parent list item, depending on the height of the graphic or text contained therein. In the case of the PGA Championship site, the parent graphics were cut shorter than the surrounding area (to conserve file weight). So, instead of appearing below the white navigational bar (as they do in the final form of the site), the drop-down menus were popping out below the graphical links.

The graphical links could have been edited with extra white space on the bottom to "push" the drop-down menus to the location desired, but that would have increased the file size of each graphic and created a "hot" link space where no content was present. The challenge, then, was to find a way to push the drop-down menus below the white navigation bar without adversely affecting or changing the existing content.

The first step was simple. Each nested unordered list (the drop-down menus) was already using absolute positioning, so a `top` property was added to push them down where they needed to be:

```
#nav li ul {
 position:absolute;
 left:-999em;
 top:20px;
}
```

This successfully moved each drop-down menu 20 pixels below its parent list item and thus below the white navigational bar. But a new problem emerged. The area between the main links and the drop-down menus (the same blank area that shouldn't have been clickable) was now disengaging the rollover when the pointer moved downward. So, the next step was to find a way to maintain the visibility of the drop-down menus whenever the mouse pointer entered this vacant area.

By default, a list element is only as tall as the content it contains. But you can change that behavior with CSS:

```
#nav li {
 position:relative;
 float:left;
 margin:0 15px 0 0;
 padding:0;
 width:auto;
 height:20px;
}
```

The important part here is the `height` property. By specifying a custom height and thus overriding the aforementioned default behavior, the invisible bounding box of each list element expands downward to fill the gap. The list items now behave as if they contain graphics 20 pixels tall, but are actually much shorter. But the browser can't tell the difference, and thus, the drop-down menus operate as expected.

To see how the list items and graphical elements are affected, take a look at Figure 3-11. Using Chris Pederick's free Web Developer extension (`http://chrispederick.com/work/web-developer`) for Firefox, the invisible bounding boxes of the list elements and images are made visible by adding a temporary black stroke. This offers a visual confirmation of the style sheet modifications and shows what the browser is displaying in real time. The extension came in handy many times during development of the PGA Championship site, and it is recommended to anyone involved with Web development and design.

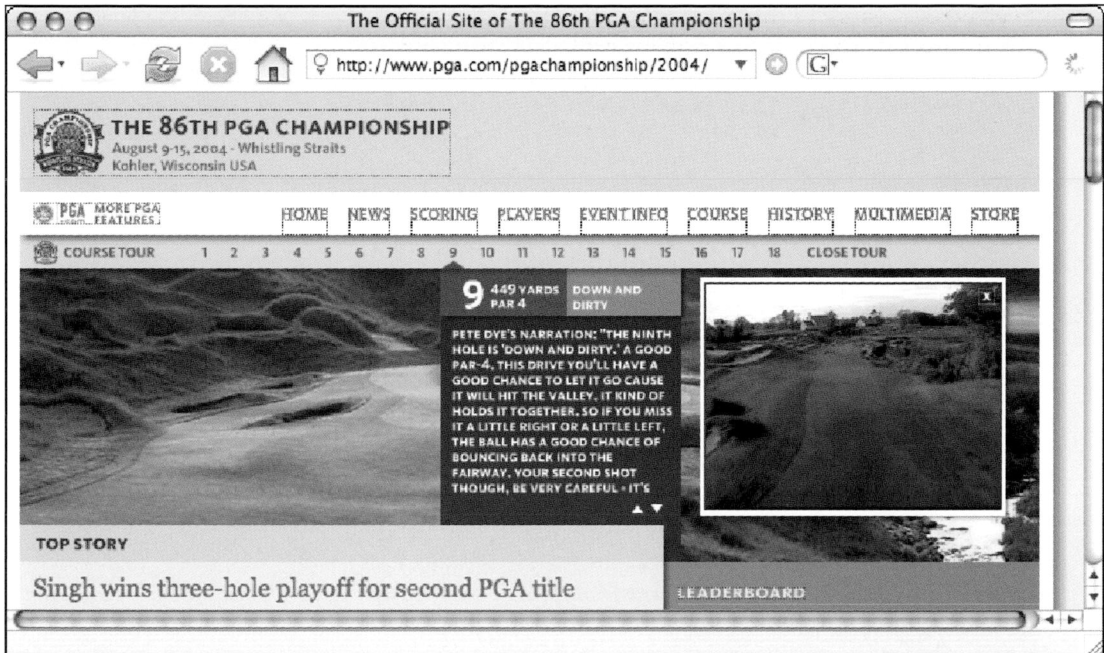


**Figure 3-11: The PGA Championship viewed in Firefox and with all list elements and images outlined using the Web Developer extension.**

## Customization: Styling the Drop-Down Menus

With the drop-down menus functioning properly and appearing in the proper place, it was time to tweak the appearance of the menu options.

To start, nested unordered lists were given a `background` color of white and assigned a uniform `width` (based on the longest menu item title) on all the drop-down menus:

```
#nav li ul {
 margin:0;
 padding:0;
 position:absolute;
 left:-999em;
 top:20px;
 background:#fff;
 width:146px;
}
```

As shown in Figure 3-12, it is easy to see the problem. The left edge of each drop-down menu is aligned with the left edge of its parent list item, and there isn't enough visual separation between each option.

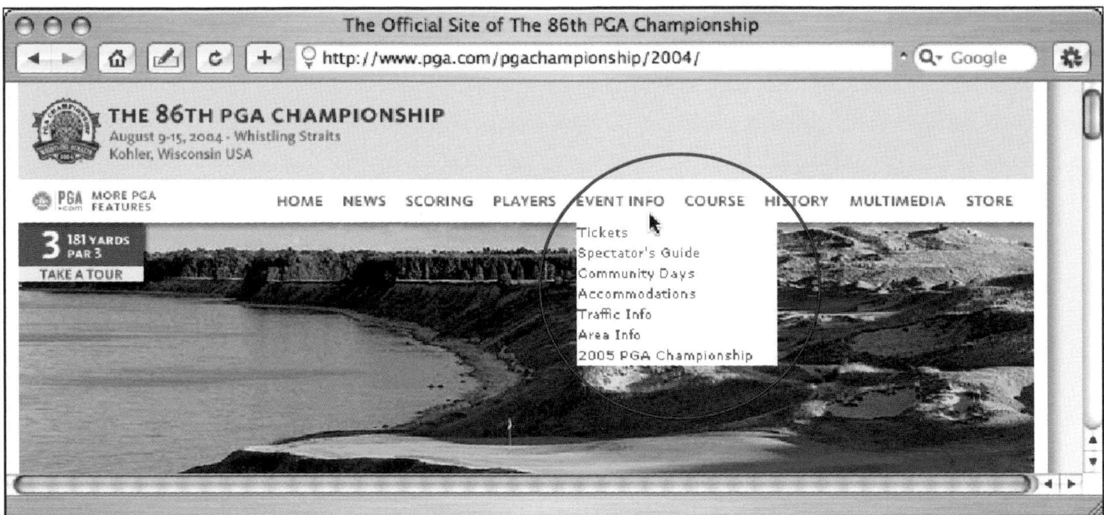


**Figure 3-12: Misaligned drop-down menu with visually bland options.**

So, some additional edits can be made to the nested list items:

```
#nav li li {
 height:auto;
 margin:0;
 padding:0;
 width:100%;
 font-size:9px;
 border-bottom:1px solid #F5F5F0;
}
```

Because the `width` of each nested list item is set to 100 percent, their boxes expand to the width of their parent element — which, in this case, is `146px`. If the default width of the list items isn't modified, the browser draws a bottom border only as long as the text contained inside. Setting the list item to a width of 100 percent, gives the menu options a uniform appearance, regardless of how much text is contained in each item.

Next, the textual content was addressed:

```
#nav li li span {
 display:block;
 margin:0;
 padding:3px 4px 3px 7px;
 position:relative;
}
```

To better control the positioning of each block of text within its respective list items, each option is wrapped with a `span` tag because `span` avoids another subclass with a unique name and semantically makes more sense than a `div`, `paragraph` tag, or what-have-you. So, the `display` properties of `span` are changed to a `block` element (which by default it is not). This allows block attributes such as `margin` and `padding`. After the `padding` is successfully tweaked, the menu appears as shown in Figure 3-13.

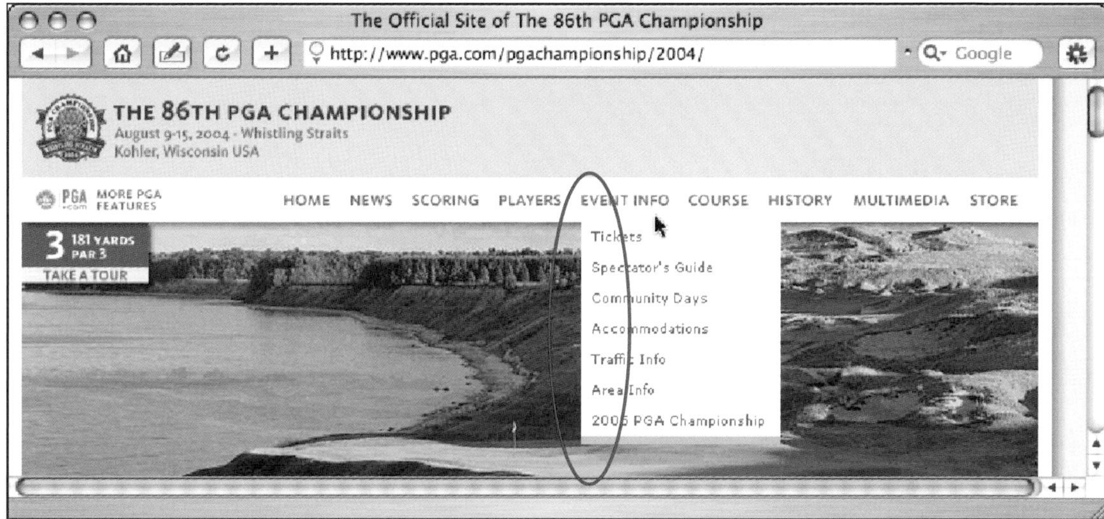


**Figure 3-13: Drop-down options styled but misaligned with left margin of the main navigation links.**

The drop-down menus look complete but one issue remains. The textual menu options are no longer aligned with the left edge of their respective parent list items. Although they don't have to be changed, it was decided that they would look better with a slight adjustment to the left. Fortunately, this is as easy as forcing each unordered list to the left, like this:

```
#nav li ul {
  margin:0 0 0 -8px;
  padding:0;
  position:absolute;
  left:-999em;
  top:20px;
  background:#fff;
  width:146px;
}
```

Thank goodness for negative values! Changing the left `margin` from zero to `-8` (the order of margin values is top, right, bottom, left) shifted each nested unordered list 8 pixels to the left (as opposed to the right if the number is positive). This brings the left edge of each textual option perfectly in line with its parent list item, as shown in Figure 3-14.

**Figure 3-14: The completed drop shadow with options fully styled and properly aligned.**

## Important Caveat

Now that we've discussed ways to modify the original source, here's a potential issue to watch out for when using Suckerfish drop-down menus. *Suckerfish requires JavaScript in IE/Windows.* Chalk this up as another example of Internet Explorer's lackluster support of CSS. Suckerfish is activated purely by CSS in Mozilla, Firefox, and Safari, but in order for it to work in Internet Explorer for Windows (IE/Windows), a little bit of JavaScript must be included in any document using the drop-down menus. The "hack" is quite small and simply oversteps IE's lack of support for the `:hover` pseudo-link element by attaching custom behaviors to the Document Object Model (DOM). But here's the rub. If your IE/Windows users have JavaScript turned off, your drop-down menus won't appear. Very few people actually turn this off, but it's a reality you should be aware of.

## Understanding Usage

With the browser support issue out of the way, the following are some real-world usability tips for implementing CSS drop-downs in your own work:

- **Tip 1: Provide backup.** Because of the cross-browser issues detailed earlier, it is imperative that your site layout include a secondary level of navigation should your drop-down menus fail to operate. Otherwise, your visitors won't be able to navigate your site. This should be standard procedure for any type of drop-down navigation — Suckerfish or otherwise.
- **Tip 2: Be careful with Internet Explorer, Suckerfish, and Flash.** When Internet Explorer for Windows encounters Flash content (whether it's an advertisement or a movie created by you), the browser pushes it to the very top of the `z-index` layer stack. What does that mean? It means that your menus could potentially appear underneath your Flash content, making it impossible for a user to click on any of the covered options. The solution is to include a `wmode` tag in Flash's object/embed code. (Details can be found at `www.macromedia.com/support/flash/ts/documents/flash_top_layer.htm`.)

- **Tip 3: Include a `z-index` property if your document has layers.** If your layout has layered objects using a `z-index` property, your Suckerfish navigation must have one as well, but on a higher level than everything else. The `z-index` can be added to either your navigation's parent unordered list element or (in the case of the PGA Championship site) you can wrap your navigation with a container `div` and apply the `z-index` to that element. Doing so raises your navigation above the rest of the fray, so the menus drop down and *over* anything they may come in contact with.

### The Bottom Line

So, after all that, you may be wondering why Suckerfish is recommended. The answer is simple. Despite the issues noted here, Suckerfish remains the most accessible, cross-browser-friendly drop-down menu solution out there. It's also far, far lighter in bytes than anything else, and it's much easier to update and maintain. If you implement the menus on a highly trafficked site (the PGA Championship site, for example, was hit millions of times per hour), then having a light drop-down menu solution is optimal.

# Engineering Web Standards–Compliant Flash Embedding

One of the common problems Web developers face when creating standards-compliant XHTML markup is embedding Flash content. Most developers simply copy and paste the standard set of `object/embed` tags Flash creates when publishing a movie. However, because they come loaded with all kinds of invalid attributes and elements, they wreak havoc on a document's conformance to Web standards, since `embed` is a proprietary element not found in any W3C specification.

Fortunately, there are workarounds. Here are the three most popular methods used today to embed standards-compliant Flash content.

## Using the Flash Satay Method

The Flash Satay method (`www.alistapart.com/articles/flashsatay`) removes the `embed` tag and removes some "unnecessary" proprietary attributes in the `object` tag. It works great, but with one *huge* caveat: Flash movies in Internet Explorer for Windows won't start until they are 100 percent loaded.

The Satay method does offer a workaround, which includes fooling Internet Explorer for Windows by embedding an empty "container" movie set to the same parameters (width, height, and so on) as the "real" movie and using the container clip to load the actual content. Internet Explorer will then successfully stream the movie, and the markup will validate, but at a cost to any developer's sanity — each and every embedded movie requires an accompanying empty container movie, thus creating a lot of extra directory trash and headaches.

## Writing the object/embed Tags Using JavaScript

In this scenario, the `object/embed` elements remain as they are but are moved to an external JavaScript file. Flash content is then written into the document using a series of `document.write` JavaScript methods. Validators (the W3C has an excellent one at `http://validator.w3.org`) see only the valid JavaScript element — not Flash's `object/embed` code contained inside — so the `object/embed` tags pass with flying colors.

This was the workaround used for the PGA Championship site. The XHTML not only remained valid but because JavaScript was used, offered an opportunity to perform some light browser or plug-in detection should alternate (non-Flash) content be required.

Once the external JavaScript file is created (too long to reproduce here — load `www.pga.com/pgachampionship/2004/js/flash_home.js` in your Web browser to see the source), it is linked in the XHTML document like this:

```
<script type="text/javascript"
src="http://www.pga.com/pgachampionship/2004/js/flash_home.js"></script>
```

This method is not without issues. First of all, Web standards purists will argue that the JavaScript file is essentially a Trojan horse that slips invalid, unsupported markup into XHTML and past the eyes of validators (which is exactly the point). Second, by relying on JavaScript to write your content, you are assuming that users have it enabled in their browsers (most everyone does, but some disable it for extra speed and to avoid ads). Finally, each and every Flash movie requires its own external `.JS` file (not a big deal with a handful of movies, but things could quickly get out of control).

## *Knowing the SWFObject*

Released a few months after the 2004 PGA Championship site, SWFObject is the most sophisticated and robust embedding method currently available. Created by Geoff Stearns, the JavaScript package is a direct response to the limitations of both of the aforementioned methods, while providing simpler markup that validates as XHTML 1.0 Transitional and up.

SWFObject offers everything a Flash developer needs — player detection, ability to offer alternate content to those without the plug-in, methods to pass additional parameters and variables through FlashVars, `div` targeting for embedding an `swf` in a specific area, and even a variable to bypass player detection and force the display of a Flash movie, whether the user has the plug-in or not.

SWFObject is also search engine–friendly, which you rarely see with Flash content. Users simply create a `div` in their document and fill it with normal HTML textual content, which can then be indexed by search engines and displayed for visitors without the Flash plug-in. If a visitor has the Flash plug-in, the `div`'s content is replaced with the Flash movie. This enables both the haves and the have-nots to easily receive rich content, without a lot of work for the Web developer.

For more information about SWFObject (which is free to download and use), see `http://blog.deconcept.com/swfobject`.

# Summary

This chapter covered a lot, from creating visual effects in Photoshop to dealing with drop-down menus to positioning elements with CSS to working around common Flash validation issues in XHTML. The techniques used here should inspire further exploration and experimentation when using CSS in your own work.

Next up is a look at the redesign of the University of Florida's Web site, including the history of the site, the challenges in updating legacy content, and a walkthrough of the CSS markup used.

# The University of Florida's UFL.edu

*A common mistake that people make when trying to design something completely foolproof is to underestimate the ingenuity of complete fools.*

*— Douglas Adams*

The University of Florida (UF) is among the world's most academically diverse public universities with fields of study across 16 colleges. UF, which traces its roots to the East Florida Seminary established in 1853, has a long history of established programs in international education, research, and service, with extension offices in all 67 Florida counties.

UF's student body has over 50,000 students and is the second largest university in the U.S. The University of Florida's Web presence has somewhat mirrored the trends you would see when looking at the Web as a whole. Shifts in the foci of Web developers (and the developers of the browsers in which they are viewed) can be seen in microcosm through the UF Web site.

In this chapter, you'll explore some of the decisions UF made with regard to its Web presence and take a look at the techniques used to carry them out.

## Looking Back at UF's First Web Site

UF posted a home page in 1995 that was typical of sites of the time. Well-built pages were generally structural in nature and light on aesthetics. The 1995 page, in fact, was rather utilitarian with links to much of the same information one would find on the current UF site (see Figure 4-1).

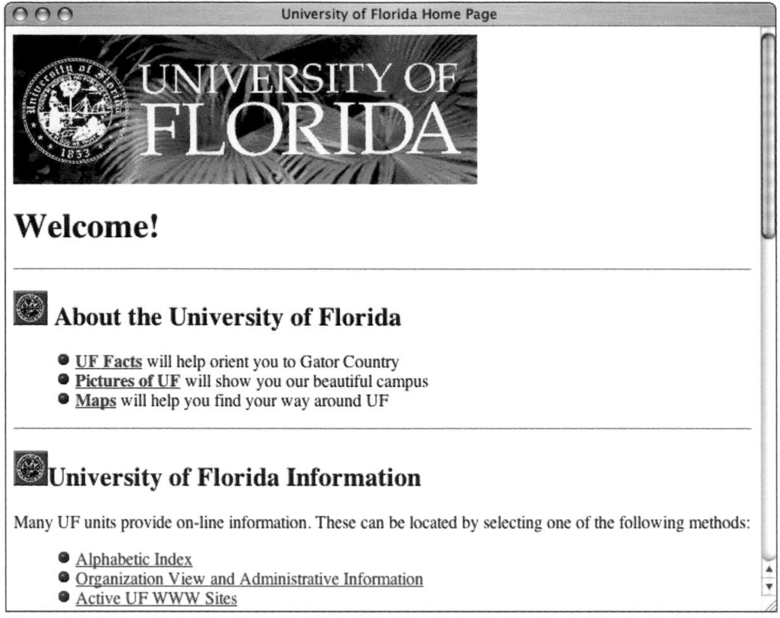


**Figure 4-1: The University of Florida home page launched in 1995.**

Here's a bit of the markup from the first UF site:

```
<H2><IMG alt=** src="images/placeholder.gif" align=bottom width="32" height="32">
About the University of Florida</H2>
<UL><IMG alt=* src="images/ball.gif" width="14" height="14">
<B><A href="#">UF Facts</A></B> will help orient you to Gator Country<BR>
<IMG alt=* src="images/ball.gif" width="14" height="14">
<B><A href="#">Pictures of UF</A></B> will show you our beautiful campus<BR>
<IMG alt=* src="images/ball.gif" width="14" height="14">
<B><A href="#">Maps</A></B> will help you find your way around UF<BR>
</UL>
<HR>
```

As you might notice, a number of semantic elements are well identified. Headings were given the proper weight, and unordered lists were marked as such. Glaringly omitted are the list item elements. Instead of the `li` element, the creators used images and `br` tags to start and end list items. This was done, presumably, to style the lists.

## Reflecting on Its Revisions

The subsequent revisions of the university's site trended toward using a role-based navigational system consisting primarily of five major groups (see Figure 4-2):

- Prospective Students

- Current Students
- Campus Visitors
- Faculty & Staff
- Alumni, Parents, & Friends

Within each of these groups, a visitor can find all the information the university thought each of the different types of visitor would need. Inside "Prospective Students" are admissions information, directions on taking a campus tour, facts about the university, and so on. Each group has similar role-targeted information. The tendency to shift to role-based navigation as a primary means of navigation was seen across both university Web sites and the Web at large.

This new graphics-heavy design did not come without a price. While UF received more positive than negative feedback in response to the aesthetics of the 1999 design, there were a number of complaints centered on the time needed to load the site. In this design, the visitor's browser had to make more than 30 HTTP requests to the UF servers for various pieces of the page: HTML, images, JavaScript, and so on. Each request lengthened the total time needed to load the site.

The more semantic markup found in the first design was lost in these revisions. The unordered lists and header elements in the first design were scrapped for multiple image maps, JavaScript rollovers, and tables.

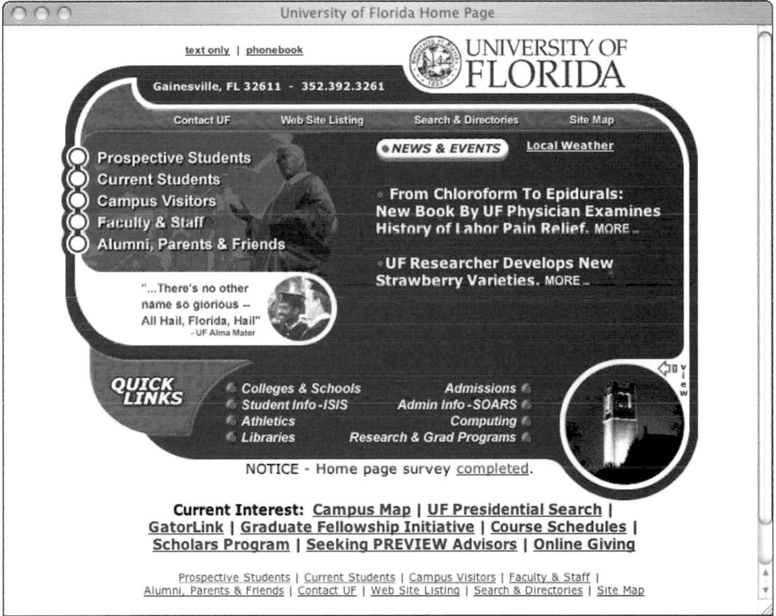


**Figure 4-2: A revision to the University of Florida home page launched in 1999.**

## Examining the Current Site

With the expansion in usage of standards-compliant browsers, UF decided to attack these problems and others with a new design (see Figure 4-3). To redesign the site, UF needed the following:

- An assessment of the university's major audiences and development of user profiles to include Web technology usage and accessibility needs
- Structuring of the information within the site
- In-depth user testing
- Reviews of peer Web sites

The current site was launched in February 2004. While the design was refined, the core design is still prominent, as shown in Figure 4-4. The site currently receives approximately 100,000 visits per day.

The remainder of this chapter provides you with a look into how this new site was developed.

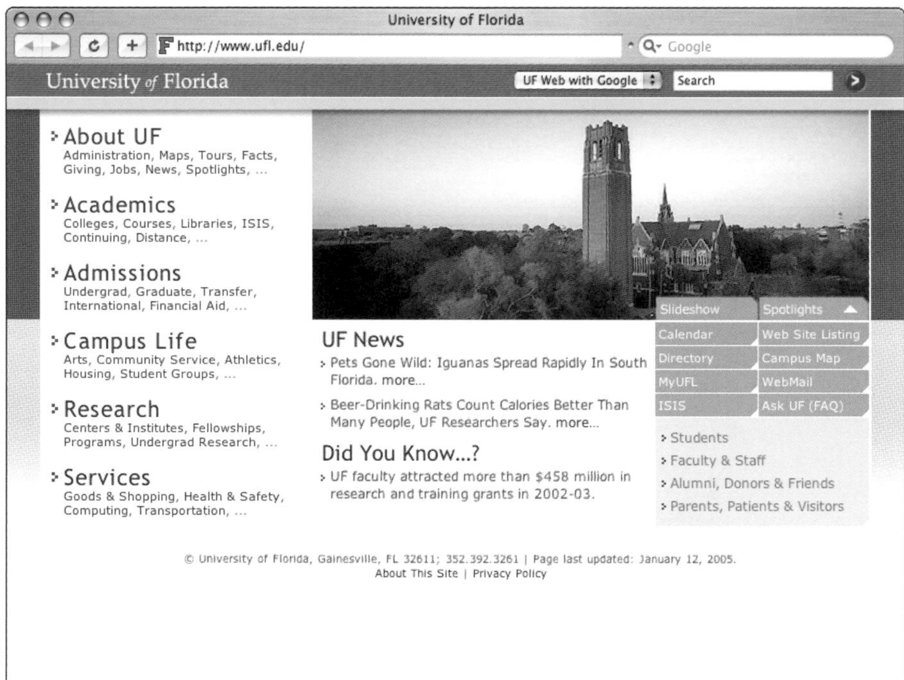


**Figure 4-3: 2004 site revision.**

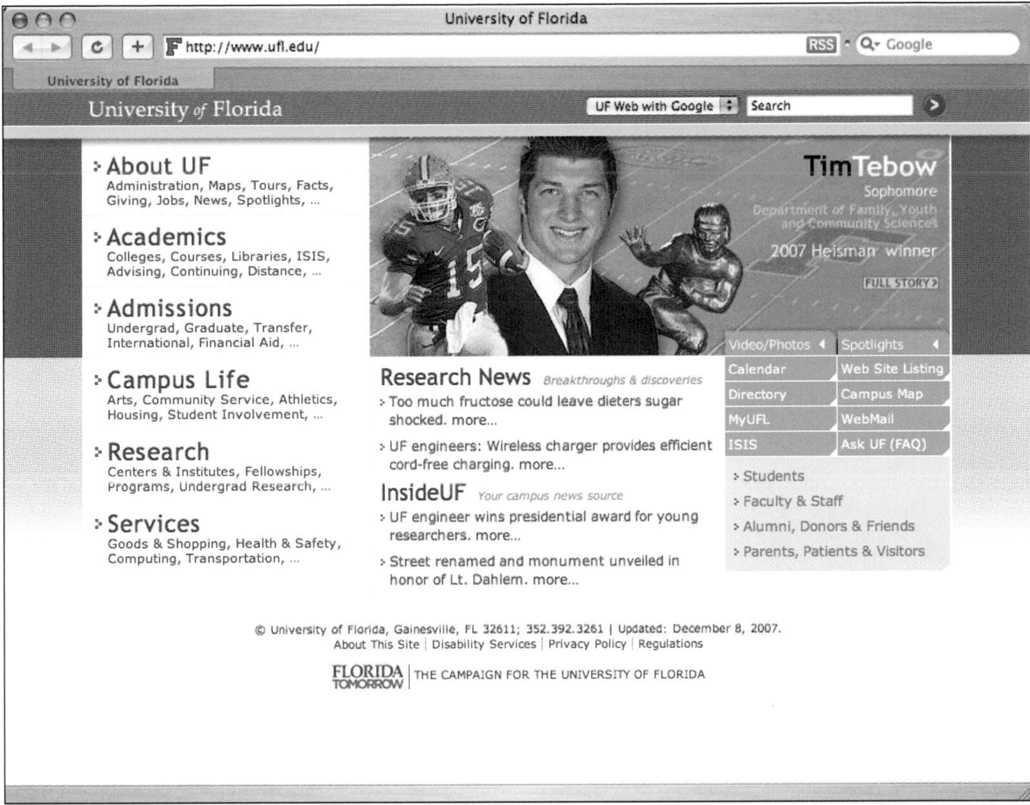


**Figure 4-4: Updated look in 2008 has only minor design enhancements.**

# Defining the Site

When identifying success for a university site, issues such as the financial bottom line and clicks-through to a shopping cart take a backseat to broader issues such as visitor satisfaction and perception. This makes identifying the goals of the sites fairly simple: Talk to the site's visitors, watch them use it, and give them what they want.

## *Building the Team*

Many members of the UF community have multiple roles. With visitors looking for so many different types of content coming through a single site, it was imperative to have the design driven by not only the site's visitors but also the members of UF's staff and faculty that deal directly with those visitors. Early on, a team representing 20 of these areas from around campus developed a nested list of the types of visitors to the UF site. For example, a main type of visitor would be "student." Within "student" would be "undergraduate," "graduate," "international," and so on. Then further nesting: "prospective graduate," "transfer undergraduate," and so on. The team then identified tasks that each type of visitor would perform.

## Starting with User Research

As with most organizations, people at UF often find themselves wearing many different hats. A staff member might also take courses and attend athletic events, while a graduate student may teach courses and be an undergraduate alumnus. This manifested itself in user research where visitors to the previous UF site would have to guess which group they fell within to find the information they were looking for.

Visitors would also choose different groups based on their desired membership, not necessarily their current role. For example, many potential UF students (namely, those in high school) would choose the Current Students link from the UF home page instead of Prospective Students. When asked, the visitors gave responses that fell into three general categories:

- "I am currently a student at my high school."
- "What does 'prospective' mean?"
- "I wanted to see what real UF students are doing, not some brochure." (This type of response was the most prevalent — and the one that was found to be the most interesting — among those potential students who chose something other than Prospective Students.)

It became clear quite quickly that the way the university classifies people, while valid and useful to the university, is not necessarily the way visitors classify themselves. This also suggests that role-based navigation should not be relied upon as the primary means of navigating the site.

UF needed to marry this look at its visitors with the current trends in university Web sites.

## Examining Ourselves

An important part of defining the site was looking at how sites throughout academia define themselves. While many university sites primarily use a role-based navigational system, the university staff knew through user research that this wouldn't be ideal for UF. That being said, the staff could use other universities' sites to ensure that all staff was staying within the *lingua franca* of academia. The phrases universities use to define different pieces of content, if agreed upon, can serve as the basis for a primary navigation.

The university staff understood from the beginning that the final structure of the UF site would be unique. However, looking at macroscopic trends like these pulled out the phrases that are most common. To look into this, UF surveyed more than a thousand university Web sites looking for commonly used terms. Idioms such as "About (University/College X)," "Academics," "Admissions," and "Alumni" quickly rose to the top. These matched up well with the user research (namely, card sorting) and were adopted as main phrases within the navigation.

> *Card sorting is a fairly low-tech (but very useful) method of enlisting a site's visitors when creating information architecture. Essentially, test participants are asked to group index cards that contain short descriptions of pieces of content and tasks from the site, and then name these new stacks. More on this methodology can be found in Mike Kuniavsky's book* Observing the User Experience: A Practitioner's Guide to User Research *(Morgan Kaufmann, 2003).*

Many sites fell prey to frequent use of acronyms and other proprietary phrases. While this is unpreventable in some cases, it should be avoided and certainly done sparingly. The university staff also noted that acronyms were very rarely defined.

# Defining Technical Specs

The increased download times created by the myriad of images of the previous design were something UF wanted to tackle without returning to the vanilla site launched in 1995. Also, the university wanted a return to (and an improvement upon) the semantics found in the initial design. If by and large the visitors' environment supported a shift to a strictly standards-compliant design, then UF's path would be to create that environment.

## Utilizing Web Standards

Early on, the decision was made to strive for a site where content and aesthetics were separated. This could be implemented only if UF knew the following:

- How many visitors would be adversely affected by taking a standards-based approach?
- How quickly are these visitors moving away from noncompliant browsers?

UF felt comfortable proceeding with standards-compliant markup and semantic use of XHTML elements because of the following:

- The steady movement of Netscape users to Netscape 7 and, ultimately, Mozilla or Firefox. (We'll explore this in greater detail later.)
- Generally speaking, users of noncompliant browsers access the Web through a slower connection. The decrease in load time (from 50K and 30 HTTP requests to 30K and, more important, only 3 HTTP requests for users of noncompliant browsers) heavily outweighs any simplification of aesthetics. This is especially true for these visitors who are regularly subjected to pages that react very poorly to ancient browsers.
- The addition of an enterprise resource management system that rejects ancient browsers to handle the university's financials forces users to move to modern browsers. (About 40 percent of UF home page traffic comes internally from students, faculty, and staff using the university's statewide network.)
- By using style sheets, users of noncompliant browsers that do not support the `@import` rule would receive a document with the browser's very simple default styling.

## Incorporating Accessibility

UF was very concerned with creating a site that was accessible to all members of the UF community through whichever medium they chose to use. This includes those who must use alternative Web browsing technologies due to hearing, visual, or mobility impairment. A standards-based approach served as a way to advance accessibility as part of the entire development process, not simply an add-on before launching a site — or even worse, realizing a site isn't accessible and creating a "text-only" version.

> *More information on assistive technologies such as screen readers, Braille displays, and talking browsers can be found in the book* Building Accessible Websites *by Joe Clark (New Riders Press, 2002).*

# Creating a Main Navigational Structure

The University of Florida has more than a million pages on the Web covering topics from aerospace engineering to zoology. Its site navigation must both (at a glance) convey the diversity of research and teaching activity at the university and allow intuitive access to all its resources.

An inherent drawback to graphical or dynamic rollovers as navigational tools is the concealing of the underlying architecture. The visitor can't scan the page's content in its entirety. The visitor must guess what items are hidden beneath each branch of the structure and then act on that guess to see if that section of navigation contains what is sought.

Although rollovers allow a site visitor to see the site structure one branch at a time, an entire architectural overview that requires no guessing on the part of the visitor can be much more useful. The six major sections that give an overview of the university are much better served by openly displaying some of their contents near the section headers (see Figure 4-5).

**Figure 4-5: The University of Florida's primary navigation.**

## The XHTML

On the UF home page, the primary navigation is not merely a means of getting from one page to another. It is some of the most important content of the page, and the markup used in the navigation should reinforce that importance.

## Unordered Lists

Grouping similar sets of information (as is done when lists are used) allows for the following:

- Styling through CSS
- Semantic grouping of similar objects
- Easier traversal through groups of content, especially in screen readers

## Nested Unordered Lists

At first glance, the UF primary navigation might seem best handled as nested, unordered lists. There is an unordered list of main topics, with each topic having a set of links that apply to it (see Figure 4-6). This would look something like the following:

```
<ul id="priNav">
 <li><a href="/aboutUF/">About UF</a>
  <ul>
   <li><a href="/aboutUF/administration.html">Administration</a>,</li>
   <li><a href="http://campusmap.ufl.edu/">Maps</a>,</li>
   <li><a href="http://virtualtour.ufl.edu/">Tours</a>,</li>
   <li><a href="/facts/">Facts</a>,</li>
   ...
  </ul>
 </li>
 <li><a href="/academics/">Academics</a>
  <ul>
   <li><a href="/colleges/">Colleges</a>,</li>
   <li><a href="http://www.reg.ufl.edu/soc/">Courses</a>,</li>
   <li><a href="http://www.uflib.ufl.edu/">Libraries</a>,</li>
     <li><a href="http://www.isis.ufl.edu/">ISIS</a>,</li>
     ...
    </ul>
   </li>
 ...
</ul>
```

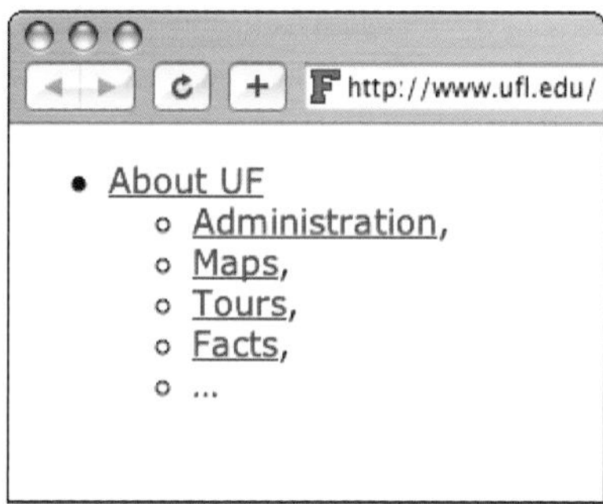


Figure 4-6: Unstyled, nested unordered lists.

Although certainly valid, the list items inside the navigation acting as headers (About UF, Administration, and so on) are not separately defined with heading elements. When treated as list items, major areas of the site are understated.

## Weighting for Semantics

To give the main headings the proper meaning within the page and site as a whole, the navigation is placed inside a `div` and represented as a series of headers followed by unordered lists (see Figure 4-7):

```
<div id="priNav">
 <h2><a href="/aboutUF/">About UF</a></h2>
 <ul>
  <li><a href="/aboutUF/administration.html">Administration</a>,</li>
  <li><a href="http://campusmap.ufl.edu/">Maps</a>,</li>
  <li><a href="http://virtualtour.ufl.edu/">Tours</a>,</li>
  <li><a href="/facts/">Facts</a>,</li>
  ...
 </ul>
 <h2><a href="/academics/">Academics</a></h2>
 <ul>
  <li><a href="/colleges/">Colleges</a>,</li>
  <li><a href="http://www.reg.ufl.edu/soc/">Courses</a>,</li>
  <li><a href="http://www.uflib.ufl.edu/">Libraries</a>,</li>
  <li><a href="http://www.isis.ufl.edu/"><acronym title="Integrated Student
Information System">ISIS</acronym></a>,</li>
  ...
 </ul>
 ...
</div>
```

**Figure 4-7: Unstyled, unordered lists with topical headers.**

The headers here assign meaning to both the current page and the entire site. This benefits users of screen readers such as Jaws and IBM's Home Page Reader, allowing rudimentary navigation from header to header. As an added bonus, many search engines give more weight to text inside headings.

Because the initial letters of Integrated Student Information System (UF's Web-based system to register for classes and pay tuition, which is seen inside the list item for Academics) form a pronounceable word ("eye-sis"), ISIS is considered an *acronym*. If the initial letters are sounded out so that each letter is pronounced (as in HTML), the word would be considered an abbreviation and the `abbr` tag would be used. The `acronym` and `abbr` elements allow contextual expansion of the text presented to the visitor. This should be done to describe the first occurrence of any acronyms or abbreviations in a document. This assists screen reader users by reading out the meaning of the abbreviations and acronyms. It also explains what would be esoteric phrases to search engines such as Google.

## The CSS

Following is the CSS:

```
* {
 padding: 0;
 margin: 0;
}

ul {
 list-style: none;
}

li {
 font-size: 11px;
 color: #444;
}

h2 {
 font-weight: normal;
 font-size: 21px;
}

a {
 text-decoration: none;
}

a:link, a:visited {
 color: #0021a5;
}

a:hover, a:active {
 color: #ff4a00;
}

acronym {
 border: 0;
 font-style: normal;
}

#priNav {
 width: 248px;
 float: left;
 padding: 6px 2px 0 0;
 margin: 0 2px;
}

#priNav h2 {
 padding: 7px 0 0 20px;
 letter-spacing: 1px;
 line-height: 22px;
```

```
 background: url(images/pointer.gif) no-repeat 9px 14px;
}

#priNav ul {
 padding: 0 0 7px 20px;
 height: 26px;
 border-bottom: 1px solid #eee;
}

#priNav li {
 display: inline;
 line-height: 13px;
 padding-right: 4px;
 float: left;
}
```

## The Images

UF uses two images to display its primary navigation: `navDropShadow.jpg` (see Figure 4-8) and `pointer.gif` (see Figure 4-9). The first is borrowed from the main HTML element container.

The `background.gif` image in the `body` element can be seen on the sides of Figure 4-3.

**Figure 4-8:** `navDropShadow.jpg.`

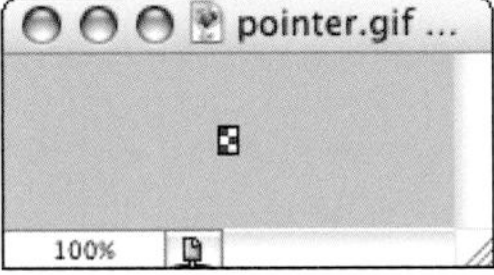


**Figure 4-9:** `pointer.gif.`

## Brick by Brick

To start, use the universal selector to set the default `margin` and `padding` to zero (0) for all elements. Margin and padding are the two most commonly used properties for spacing out elements. A `'margin'` is considered the space outside of the element, and `'padding'` is the space inside the element.

```
* {
 padding: 0;
 margin: 0;
}
```

Next, remove the default bullets from all unordered lists and shine up the `h2` and `li` elements:

```
ul {
 list-style: none;
}
li {
 font-size: 11px;
}
h2 {
 font-weight: normal;
 font-size: 21px;
}
```

UF's official colors are orange and blue, so turn all links UF blue and set the hover and active states to UF orange:

```
a:link, a:visited {
 color: #0021a5;
}
a:hover, a:active {
 color: #ff4a00;
}
```

The UF home page is very link-heavy (`ufl.edu` has more than a million pages) and having every word on the page underlined could be a bit messy, so the underline on all links:

```
a {
 text-decoration: none;
}
a:link, a:visited {
 color: #0021a5;
}
a:hover, a:active {
 color: #ff4a00;
}
```

Several `acronym` elements are used on the site. Keeping the default `border-bottom` that some user agents apply would be distracting and draw the eye to the links that have acronyms. You don't want that, so remove the underlining effect from `acronym` too:

```
acronym {
 border: 0;
}
```

## Building the Box

The primary navigation has a fixed width, so set that first:

```
#priNav {
 width: 248px;
}
```

You use a left float to ensure that the navigation will appear on the left and the rest of the content to the right:

```
#priNav {
 width: 248px;
 float: left;
}
```

The content container uses a padding of 2 pixels on the left and right that should be matched here by adding a similar margin to the right side of the primary navigation. Use margin instead of padding to keep the writable area of the box 2 pixels from the edge of the main container and 2 pixels from the main content area:

```
#priNav {
 width: 248px;
 float: left;
 margin-right: 2px;
}
```

To give the header's drop-shadow gradient some room and keep the text from running to the right edge of the section dividers, add padding to the top and right of the navigation:

```
#priNav {
 width: 248px;
 float: left;
 padding: 6px 2px 0 0;
 margin-right: 2px;
}
```

That'll do it for the primary navigation's container. Let's move on to styling the section elements.

## Styling the Section Headers

Each h2 in the primary navigation covers one of the six major areas of UF's site. You've already set the font properties for the h2 element globally, but here you let it breathe a little by adding positive letter-spacing:

```
#priNav h2 {
 letter-spacing: 1px;
}
```

The bounds are well set for the width of the section header by the primary navigation container, so you don't need to set it explicitly here. That being said, the h2 element must be given some padding from the top and left edge of the section dividers:

```
#priNav h2 {
 padding: 7px 0 0 20px;
 letter-spacing: 1px;
}
```

The background-image, background-repeat, and background-position properties can be combined in the background property. You do it, in this case, to put a bullet (pointer.gif) in front of each h2. The upper-left corner of the bullet is placed 9 pixels to the right of and 14 pixels below the upper-left corner of the padding area you just set. The `background-color` and `background-attachment` properties can also be combined in the `background` property, but they are not needed here.

```
#priNav h2 {
 padding: 7px 0 0 20px;
 letter-spacing: 1px;
 background: url(images/pointer.gif) no-repeat 9px 14px;
}
```

To ensure that descenders (the portion of a letterform that drops below the baseline in letters such as *p* and *y*) don't affect the lines below them, define the `line-height`:

```
#priNav h2 {
 padding: 7px 0 0 20px;
 letter-spacing: 1px;
 line-height: 22px;
 background: url(images/pointer.gif) no-repeat 9px 14px;
}
```

### Styling the Lists

To style the unordered lists below each heading, start by adding the vertical complement of the padding set for the `h2` elements to the `ul`. (The `h2` element is a block element by default.)

```
#priNav ul {
 padding: 0 0 7px 20px;
}
```

Next, to place the `li` elements one after the next inside the `ul` block, override the `li` elements' default `block` state to display it `inline`:

```
#priNav li {
 display: inline;
}
```

To set the height of the list, add the `height` property to the `ul` elements and `line-height` to the `li` elements:

```
#priNav ul {
 padding: 0 0 7px 20px;
 height: 26px;
}

#priNav li {
 display: inline;
 line-height: 13px;
}
```

Now add the border that separates each section:

```
#priNav ul {
 padding: 0 0 7px 20px;
 height: 26px;
```

```
 border-bottom: 1px solid #eee;
}

#priNav li {
 display: inline;
 line-height: 13px;
}
```

That was fairly straightforward, wasn't it? The changes kept the semantics of the primary navigation intact and styled the headers and subsequent lists to match the desired design.

With the primary navigation handled, let's look at another type of unordered list: supplementary navigation.

# Making the Supplementary Navigation

A supplementary navigation does exactly what it sounds like it would do. It supplements the primary navigation with links to sections that are brought up for lower sections in a navigation's hierarchy for the benefit of the users. The supplementary navigation discussed here consists of two parts: the utility navigation and the role-based navigation (see Figure 4-10).

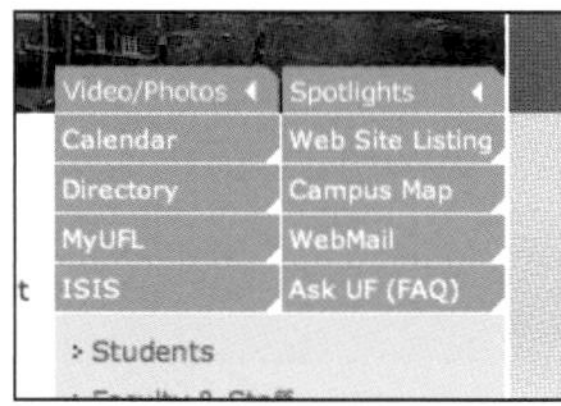


**Figure 4-10: UF's supplementary navigation.**

*Note that the Video/Photos and Spotlights buttons are part of the Flash animation, not the supplementary navigation.*

## *The XHTML*

Because the supplementary navigation is made up of two distinct parts, you define each separately. The structures that house both of them are quite similar. Let's look at the utility navigation first.

### *Utility Navigation*

Utility navigation is simply a set of links to frequently used tools. At UF, this includes a map of the campus, calendar of events, campus directory, ufl.edu email access, and so on. In the past, groups of disparate utilities were often handled using pipes or images to separate items. This neither adds meaning to the items used for separation nor allows for the function afforded by the browser.

The best method of applying a sensible grouping to these types of utilities is through (you guessed it) an unordered list. The list you'll create looks like this:

```
<ul id="utilNav">
 <li><a href="http://calendar.ufl.edu/">Calendar</a></li>
 <li><a href="/websites/">Web Site Listing</a></li>
 <li><a href="http://phonebook.ufl.edu/">Directory</a></li>
 <li><a href="http://campusmap.ufl.edu/">Campus Map</a></li>
 ...
</ul>
```

Each utility gets its own list item inside a containing `ul` with the `id` of `utilNav`. That's the first part of the supplementary navigation; let's handle the second part.

## Role-Based Navigation

Moving away from role-based navigation as a primary means of navigation in the design was discussed earlier in the chapter. That being said, UF did not want to completely remove that as a means of grouping information.

You can keep the role-based navigation but downplay its importance by moving it down the page in the XHTML and placing it in a box in the bottom-right corner of the design:

```
<ul id="roleNav">
 <li><a href="/students/">Students</a></li>
 <li><a href="/facstaff/">Faculty &amp; Staff</a></li>
 <li><a href="/friends/">Alumni, Donors &amp; Friends</a></li>
 <li><a href="/visitors/">Parents, Patients &amp; Visitors</a></li>
</ul>
```

Similarly to the utility navigation, each role is a list item inside an unordered list called `roleNav`.

## Wrapping the Two Together

Now that you've created the utility and role-based navigation, you can group them together as supplementary navigation. Simply wrap everything in a `div` called `suppNav`:

```
<div id="suppNav">
 <ul id="utilNav">
  <li><a href="http://calendar.ufl.edu/">Calendar</a></li>
  <li><a href="/websites/">Web Site Listing</a></li>
  <li><a href="http://phonebook.ufl.edu/">Directory</a></li>
  <li><a href="http://campusmap.ufl.edu/">Campus Map</a></li>
  ...
 </ul>
 <ul id="roleNav">
  <li><a href="/students/">Students</a></li>
  <li><a href="/facstaff/">Faculty &amp; Staff</a></li>
  <li><a href="/friends/">Alumni, Donors &amp; Friends</a></li>
  <li><a href="/visitors/">Parents, Patients &amp; Visitors</a></li>
 </ul>
</div>
```

This works, but the two navigational groups lack definition. You must provide headers that describe what is inside each list to both utility and role-based navigation.

```
<div id="suppNav">
 <h2>Frequently Used Sites</h2>
 <ul id="utilNav">
  <li><a href="http://calendar.ufl.edu/">Calendar</a></li>
  <li><a href="/websites/">Web Site Listing</a></li>
  <li><a href="http://phonebook.ufl.edu/">Directory</a></li>
  <li><a href="http://campusmap.ufl.edu/">Campus Map</a></li>
  ...
 </ul>
 <h2>Information For:</h2>
 <ul id="roleNav">
  <li><a href="/students/">Students</a></li>
  <li><a href="/facstaff/">Faculty &amp; Staff</a></li>
  <li><a href="/friends/">Alumni, Donors &amp; Friends</a></li>
  <li><a href="/visitors/">Parents, Patients &amp; Visitors</a></li>
 </ul>
</div>
```

You have a well-structured pair of lists to work with now, so let's polish them up.

# The CSS

There are three distinct items with which to work: the utility navigation, role-based navigation, and the supplementary navigation container. The container should be dealt with first.

## Styling the Supplementary Navigation

The first thing to do is place a limit on the width of the supplementary navigation container, `suppNav`:

```
#suppNav {
 width: 200px;
}
```

The entire supplementary navigation must be moved outside the normal flow and off to the right side of the page. To do that, you place the container absolutely:

```
#suppNav {
 width: 200px;
 position: absolute;
 top: 195px;
 right: 2px;
}
```

You added headers to each of the two navigational groups, but you're about to start styling each of those groups. This styling should be enough to separate the lists from the information around them, so hide the headers inside the supplementary navigation:

```
#suppNav h2 {
 display: none;
}
```

Because this style is inside the style sheet brought in through `@import`, the headers will still be displayed in their proper formatting not only in search engines but in ancient browsers as well.

This styled supplementary navigation `div` gives you a good container in which to place your utility and role-based navigation.

## Styling the Utilities

You want the list of utilities to flow and fill up the width of the container. Start by setting the `li` element to display inline as you did with the lists inside the primary navigation:

```
#utilNav li {
 display: inline;
}
```

Next, you must build the box inside of which each of the utilities will reside. Because you have an exact width and height to specify for each box, you set both. To take advantage of the default center vertical alignment inside the box, use the `line-height` attribute to set the height.

```
#utilNav li {
 width: 99px;
 line-height: 21px;
 display: inline;
}
```

The container is 200 pixels wide, allowing you to give the list items some space. The 1-pixel margin added to the left should be matched by a 1-pixel margin on the bottom:

```
#utilNav li {
 width: 99px;
 line-height: 21px;
 margin: 0 0 1px 1px;
 display: inline;
}
```

With your list items sized and spaced, you're ready to handle the links inside them. To have the `a` element handle the rollover properly, the default display type must be overridden by rendering it as a `block`. The size of the box that holds the link should match the size of the box created by the list item, so size the `a` element accordingly:

```
#utilNav li a {
 width: 99px;
 height: 21px;
 display: block;
}
```

To give the text inside a little padding to the left — and to avoid the hassles caused by differences in box model interpretations — indent the text in lieu of padding it:

```
#utilNav li a {
 text-indent: 3px;
 width: 99px;
```

```
  height: 21px;
  display: block;
 }
```

To shine up the links, add some color and an image. Placing the image in the lower-right of each link bevels the corner at 45 degrees:

```
 #utilNav li a {
  text-indent: 3px;
  width: 99px;
  height: 21px;
  color: #fff;
  display: block;
  background: #94a2d9 url(images/chamfer.gif) no-repeat right bottom;
 }
```

Adding a splash of feedback to the links is as simple as setting the hover state. Here you make them change color slightly by changing the `background-color` but leaving the `chamfer` image intact:

```
 #utilNav li a:hover {
  background-color: #566cc3;
 }
```

## That Tricky Box Model

Using list items can cause problems in Internet Explorer 5 for Mac and Windows. Indenting the text inside the links instead of padding them fixes the rendering in all of the browsers except IE5. When text is indented inside list items, IE5 creates a *de facto* margin outside the box equal to the size of the indentation, thus making the effective size of the box wider and throwing off the proper wrapping inside the container.

A quirk in these browsers can fix the problem as easily as it was created. To trick IE5 for Mac and Windows into gobbling up the extra girth it creates, simply float everything left:

```
 #utilNav li {
  width: 99px;
  line-height: 21px;
  margin: 0 0 1px 1px;
  display: inline;
  float: left;
 }
 #utilNav li a {
  text-indent: 3px;
  width: 99px;
  height: 21px;
  color: #fff;
  display: block;
  background: #94a2d9 url(images/chamfer.gif) no-repeat right bottom;
  float: left;
 }
 #utilNav li a:hover {
  background-color: #566cc3;
 }
```

By the way, notice that you didn't need to style the `#utilNav ul` element at all in making the design work. To style the next navigational item, you make use of the `ul` element.

## *Styling the Roles*

The role-based navigation has some similarities to the utility navigation you just styled, but it also has quite a few differences. You want to give the effect of text inside a containing box, not individual buttons for each list item. In this case, you handle some of the manipulation inside the unordered list element.

The method used in the utility navigation to get around the extra width caused by text indentation in Internet Explorer 5 for Mac and Windows has its repercussions here. Because the utility list items were floated left, the point at which the browser renders the current element never moved. You get around this by clearing any elements that are floated to the left:

```
ul#roleNav {
 clear: left;
}
```

The `ul` element should stretch to fit the width of its container, so there is no need to set a width. The height will be handled naturally as well. To make the left side of the role-based navigation line up with the left side of the individual list item boxes created earlier, add a 1-pixel left margin:

```
ul#roleNav {
 clear: left;
 margin-left: 1px;
}
```

The `chamfer.gif` image used to bevel the corner of the utility list items can be reused here to bevel the corner of the role list container:

```
ul#roleNav {
 background: #dbe0f2 url(images/chamfer.gif) no-repeat right bottom;
 clear: left;
 margin-left: 1px;
}
```

The list box needs some room to stretch top and bottom, so add 6 pixels:

```
ul#roleNav {
 padding: 6px 0;
 background : #dbe0f2 url(images/chamfer.gif) no-repeat right bottom;
 clear: left;
 margin-left: 1px;
}
```

To create some spacing between the list items and vertically center each of the items, set the `line-height`:

```
ul#roleNav li {
 line-height: 22px;
}
```

To remove extra spacing created by IE5 below each of the list items, fool it into gobbling up the space by setting `display` to `inline`:

```
ul#roleNav li {
 line-height: 22px;
 display: inline;
}
```

As with the links inside the utility list, you should set the `height` of the links inside the list items. The `display` property should also be overridden here to `block`. Like the list items and the unordered list they are in, this will stretch to fit the width of the container.

```
ul#roleNav li a {
 height: 22px;
 display: block;
}
```

To move the text off the left side of the box, add a `padding-left` large enough to give the bullets you will add some breathing room:

```
ul#roleNav li a {
 padding-left: 16px;
 height: 22px;
 display: block;
}
```

As you did in the primary navigation, place a bullet inside the left padding using a background image 8 pixels from the left edge and centered vertically. (When the second parameter of the `background-position` property is omitted, it defaults to `center`.) Set the color and size of the font too:

```
ul#roleNav li a {
 padding-left: 16px;
 font-size: 12px;
 height: 22px;
 display: block;
 color: #596ec4;
 background: #dbe0f2 url(images/pointer_small.gif) no-repeat 8px;
}
ul#roleNav li a:hover {
 color: #0021a5;
}
```

## The Final Outcome

Here you have it — a complete look at the style behind the supplementary navigation:

```
#suppNav {
 width: 200px;
 position: absolute;
 top: 195px;
 right: 2px;
}
#suppNav h2 {
 display: none;
```

```
}
#utilNav li {
 width: 99px;
 line-height: 21px;
 margin: 0 0 1px 1px;
 display: inline;
 float: left;
}
#utilNav li a {
 text-indent: 3px;
 width: 99px;
 height: 21px;
 color: #fff;
 display: block;
 float: left; /* For IE5 */
 background: #94a2d9 url(images/whiteCornerNik.gif) no-repeat right bottom;
}
#utilNav li a:hover {
 background-color: #566cc3;
}
ul#roleNav {
 padding: 6px 0;
 background : #dbe0f2 url(images/whiteCornerNik.gif) no-repeat right bottom;
 clear: left;
 margin-left: 1px;
}
ul#roleNav li {
 line-height: 22px;
 display: inline;
}
ul#roleNav li a {
 padding-left: 16px;
 font-size: 12px;
 height: 22px;
 display: block;
 color: #596ec4;
 background: #dbe0f2 url(images/pointer_small.gif) no-repeat 8px;
}
ul#roleNav li a:hover {
 color: #0021a5;
}
```

That's it. That's the list.

# Revisiting Flash Embedding

UF wanted to display a rotating series of three spotlights on faculty (see Figure 4-11) and decided that Flash (instead of Java or JavaScript image rotators) was the way to do it.

Using Flash also meant that it couldn't be a deal breaker. In other words, if the visitor doesn't have Flash installed, the site still must function properly. To be appropriate for this site's audience, Flash must be an augmentation of the site's content — not a barrier to those without Flash.

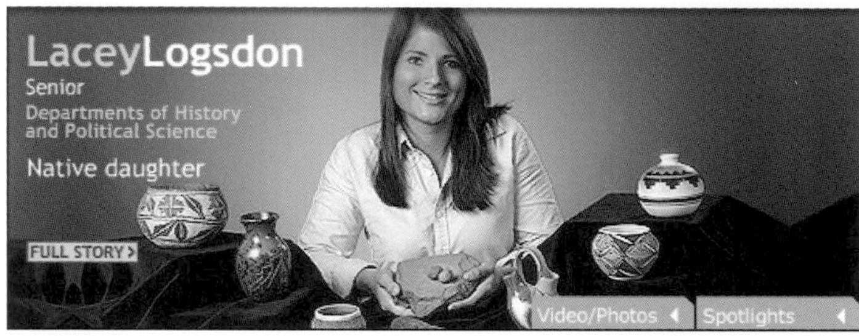

**Figure 4-11: Examples of Flash spotlights used on the UF site.**

The previous chapter discussed methods of properly including Flash in your designs. Let's look at one of these in more detail: Flash Satay (`www.alistapart.com/articles/flashsatay`).

## Back to Flash Satay

As discussed in Chapter 3, the Flash Satay method of including Flash in Web sites addresses the `embed` element used by older browsers and the proprietary attributes commonly used inside the `object` element.

To better understand what we're trying to do here, take a look at what a typical piece of markup to include Flash on a page would look like:

```
<object classid="clsid:D27CDB6E-AE6D-11cf-96B8-444553540000"
codebase="http://download.macromedia.com/pub/shockwave/cabs/flash
/swflash.cab#version=6,0,0,0" width="516" height="194" id="movie">
 <param name="movie" value="spotlights.swf">
  <embed src="spotlights.swf" width="516" height="194"
   name="movie" type="application/x-shockwave-flash"
```

```
    plug inspage="http://www.macromedia.com/go/getflashplayer">
</object>
```

The Flash Satay method takes a big chunk out of this and leaves you with some rather clean markup:

```
<object type="application/x-shockwave-flash" data="loader.swf" width="516"
height="194">
 <param name="movie" value="loader.swf" />
</object>
```

This new loader movie (a small file of around 4K) simply loads the larger movie with all the content (see Figure 4-12). This gets around an issue in IE for Windows in which the movie loaded in the object parameter won't stream, causing the visitor to have to wait until the entire Flash movie has loaded before it starts.

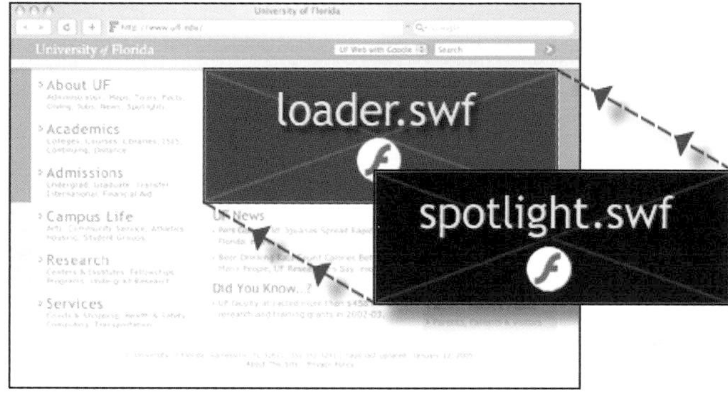


**Figure 4-12: Flash Satay uses a loader movie in addition to the main Flash content.**

If the visitor does not have Flash installed, UF wants alternate content in its place. The `object` module has a very useful method of allowing you to provide that by simply adding the alternate content after the first parameter. In this case, you place an image of a campus landmark, as shown in Figure 4-13.

```
<object type="application/x-shockwave-flash" data="loader.swf" width="516"
height="194">
 <param name="movie" value="loader.swf" />
 <img src="images/tower.jpg" alt="Century Tower Photo and University Auditorium"
width="516" height="194" />
</object>
```

Elsewhere on the page in the primary navigation, there is a link to the same XHTML-based spotlights that the Flash-based spotlight movie links to. So, if a visitor does not have Flash installed or enabled, the same content is still accessible to the Spotlight section.

This works well for all modern browsers, or so it would seem. An unfortunately widespread glitch caused by a corrupt Flash Player Active X control when users of IE 5.5 upgraded from IE 5.01 causes a text area to be rendered instead of the requested object (in this case, the Flash spotlights loader) in the absence of the `classid` attribute. For IE to play nicely with the new, sleek, standards-compliant markup, you need to resort to a little trickery.

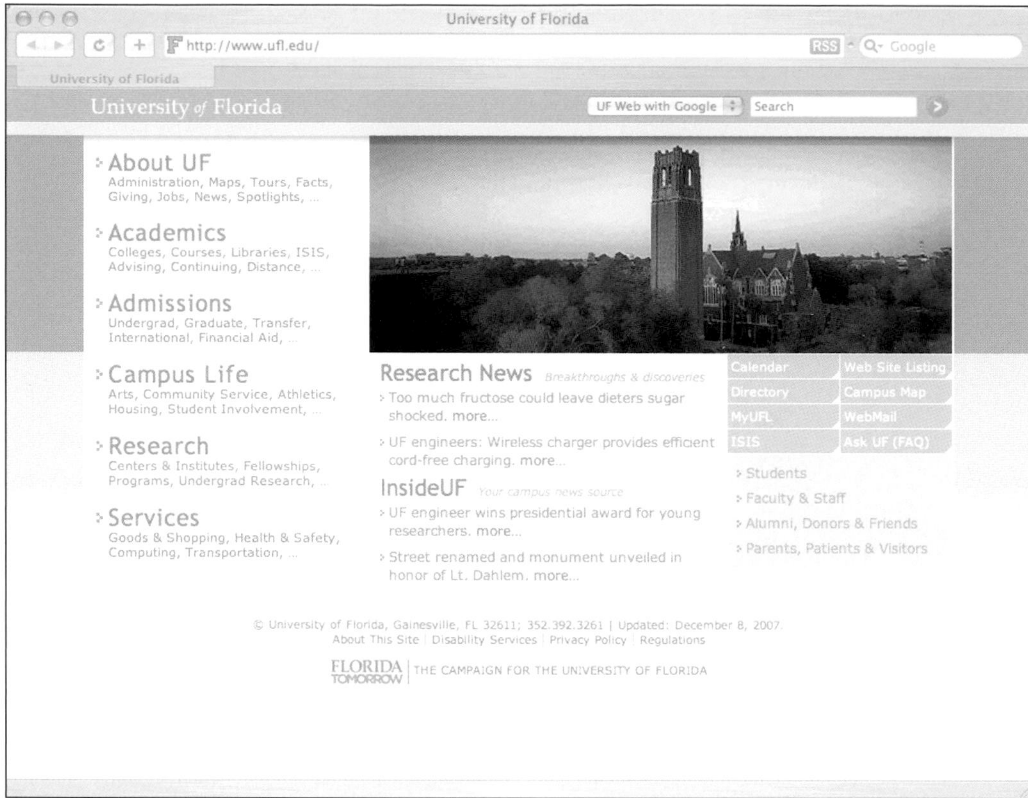


**Figure 4-13: Elements passed after the movie parameter are used as alternate content.**

# *Server-Side Detecting with Flash Satay*

Flash Satay suggests using the `object` element without an `embed` attribute to allow standards-compliant additions of Flash content to XHTML. UF took the Flash Satay method of Flash inclusion described earlier and circumvented problems in IE 5.5 by making a minor revision — server-side browser detection.

## *Apache and the BrowserMatch Directive*

To handle the `classid` attribute properly, you must pass it only to visitors using Internet Explorer for Microsoft. You can discern what browser a visitor is using (for the most part) through the request it makes to the server for a Web page. The server normally records some basic information about the request: the name of the file, the time, whether the request was successful, the size of the file, and (most important for your needs here) the type of browser.

The method used here assumes that the site is hosted on an Apache Web server. Approximately half of all Web sites (including the UF site) are hosted using the Open Source Web server software Apache. This method can be modified for usage by sites hosted on Microsoft's IIS or other Web servers.

To begin, create or locate the `.htaccess` file in either the root directory of the site or in the directories where the documents are that use Flash. The `.htaccess` file is a simple text file containing directives that configure how a server handles documents and directories. If not done already, tell the server to parse the type of document used. If as here you are using (X)HTML documents, you do this by adding an `AddHandler` directive for the suffix of your content to the site's `.htaccess` file:

```
AddHandler server-parsed .html
```

If the content is already in a server-parsed format, the `AddHandler` directive is not needed.

Now set an environment variable that will allow you to identify the content in the documents (namely, the `classid`) you pass to Internet Explorer for Windows. Add the following line in the `.htaccess` file:

```
BrowserMatch MSIE msie
```

This directs the server to set an environment variable called `msie` to `true` if the `User-Agent` is `MSIE` (Internet Explorer for Windows).

Take another look at the markup as it is now:

```
<object type="application/x-shockwave-flash" data="loader.swf" width="516"
height="194 classid="clsid:D27CDB6E-AE6D-11cf-96B8-444553540000">
 <param name="movie" value="loader.swf" />
 <img src="images/tower.jpg" alt="Century Tower" width="516" height="194" />
</object>
```

Because you now have a variable that lets you know when the visitor is using IE for Windows, you can selectively add the `classid` back in by checking for the `msie` variable. The code to tell the server to do so looks like this:

```
<object type="application/x-shockwave-flash" data="loader.swf" width="516"
height="194"
<!--#if expr="${msie}"-->
classid="clsid:D27CDB6E-AE6D-11cf-96B8-444553540000"
<!--#endif --> >
<param name="movie" value="loader.swf" />
<img src="images/tower.jpg" alt="Century Tower" width="516" height="194" />
</object>
```

*Using the BrowserMatch directive is explained in more detail in the Apache documentation describing the* `mod_setenvif` *module at* `http://httpd.apache.org/docs/mod/mod_setenvif.html`.

## Drawbacks and Barriers to Flash Satay with Server-Side Detection

As is mentioned in Chapter 3, if a site has a sizeable number of Flash movies, then the creation of container movies for each one can become cumbersome. The UF site uses a small number of Flash movies (well, just one), so that's okay.

For the method described here, the site's server must be configured to allow directives and the content creator must have access to create those permissions. This is the case at UF.

The directive must parse through each page served, placing an additional (though nominal) load on the server. This wasn't an issue for UF because it already parses every page to allow for server-side includes (SSIs).

# Looking for Missteps

After going through a seven-month process to redesign its site, UF found some things it would do differently.

## Leading Only by Example

When UF released the new site, colleges and departments around campus were clamoring to incorporate the techniques and manner of design used on the home page. To stay on schedule, the site was launched without the completion of a definitive style guide and set of templates to be distributed across campus.

A set of templates has since been developed, but the delay stymied campus Web development. The time to manage a shift in how UF develops Web sites was when its most visible section was going through that change.

## "Force of Habit" or "Who Moved My Input Field?"

With any redesign, especially on a site with a large number of repeat visitors, managing change becomes critical to acceptance. There are often users (especially staff members) whose site usage is something like this:

> *"I go to the home page and click Link X, scroll down and click Link Y, type what I need into Box Z, and click Go."*

While a well-tested redesign should certainly create a more usable site for any new visitor, repetitive users of the site (like the one quoted here) will likely react violently to an interruption in their Pavlovian conditioning.

Mismanagement and lack of attention to the transition of these repeat visitors can lead to a great deal of angst and wasted resources.

While the site was shared with the test audiences, a protracted public beta might have alleviated some of the growing pains that came along with the redesign.

# Summary

The evolution of the University of Florida Web site provided a look into some of the challenges that await changing Web sites, the decisions UF made to combat them, and the techniques that did the job. You looked at styling headers and unordered lists in different types of navigation and why they should be used. You also saw some modifications to widely used Flash markup to allow for both standards compliance and across-the-board application. We hope this will help you tackle your next big project.

# 5

# Stuff and Nonsense Ltd.: Strategies for CSS Switching

*I have a switch in my apartment that doesn't do anything. Every once in a while I turn it on and off. On and off. On and off. One day I got a call from a woman in France who said "Cut it out!"*

*— Stephen Wright*

This is the chapter where we tell you to forget all that you have learned about CSS so far, to look beyond the surface of the pool and discover the truth within the truth . . . or something like that. (Honestly, we're more fun at parties than we might seem.)

After four chapters, it's worth remembering that as convenient as it is to site designers, cascading style sheets can also drastically improve the online experience for the users of your sites. In Chapter 1 you saw briefly how the cascade is written with users' needs in mind, and that user style sheets are ultimately given precedence over the author style sheets you write. The authors of the specification didn't do this to spite those that design for the Web, but rather to empower those who read it.

After all, the true wonder of the Web is its promise of universal access: an avenue through which a user can gain instant and complete entry to any topic, from anywhere in the world. In fact, much of the mantle you don as a Web designer is to honor that promise — to make sites that are at once visually compelling *and* with an interface that presents no barrier to entry.

However, designers have slowly come to realize that their understanding of their audience has been incomplete at best. In the early days of the Web, development was focused on having sites "look right" on contemporary desktop browsers. But in recent years, the understanding of users' needs has matured. People with physical, hearing, visual, or cognitive disabilities have always been using Web sites; it's just taken designers some time to realize it. So, it's only of late that the definition of "accessibility" has flowered, and site-building techniques have followed suit.

Some designers may tell you that building an accessible site means building a boring site, yet accessibility isn't about larger fonts and creating high-contrast guidelines. Some users of the Web can read only smaller texts, while others can see only yellow text on a black background. Rather, many of the design techniques explored throughout this book — semantic, well-structured markup, a separation between content and presentation — can and will afford you incredible leverage in building professional, inspiring designs *and simultaneously* improve the accessibility of your sites for all of your users, not just a select few. In short, you can better realize the Web's potential for universal access, and make some ultra-sexy sites to boot.

This chapter is not a manifesto on accessibility, space allotments, and our meager skills being the largest impediments. Instead, you'll explore different techniques for democratizing your design through the use of *style sheet switching*. By applying a different CSS file to a markup document, you can drastically change any or all aspects of its design — the layout, typography, or color palette. This technique may hold incredible appeal to designers because it exponentially decreases the amount of overhead required to redesign a site. But, as you'll see, this technique can wield incredible benefits to your site's users, allowing them fine-grained control over a page's presentation and, in turn, better access to the content therein. After all, it's about throwing the gates as wide open as possible.

Let's dive right in.

# Laying the Foundation

As with other chapters, begin with a valid XHTML document. For the purposes of the style sheet–switching experiments, the document in Listing 5-1 will do nicely.

**Listing 5-1: The Markup Foundation for Style Switcher Experiments**

```
<!DOCTYPE html PUBLIC "-//W3C//DTD XHTML 1.0 Transitional//EN"
"http://www.w3.org/TR/xhtml1/DTD/xhtml1-transitional.dtd">

<html xmlns="http://www.w3.org/1999/xhtml">
<head>

<title>Always offer an alternative.</title>

<meta http-equiv="Content-Type" content="text/html; charset=utf-8" />

</head>

<body>

<div id="container">
  <div id="content">
    <h1>Always offer an alternative.</h1>

    <p><span class="lead">Lorem ipsum dolor sit amet,</span> consectetuer
adipiscing elit. Nullam tortor. Integer eros...</p>

    <p id="blurb">This is, as they say, a &#8220;pull quote.&#8221;</p>
```

```
    <p>Donec id nisl...</p>

    <h2>Additionally, you might consider...</h2>

    <p><img src="portrait.png" alt="An author's handsome (if pixellated) mug"
class="portrait" />  Quisque sit amet justo. Cum sociis...</p>
  </div>
</div>

</body>
</html>
```

By now, this sort of markup should seem rather old hat to you. The markup is simple, yet well meaning, with proper heading elements (`h1` and `h2`) applied to suit their position in the (admittedly nonsensical) document's outline. Paragraphs have been marked up as such via the `<p>` element, with one earmarked with an `id` of "blurb" so that you might later style it differently than its siblings. And just to spice up the layout a bit, it includes a pixel illustration of one of this book's authors. (Sorry, no prizes are available for guessing which one it is.)

Figure 5-1 shows you just how humble this beginning is.

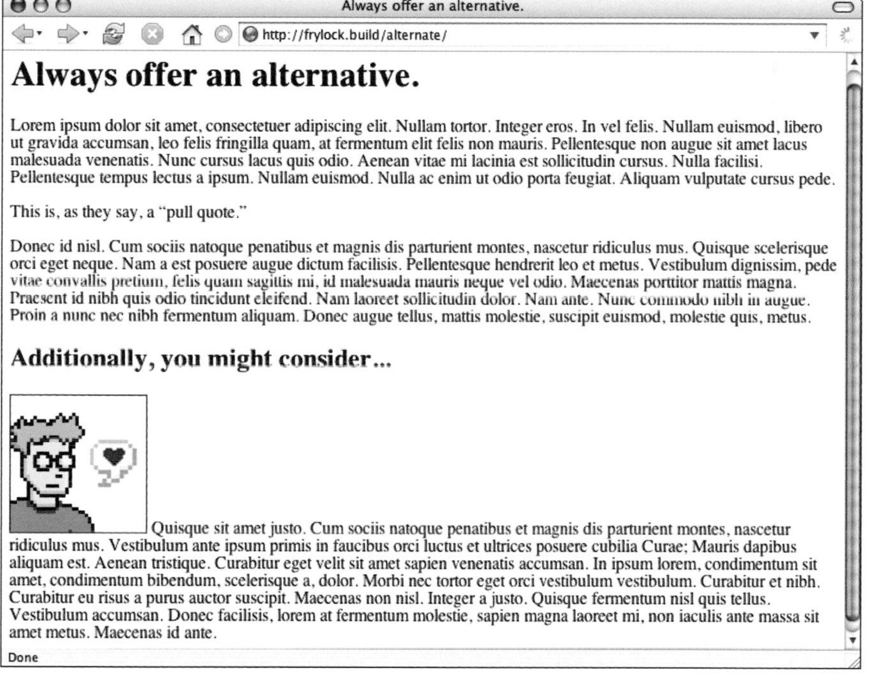


**Figure 5-1: The unstyled XHTML document, partying like it's 1994.**

As always, you can apply a rough style sheet to this document and slap a bit of mascara on that otherwise unimpressive wall of serifs. So, create a new style sheet called `core.css`, and include the rules in Listing 5-2.

**Listing 5-2: The core.css Style Sheet**

```
/* default font and color information */
body {
  background: #FFF;
  color: #444;
  font: 62.5%/1.6em "Lucida Grande", Verdana, Geneva, Helvetica, Arial, sans-serif;
}
/* END default font and color information */

/* default link rules */
a {
  color: #C60;
}

a:hover {
  color: #F60;
  text-decoration: none;
}
/* END default link rules */

/* headings */
h1, h2 {
  color: #B61;
  line-height: 1em;
  font-weight: normal;
  font-family: Helvetica, Arial, Geneva, Verdana, sans-serif;
  margin: 1em 0;
  padding: 0;
}

h1 {
  font-size: 2.2em;
}
/* END headings */

/* container */
#container {
  margin: 0 auto;
  max-width: 60em;
}
/* END container */

/* content */
#content h2 {
  font-size: 1.2em;
  text-transform: uppercase;
}

#content p {
  font-size: 1.1em;
  line-height: 1.6em;
}
```

```
#content img.portrait {
  float: right;
  margin: 0 0 1em 1em;
}

#content span.lead {
  text-transform: uppercase;
}

#content #blurb {
  background: #FFC;
  border: 1px dotted #FC6;
  color: #000;
  font-size: 1.5em;
  line-height: 1.4em;
  padding: .5em;
  text-align: center;
}
/* END content */
```

That was a bit of a rush, wasn't it? Rather than adding a few selectors at a time and discussing the visual result, this chapter focuses less on the techniques the style sheet contains than on the end result gained by switching them. After all, this CSS is merely a placeholder, one that could easily be replaced. With that said, you won't examine every detail of the file, although there are a few techniques worth noting:

- `#container { margin: 0 auto; }` — While you may be tut-tut-ing the use of a `div` with no real semantic worth, `#container` establishes a handy means of controlling the width of the content within it. Setting left- and right-side "auto" margins (`0 auto;`) allows you to horizontally center the `div` within its parent element — namely, the `body` of the markup.

  There's only a slight issue with this approach. Versions 5.*x* of Internet Explorer on Windows doesn't properly implement auto-margins and therefore does not understand this rule. As a result, you need to apply `text-align: center;` to the `body` element. Granted, this is an incorrect interpretation of the `text-align` property (designed to control the inline content of a block, and not the block itself), but it nonetheless puts IE5/Windows back in its place. However, by applying `body { text-align: center; }`, IE5/Windows also centers all of the text on the page. Thankfully, once you set `#container { text-align: left; }`, your work is done.

- `#container { max-width: 60em; }` — Setting the max-width property completes the effect, ensuring that the `#container` element never gets larger than 60ems. If the user reduces the size of his or her window to less than the width of `#container`, the `div` will shrink accordingly. In short, it's a no-hassle way to gain a truly flexible layout.

  The largest drawback to the `max-width` property is Internet Explorer's complete lack of support for it. Neither the Macintosh nor the Windows version of that browser will understand `max-width`. As a result, you have to serve up a defined width to IE. For this example, it's `width: 60em;`, but you might opt to choose a more flexible percentage width. Serving this alternate value to IE and IE alone can be done through the judicious use of a CSS hack, or (a favorite method) by placing the "incorrect" value in a separate style sheet with browser-specific hacks. Chapter 2 discusses both of these options in more detail.

- `body { font: 62.5%/1.6em "Lucida Grande", Verdana, Geneva, Helvetica, Arial, sans-serif; }` — The font property that's set on the body element is actually a shorthand property. It declares the `font-size` (62.5%), `line-height` (1.6em), and `font-family` (`Lucida Grande, Verdana, Geneva, Helvetica, Arial, sans-serif;`) in one handy-dandy property/value pair. And because these values are inherited by the body's descendant elements, you've immediately applied a basic type profile to the entire document with this one rule.

The 62.5 percent value for `font-size` is a technique first publicized by Web designer Richard Rutter ("How to Size Text Using ems," `http://clagnut.com/blog/348`). Because the default text size for all modern browsers is 16 pixels, setting `font-size: 62.5%;` on the body nets you a default type height of 10 pixels ($16 \times 0.625 = 10$). From there, sizing descendant elements with ems (a relative unit of measurement) becomes much more logical: 1em is 10px, 1.6em is 16px, .9em is 9px, and so forth. Rather than using pixels throughout the document (which IE users cannot resize), this method gives you a near-pixel-perfect replacement for the typesetting — and allows users to resize text to a size that suits their needs.

- `#content img.portrait { float: right; }` — The oh-so-handsome pixel portrait is aligned flush with the right edge of its containing paragraph. But rather than resorting to deprecated markup techniques such as `<img src="blah.gif" align="right" />`, you use the powerful CSS `float` model to achieve the same effect. (Recommended reading: CSS guru Eric Meyer's excellent article, "Containing Floats," at `http://complexspiral.com/publications/containing-floats`.)

You could easily paste this entire chunk of code into a `<style type="text/css">...</style>` block in the head of the document, but of course that would muddy the markup with presentational information — and honestly, who wants to hunt down style information across a few hundred XHTML documents? That's right; some call it "adhering to a strict separation between structure and style." It could also be called "lazy." Either way you think of it, maintaining that separation makes it a lot easier for you and others to work with the site.

So, create a second style sheet, and name it `main.css`;. At the top of that new file, use the `@import` command to invoke the `core.css` file, like this:

```
@import url("core.css");
```

This effectively creates a "wrapper" style sheet — a CSS file that acts as a gateway to other style sheets. With the `main.css` file in hand, you can now include it — and with it, `core.css` — in the XHTML with one simple `link` element, placed in the `head` of your document:

```
<link rel="stylesheet" href="main.css" type="text/css" />
```

And *voilà*! A rather plain-looking document suddenly gets a bit of personality (see Figure 5-2).

You might be scratching your head after creating this seemingly superfluous `main.css` file, but rest assured, there are some very good reasons for putting it in place. Although it wasn't designed as such, the `@import` rule is a kind of litmus test for a browser's support of advanced CSS techniques. Legacy browsers that have broken CSS implementations don't understand the `@import` rule and will simply disregard it. This allows you to serve up high-octane style sheet rules to modern browsers, while such antiquated browsers as versions 4 and below of Netscape and Internet Explorer will simply ignore the style sheets that they wouldn't otherwise understand.

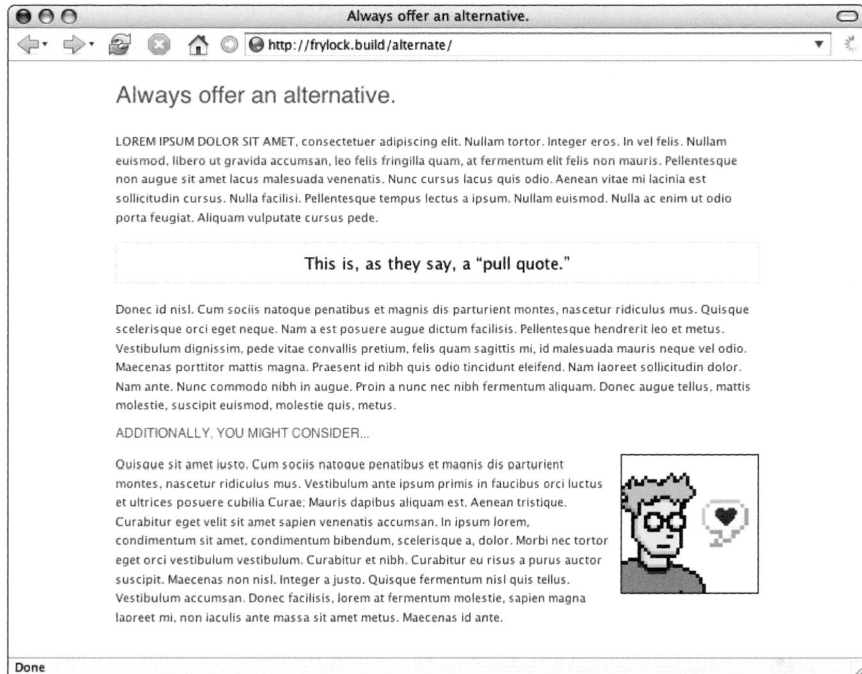


**Figure 5-2: Applying some basic styles to the XHTML makes it a bit more readable.**

An added benefit to this intermediary style sheet is that you can place multiple `@import` rules therein. This could come in handy if you needed to break your site's presentation into multiple files (for example, one for layout, another for color, yet another for typography). Or even better, you can use this technique to manage your various CSS hacks, as you saw in Chapter 2. As you test the CSS in Listing 5-3, you may find that the different versions of Internet Explorer (both on the Macintosh and Windows platforms) break different aspects of the layout. While you could use a battery of style sheet hacks within the `core.css` file to serve up alternative property values to these browsers' broken CSS implementations, Listing 5-3 shows how you might use the wrapper style sheet to include browser-specific CSS hack files that allow you to keep the `main.css` file clean and hack-free.

**Listing 5-3: Revised core.css File with Intelligent Hack Management**

```
@import url("core.css");

/* Import WinIEx-only bugs - hide from Mac IE5 \*/
@import url("hacks.win.iex.css");
/* END hide from Mac IE5 */

/* Import Win IE5x hacks */
```

*Continued*

**Listing 5-3** *(continued)*

```
@media tty {
     i{content:"\";/*" "*/}} @import 'hacks.win.ie5.css'; /*";}
}/* */

/* Import Mac IE5 hacks */
/*\*//*/
@import url("hacks.mac.ie5.css");
/**/
```

You've already explored the CSS hacks needed to get the page looking good in less-than-CSS-savvy browsers, and triaging the different hacks into browser-specific files is an excellent way to keep your `core.css` file clean and hack-free. If you ever decide to drop support for a certain browser, you now need to remove only a few lines from `main.css` — definitely a more appealing thought than scouring the primary style sheet rules line by line, looking for CSS hacks. Again, it's equal parts "strategic" and "lazy" here at CSS Best Practices Headquarters.

With the CSS and XHTML firmly in place, let's delve into the mechanics of style sheet switching.

# CSS Switching

One fault of the example page's current design is that legibility wasn't one of the guiding design goals. The contrast is a bit light because it uses a near-black color for the text against the `body`'s white background. And the default font size of 62.5 percent of the browser's default (or roughly 10 pixels) might be difficult to read for users suffering from visual impairments. (Even a reader with slight myopia might have to work at reading the content.) How can you improve the design to make it more legible, without sacrificing the original vision?

To begin, create a separate style sheet that addresses some of these possible pitfalls. In Listing 5-4 provides a new CSS file named `contrast.css`.

**Listing 5-4: The contrast.css Style Sheet**

```
body {
  background: #000;
  color: #DDD;
}

h1, h2 {
  color: #FFF;
  font-weight: bold;
}

#content {
  font-size: 1.1em;
}

#content h2 {
  font-size: 1.6em;
```

```
    text-transform: none;
  }

  #content #blurb {
    background: #222;
    border-color: #444;
    color: #FF9;
  }

  span.lead {
    font-weight: bold;
  }
```

Now simply add a `link` to the new `contrast.css` file in the `head` of the markup, like this:

```
<link rel="stylesheet" href="main.css" type="text/css" />
<link rel="stylesheet" href="contrast.css" type="text/css" />
```

When you reload the document in your browser, you'll see that the landscape has changed pretty drastically, as shown in Figure 5-3.

First and foremost, it's worth mentioning that because the two CSS files are being included in tandem, you don't need to use `contrast.css` (Listing 5-4) to re-declare any of the layout or type rules established in `main.css`. Rather, you can simply selectively override individual rules and/or property values and let the rules of specificity handle which rules cascade to the user.

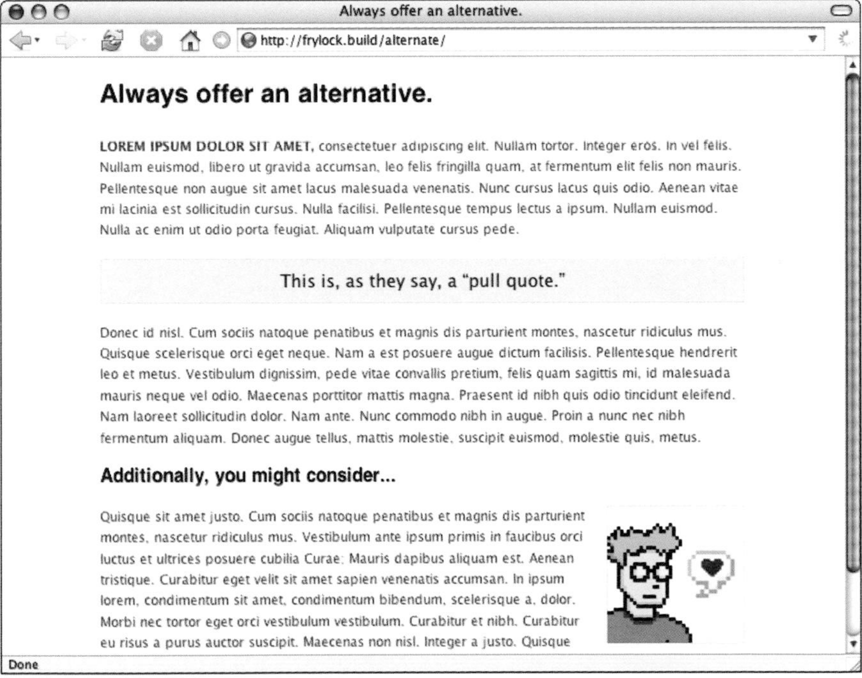


**Figure 5-3: A supplementary style sheet provides heightened contrast and an increased font size.**

From a purely aesthetic point, you've instantaneously changed the presentation of the markup — and all by including the new `contrast.css` file. The text size has been increased very slightly (from 1em to 1.1em), and the colors on the pull quote have been changed to reflect the new palette. The completed effect feels much more nocturnal — but more importantly, you've created a style sheet that allows users to enjoy a higher level of contrast, as well as a slightly more legible type size.

The original question is still unanswered: How do you switch between the two style sheets?

# The Mechanics: How It's Supposed to Work

Thus far, you've associated two separate CSS files with one document. Currently, both files are being read and applied to the document with equal weight, with the rules of specificity resolving any conflicts that may arise between the two. However, to accommodate more complex scenarios than the one you currently have, the HTML and CSS specifications provide structured guidelines for how multiple style sheets interact. Web page authors are given a number of ways to prioritize the style sheets you include via the `link` element. Let's examine the three different classes of style sheets — persistent, preferred, and alternate — and see how they might apply to the switching scenario.

## Persistent Style Sheets

*Persistent* style sheets are always enabled. Think of them as CSS that is "turned on" by default. The persistent CSS file is applied in addition to any other style sheets that are currently active, and acts as a set of shared style rules that every other style sheet in the document can draw upon.

Each `link` element with a `rel` attribute set to `"stylesheet"` is a persistent style sheet — and, in fact, you've created two already:

```
<link rel="stylesheet" href="main.css" type="text/css" />
<link rel="stylesheet" href="contrast.css" type="text/css" />
```

As you add additional kinds of style sheets, any `link`s that you designate as persistent will act as the baseline, sharing their rules with all other included CSS files.

## Preferred Style Sheets

You can designate a style sheet as *preferred* by adding a `title` to a persistent style sheet, like this:

```
<link rel="stylesheet" href="main.css" type="text/css" />
<link rel="stylesheet" title="Higher Contrast" href="contrast.css" type="text/css"
/>
```

Additionally, you can specify multiple "groups" of preferred style sheets by giving them the same `title` attribute. This allows the user to activate (or deactivate) these groups of CSS files together. Should more than one group be present, the first group takes precedence.

Much as with persistent style sheets, preferred CSS files are enabled by default. So, in the previous example, the `contrast.css` file would be enabled when the user first visits the page (borrowing, as it did before, from the persistent `main.css` file). However, preferred style sheets are disabled if the user selects an alternate style sheet.

## Alternate Style Sheets

An *alternate* style sheet can be selected by the user as, well, an alternative to a CSS file marked as preferred by the site's author. To designate a `link` as an alternate style sheet, it must be named with a `title` attribute, and its `rel` attribute set to `"alternate stylesheet"`. As with preferred style sheets, you can group `links` together by giving them identical `title` attributes. So, in short, this is what you've been looking for — a means by which you can allow users to select the design that best suits their needs. If you do, in fact, want `main.css` to be the default and `contrast.css` to be an optional, alternate CSS file, you would update the two `link` elements to match:

```
<link rel="stylesheet" href="main.css" type="text/css" />
<link rel="alternate stylesheet" title="Higher Contrast" href="contrast.css"
type="text/css" />
```

Now, viewing the page in a browser that supports style sheet switching, the user can finally control the display of the page. Browsers such as Firefox or Opera include an option to select the new alternate style sheet, as shown in Figure 5-4.

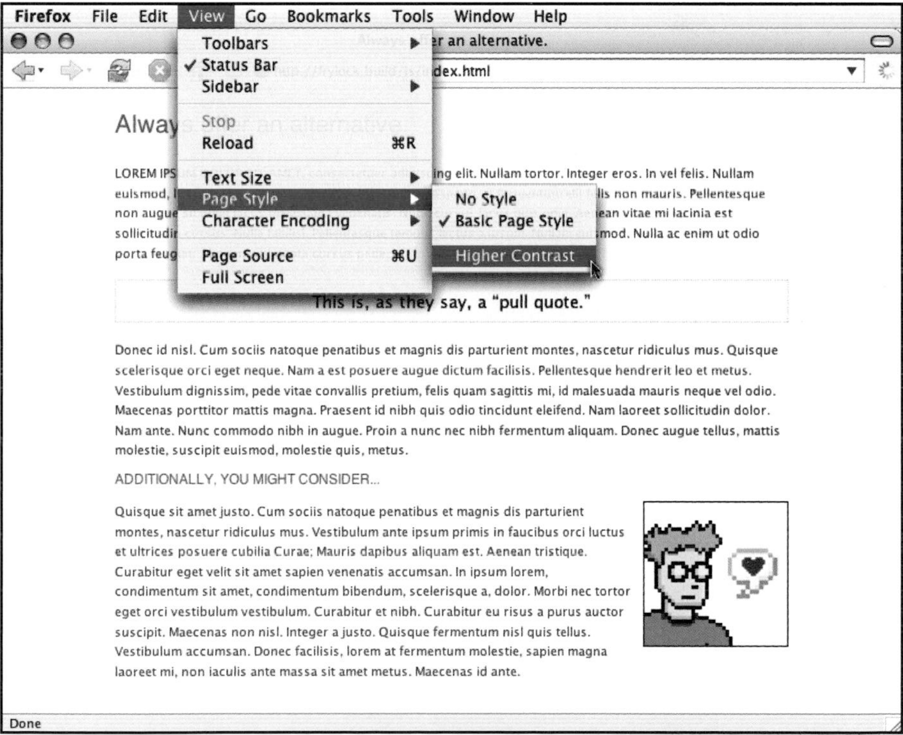


**Figure 5-4: By changing the `rel` attribute of the second link element to "alternate stylesheet" and supplying a title, you implement some basic style switching.**

Once the user selects Higher Contrast from the menu, the alternate style sheet with that title — namely, `contrast.css` — becomes active. And that's the solution we were looking for. The original design is the active default, but you've created the means by which users can select another design altogether. Using this method, you can add even more alternate CSS options. For instance, create a file named `hot.css` and use the rules in Listing 5-5.

**Listing 5-5: The hot.css Style Sheet**

```
body {
  background: #000 url("bg-stylish.jpg") no-repeat 50% 0;
  color: #DDD;
}

h1, h2 {
  color: #FFF;
  font-weight: normal;
  text-align: center;
  text-transform: none;
}

#content {
  font-size: 1.1em;
}

#content h1 {
  font: 2.6em Zapfino, "Gill Sans", Gill, Palatino, "Times New Roman", Times,
serif;
  margin: 200px 0 70px;
}

#content h2 {
  font: 1.6em "Gill Sans", Gill, Palatino, "Times New Roman", Times, serif;
  margin: 1.4em 0;
  text-transform: uppercase;
}

#content #blurb {
  background: #222;
  border-color: #444;
  color: #FF9;
}

span.lead {
  font-weight: bold;
}
```

Now, by applying what you've learned about alternate style sheets thus far, you can easily present `hot.css` to your users as another user interface option:

```
<link rel="stylesheet" href="main.css" type="text/css" />
<link rel="alternate stylesheet" title="Higher Contrast" href="contrast.css"
type="text/css" />
<link rel="alternate stylesheet" title="Gratuitous CSS" href="hot.css"
type="text/css" />
```

If the users have the capability to select an alternate CSS file from their browsers, they'll be able to see the new styles, as shown in Figure 5-5. And, as before, the change is a fairly drastic one — but you've finally allowed the users to choose an appealing design and tailor the content to meet their needs.

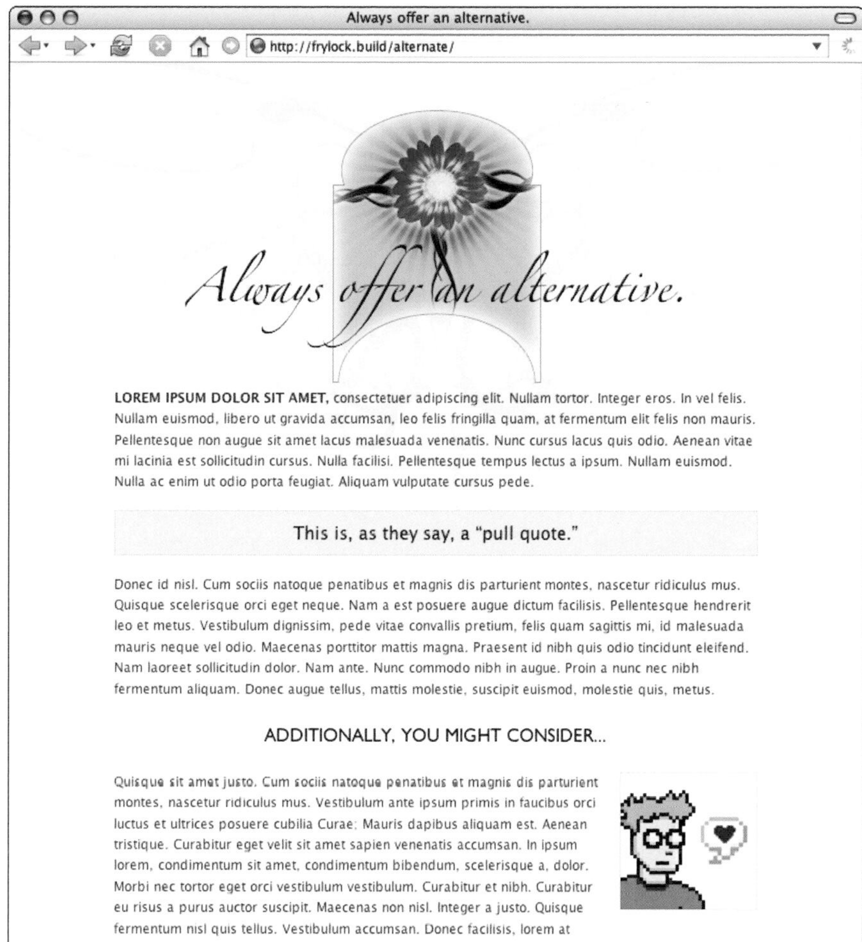


**Figure 5-5: Understanding how the cascade works enables you to build even more complexity into your alternate CSS documents.**

## Another Solution You (Almost) Can't Quite Use

As with some of the most promising features of CSS, adoption of alternate style sheets would be more widespread if browser support were more robust. As of this writing, the number of browsers that natively allow users to select alternate style sheets is limited to Gecko-based browsers such as Mozilla and Firefox, and the Opera browser. For example, Apple's Safari has no way to select alternate or preferred style sheets. And, you guessed it, Internet Explorer (the browser known and loved the world over) won't allow users to select the alternate user interfaces you build for them. If the world's most popular browser keeps this feature out of the hands of your users, you have a bit more work to do.

Furthermore, the browsers that *do* natively support alternate style sheet switching have only limited switching functionality. These browsers do allow the user to easily switch between the default CSS and any alternates provided by the author, but they do not remember the user's selection. This means that, if a reader selects an alternate style sheet and then reloads the page or leaves and returns to it, the browser will have forgotten the earlier choice and will reinstate the default style.

Obviously, neither of these scenarios will work for your users. Fortunately there are some additional steps you can take to bring the full benefits of CSS switching to them.

# The Reality: How It Can Work Today

It's established, then, that most of your audience won't be able to use in-browser CSS switching so you must build an interface into your page that allows users to overcome these limitations. Now, you might realize that the two client-side technologies you've been studying up to this point aren't especially well equipped to handle this. While XHTML and CSS excel at describing and styling content, respectively, neither was designed to *interact* with the user. Sure, you can use XHTML to build a list of links on the page as follows:

```
<div id="switcher">
  <ul>
    <li id="style-default"><a href="styleswitch.html">Default style</a></li>
    <li id="style-contrast"><a href="styleswitch.html">Higher Contrast</a></li>
    <li id="style-hot"><a href="styleswitch.html">Gratuitous CSS</a></li>
  </ul>
</div>
```

And you can add some CSS to `core.css` to style them accordingly, as shown in Figure 5-6:

```
/* switcher styles */
#switcher ul {
  text-align: right;
  list-style: none;
}

#switcher ul li {
  border-left: 1px solid;
  list-style: none;
  display: inline;
  padding: 0 0 0 1em;
  margin: 0 1em 0 0;
}

#switcher #style-default {
  border-left: 0;
  padding-left: 0;
}

#switcher ul a.now {
  color: #000;
  font-weight: bold;
```

```
    text-decoration: none;
  }
  /* END switcher styles */
```

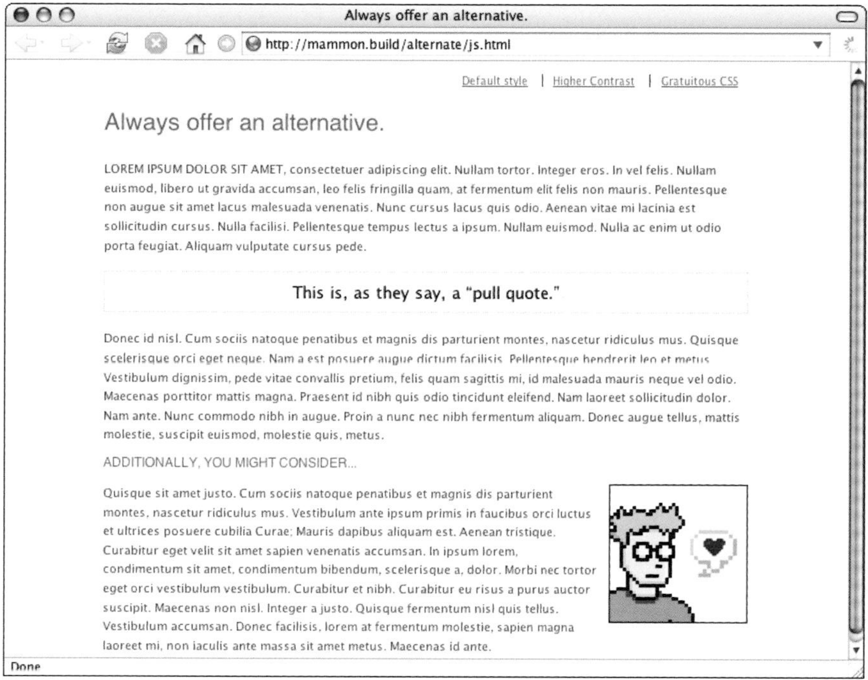


**Figure 5-6: Links for a switcher are added to the top of the page, but all they can do at the moment is look pretty.**

However, what happens when the user clicks on those links? If your answer was something akin to "zilch," you win the blue ribbon. XHTML and CSS can't really *do* anything when you're talking about responding to a user's actions. They can, in turn, affect the content and the presentation of the page, but when the user tries to click a link to change the active style sheet, that's when you need to turn to the third tool in the standards-savvy designer's toolkit: JavaScript.

## Jumping on the JavaScript Bandwagon

To put it simply, JavaScript was created as a client-side scripting language. JavaScript (or JS, to use the parlance of lazy typists everywhere) is a language designed to add a layer of interactivity into your Web pages. When a user visits a Web page that has some JavaScript code in it, the browser reads the JS and follows any instructions that might be contained therein. Those instructions might tell the browser to display helpful messages to a user as he or she completes a form, or to perform basic validation on the data he or she enters there. You can even use JS to instruct the browser to perform a certain action when the user clicks a link. In short, JavaScript is the means by which you bridge the divide between your content and your users, allowing the latter to fully interact with the former.

Sounds intimidating (and more than a little stuffy), doesn't it? Perhaps it's best to just dive right in.

## Gathering Requirements

Before you begin a lick of coding, you want to make sure that you understand exactly what it is that you're building. Just as requirements gathering is beneficial to a client project (as discussed in Chapter 1), the smallest development gig can benefit from some sort of needs analysis. With a better understanding of what you need to build and what it needs to achieve, you can code quicker and more efficiently — two qualities that will make your clients and you quite happy.

So let's take a quick inventory of what you're working with:

- There are three `link` elements in the `head` of the XHTML document that include screen-specific CSS files: a persistent style sheet (`main.css`), and two alternate style sheets (`contrast.css` and the ultra-swank `hot.css` ).
- Accordingly, at the top of the document is a list of three anchors, each corresponding to a different style sheet. Granted, these anchors are about as useful as a road map in the desert, but you're going to change that shortly.

So, what exactly should your function do? Ideally, when a user clicks a link:

1. The function should cycle through each of the `link` elements in the `head` of our XHTML and inspect those that link to style sheets *and* have a title.
2. If the `link` matches the link that the user selected, it should be set to be the "active" CSS.
3. Otherwise, the `link` should be set to "disabled," which will prevent the browser from loading the style sheet.
4. Once the function has finished setting the active link element, it should remember the user's choice. The style sheet the user selected will, therefore, remain "active" as the user browses through the site, and the choice will be remembered if the user returns to your site during a later browsing session.

How will you do all of this? Well, the solution ultimately involves a fair amount of pixie dust and happy thoughts — but you shouldn't get too far ahead of yourself.

## Building the Switching Function

With your goals firmly in mind, you can begin building your style sheet functions. First, create a new file called `scripts.js`, and include the following markup in the head of the XHTML document:

```
<script type="text/javascript" src="scripts.js"></script>
```

Much as you use the `link` element to include external CSS files for your site's presentation, you can use the `script` element to reference an external JavaScript file. And, in that file, you can write in the first lines that will power the CSS switcher. If JavaScript syntax looks a bit intimidating, don't worry. We'll only touch on some of the highlights.

```
// activeCSS: Set the active stylesheet
function activeCSS(title) {
  var i, oneLink;
  for (i = 0; (oneLink = document.getElementsByTagName("link")[i]); i++) {
    if (oneLink.getAttribute("title") && findWord("stylesheet",
oneLink.getAttribute("rel"))) {
```

```
        oneLink.disabled = true;
        if (oneLink.getAttribute("title") == title) {
          oneLink.disabled = false;
        }
      }
    }
  }

  // findWord: Used to find a full word (needle) in a string (haystack)
  function findWord(needle, haystack) {
    return haystack.match(needle + "\\b");
  }
```

In this code snippet, you have two JavaScript *functions*, which are basically discrete chunks of functionality: `activeCSS()` and `findWord()`. Each function contains a series of instructions that are passed to the browser for processing. For example, here's what happens when `activeCSS` is invoked:

1. An *argument* (or variable) is passed to it with the title of the desired "active" style sheet.
2. The function assembles a list of all `link` elements in your document (`document.getElementsByTagName("link")`) and proceeds to loop through them, checking to see whether the title of the link matches the title of the function's argument.
3. When a match is found, the function then evaluates the `rel` attribute to see if the word "stylesheet" is present. The `findWord()` function is used here to search the `rel` for a whole-word match only. This means that if someone accidentally types `rel="stylesheets"` or the like into a `link` element, your function ignores them.
4. Each link that meets the criteria in step 2 will be disabled (`oneLink.disabled = true;`).

Admittedly, this is a bit of a gloss of the functions' syntax. JavaScript is a robust and rewarding language, but you're nonetheless forced to breeze through some of its subtleties to get back on the CSS track. However, the preceding list demonstrates the high-level concepts at play in the code you've created and should provide a fine starting point for those interested in further exploring JavaScript's elegant syntax.

While these two functions enable you to switch your CSS, they simply lie dormant until they are *invoked* (or called) by your markup. You want the switcher to fire when a user selects a link from the `#switcher` list, and the easiest place to do that is within the anchors of the style switcher list:

```
<div id="switcher">
  <ul>
    <li id="style-default"><a href="styleswitch.html"
onclick="activeCSS('default'); return false">Default style</a></li>
    <li id="style-contrast"><a href="styleswitch.html"
onclick="activeCSS('Higher Contrast'); return false">Higher Contrast</a></li>
    <li id="style-hot"><a href="styleswitch.html"
onclick="activeCSS('Gratuitous CSS'); return false">Gratuitous CSS</a></li>
  </ul>
</div>
```

The `onclick` attribute introduced here is called an *event handler*. When the user performs a certain action or "event" (in this case, a mouse click), the JavaScript contained in the attribute value is fired. So, in the preceding example, when the `onclick` handler detects that a user has clicked on the anchor, it fires the `activeCSS()` function.

*You could argue that using these event handlers, such as* `onclick`*,* `onblur`*,* `onmouseover`*, and so on is analogous to relying on the* `style` *attribute — that these inline attributes blur the separation of structure and behavior, and they can easily increase the cost of maintenance and support. Rather than editing your XHTML to reflect any changes in the JavaScript, it would instead be possible to use more modern JS to automatically generate the event handlers your links will need and, therefore, keep the necessary divide between your markup and your scripting. For more information, look up Peter-Paul Koch's "Separating behavior and structure" (*`http://digital-web.com/articles/separating_behavior_and_structure_2`*).*

Look closely at the three different event handlers, and you'll see that each reference to `activeCSS()` differs slightly in that it includes in parentheses the title of the style sheet the link should activate. This is the *argument* mentioned earlier and is the string of text that the `activeCSS()` function compares to the `title` of each `link` element.

*You may have noticed that after the call to the* `activeCSS()` *function, the* `onclick` *handler contains some additional text:* `return false;`*. This plays a very small (but integral) part in the switcher because it tells the handler not to follow the URL referenced in the anchor's* `href` *attribute. Otherwise, the user would end up deposited on* `styleswitch.html` *after clicking any of the links.*

Let's just run through the steps that occur when a link is clicked. Assume that a user selects the third anchor, the `onclick` handler that contains the `activeCSS('Gratuitous CSS');` reference:

1. The three `link` elements are compiled into an array, and the function proceeds to loop over each of them. Remember that only those `link`s that contain `title`s *and* that have a `rel` attribute that contains the word "stylesheet" will be examined. This leaves you with the `link`s for `contrast.css` and `hot.css`.
2. The first `link` element has a `title` of "Higher Contrast." The function disables the `link` element, which stays disabled because its `title` doesn't match the function's argument ("Gratuitous CSS").
3. The second link element has a title of "Gratuitous CSS." The function disables the `link` element, but because the `title` *does* match the function's argument, the link is *immediately* reactivated.

And *voilà*! Figure 5-7 shows the results of each alternate style sheet.

Although you have successfully built a function to switch between the different CSS files, you're only halfway there. If the user refreshes the page or leaves the current one after selecting a new alternate style sheet, the choice is forgotten, and the default style sheet is restored. Let's put a little memory into the JavaScript functions.

## Baking a JavaScript Cookie

As you've seen with the not-quite-finished CSS switcher, the browsers don't seem to remember anything about a page once you've left or refreshed it. That is by design. The HTTP standard (which is the protocol over which the Web's pages are transferred from a server to your desktop) was designed to be "stateless." This means that each time you visit a page, the Web server considers it to be your first time, every time. Thankfully, there's a way to fill this memory gap. It's called a *cookie*, and it's less fattening than its baked namesake.

**Figure 5-7: With the JavaScript-enabled style switcher in place, users can now select a look that best suits their needs.**

A cookie, as you probably know, is a small text file that is sent by a Web server to a user's browser; it contains small bits of important information about that user's browsing session. Cookies may contain user preferences, registration information, the items placed in an online shopping cart, and so on. Once it receives a cookie, the browser saves the information on the user's computer and sends it back to the Web server whenever the user returns to that Web site.

You can use JavaScript to set and read cookies, so by adding a few more JavaScript functions to those you've already written, you can build an improved style sheet switcher — one that will respect your user's preferences across multiple pages on or visits to your site.

First, you need to set a cookie containing your user's style preference, and then you have to enable that cookie to be read later. So, let's add `setCookie()`, a new cleverly named function, to the `scripts.js` file:

```
// Set the cookie
function setCookie(name,value,days) {
  if (days) {
    var date = new Date();
    date.setTime(date.getTime()+(days*24*60*60*1000));
    var expires = ";expires="+date.toGMTString();
  } else {
    expires = "";
  }
  document.cookie = name+"="+value+expires+";";
}
```

And now, in the original `activeCSS()` function, you can add a single line (`setCookie...`) to store the user's preferences in a cookie on the user's computer:

```
// Set the active stylesheet
function activeCSS(title) {
  var i, oneLink;
  for (i = 0; (oneLink = document.getElementsByTagName("link")[i]); i++) {
    if (oneLink.getAttribute("title") && findWord("stylesheet",
oneLink.getAttribute("rel"))) {
      oneLink.disabled = true;
      if (oneLink.getAttribute("title") == title) {
        oneLink.disabled = false;
      }
    }
  }
  setCookie("mystyle", title, 365);
}
```

With this one line, half of your work is finished! The `setCookie()` function accepts three arguments: a name for the cookie (so that you can reference it later), the value to be stored in the cookie, and the number of days until the cookie expires. The previous code snippet creates a cookie named `"mystyle"`, the value of which is set to the value of the `title` argument of `activeCSS()`. This means that if a user selects a link that specifies `activeCSS('Higher Contrast')` in its `onclick` handler (that is, it invokes `activeCSS` with a `title` argument of `Higher Contrast`), then your `"mystyle"` cookie will have a value of Higher Contrast.

*In the* `setCookie()` *function, specifying the number of days until cookie expiration is optional. Because the argument is optional, you could leave it out entirely. However, omitting it causes the* `setCookie()` *function to create a* `"mystyle"` *cookie that expires at the end of the user's session — causing the user's preference to be lost as soon as he or she closes the browser. In the preceding example, the* `"mystyle"` *cookie is set to expire in 365 days, or one calendar year.*

With this lone call to `setCookie()`, you've managed to store the user's selection from the list of style sheet anchors. But how do you read the cookie and honor the preference? Simply add the following lines to the `scripts.js` file:

```
window.onload = initCSS;

// initCSS: If there's a "mystyle" cookie, set the active stylesheet when the page
loads
function initCSS() {
  var style = readCookie("mystyle");
  if (style) {
    activeCSS(style);
  }
}

// Read the cookie
function readCookie(name) {
  var needle = name + "=";
```

```
    var cookieArray = document.cookie.split(';');
    for(var i=0;i < cookieArray.length;i++) {
      var pair = cookieArray[i];
      while (pair.charAt(0)==' ') {
        pair = pair.substring(1, pair.length);
      }
      if (pair.indexOf(needle) == 0) {
        return pair.substring(needle.length, pair.length);
      }
    }
    return null;
  }
```

With these last lines of JavaScript in place, you're finally finished. The new function, `initCSS()`, has two simple tasks. First, it checks to see if there is a `"mystyle"` cookie on the user's machine (`var style = readCookie("mystyle");`). If one is present (`if (style)`), then the `activeCSS()` function is invoked with the value of the user's cookie as its argument.

The second task is hidden in a rather innocuous-looking line of this code snippet that does the heavy lifting: `window.onload = initCSS;` fires the `initCSS()` function when the document finishes loading in the user's browser. Now, as the user moves between the pages of your site, or when the user returns during a later session, you can immediately poll for the presence of a `"mystyle"` cookie as each of your pages comes up. As the user makes selections from your style switcher, your pages will honor them, allowing the user to tailor not only individual pages, but an entire *site* to his or her browsing needs.

Listing 5-6 shows the complete JavaScript file.

**Listing 5-6: Complete scripts.js File that Powers the JavaScript-Enabled CSS Switcher**

```
/*
  Onload
*/
window.onload = initCSS;

// initCSS: If there's a "mystyle" cookie, set the active stylesheet when the page
loads
function initCSS() {
  var style = readCookie("mystyle");
  if (style) {
    activeCSS(style);
  }
}

/*
  Switcher functions
*/
// activeCSS: Set the active stylesheet
function activeCSS(title) {
  var i, oneLink;
```

*Continued*

**Listing 5-6** *(continued)*

```
  for (i = 0; (oneLink = document.getElementsByTagName("link")[i]); i++) {
    if (oneLink.getAttribute("title") && findWord("stylesheet",
oneLink.getAttribute("rel"))) {
      oneLink.disabled = true;
      if (oneLink.getAttribute("title") == title) {
        oneLink.disabled = false;
      }
    }
  }
  setCookie("mystyle", title, 365);
}

// findWord: Used to find a full word (needle) in a string (haystack)
function findWord(needle, haystack) {
  var init = needle + "\\b";
  return haystack.match(needle + "\\b");
}

/*
  Cookie functions
*/

// Set the cookie
function setCookie(name,value,days) {
  if (days) {
    var date = new Date();
    date.setTime(date.getTime()+(days*24*60*60*1000));
    var expires = ";expires="+date.toGMTString();
  } else {
    expires = "";
  }
  document.cookie = name+"="+value+expires+";";
}

// Read the cookie
function readCookie(name) {
  var needle = name + "=";
  var cookieArray = document.cookie.split(';');
  for(var i=0;i < cookieArray.length;i++) {
    var pair = cookieArray[i];
    while (pair.charAt(0)==' ') {
      pair = pair.substring(1, pair.length);
    }
    if (pair.indexOf(needle) == 0) {
      return pair.substring(needle.length, pair.length);
    }
  }
  return null;
}
```

# Down with PHP

There's one fairly large drawback to the JavaScript solution. How do you know that the user has JavaScript on his or her machine? Okay, we can almost hear the snorts of derision from here — after all, JavaScript is the new black, right? What browser *doesn't* have this ultra-cool language available to it? Quite a few, as it turns out.

Internet statistics repositories suggest that anywhere from 6 percent to 10 percent of all Web users are browsing without JavaScript. It's true; it does sound like betting odds — 1 in 10 isn't so bad, right? Well, once you remember that there are millions of people in that group of "6 percent to 10 percent," the demographic starts to look a little different. And, regardless of exactly how many people browse without JavaScript, why should you exclude any from accessing your site, especially when it's incredibly easy to replicate the same functionality with server-side programming, as you'll soon see.

Rather than relying on client-side code that may or may not be available to your users, you can build a script that resides on your Web server to handle the style switching. Because you'll be working in a server-side environment, you can stop worrying about whether JavaScript is active on your users' computers. As long as the users can accept cookies, the server-side script will handle the style sheet switching logic with ease.

Of course, there are nearly as many server-side programming languages as there are authors on this book. For this project, use PHP (`www.php.net`). It's a wildly popular, open source (read: "free") programming language that is available on a staggering number of today's Web servers. Because of its popularity, its speed, and its robust feature set, it makes a fine choice for this chapter's experiments.

> *Of course, PHP isn't a magic bullet — if it's not installed on your Web server, you can't take advantage of it. Contact your server's administrator to see if it's installed on yours — otherwise, if you want some help getting PHP installed on your machine, there are plenty of resources available.*
>
> *The official PHP documentation (`www.php.net/docs.php`) is possibly the best place to start — although in all honesty, its installation instructions (while very clearly written) are a bit intimidating for those of us somewhat lacking in the `133t`-ness category. If you find yourself a bit lost among the configuration instructions, we recommend resorting to your favorite search engine. A search for "install php windows" or "install php mac" will yield hundreds of (we hope) easy-to-read results, yet another testament to PHP's popularity as a powerful, robust programming language.*
>
> *Additionally, Mac OS X users can avail themselves of easy-to-install packages. We recommend Server Logistics' feature-rich PHP installer (`www.serverlogistics.com/php4.php`), but other comparable packages are available. The drawback to such packages is that they limit the amount of control you can exercise over PHP's configuration. If an "as-is" installation isn't appealing to you, then the official documentation is the best resource out there.*

## Creating the Script

Once you have PHP up and running on your server, you can get to work. To begin, modify your XHMTL — specifically, the unordered list that contains the different style sheet options. Whereas you previously used `onclick` handlers to do the dirty work, the landscape has changed somewhat:

```
<ul>
  <li id="style-default"><a href="switch.php?style=">Default style</a></li>
```

```
  <li id="style-contrast"><a href="switch.php?style=contrast">Higher
Contrast</a></li>
  <li id="style-hot"><a href="switch.php?style=hot">Gratuitous CSS</a></li>
</ul>
```

Now, all of your links are pointing to a file named `switch.php` — but what's all of that `?style=` stuff in the links? The text that follows the question mark in the `href` is known as a *query string* and allows you to pass parameters to your CSS switcher script. Query string parameters always come in name/value pairs, like this:

```
file.name?name=value
switch.php?style=contrast
```

To pass multiple name/value pairs to a script, concatenate them with ampersands (&), like this:

```
Switch.php?style=contrast&amp;font=serif&amp;css=cool
```

*In HTML, ampersands have a special meaning. They signal the start of character entities, codes that represent special characters in HTML. For example,* `©` *is the entity for ©,* `™` *displays ™ in your browser, and so forth. When you want a literal ampersand to appear, as in this query string, you need to use* `&`*, which is the proper entity reference. Otherwise, your HTML will be invalid, and your query string may break — two options that aren't at all appealing.*

You'll see shortly how these parameters play a part in the style switcher, but for now create the `switch.php` file, and paste in the following code:

```
<?php
$domain = "my-site-here.com";

if (stristr($_SERVER['HTTP_REFERER'], $domain)) {
  $bounce_url = $_SERVER['HTTP_REFERER'];
} else {
  $bounce_url = "http://$domain/";
}

setcookie('mystyle', $_GET['style'], time() + 31536000);

header("Location: $bounce_url");
?>
```

And that's it. No, really — this won't be evolving into 80 lines of code over the next 50 pages, we promise. In JavaScript, you had to write custom functions to handle some of the basic tasks that the style switcher tackled. But many of these common tasks (such as reading and writing cookies) are already a part of the language. By using these built-in functions, you can cut down drastically on code bloat and get the style sheet switcher out the door as quickly as possible.

The meat of this code is the antepenultimate line of code:

```
setcookie('mystyle', $_GET['style'], time() + 31536000);
```

You had to create a custom function to set a cookie in JavaScript, but PHP does the hard work for you. Its `setcookie()` function is readily available to you and snaps nicely into the script. The one overlap with the JavaScript `setCookie()` function is that you're also passing three arguments to the function, the first two being the most critical. The first argument is, as before, simply the name for the cookie — `"mystyle"` in this case.

The second argument (`$_GET['style']`) defines what's actually stored as the value of the `"mystyle"` cookie. The `$_GET` variable is actually a named list, or *associative array*, of all the parameters passed to the page in a query string. For instance, assume that the `switch.php` page is called with the URL `http://my-site-here.com/switch.php?style=hot&css=cool`. The value of `$_GET['style']` is what follows the equal sign in the `style=hot` name/value pair, or `"hot"`; similarly, `$_GET['css']` would return a value of `cool`. As a result, the `setcookie()` function will build a `"mystyle"` cookie with a value of `hot`, which is exactly what you (and your users) want.

The third argument — `time() + 31536000` — may look like you need a decoder ring to make sense of it, but it's not quite as intimidating as it might seem. The `time()` function simply returns the current time, measured in seconds from midnight on January 1, 1970 — also called "the Unix Epoch," a common point of reference for functions dealing with time-based tasks. Once you have the current time, you're adding a year's worth of seconds to it (60 seconds × 60 minutes × 24 hours × 365 days = 31536000). Essentially, you're getting the time that is exactly one year later than when the cookie was set and using that to determine when the cookie expires.

Once the cookie's been set, you simply redirect the user back to `$bounce_url`, which was set at the beginning of the file. There's some extra processing at the top of `switch.php`, examining the user's referrer (the URL of the page he or she was visiting before being sent to `switch.php`). If the user was referred from a page on your `$domain` (`if (stristr($_SERVER['HTTP_REFERER'], $domain))`), you'll simply redirect the user to it. However, if another site decided to link directly to your style switcher, you'll set `$bounce_url` to your homepage (`$bounce_url = $_SERVER['HTTP_REFERER'];`).

The cookie is set and the user is redirected back to your site. What happens next? You need to set up some sort of logic for handling the cookie you've just baked. Let's dive right in and see what we can uncover.

## Eating the Cookie

This step requires inserting some PHP code directly into your XHTML — nothing onerous, but you first need to convert your markup document into one that your PHP server can read. To do so, simply rename the file, and change its `.html` extension to `.php` — if your system administrator has done his or her job properly, this should be all that's required to ready your XHTML for a little PHP-fu.

Once you've changed the file extension, insert the following code in the `head` of your document:

```
link rel="stylesheet" href="main.css" type="text/css" />
<?php
if ($_COOKIE['mystyle']) {
?>
<link rel="stylesheet" href="<?= $_COOKIE['mystyle']; ?>.css" type="text/css"
media="screen" />
<?php
```

```
}
?>

<link rel="alternate stylesheet" title="Higher Contrast" href="contrast.css"
type="text/css" />
<link rel="alternate stylesheet" title="Gratuitous CSS" href="hot.css"
type="text/css" />
```

When the markup document is loaded in the browser, the snippet of PHP is inserted into the `head`. If no `"mystyle"` cookie has been set (or if the value is just an empty string), then none of the code wrapped in the `if { ... }` statement runs. However, if your cookie *is* present, then a new `link` element is printed into your markup. Let's expand on that.

According to the query strings put in place in the `#switcher` unordered list, the two possible values for the `"mystyle"` cookie are `hot` and `contrast`. As a result, if you click a link with an `href` of `switch.php?style=hot`, the `link` element will be:

```
<link rel="stylesheet" href="hot.css" type="text/css" />
```

And with that, you've successfully completed the PHP style sheet switcher. Building on the goals and concepts outlined for the JavaScript switcher, you've now implemented a solution that allows your users to select a design at their leisure, with a much lower technical barrier for entry.

# CSS beyond the Browser

Your document is now looking quite fetching when viewed in a modern desktop browser, and you've explored a few different ways to allow users to change your site's presentation layer. What happens when you take that document outside of the browser context? What happens when you try to print one of your hyper-stylized designs?

Figure 5-8 shows a preview of the Gratuitous CSS skin.

As you can see, a little too much of the design shows through when it's printed, but not enough to be particularly effective. Gone are the page's background color and graphic, which printers won't render by default. Additionally, the rules that govern the page's layout are still fully intact. The content appears to have been pushed down the page for no good reason. The white space at the top doesn't serve any purpose and instead clips the amount of text visible on the page. Furthermore, the small sans-serif face that's used for the body copy might be fine onscreen (where the user can increase the size of the type as he or she sees fit), but it's less than ideal for paper. Serif faces are generally used to improve legibility when reading a page offline, and something a few points taller than the current type size might not hurt. In short, this printed version isn't exactly appealing.

Ultimately, you should create a separate design for the printed version of your page — one that emphasizes legibility over style, yet without sacrificing aesthetics altogether. Historically, this has required no small amount of overhead on your part. The days of separate, print-only versions of pages still loom large in memory. Keeping these "design-light" pages in sync with their "design-full" counterparts was an incredibly time- and resource-consuming affair that often required complicated scripts, grueling hours of manual editing, and occasionally more than a little late-night swearing at the computer monitor.

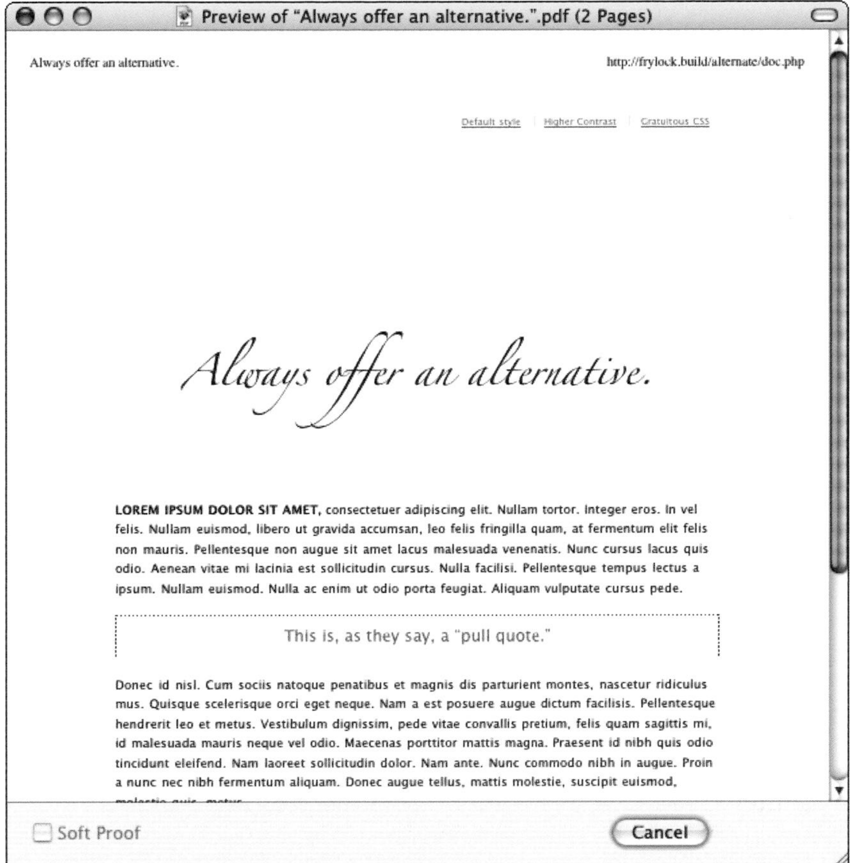


**Figure 5-8: You can definitely do better.**

# Media Types: Let the Healing Begin

The authors of the CSS specification anticipated this problem. They introduced the notion of *media types*, a means of classifying style sheets to deliver different designs to different devices such as printers, computer monitors, screen readers, handheld Internet-ready devices, and the like. Simply by earmarking your three `link` elements as containing "screen"-specific designs that should be delivered only to full graphic browsers (such as IE or Firefox), you can avoid some of the unpleasantness you saw earlier. To do so, simply specify a value of `"screen"` in the `link`'s `media` attribute:

```
<link rel="stylesheet" href="main.css" type="text/css" media="screen" />
<link rel="alternate stylesheet" title="Higher Contrast" href="contrast.css"
type="text/css" media="screen" />
<link rel="alternate stylesheet" title="Gratuitous CSS" href="hot.css"
type="text/css" media="screen" />
```

Now when you preview the document in its print view, things look quite a bit different (see Figure 5-9).

Always offer an alternative. http://frylock.build/alternate/

**Always offer an alternative.**

Lorem ipsum dolor sit amet, consectetuer adipiscing elit. Nullam tortor. Integer eros. In vel felis. Nullam euismod, libero ut gravida accumsan, leo felis fringilla quam, at fermentum elit felis non mauris. Pellentesque non augue sit amet lacus malesuada venenatis. Nunc cursus lacus quis odio. Aenean vitae mi lacinia est sollicitudin cursus. Nulla facilisi. Pellentesque tempus lectus a ipsum. Nullam euismod. Nulla ac enim ut odio porta feugiat. Aliquam vulputate cursus pede.

This is, as they say, a "pull quote."

Donec id nisl. Cum sociis natoque penatibus et magnis dis parturient montes, nascetur ridiculus mus. Quisque scelerisque orci eget neque. Nam a est posuere augue dictum facilisis. Pellentesque hendrerit leo et metus. Vestibulum dignissim, pede vitae convallis pretium, felis quam sagittis mi, id malesuada mauris neque vel odio. Maecenas porttitor mattis magna. Praesent id nibh quis odio tincidunt eleifend. Nam laoreet sollicitudin dolor. Nam ante. Nunc commodo nibh in augue. Proin a nunc nec nibh fermentum aliquam. Donec augue tellus, mattis molestie, suscipit euismod, molestie quis, metus.

**Additionally, you might consider...**

Quisque sit amet justo. Cum sociis natoque penatibus et magnis dis parturient montes, nascetur ridiculus mus. Vestibulum ante ipsum primis in faucibus orci luctus et ultrices posuere cubilia Curae; Mauris dapibus aliquam est. Aenean tristique. Curabitur eget velit sit amet sapien venenatis accumsan. In ipsum lorem, condimentum sit amet, condimentum bibendum, scelerisque a, dolor. Morbi nec tortor eget orci vestibulum vestibulum. Curabitur et nibh. Curabitur eu risus a purus auctor suscipit. Maecenas non nisl. Integer a justo. Quisque fermentum nisl quis tellus. Vestibulum accumsan. Donec facilisis, lorem at fermentum molestie, sapien magna laoreet mi, non iaculis ante massa sit amet metus. Maecenas id ante.

**Figure 5-9: The print document is messed up royally. Thankfully, this is only laying the foundation.**

It might not look like it, but this is, in fact, progress. By adding the `media="screen"` attribute to your `links`, you've wedded your designs to one context — the browser — and divorced them from all others. So when viewing your document in a different media type (such as a printer), you see the raw, unstyled content.

> *You can also specify multiple media types for any given* `link` *element. For example, the Opera browser (*`www.opera.com`*) respects the "projection" media type when browsing in its full-screen viewing mode. As a result, it disregards any CSS reserved exclusively for the "screen" media. If you want to reuse your screen-specific style sheet in a projection environment, you can simply append it to the media attribute with a comma:* `<link rel="stylesheet" href="main.css" type="text/css" media="screen, projection" />`.

Of course, while you can deny styles to nonbrowser devices, you can also deliver styles exclusively to them. After all, there's no reason to suffer through an unstyled printout when your onscreen design is so robust. With that, let's create a style sheet called `print.css`, as shown in Listing 5-7.

**Listing 5-7: The print.css Style Sheet**

```
body {
  background: #FFF;
  color: #000;
  font: 12pt/1.4em Georgia, Garamond, "Times New Roman", Times, serif;
}

h1, h2 {
  font-weight: normal;
  margin: 1em 0;
  padding: 0;
  text-transform: small-caps;
}

img.portrait, #switcher {
  display: none;
}

#blurb {
  background: #CCC;
  border: 1px solid #999;
  float: right;
  font: 16pt/1.5em Helvetica, Arial, Geneva, Verdana, sans-serif;
  margin: 0 0 1em 1em;
  padding: 1em;
  text-align: right;
  text-transform: small-caps;
  width: 10em;
}
```

Fairly simple, isn't it? When creating a print-specific style sheet, you use the same syntax and tactics discussed throughout the book. Whether applied in the browser or on a piece of paper, it's still CSS. Granted, there are a few things to consider when designing for print:

- **Controlling type size** — Perhaps the most striking thing about the print-specific style rules is that you use points to control the size of the type. While points are an absolute measure of font size, you'll use them to show the only acceptable context for their use: print styles. When designing for the screen, avoid points like the plague because of browsers' inconsistent rendering of point sizes. For print, however, points are ideal.
- **Pruning the useless** — Certain aspects of your markup probably don't need to be displayed in the printout. Perhaps you want to spare users from printing out the photo of that ugly mug, for instance. And of course, the links for the in-browser style sheet switcher are wholly pointless. With your print-specific style sheet, it's a simple matter of specifying `img.portrait, #switcher { display: none; }`. Through the magic of media types, these two elements will still be available onscreen, but removed from the printed version.

After creating your print-specific style sheet, include it in the `head` of the document. As always, you'll use a `link` to do so, but take extra care to specify the correct media type — namely, `"print"`:

```
<link rel="stylesheet" href="main.css" type="text/css" media="screen" />
```

```
<link rel="stylesheet" href="print.css" type="text/css" media="print" />

<link rel="alternate stylesheet" title="Higher Contrast" href="contrast.css"
type="text/css" media="screen" />
<link rel="alternate stylesheet" title="Gratuitous CSS" href="hot.css"
type="text/css" media="print" />
```

When you try printing again, the results should be a bit more pleasing to the eye. This time around, the screen-specific style sheets will be ignored, and your `print.css` will be allowed to control the presentation. As you can see from Figure 5-10, that assumption seems to be pretty much spot-on.

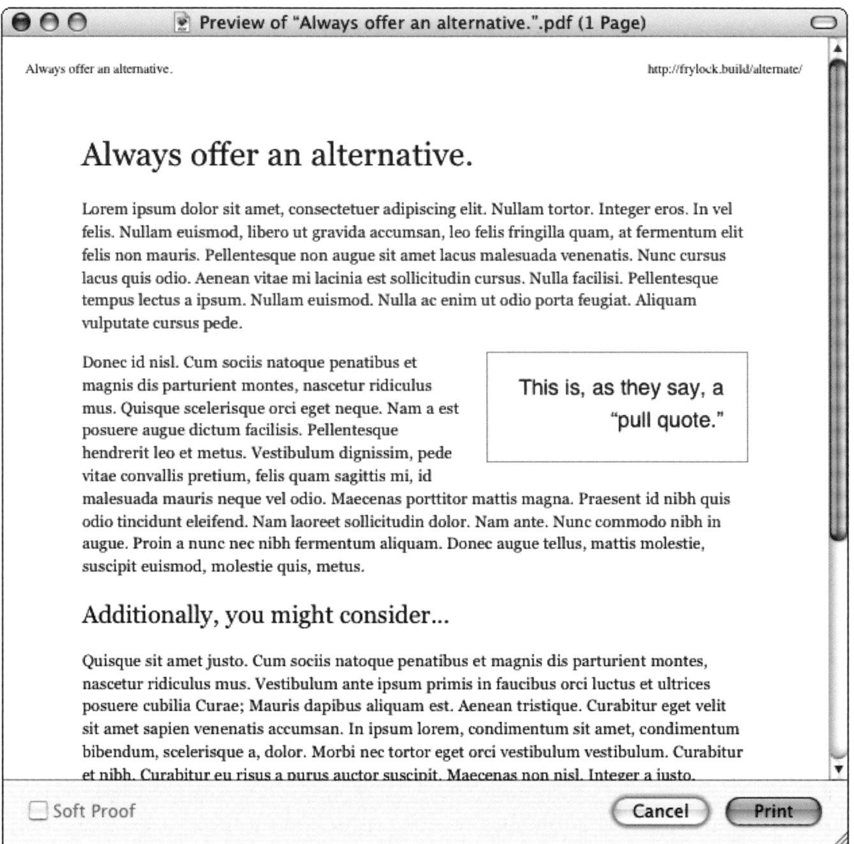


**Figure 5-10: And here it is, with the print-specific style sheet in place.**

The minuscule, sans-serif typeface has been replaced with a much more attractive serif face. Of course, you probably don't want to settle for the Model-T of fonts, so you'll opt to use the much more attractive Garamond or Georgia for your page's print version. And although you previously styled the `#blurb` paragraph as a full-column block on its own row, here you use the float model to pull it out of the document flow and give your pull quote much more of an "in-content" feel.

All of this has happened independently of the progress you've made with your onscreen designs. Essentially, your use of media types has enabled you to create two separate and distinct "views" of your page: the onscreen (aesthetically rich) version and the offline (content-over-panache) printed view. One markup document is displayed on multiple devices. Style sheets allow you to realize the promise of device independence, all the while keeping you from those late-night sessions of yelling at your computer monitors.

### The Problem with Choice

Now that you've implemented your media-specific designs, you are, in some respects, back at square one. You've given your users the capability to choose an onscreen design that works most effectively for them, but you've imposed a print-specific style sheet on them, with no option to change it. Do your users have to sacrifice choice in nonscreen media?

In short, the answer is, "No." You could go back to your JavaScript- and PHP-enabled style switchers and add in cases for print-specific styles. Of course, given the number of different media possibilities, your scripts (and the UI you present to your users) could become prohibitively large and difficult to maintain. What you need, then, is an elegant, scalable solution that allows you to easily and quickly manage alternate styles for multiple media types — and all without sacrificing usability.

## Stuff and Nonsense: Building a Better Switcher

We're lucky that certain innovative folks are already thinking along these lines. Enter Stuff and Nonsense (`www.stuffandnonsense.co.uk`), a design studio based in Wales, UK. (Figure 5-11 shows its home page.) A quick browse through the studio's portfolio (`www.stuffandnonsense.co.uk/work`) leads to two separate realizations: first, the studio has done beautiful, eye-catching work for such globally recognized brands as Disney and the World Wildlife Fund; second, the design of each of its portfolio sites is driven by cascading style sheets and built on a foundation of valid XHTML.

Obviously, Web standards are a passion at Stuff and Nonsense. But as you browse through its site, an obvious respect for its users' needs runs equally deep. Featured on the Accessibility page is a link inviting users to "Customise the look of this site" (`www.stuffandnonsense.co.uk/company/iotbs`), as shown in Figure 5-12. On the resulting page, users can select various style options not only for their in-browser experience but for printing as well. Whether a user prefers reading printed documents in either a small sans-serif typeface or a larger serif, Stuff and Nonsense has given him or her the capability to choose. Furthermore, the user's preferences are stored in a cookie so that they persist throughout the time spent visiting the site. The user can browse to or print any page on the site and is presented with the design that best meets his or her needs throughout the stay.

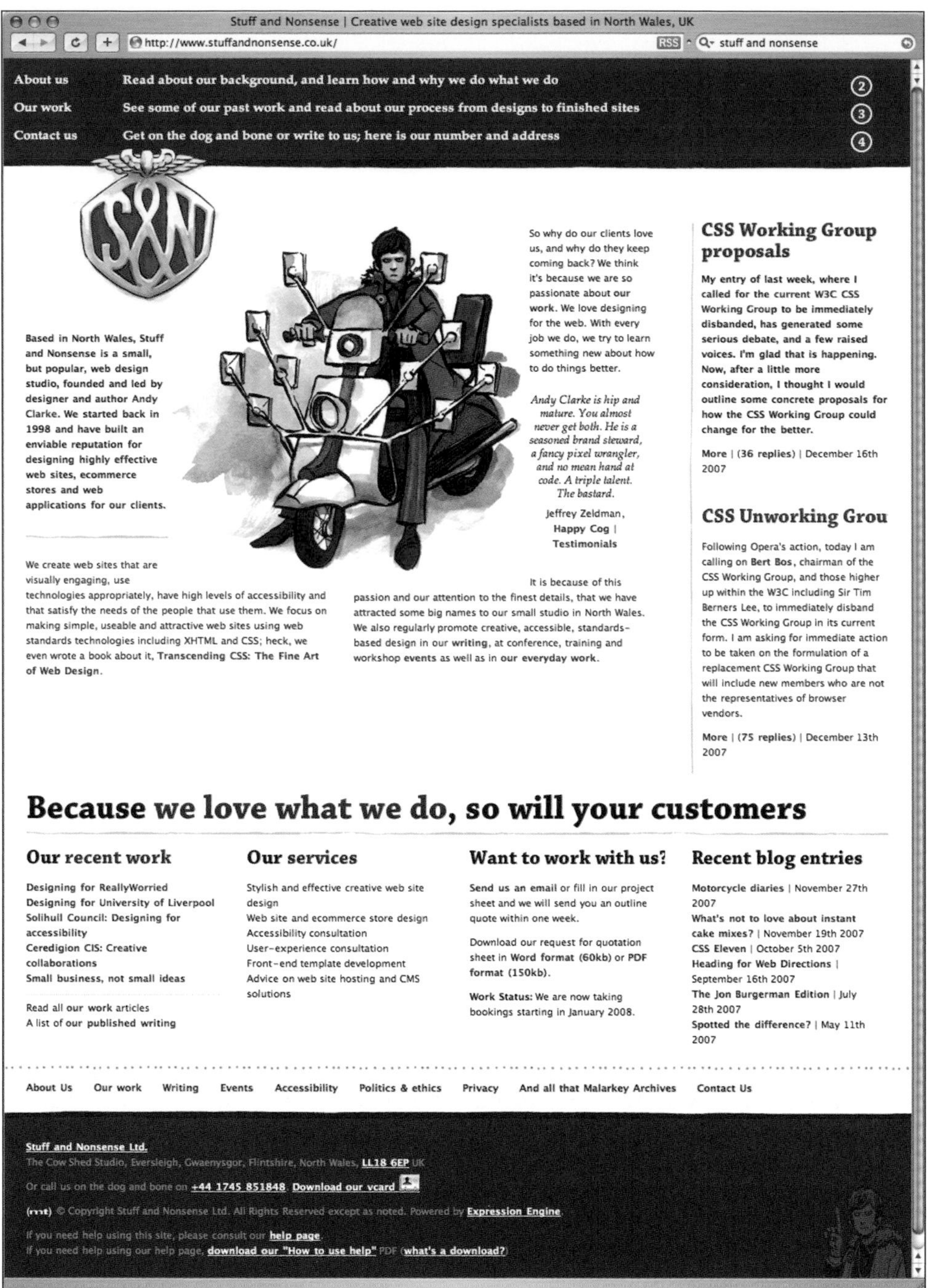


Figure 5-11: The home page of Stuff and Nonsense, a well-respected design boutique based in the UK.

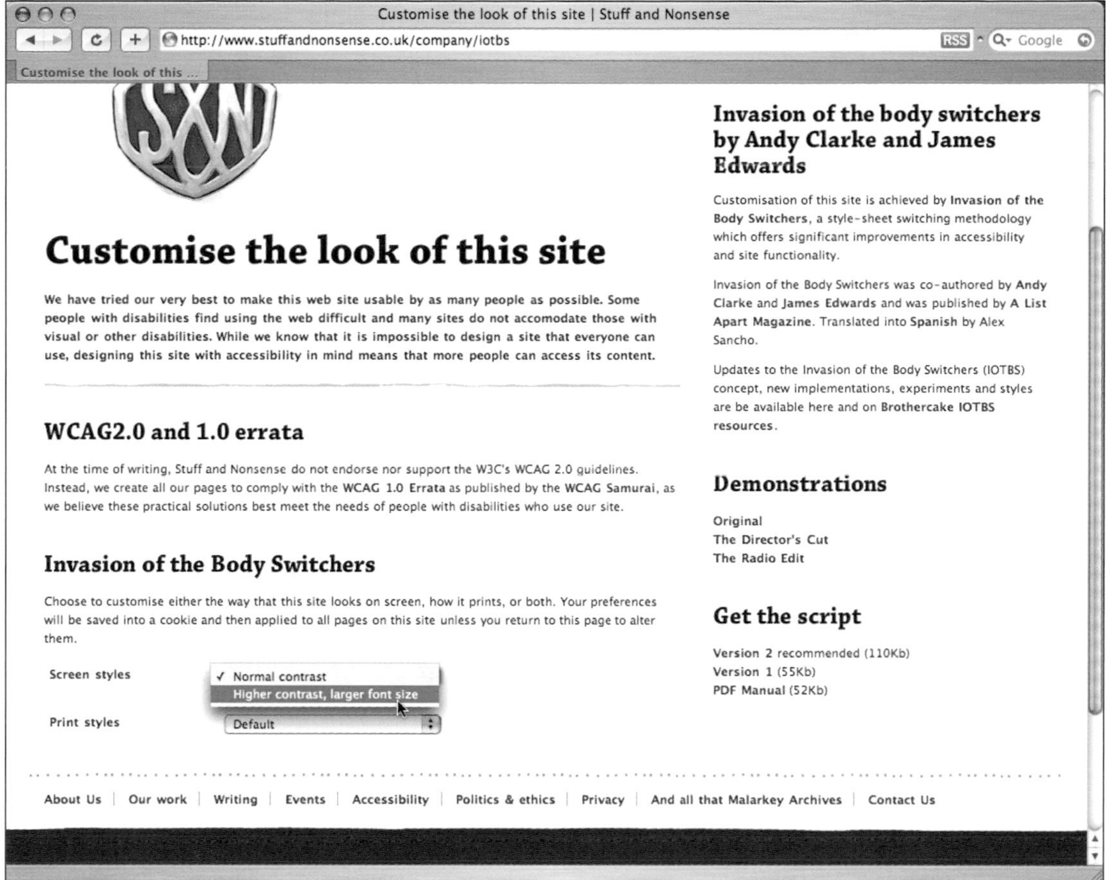


**Figure 5-12: The "Invasion of the Body Switchers"-style switcher allows users to select style options for screen, print, or any other media type through one simple interface.**

This is the oddly named yet feature-rich "Invasion of the Body Switchers" (IOTBS)–style switcher. Its name derived from how its switching functionality is powered by switching the `class` attribute on the `body` element. It's quite possibly the perfect style switcher, and the authors of IOTBS have made it freely available for download at `http://stuffandnonsense.co.uk/resources/iotbs.html`. Remarkably easy to install and configure, IOTBS affords maximum convenience to site owners and users alike. It even generates its entire interface via JavaScript, ensuring that users unable to take advantage of CSS switching won't be presented with nonfunctional markup.

With a tool like IOTBS in your arsenal, you can avail yourself of more of the true power of media-specific style sheets. Its easy-to-install interface will have your users thanking you. They can now sand the rough edges that don't meet their needs and tailor your site into something truly usable.

# Meet the Designer: Andy Clarke

With that brief introduction to IOTBS, meet one of the minds behind it: the creative director of Stuff and Nonsense, Andy Clarke. Andy is a rare breed of Web professional. A multitalented designer, developer, and writer, Andy has been the creative director of Stuff and Nonsense since founding it in 1998. As one-half of the team that brought the Web such an ingenious approach to style switching, Andy was gracious enough to answer a few brief questions about accessibility, high-caliber design, and how the two aren't mutually exclusive.

**Q:** *Andy, it's great to have you for this little chat. How is it, then, that you moved into Web design?*

**A:** Well, it's a long story, and I won't bore you with all of it. When I left college (having studied for a degree in Fine Art), I worked in various jobs, but was always involved in the arts and always with technology. I was one of the first people in the UK to work with professional digital cameras and before that, with electronic retouching, in the dark days before Photoshop! My background in art always let me keep a creative eye on the job, and when I got the chance to move to a creative advertising agency in London, I jumped at the chance.

This was a time when the Web was beginning to "get commercial," and I saw very early that the Web done well is just like advertising: communicating messages and getting an audience to identify with a client. Then, in 1998, I moved away from London, and before long, people began asking, "Can you do . . .?" Seven years later, I'm very lucky in that they haven't stopped asking.

**Q:** *The client list of your studio, Stuff and Nonsense, features an impressive array of brand names, including (but not limited to) the Disney Store UK and World Wildlife Federation UK. Even more impressive is the fact that all of your portfolio work is both crisply designed and built with XHTML/CSS. Why Web standards?*

**A:** Why not? I don't see either Web standards or (for that matter) accessibility as issues. I believe that they are simply part of doing the job "right." One of the things that I have learned in working with clients at Stuff and Nonsense is that they rarely care "how" a job is done. What matters to them is successfully connecting with their target audience.

You mentioned Disney Store UK and I think that it is fair to say that like most clients, they did not ask for a standards-compliant site. But they were looking for reductions in download times, an altogether faster shopping experience, and easier ways for them to update their site. Implementing the design with Web Standards technologies fit the bill and achieved their goals perfectly.

The Disney Store UK site was developed using the Karova Store platform (`www.karova.com`), which not only separates the presentation tier from the rest of site but also has an XML architecture rather than a database backend. XML is transformed into XHTML through XSLT, the end result being a site that is extremely flexible and will allow Disney Store UK new opportunities to deliver their content in the future, including through RSS feeds. At the end of the day, what matters to most clients is not the "tools," but the solutions offered to them. Web standards offers more solutions and that is why Stuff and Nonsense develops only with standards.

**Q:** *So, tell us a bit about this clever little thing you cooked up. Something about a style sheet switcher, we understand?*

**A:** You're referring to "Invasion of the Body Switchers" (IOTBS), the style sheet switcher that I wrote about on A List Apart magazine (`www.alistapart.com/articles/bodyswitchers`)? Well, I can't take credit for the really clever stuff. The technical genius behind IOTBS was my good friend James Edwards (`www.brothercake.com`), who took my concept and made it work.

One of the important aspects of Web standards is the ability for designers to work on presentations through CSS without changing the underlying markup (HTML or XHTML) of a Web page. Nowhere is this demonstrated better than on Dave Shea's CSS Zen Garden (`www.csszengarden.com`), where we see different designs of the same page made possible through using CSS style sheets.

"Switching" style sheets can be necessary for all sorts of reasons. Perhaps a client would like to offer visitors the ability to switch between a fixed-width or a "liquid" layout that fills the window — designer and author Dan Cederholm offers just such a choice on his site, SimpleBits (`www.simplebits.com`). Alternatively, you may wish to offer visitors with low vision an "accessible" design. The possibilities are endless and sometimes the aims and results are serious, sometimes just geeky gimmicks.

Server-side and JavaScript style sheet switchers have been around for years. But what makes "Invasion of the Body Switchers" different is the ability to independently switch screen, printer, and other media styles. All with only one CSS and one JavaScript file. I'm very proud of IOTBS, and I hope that it will help convince more designers that working with standards can expand their creative options.

**Q:** *We see that it's used heavily on the site of Stuff and Nonsense (`www.malarkey.co.uk`). Have you used it on any professional projects? Is this something that's important to clients?*

**A:** What is becoming increasingly important to our clients is offering visitors choices. Style sheet switchers such "Invasion of the Body Switchers" can be used to offer separate design themes to different visitor groups. But by using CSS "display properties," we can also hide and reveal content.

This has been put to great effect in several recent projects that target young people. By using the possibilities opened up by CSS and IOTBS, we no longer have to code three or more versions of an XHTML document or even an entire Web site. This reduces development times, makes our business more efficient, and ultimately saves the client money. Everyone is happy.

**Q:** *Some designers might find it unsettling to allow users to, well, essentially revise their sites' design. What would you say to them? Why should we let our users have greater control over the design of our pages?*

**A:** As designers or developers of Web sites, we need to remember who we are working for. Of course, it is our client who puts our food on the table, but our work is ultimately judged by site visitors. The happier they are, the happier our clients will be and the better the chance that they will come back.

The Web is unlike any other media. In television the picture stays pretty much the same no matter what size screen you are viewing on. CRT, LCD, or Plasma, 17-inch portable or 52-inch widescreen, things stay pretty much the same. On the Web, we do not simply "sit back and watch." We have more control over how the content is delivered and Web designers must remember that visitors' opinions matter more than their own.

**Q:** *After poking around a bit, it seems that there have been a number of style switchers published online. Some of them rely on client-side JavaScript (as yours does), whereas others rely on some back-end coding. Is there a clear benefit to either approach?*

**A:** Now you're getting all technical on me! I'm only a humble designer! Many different solutions are available to implement style sheet switching; some of them are "server side" (relying on backend languages such as PHP) and others like "Invasion of the Body Switchers" are "client side," using languages such as JavaScript. Which solution a developer chooses depends on the environment in which the site is running and the specific needs of the client.

It's only a personal preference, but as style sheet switching is a "client function," I prefer to use client-side solutions. That said, I can give you the exclusive news that there will be a server-side version of "Invasion of the Body Switchers" coming very soon.

So, I suppose that begs the question: What is it that makes your client-side switcher stand apart from the crowd?

"Invasion of the Body Switchers" takes a new approach to style sheet switching. Our approach does require abandoning conventional "style sheet" and "alternate style sheet" semantics, but this doesn't trouble me, because:

1. Many browsers do not implement native style sheet switching.
2. Those that do not apply any persistence to a selected alternate style sheet.

Other solutions rely on multiple style sheets, using `<link />` elements and "style sheet/alternate style sheet" semantics. This adds extra server calls, but more important, it does not allow for different media styles to be selected independently of each other.

"Invasion of the Body Switchers" lets us target different media types independently and gives site visitors a simple interface from which select their preferences, all saved into a cookie until they change their mind.

IOTBS works by adding one or more unique class names to the page's `<body>` tag. Styles are then defined using descendant selectors. The end result gives users much greater control over the output of your Web pages.

**Q:** *Interesting, so what are these "media types" you speak of? Why should the CSS-savvy Web designer care about them?*

**A:** It's sometimes hard for designers who come to the Web from other media to understand that that not only is their work not viewed "pixel perfect" by everyone but that people access Web content through different media. Sometimes that media is our good friend the computer monitor; sometimes it is an Internet kiosk at the airport; sometimes a handheld computer, a projected image, or even a mobile phone. Some people find it more difficult to read from a screen and like to print out pages.

In the past, preparing for all these different media types would have been cost-prohibitive, if not impossible, as it required making different versions for different viewing devices. But, with the advent of technologies that support common standards, we can create content that can be written once only, and then styled for different media output, all through the magic of CSS.

**Q:** *Stepping back a bit, we'd be interested to hear a bit more about your design process. How do you usually work?*

**A:** Our first job is to understand what the client is trying to communicate to his or her audience. We also get a feel for the "personality" of the company and look at their brand values (even if they haven't done so themselves) so that we can match the tone of the design to the personality and brand values. Effective design for the Web is about effective communication between a client and their audience. That is why we focus on what and how to communicate, before we think about technical or creative issues.

We start by developing paper prototype designs, from sketches to layouts made in either Photoshop or Macromedia Fireworks. These layouts begin as simple wireframes and from them we build markup guides, often on paper, which our developers use as their XHTML structure.

Some time ago, I developed a set of naming conventions for our site development, specific names for `<div>`s and classes that relate to content rather than presentation (`#branding` rather than `#header`, and so on). We stick tightly to these conventions so that the entire team understands what a particular CSS rule relates to. We also have conventions for the naming of images and this also speeds development.

Our graphic layouts then develop into production art for our design team and it is rare that our final Web pages do not match the graphic layout exactly. We also get approval from the client at each stage and always work within our internal convention framework to ensure that development is as efficient as possible.

**Q:** *And what about inspiration? When you're staring down a tight client deadline, from where do you get your ideas?*

**A:** I'm a real pop culture junkie. I love trashy pulp detective novels such as Mickey Spillane's Mike Hammer. I love comics even more and works by comic artists such as "Sin City's" Frank Miller and "Concrete" creator Paul Chadwick are a few of my passions.

You might find it unusual to hear that I am also passionate about political art from Soviet-era Russia, China, and Cuba. I find the cult of personality fascinating and across recent history there have been many terrific examples where political art in the form of posters or statues becomes almost "high" art. The most recent examples I have seen have come from pre-invasion Iraq.

I suppose that if I think about it, what these examples have in common is that they are both designed to engage an audience, drawing them into a different world. Again, it's about communicating messages . . . and so we get back on to the subject of the Web.

**Q:** *Are there any CSS issues that you face more regularly than others? How do you work through them?*

**A:** CSS issues are becoming rarer for me and when one does raise its ugly head, there is usually a solution to be found by doing a quick bit of Googling. Many people with far bigger brains than mine — Brothercake, Dave Shea (`http://mezzoblue.com`), Doug Bowman (`http://stopdesign.com/`), and John Gallant immediately spring to mind — have found solutions to browser bugs and behaviors I would never have dreamt existed. Of course, there are times when I curse one browser or another and yell, "This would be soooo much easier with tables!" But those outbursts are getting rarer.

There are now ways to fix or work around almost every CSS issue, and when one does appear unexpectedly, it is important to take a logical approach, as sometimes one element in combination with another will trigger a problem.

Validation is extremely important and ensuring that my code validates is always my first move before I even open a CSS file. If my code and CSS both validate and the problem still appears, I deconstruct the page, removing elements in turn so that I can see which element is straining my sanity.

Many browser bugs are now so well known that entire sites such as John Gallant's Position Is Everything (`www.positioniseverything.net`) are dedicated to them. If an answer can't be found on PIE or on many other sites, I recommend asking a question of the many experts who contribute to Eric Meyer's (`www.meyerweb.com`) excellent CSS-D mailing list (`http://css-discuss.org`). Ask nicely and you're likely to find a helpful soul with a solution.

**Q:** *What exactly do you look for in a "successful" site design? Are there any design principles you hold especially dear?*

**A:** I suppose that I'm not the best person to judge whether or not a design is successful, but I do listen to feedback from clients and their customers. What matters to me is that the project has made good business for the client who pays my wages. That way, I hope that they will keep coming back.

When I look back on many of the designs I have made, it is always the clearer, simpler ones that I like the most. I take the approach that no amount of design "fairy dust" can transform a poor content site into a successful site. So, I work with clients on ensuring that content always come first.

Working from content outward is always better than trying to "shoehorn" content into a preconceived design or layout, and that is why I often spend more time on planning and wireframing a site before I contemplate the design look-and-feel.

**Q:** *Any last words you'd care to share with us?*

**A:** "When I didn't know what color to put down, I put down black. Black is a force: I depend on black to simplify the construction." Actually not my words, but those of artist Henri Matisse.

# Summary

Well, that was something of a whirlwind, wasn't it? With a heightened understanding of media-specific CSS and three different style-switching strategies, you've covered no small amount of ground. Yet, as with much of this book, this chapter is but a road map to some incredibly rich landscapes. As a result, it's going to feel like quite a gloss. We could fill an entire chapter on each of these topics, and recommend further research on any of these CSS switching strategies. What you'll gain is that your Web sites will be available to a much wider audience.

In the next chapter, you apply the techniques and strategies discussed throughout the book to a real-world site design. Exciting, yes?

# 6

# Adventures of CindyLi.com: Blog Modifications

*Art is not a handicraft, it is the transmission of feeling the artist has experienced.*

*— Leo Tolstoy*

CSS is a powerful tool, and in this chapter you will see how the CindyLi.com Web site was conceptualized and implemented as well as how it was created (and manipulated) with CSS. In this chapter you learn how to use CSS markup to design/redesign your site and/or blog. To view the site, open your browser to `www.cindyli.com`, as shown in **Figure 6-1**.

## Blogs

A blog (short for Web log) is a kind of online journal in which entries are commonly displayed in reverse chronological order. A blog can be an entire Web site, or it can be a component or element that you add to your Web site.

The term blog is also used as a verb. "After the news last night, I blogged about how I felt about it," for example. A blog is considered personal, and some are even online diaries. Most blogs contain many media elements such as text, graphics or images, and hyperlinks, as well as audio and video clips. Podcasts are also found in many blogs.

The only rule to blogging (if there were rules) is that all content should be related to the blog's topic. Many blog hosts provide their readers with the capability to leave comments on their pages so that the blog's topic can be discussed by others.

In this chapter's example (CindyLi.com), you learn how a simple blog can be designed and then enhanced by CSS. To set up your own blog (or learn more about them), please visit the following links:

- **Technorati** — `http://technorati.com`
- **Blogger** — `http://blogger.com`
- **WordPress** — `http://wordpress.org`

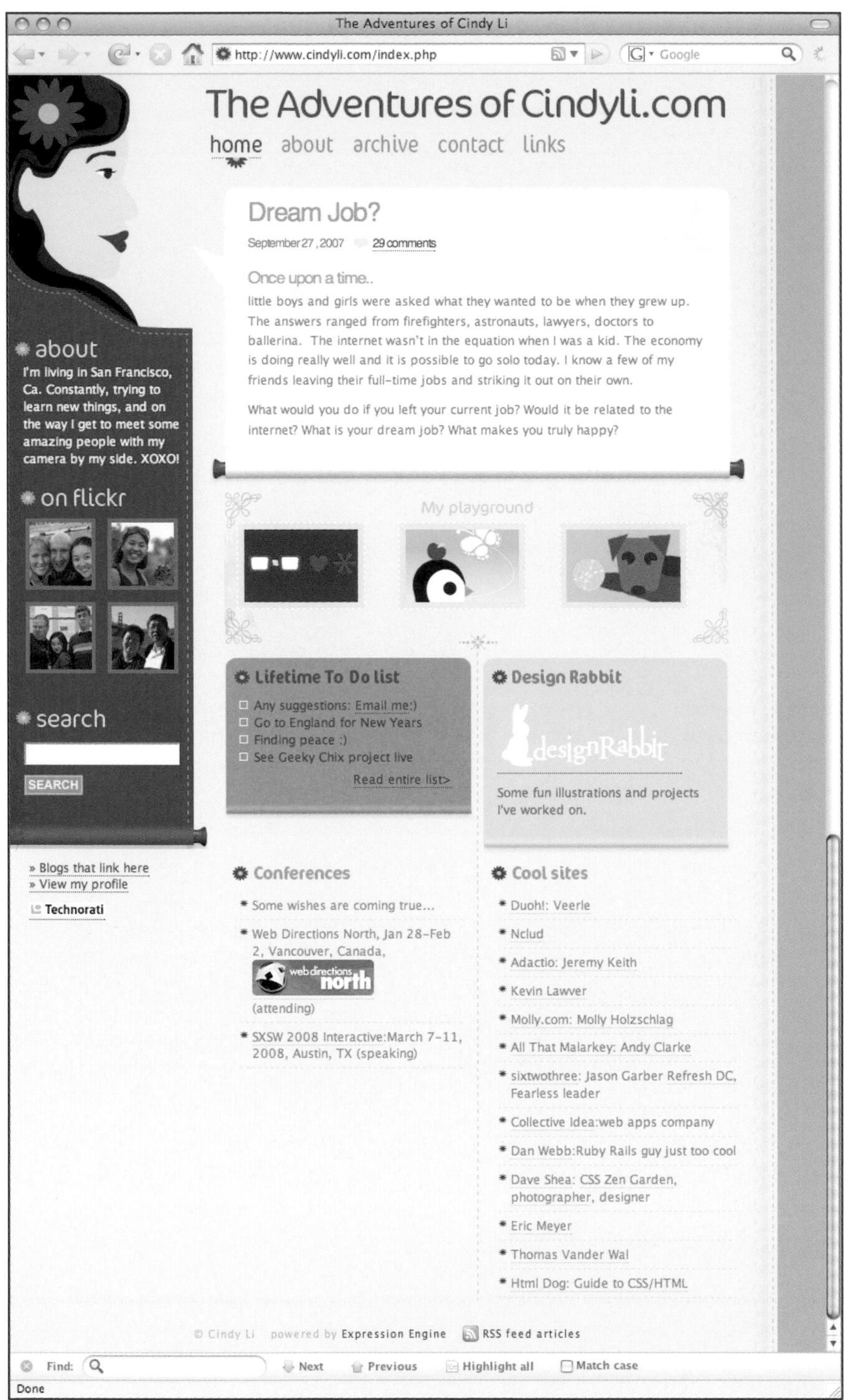


**Figure 6-1: The finished Web site of CindyLi.com.**

# CSS: Cindy Li Starts to Blog

Let's start with a brief history of CindyLi.com so you will be able to see how the design evolved.

CindyLi.com was a simple text blog that developed into an extremely visual and functional design incorporating the owner's (Cindy Li) personal data and a lifetime to-do list for bloggers to comment on. Through the use of CSS (and with the capability to design and make graphics), the site took on new life in a stunning visual concept.

CindyLi.com is unique in that it's easy to use, fun, and uses the blog feature in a really artistic way. It also captures everything that is important to its host, making it highly functional as well as interactive. The blog's owner, artist Cindy Li, was inspired while attending the 2006 South by Southwest (SXSW) Interactive Festival. Cindy blogged every SXSW session and uploaded it to her WordPress-powered blog every night. She was immediately motivated by the amount of traffic that suddenly came to her site and enjoyed interactively sharing her thoughts and opinions. Because of this, she was motivated to make her blog bigger and much better — and even to use it to promote her other art offerings. Being an artist, it was important that the blog not only capture the essence of her ideas but represent her artistically in a unique way and be functional as well.

Enter CSS. The plan was to combine a lifetime to-do list, a blog roll, a list of upcoming conferences, and photos into a very high-end look-and-feel while maintaining the "fun" aspect.

As you will see in this chapter, CindyLi.com started as nothing more than a design template that you can download yourself and install and set up within minutes. Figure 6-2 shows a blog design template manipulated into Cindy's first effort.

# Design Elements

The most important element of a Web site — or at least what needs to be done first — is the site's layout and design. No Web site should be put up without a solid plan. A good plan saves you time and provides goals for what you expect to achieve. To create CindyLi.com, the first step was to create a layout. A layout can be as simple as just setting up the site itself as a text-based blog and growing it from there. There's no harm in starting small and then adding to the site. The only design step that you should take is to make sure that you start with a blogging tool that enables you to grow as you learn.

## *Creating a Layout*

A solid design (and layout for the design) is usually developed using tools such as Adobe's Photoshop and Illustrator. Although these topics are not covered in this book, most CSS users (especially the more experienced) are extremely familiar with them. These are some sites that can be used to learn how to do layouts as well as other design work with Photoshop and Illustrator:

- `http://tutorialoutpost.com`
- `http://photoshopzilla.com`
- `http://photoshopcamp.com`

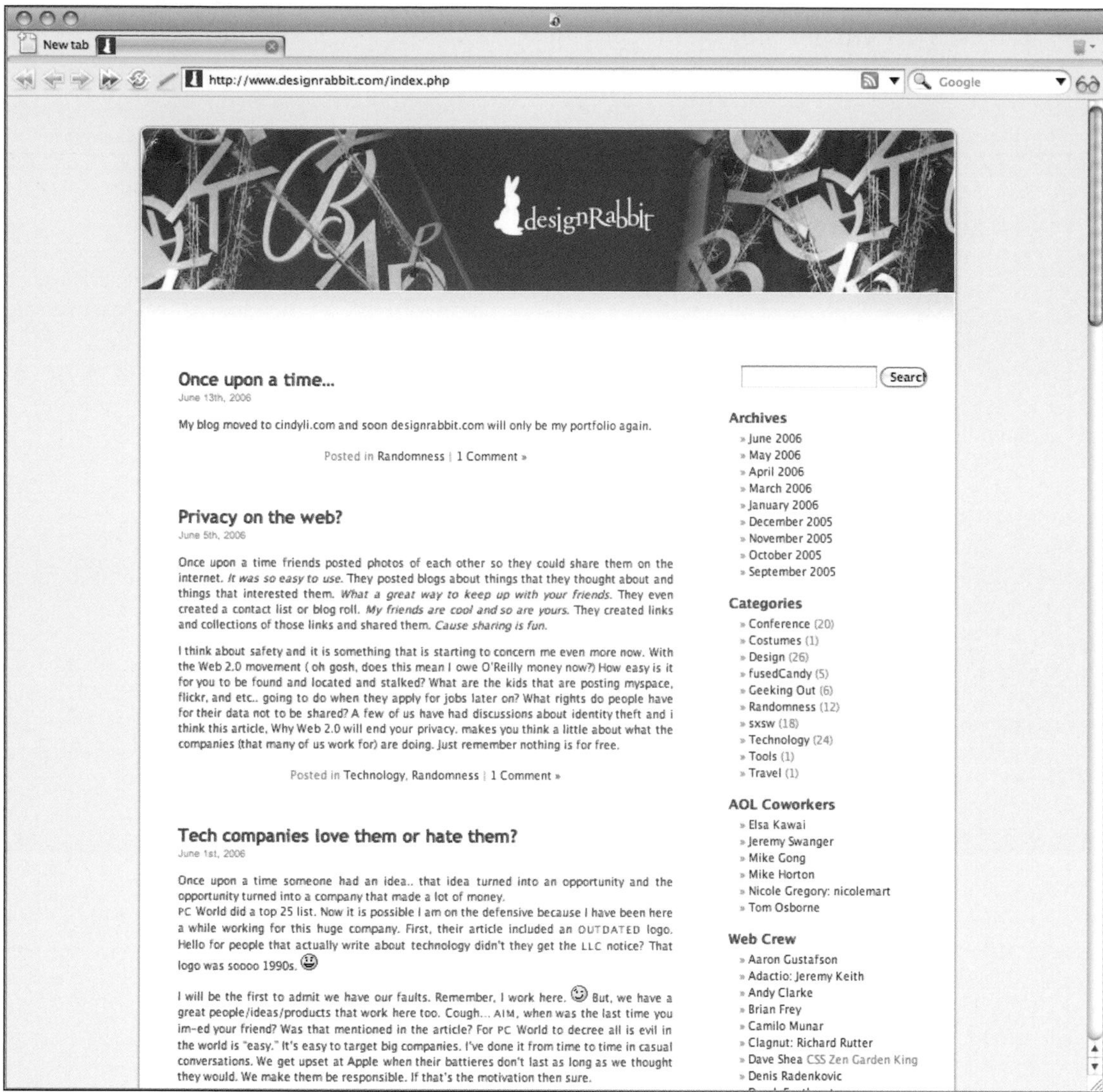


**Figure 6-2: A WordPress blog design template with an added header graphic.**

Laying out a site graphically gives you a good idea visually of what the end result will be. This is a great way to make changes before coding (meaning that you wouldn't have to make changes to the code later when you find that you don't like the design).

## Laying Out the Design

With every project, even a blog, the designer needs to create a list of elements that the site should have. This content inventory list must include what you want both visually and functionally. CindyLi.com was to reflect the owner's Taiwanese-American heritage, for example, so colors and elements needed to be considered for the overall layout.

**Always set requirements for a design or redesign early in the project. Designing becomes easier when parameters such as color and logos are determined up front.**

As Cindy Li did (see Figure 6-3), settle on a specific color palette, and then use it to determine and create the base colors for your site. Logos or any other marketing elements should also be considered as key elements for a Web site.

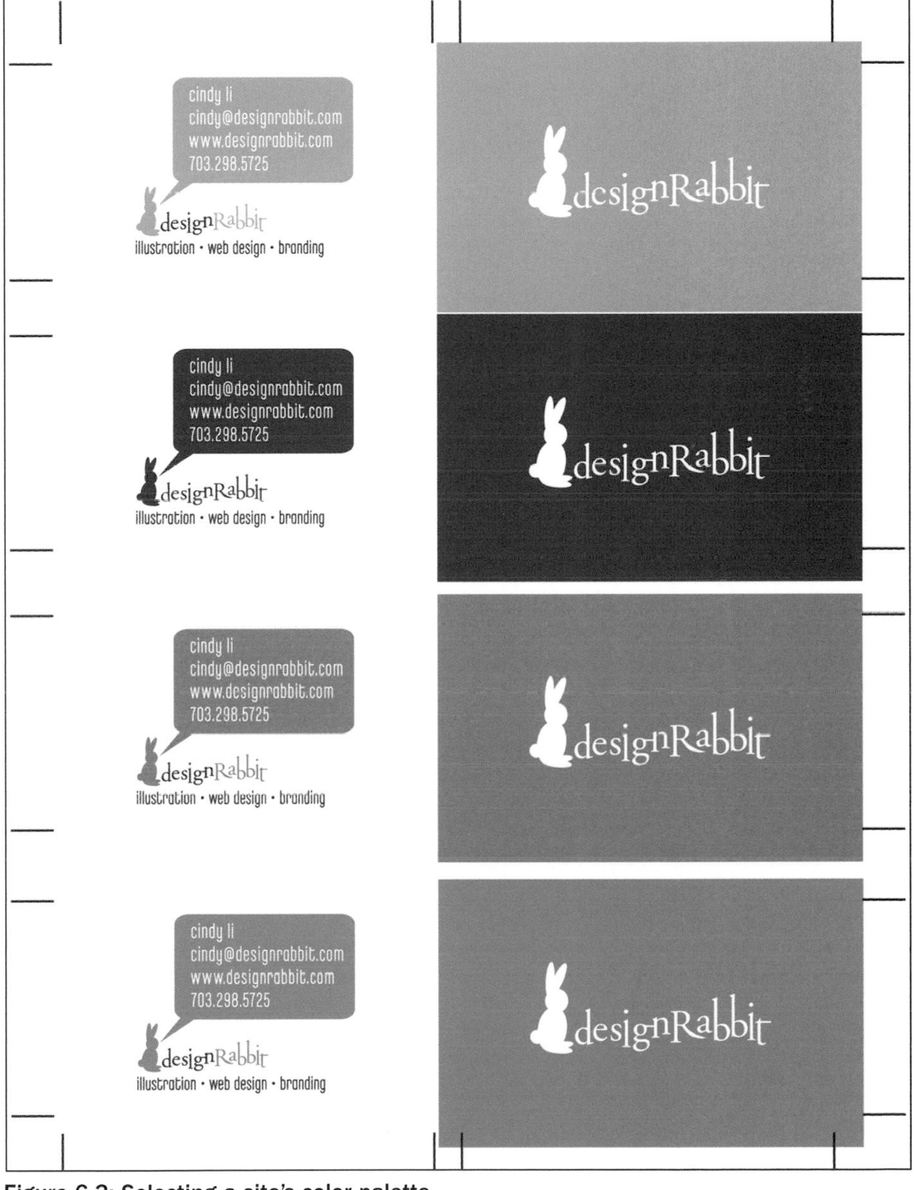


**Figure 6-3: Selecting a site's color palette.**

# Creating the Site

Once your basic plan is set, your first step is to create the graphics so that you know their sizes and how much space they will take up.

Use a vector-imaging tool such as Adobe Illustrator to create your graphics. The software enables you to adjust the size of elements or reuse them without a loss of quality. There are other software products you can find online and use as well. Here are a couple of links you can use to learn how to do layouts (as well as other design work) with Photoshop and Illustrator:

- `http://grafx-design.com/phototut.html`
- `http://gimp.org`

When the illustration is ready, you can import it into Adobe Photoshop or a similar tool to create a layout of your Web site for final proofing and editing. Complete your layout, decide whether you like the design (if you don't, start over), and make a plan for creating it. The next step is to deploy it.

## Designing the Navigation Bar

There are three main points to consider when designing navigation for a site:

- **Functionality** — If a visitor cannot find the links to navigate your site, then you did not design it correctly.
- **Logic** — It is important that your site's navigation make sense. Contact, for instance, is a great term used to welcome those who want to email or call you on a phone. Using terms that make no sense or are hard to determine ruins the natural flow of your site and makes it difficult to access and find information.
- **Navigation features such as buttons and bars** — These features enable your users to find their way through your site quickly and easily. They remain consistent and usable on every page and are especially useful in lengthy pages.

Figure 6-4 shows the navigation bar designed for CindyLi.com, including both states — regular and rollover.

**Figure 6-4: A navigation bar.**

### Sizing

To create a navigation bar in Adobe Photoshop, open Photoshop, type the navigation text, and give each state 20 pixels of space. The height is based on the larger state — in this case the rollover state (the pink text with the daisy and dashes) with extra vertical space.

The width of the navigation image is dependent on the characters in the navigation bar, so set the final image size by selecting Image ➪ Image Size, as shown in Figure 6-5. The size for CindyLi.com is 350 pixels by 74 pixels. If you have larger words for your own navigation, the image's width will be wider.

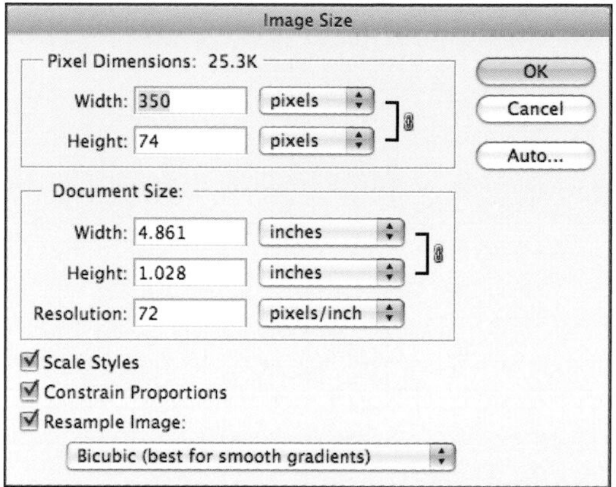


**Figure 6-5: Image Size window in Adobe Photoshop.**

## *Coloring*

Fill the image window with the appropriate background color by selecting Edit ➪ Fill. You can pick the Color option in the Contents field area (double-click the swatch in the Photoshop toolbar). The Color Picker opens (see Figure 6-6). For CindyLi.com, the light blue color with the hexadecimal value of #d6ebf7 and RGB values R:214, G:235, B: 247 was chosen.

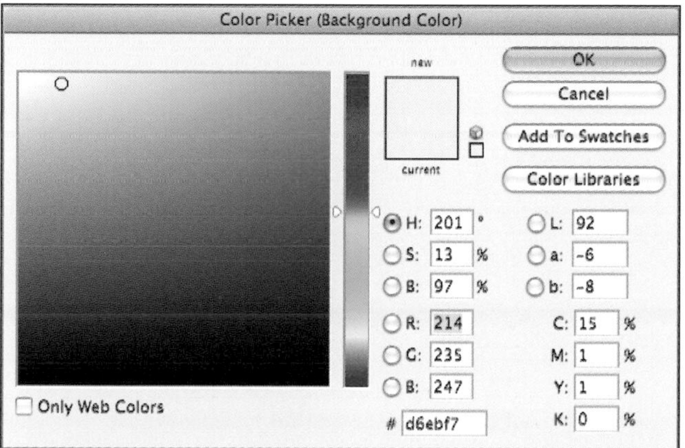


**Figure 6-6: Adobe Photoshop color picker for background color.**

With the color selected, click OK, and the image is filled with the color, as shown in Figure 6-7.

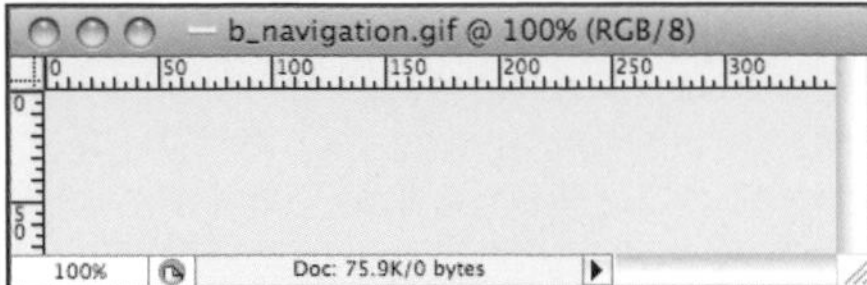


Figure 6-7: Adobe Photoshop fill example with background color.

The next stage is to pick the color for the navigation text. Double-click the swatch in the Photoshop toolbar to open the Color Picker. For CindyLi.com, a darker shade of blue (set to hexadecimal value of #497690 and an RGB value of R:73, G:118, B:144) was selected, as shown in Figure 6-8. The darker color provides contrast with the background and increases legibility of the words.

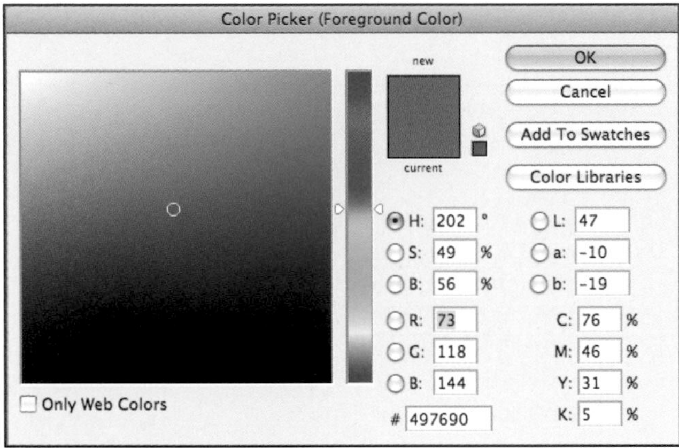


Figure 6-8: Adobe Photoshop Color Picker window for blue.

## Text

Set the font and point size for your text; CindyLi.com uses 24-point Cocon font. Type in the words for the navigation bar — in this example: home about archive contact links. The result is a string of words, as shown in Figure 6-9.

Figure 6-9: Navigation typed with the Cocon font in blue.

# Making the Rollover Graphics

With the main navigation labels in place, the creation of the rollover graphics is next. First, duplicate the text layer in Photoshop and position a new text layer 20 pixels below the original text labels.

Pick one of the colors from your original color scheme — a dark pink (see **Figure 6-10**) with the hexadecimal value of #ad0066 and RGB of R:173, G:0, B:102 is used in CindyLi.com.

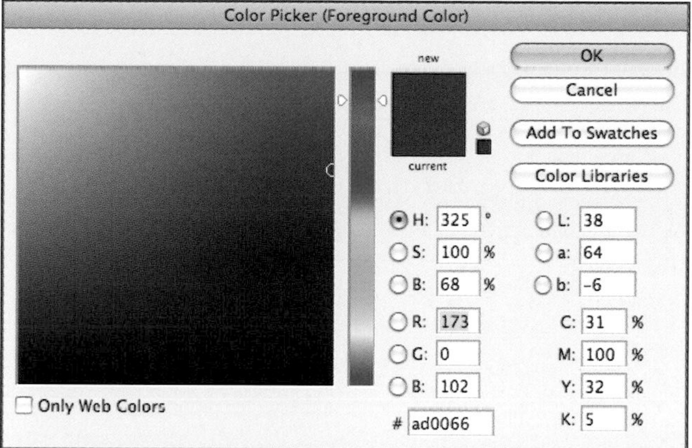


**Figure 6-10:** Adobe Photoshop Color Picker window for hot pink.

The new text is filled with the new color, as shown in **Figure 6-11**.

**Figure 6-11:** Navigation typed with the Cocon font in hot pink.

To accentuate the rollover and selected states for the navigation, incorporate more graphics such as flowers used in CindyLi.com. Using Illustrator, you can draw the graphic you want and then import it into Photoshop as an image for use on the site. That's how the navigation bar shown in the **Figure 6-12** was created.

**Figure 6-12:** The final navigation image.

## Setting Up the Navigation Markup and CSS

The graphics for the navigation are now in place. The following CSS markup controls how the navigation links work:

```
<ul id="nav">
 <li id="home"><a href="http://www.cindyli.com/index.php" title="This link takes
you back to the homepage">home</a></li>
```

```
 <li id="about"><a href="http://www.cindyli.com/index.php/site/about/" title="Find
out a bit more about this weblog and myself">about</a></li>
 <li id="archive"><a href="http://www.cindyli.com/index.php/site/archives/"
title="Browse the archive">archive</a></li>
 <li id="contact"><a href="http://www.cindyli.com/index.php/site/contact/"
title="Contact information">contact</a></li>
 <li id="links"><a href="http://www.cindyli.com/index.php/site/links/" title="List
of websites that are cool">links</a></li>
</ul>
```

With the navigation in place as an unordered list, you then move the text out of the way so that the images in the navigation bar can be seen. (Although the text will be moved, it is still visible to screen readers.)

Here's the CSS that sets the width and height of the navigation elements:

```
ul#nav {
 width:350px;
 height:36px;
 padding:0 0 0 5px;
 margin-bottom:19px;
}
```

The following code moves all the `li` elements as block-level elements so that the navigation elements are set in a horizontal line. It also indents the text in each list item to the far right by an extreme negative indent:

```
ul#nav li {
 padding:0;
 margin:0;
 display:block;
 float:left;
 text-indent:-9999px;
}
```

All of the buttons are going to have a height of 37 pixels; it's easy to set that in CSS. However, because of the varying length of each word in the navigation bar, the width for each button needs to be determined and set individually. The following table shows the width needed for each button. You could determine these measurements for yourself by using Photoshop's measurement tools.

| Button | Label | Width |
|---|---|---|
| 1 | home | 60 pixels |
| 2 | about | 70 pixels |
| 3 | archive | 85 pixels |
| 4 | contact | 80 pixels |
| 5 | links | 55 pixels |

With the measurements in hand, use the following code to place the whole navigation menu into the background of each anchor item:

```
ul#nav li a {
 border:0;
 display:block;
 text-decoration:none;
 background:transparent url(../images/b_navigation.gif) no-repeat;
}
```

To position the background image using width and height CSS properties for each navigation menu item, you must utilize the ID attributes on each list item within the navigation menu. The first navigation menu option, home, as shown in **Figure 6-13**, is set up in the following CSS:

```
li#home a {
 width:60px;
 height:37px;
}
```

The about menu option (see **Figure 6-14**) is set up in the following CSS:

```
li#about a {
 width:70px;
 height:37px;
}
```

Here's the CSS that sets up the archive navigation menu option, shown in **Figure 6-15**:

```
li#archive a {
 width:85px;
 height:37px;
}
```

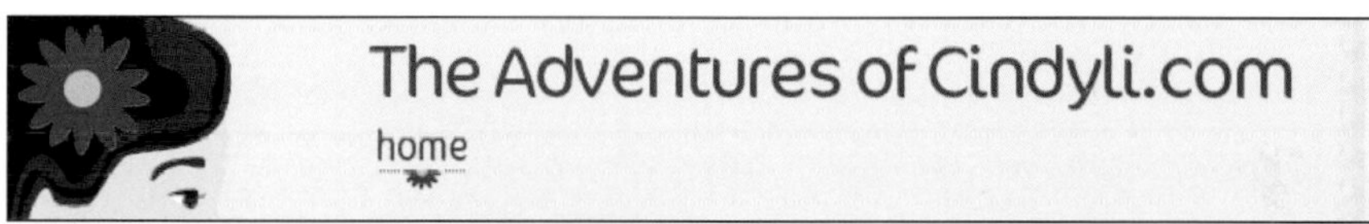


**Figure 6-13:** The home navigation added.

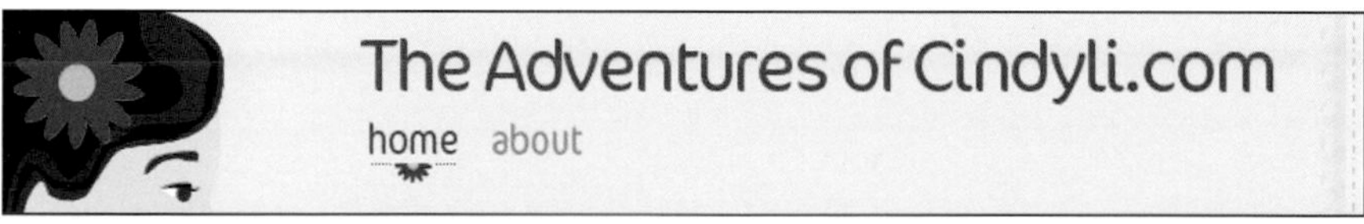


**Figure 6-14:** about navigation added.

**Figure 6-15:** archive navigation added.

The contact navigation menu option (see Figure 6-16) is set up in the following CSS:

```
li#contact a {
 width:80px;
 height:37px;
}
```

And here's the CSS that sets up the links navigation menu option, shown in Figure 6-17:

```
li#links a {
 width:55px;
 height:37px;
}
```

**Figure 6-16: contact navigation added.**

**Figure 6-17: links navigation added.**

## *Integrating the Rollovers*

With the base navigation menu set up, the next step is to create its rollover and active states. To pull this off, you need to calculate how to move the image in the size created in the previous section. The following table summarizes this information:

| Button | Label | Rollover (Hover) State Size | Note |
|---|---|---|---|
| 1 | home | 0px, -37px | It fits into the space that was created, which is 37px in height. |
| 2 | about | -60px, -37px | This button is moved -60px is because the first button has a width of 60px. |
| 3 | archive | -130, -37 | This button's width depends on the two earlier buttons' widths (60px + 70px = 130px). |
| 4 | contact | -215, -37 | This button's width depends on the three earlier buttons' widths (60px + 70px + 85px = 215px). |
| 5 | links | -295, 037 | This button's width depends on the four earlier buttons' widths (60x + 70px + 85px + 80px = 295px). |

With the measurements in hand, the code for creating the rollover effect looks like this:

```
/* Main navigation "hover" */

li#home a:hover, li#home a:focus {
 background-position:0px -37px;
}
li#about a:hover, li#about a:focus {
 background-position:-60px -37px;
}
li#archive a:hover, li#archive a:focus {
 background-position: -130px -37px;
}
li#contact a:hover, li#contact a:focus {
 background-position: -215px -37px;
}
li#links a:hover, li#links a:focus {
  background-position: -295px -37px;
}
```

To create the visited state you use the same values as in the previous example for the code, except that the second value, the background vertical placement, changes. You need to move the graphic vertically by setting the value from -37px to 0px. The code looks like this:

```
li#about a:link, li#about a:visited {
background-position:-60px 0px;
}
li#archive a:link, li#archive a:visited {
background-position: -130px 0px;
}
li#contact a:link, li#contact a:visited {
 background-position: -215px 0px;
}
li#links a:link, li#links a:visited {
 background-position: -295px 0px;
}
```

To automatically trigger the rollover or hover state on the page the visitor is viewing, you append the `body` element for each section appropriately. For example, the `body` element for the about page looks like this:

```
<body id="about-page">
```

The last bit of CSS code changes the navigation for each page using a descendant selector with two ID selectors. (This selector has a high specificity value that overrides the rollover or hover effect of the navigation, preventing the rollover effect from occurring on the page.)

```
/* Main navigation "active"
---------------------------------------------------*/
body#home-page ul#nav li#home a {
 background-position: 0px -37px;
}
body#about-page ul#nav li#about a {
background-position: -60px -37px;
}
```

```
body#archive-page ul#nav li#archive a {
 background-position: -130px  -37px;
}
body#contact-page ul#nav li#contact a {
 background-position: -215px -37px;
}
body#links-page ul#nav li#links a {
 background-position: -295px -37px;
}
```

# Setting the Speech Bubble

The main content portion of Cindy's new Web site posed an interesting problem. The speech bubble needed to be a vertical growing space.

To do this you create the header graphic, which includes the balloon tail often seen in word balloons, as shown in Figure 6-18.

**Figure 6-18: Speech bubble top graphic with a Chinese character "to create."**

The bottom of the text scroll also needs to be created for the bottom of the word balloon. Having reference photos always helps, especially when you are trying to get the light source correct. The photo shown in Figure 6-19 is a good example of the way the light and shadow should be drawn.

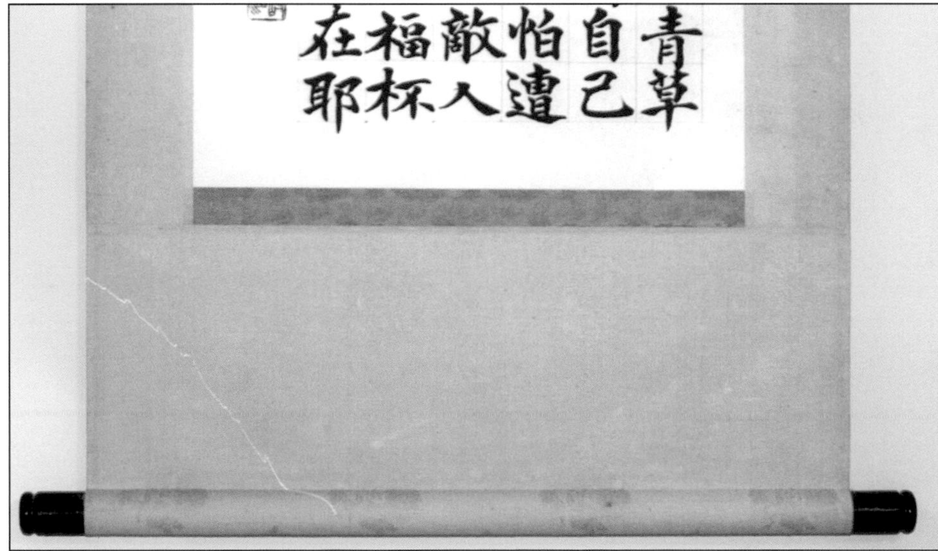


**Figure 6-19: Scroll used for a light source.**

In this example, the edge of the scroll needed to be adjusted. A different one was selected, as shown in Figure 6-20.

**Figure 6-20: Bottom scroll graphic.**

With the top and bottom graphic of the main content portion created, you add an image tile to place behind the content portion so that, as the amount of content expands with different posts, the word balloon/scroll image appears as one cohesive image.

The tile image size is 531px by 1px (see Figure 6-21). The 1-pixel height is all you need to repeat the background tile.

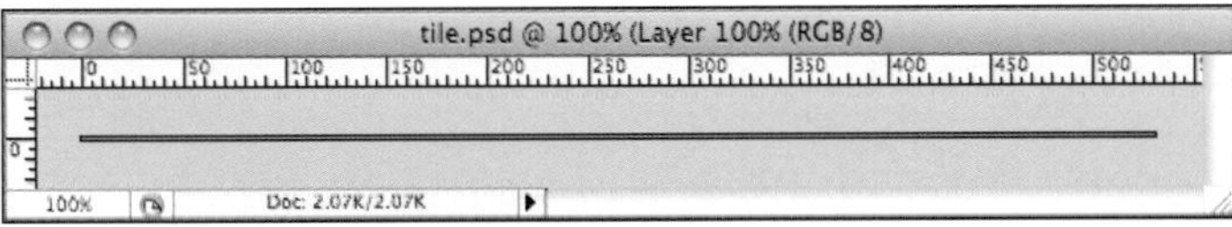


**Figure 6-21: Scroll tile in Adobe Photoshop.**

## Coding the Speech Bubble

Now you're ready to turn your attention to coding the speech bubble. The first task is to get the markup in place. The following HTML is set up using a series of nested of DIV elements:

```
<div class="bubble">
 <div class="inner-bubble">
   <div class="inner-bubble2">
    <div>
… Blog post here…
     </div>
   </div>
 </div>
</div><!--// bubble -->
```

These four DIV elements allow the images to become attached and create the speech bubble.

The first part of the bubble is the bottom portion as shown in Figure 6-22, which is set up in the CSS as follows:

```
/* bubble
-------------------------------------------------------*/
.bubble {
 background: url(../images/bg_bubble_bottom.gif) no-repeat bottom left;
}
```

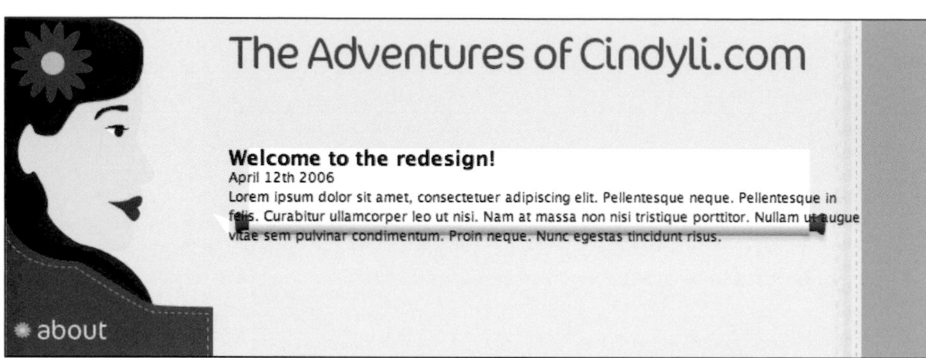


**Figure 6-22: Bottom `div` loaded.**

The code required to flesh out the bubble needs to be created in three parts. The first part creates the bottom `div`. The second part is the top (`.bubble .inner-bubble`). The third part is the middle (`.bubble .inner-bubble .inner-bubble2`), which is the tile that will be repeated as the content grows. These three sections of code are combined as follows:

```
.bubble .inner-bubble {
 width: 520px;
 padding:102px 0 38px 0;
 background: url(../images/bg_bubble_top.gif) no-repeat;
}
.bubble .inner-bubble .inner-bubble2 {
 padding:1px 20px 0 40px;
 background: url(../images/bg_bubble_tile.gif) repeat-y;
}
.bubble .inner-bubble .inner-bubble2 div {
margin-top:-90px;
}
.bubble .inner-bubble .inner-bubble2 div.flickr_badge_image {
 margin-top: 0px;
}
.bubble img {
padding:4px;
margin-right:29px;
border:1px dashed #fff;
```

```
background-color:#badbef;
float: left;
}
.bubble p.centered img {
float: none;
}
.bubble ul li {
color: #666;
background: url(../images/bullet_star-pink.gif) no-repeat 0px 3px;
padding:0 0 8px 12px;
margin-top:8px;
border-bottom:1px dashed #a8cfe4;
}
```

## Reapplying the Effect

The CindyLi.com Web site uses the scroll technique in a couple of other places: the Lifetime To Do list and the Design Rabbit graphics (see Figure 6-23).

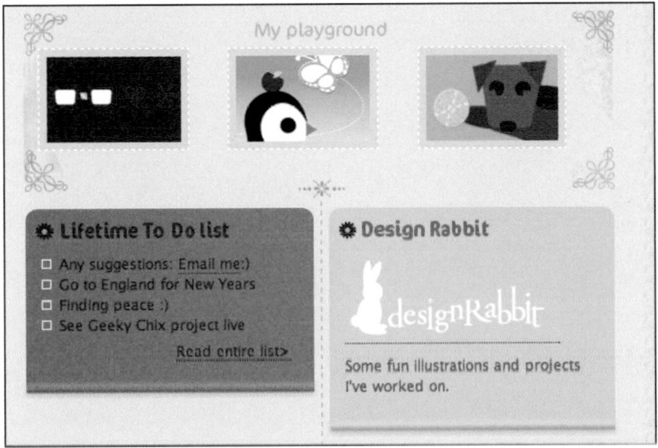


Figure 6-23: Additional applications of scroll technique.

## Putting on the Flickr Badge

Next to be added to the Cindyli.com blog Web site is a Flickr badge, which allows a set number of photos from your Flickr account to be posted to any Web page.

To get started, go to the Flickr badge maker page, `http://flickr.com/badge.gne`, as shown in Figure 6-24. (You will need a Flickr account, but getting one is fast and free.)

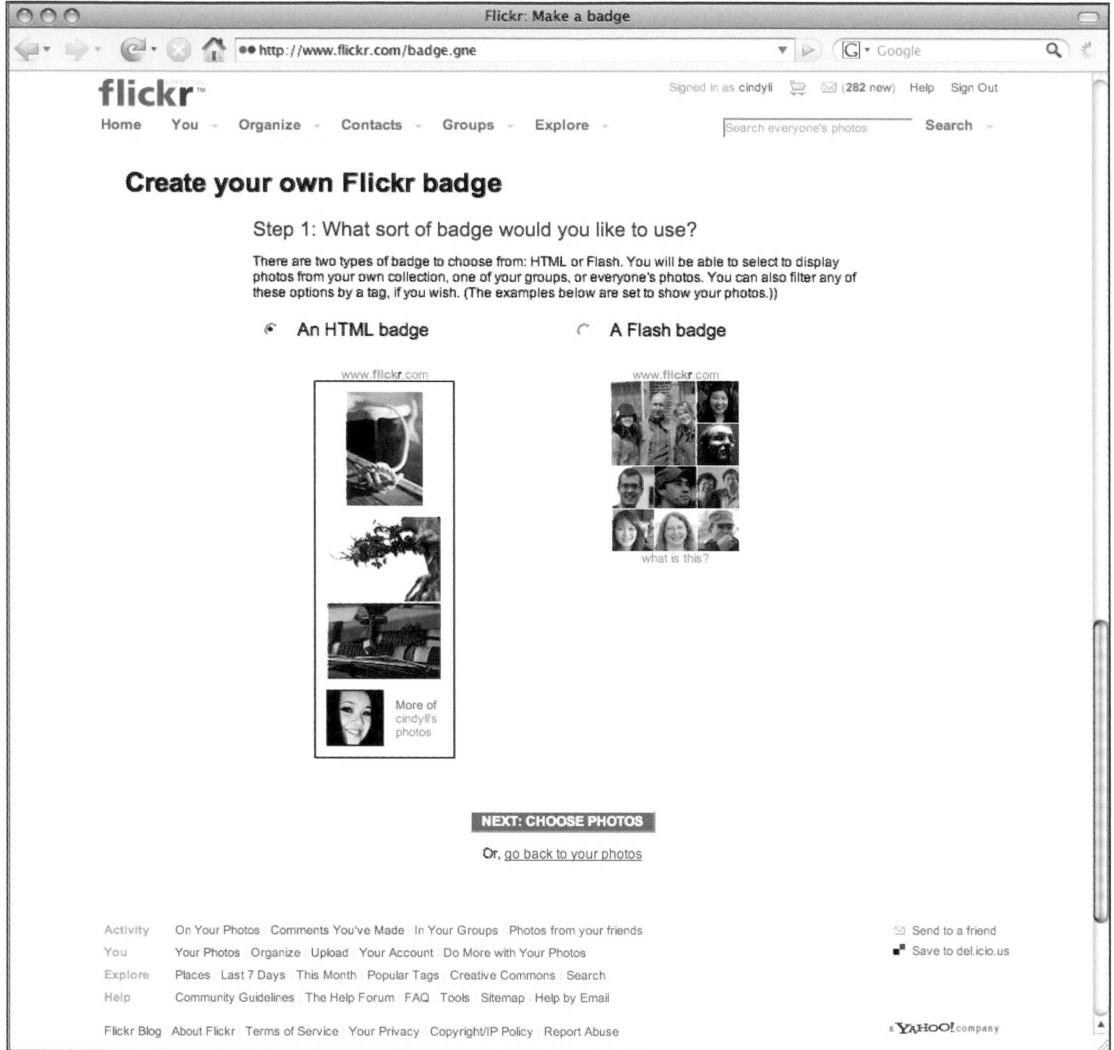


**Figure 6-24:** Flickr's create-your-own-badge Web page.

The Flickr badge settings allow 1, 3, 5, or 10 photos to be shown at one time. For the CindyLi.com, it was decided that four would be used, so the three-photo example as shown in Figure 6-25 was selected, and a modification was required.

The code in the box on the Flickr page works if you want to use the Flickr badge example that's displayed:

```
<script type="text/javascript"
src="http://www.flickr.com/badge_code_v2.gne?count=3&display=latest&size=s&layout=x
&source=user&user=43082001%40N00">
</script>
```

However, as noted, Cindy needed to tweak the variables in the string to suit her needs.

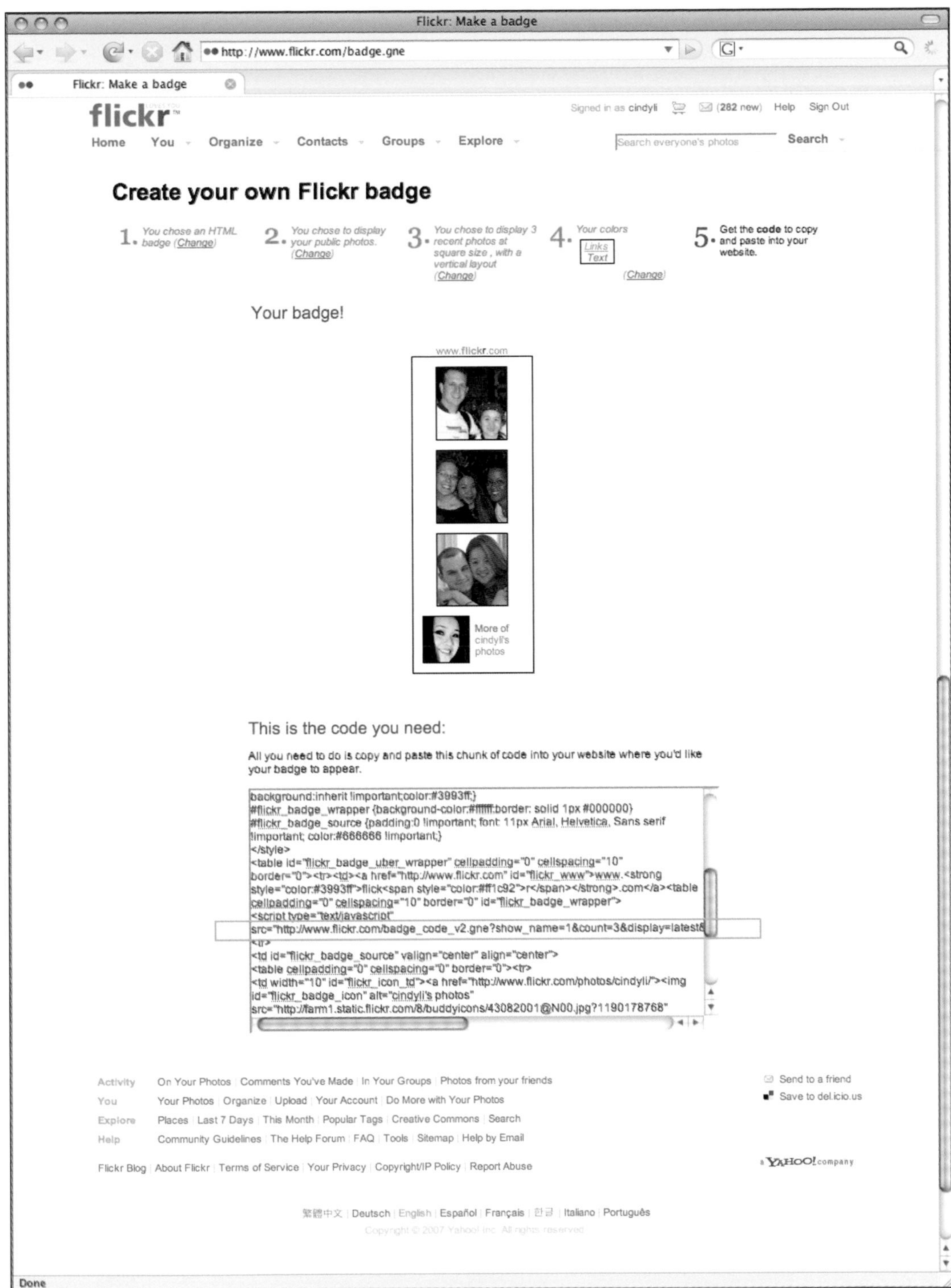

Figure 6-25: Grabbing the code from Flickr's Web site

To modify your variables, copy and paste that code directly into your template or Web document. Then copy the user number, which in Cindy's case was `"43082001%40N00."` (Note that the ampersands need to be changed into `"&"` for it to be valid XHTML code.) Adjust the `"count=3"` to `"count=4"` to display four pictures on your site:

```
<script type="text/javascript"
src="http://www.flickr.com/badge_code_v2.gne?count=4&amp;display=latest&amp;size=s&
amp;layout=x&amp;source=user&amp;user=43082001%40N0">
</script>
```

Then you wrap a `div` for the Flickr badge in the CSS file (Figure 6-26 shows the result of this new code):

```
<div id="flickr">
 <h2>Flickr Badge</h2>
 <script type="text/javascript"
src="http://www.flickr.com/badge_code_v2.gne?count=4&amp;...">
 </script>
</div>
```

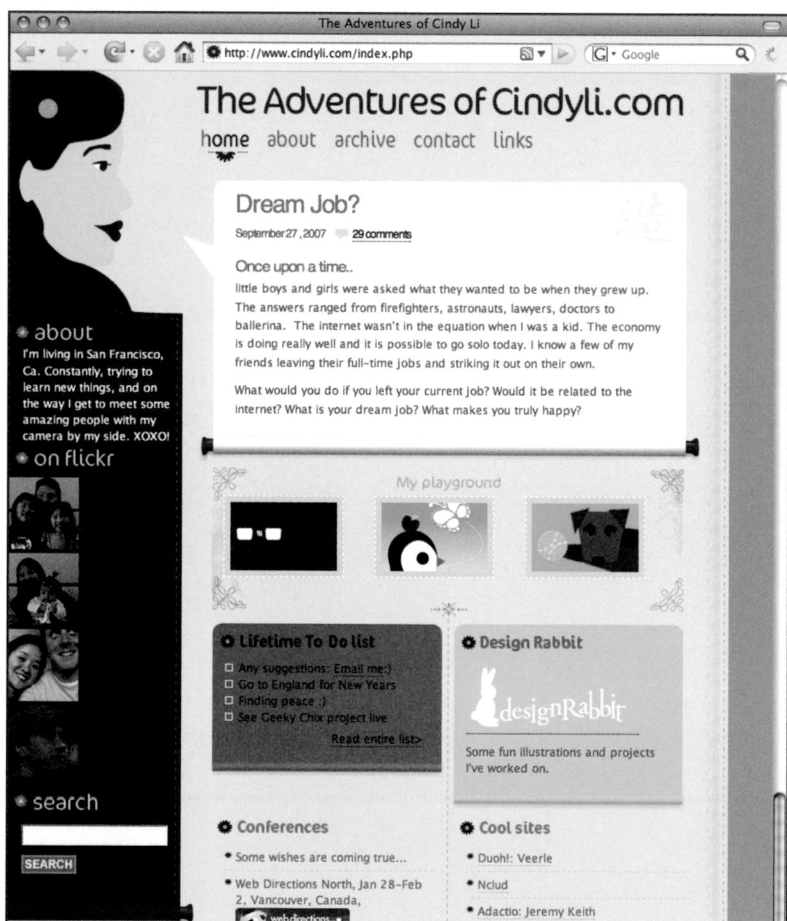


**Figure 6-26: Unstyled Flickr photos within the blog design.**

To sit the images within the pink scroll area on the left, a `div` area of 200px × 200px is needed. Padding is set to 5 pixels and the margin to 10 pixels. Margins are created so the Flickr images are in two rows with two photos in each row. Figure 6-27 shows the finished photo section.

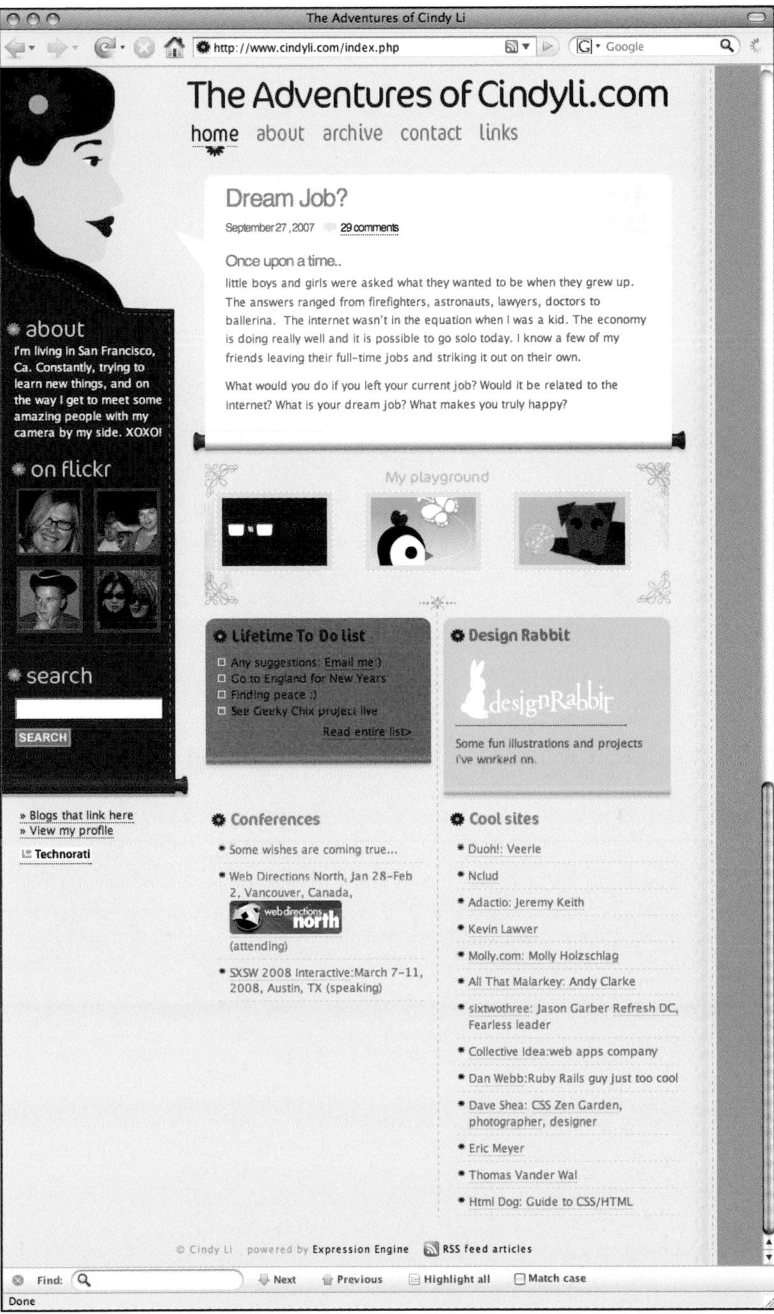


**Figure 6-27: Styled Flickr photo.**

The old saying goes your team is as strong as the weakest link. If you view your Web site as a chain, adding a third-party Web site means that you have another chain. Dealing with your site's uptime is important, but if the third-party's site is down, there's not much you can do. In the case of the photos on Cindy's page, if Flickr badge service is down, there will be empty squares on Cindy's site, as shown in Figure 6-28.

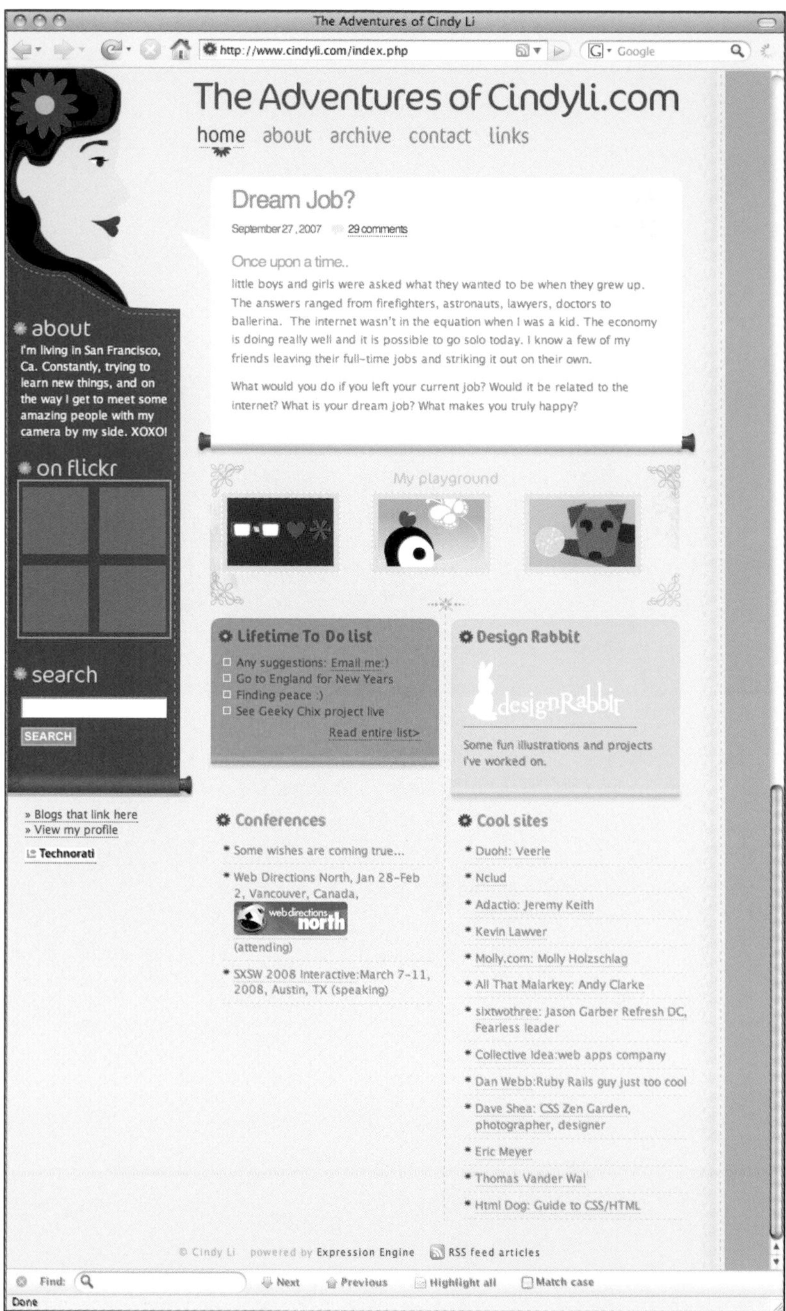


**Figure 6-28: Example of what the blog looks like when Flickr is down.**

## Check Box Styling

CindyLi.com's Lifetime To Do List is basically an unordered list with check boxes (see Figure 6-29).

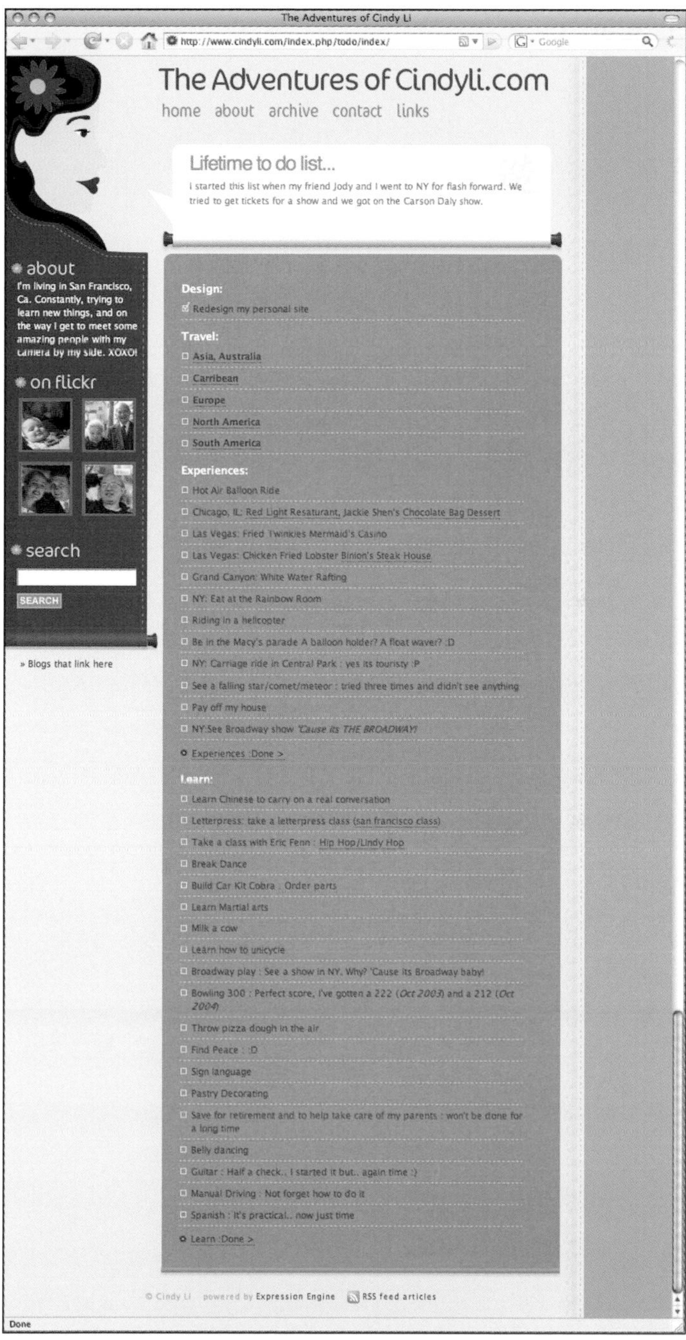


**Figure 6-29: Lifetime To Do list page example.**

To make it work, two check boxes must be created — one with a check in it and one without. Figure 6-30 shows a check box with a checkmark in Photoshop.

Cindy created her check boxes in Photoshop with the settings shown in Figure 6-31.

In Adobe Photoshop Creative Suite (CS) 3, create a 11-pixel × 13-pixel image, in RGB. The height is dependent on the height of the check in the box. The check mark extends outside of the 8-pixel × 8-pixel check box.

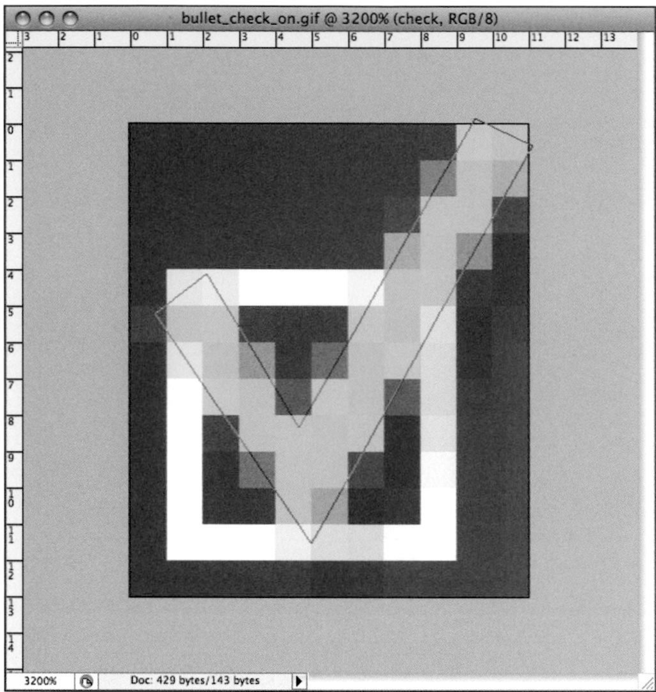


**Figure 6-30: Checked box.**

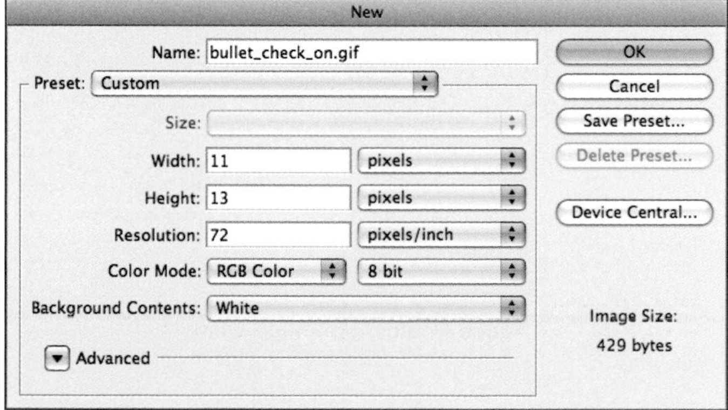


**Figure 6-31: Adobe Photoshop Create New Image dialog.**

For this image, Cindy used orange #f6851f, R: 246, G: 133, B: 31, to fill the background, as shown in **Figure 6-32**.

Create a new layer by clicking the icon on the bottom that is in between the folder icon and the trash can icon on the Layers window, as shown in the bottom-right of **Figure 6-33**, or select Layers ➪ New Layer.

Next, create an 8-pixel box by holding down the shift key when using the Rectangular Marquee Box shown in **Figure 6-34**.

The white 8-pixel square is 1 pixel from the left and 1 pixel from the bottom, as shown in **Figure 6-35**.

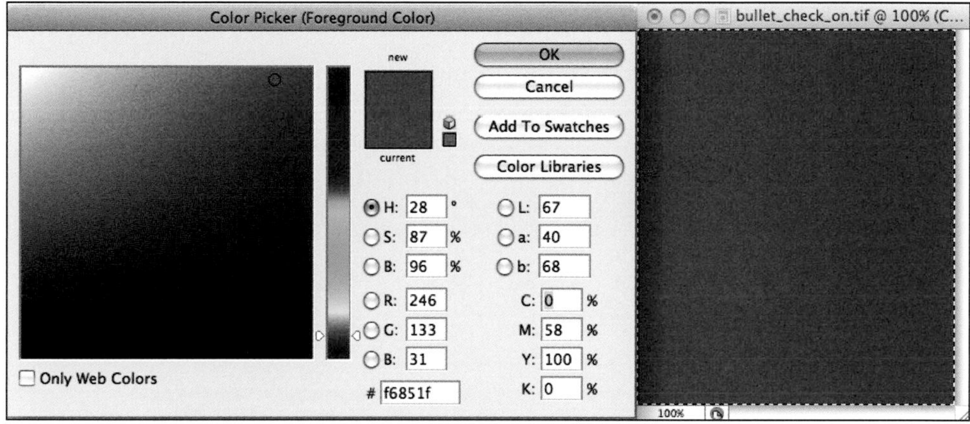


**Figure 6-32:** Adobe Photoshop Color Picker window for orange background.

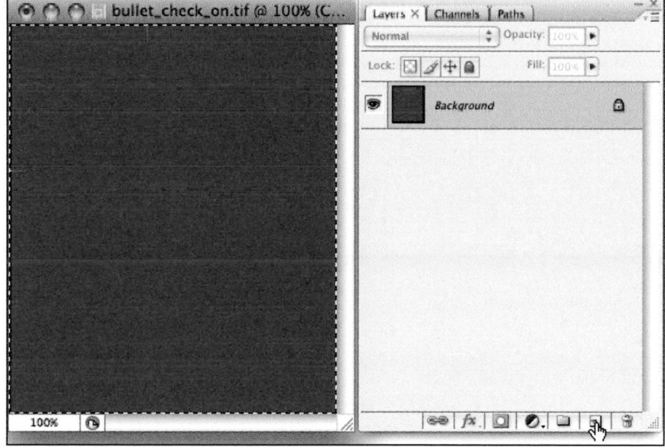


**Figure 6-33:** Adobe Photoshop image window.

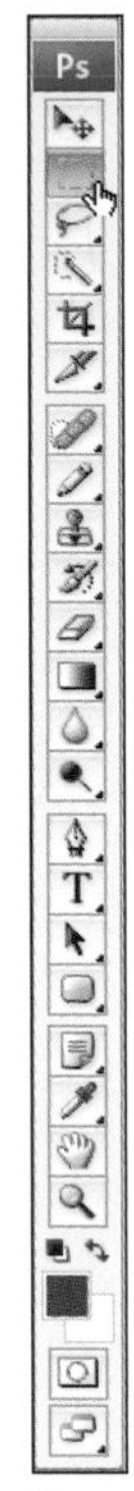

**Figure 6-34:** Adobe Photoshop toolbar with marquee tool selected.

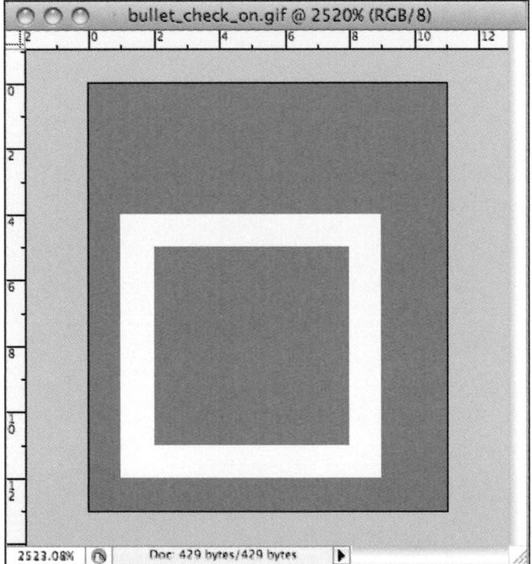


**Figure 6-35:** Example of the square white box in the orange background.

Create another layer for the check box and use the vector tool create an arrow. Then select a color for the arrow; CindyLi.com uses #d1ff44, R:209, G:255, B:68, as shown in Figure 6-36.

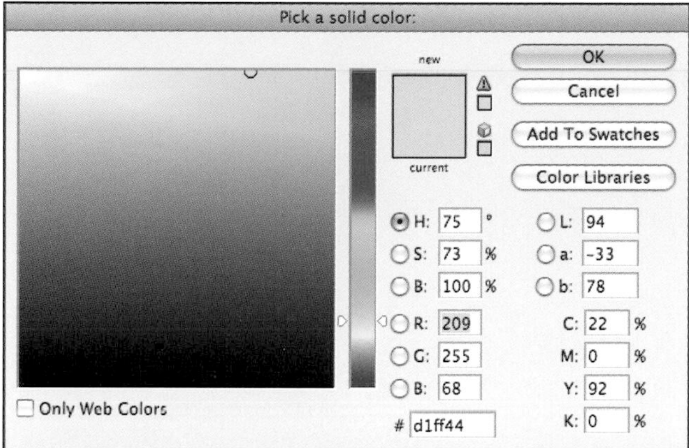


**Figure 6-36: Adobe Photoshop Color Picker for the fill color in the arrow.**

Then create a drop shadow for the check box with the following settings (see Figure 6-37):

| Setting | Value |
|---|---|
| Blend mode | Multiply |
| Opacity | 20% |
| Angle | 120° |
| Distance | 2px |
| Spread | 0% |
| Size | 0px |

Next save the file as `bullet_check_on.gif`.

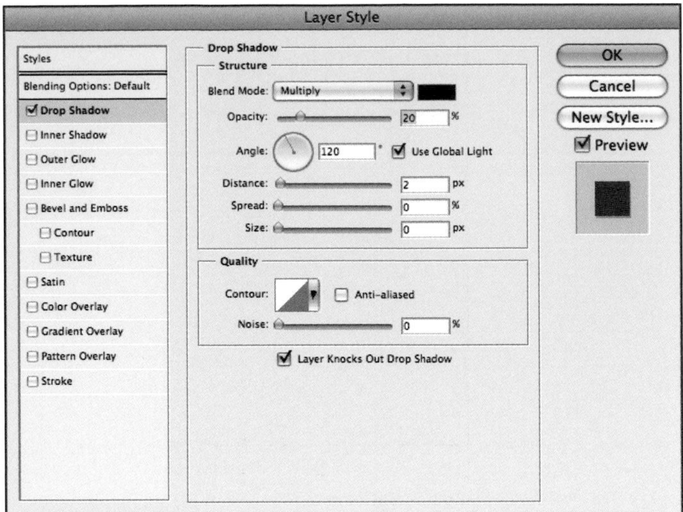


**Figure 6-37: Adobe Photoshop Layer Style settings for the arrow drop shadow.**

To create the unchecked box (see Figure 6-38), turn off the layer with the check (see Figure 6-39) and save the image as `bullet_check_off.gif`.

Here's the HTML code for the to-do list on the main CindyLi.com page:

```
<h2>Lifetime To do List</h2>
<ul>
 <li class="done">Finish blog design</li>
 <li class="undone">Go to England for New Years</li>
 <li class="undone">Finding peace :) </li>
 <li class="undone">See Geeky Chix project live</li>
</ul>
```

**Figure 6-38: Box without check in it.**

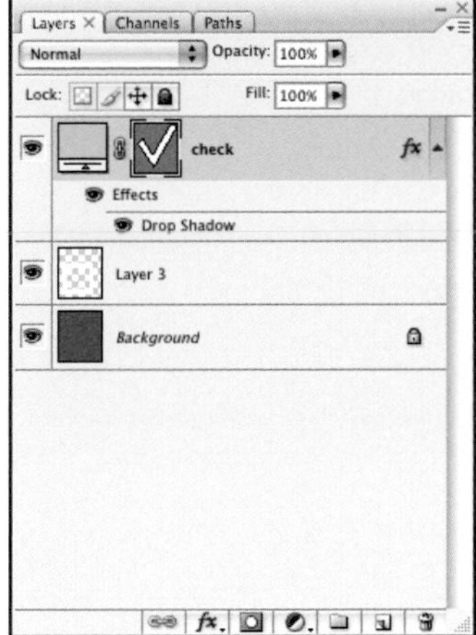


**Figure 6-39: Adobe Photoshop layers window.**

Notice that `li` elements are marked with a `class` attribute. The value states whether the to-do item is done or undone. That `class` attribute is how Cindy applies the appropriate graphic to the bullet point.

To design the check list with CSS as shown in Figure 6-40, the following code is used:

```
.lifetime li {
 color:#952300;
 padding-left:15px;
 background: url(../images/bullet_check_off.gif) no-repeat;
}
.lifetime  li.done {
 background: url(../images/bullet_check_on.gif) no repeat;
}
```

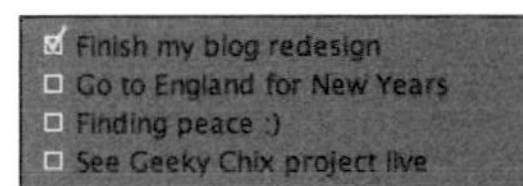


**Figure 6-40: Example of the Lifetime To Do list with one item checked as completed.**

# Summary

This chapter covered the essentials of turning a basic template blog-based Web site into a highly functional work of art. You saw how to use CSS to help build this site and make it as functional as it is. You also learned how to lay out a Web site design as well as how to set up and launch a blog and then customize it.

In addition, you examined how to create a vertically growing speech bubble that consisted of a header and a footer, how to create W3C-valid code for the Flickr badge, and how to create check boxes that you can turn on and off. This chapter also showed you how to build navigation bars, create effects, and add elements using CSS.

# 7

# AIGA Cincinnati: HTML Email Templates

*Mail your packages early so the post office can lose them in time for Christmas.*

*— Johnny Carson*

American Institute of Graphics Artists (AIGA) was founded in 1914 to promote designing as "professional craft, strategic tool and vital cultural force." With more than 16,000 members nationwide and 56 local chapters, AIGA is one of the oldest and strongest design-related organizations in the country.

Local chapters such as AIGA Cincinnati are formed throughout the country to develop better relationships with its members and provide job banks and discounts on products and services, as well as put on conferences and offer networking opportunities and workshops.

To help promote its activities, AIGA Cincinnati wanted to improve its email messages to its members to raise awareness of events and, in turn, increase the level of participation. To this end, they wanted to use HTML email templates. These custom-designed layouts cover most of their activities every year (happy hour events for networking, mentoring programs for design students, and design competition) but are flexible enough to be adapted for new events as they crop up.

## Dealing with HTML Email

Email was initially created for sending plain text; the use of HTML email to send images and markup over the Internet is only a natural progression from plain-text email because businesses and consumers wanted a better, richer experience in their email.

Now, almost all the popular email clients can read HTML email. Instead of plain text, most of those clients have their email composing settings set to create HTML email by default. It's very likely that users don't know that they are sending HTML email or that there is an option to "go back" to sending plain-text emails.

HTML email marketing is more effective than regular plain-text emails and other forms of advertising (see `http://email-marketing-reports.com/basics/why.htm`) because of higher click-through rates, the ability to include images of products, direct links to company Web sites, and so on.

However, the downside is that support for HTML email in email clients varies and is not as robust as that found in Web browsers like Safari or Internet Explorer for Windows 7. The situation is much like it was during the Browser Wars of the 1990s, where the code of a Web page would break in one browser and work fine in another.

Today, email clients are in a similar situation. At the time of this writing, the email clients marked as having poor Web standards per the Email Standards Project, mentioned later in the chapter, include Apple .Mac, Google Gmail, Lotus Notes 8, Microsoft Outlook 2007, and Windows Live Hotmail.

Through the implementation of Web standards and nudging of the Web Standards Project and fellow Web developers, the browser vendors focused on implementing HTML and CSS correctly. Through a similar effort, the recently formed Email Standards Project (see `www.email-standards.org`) is encouraging vendors and developers alike to make the changes needed for full support for standards in HTML email.

# Producing the Template

The design for AIGA Cincinnati's templates, shown in Figure 7-1, came from designer Joe Napier.

Since HTML email involves sending mini–Web pages to an environment where CSS support can be sketchy at best, HTML tables are used to control the layout. While using an HTML table layout is normally ill-advised for today's Web browser development, it's a good path to take here. Why is that?

HTML table layouts don't rely on CSS support in HTML email clients. A basic HTML table layout provides a better chance that the content of the email will be positioned where it needs to be, no matter what the level of support there is for CSS in the email client.

This is not to say that CSS is totally ignored. For HTML email templates like this project, CSS will be used to define the typography, color, and minor positioning of elements through margins and padding.

## *Printing the Design*

The first thing to do is to print the design. Use a pencil or marker with a rule to draw out the table cells for a table that encompasses the entire layout. This provides a rough estimate of how many table rows and columns are needed. This method allows the designer to get a rough idea of the HTML table structure, as shown in Figure 7-2.

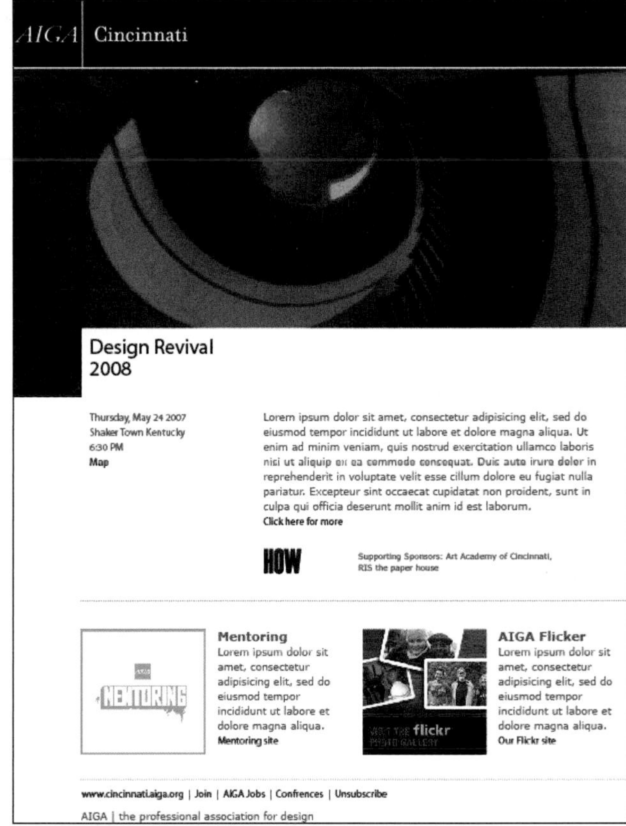


**Figure 7-1: The HTML email template.**

## Creating the HTML Table Layout

With the HTML table structure known, the next step is to work on the design into Photoshop. Open the slice tool to draw the table cells. The Slice Tool (see Figure 7-3) defines the boundaries of several graphics within a Photoshop file.

Thanks to the snapping feature, lining up cells is very easy to do. The lines from previously drawn shapes are used as guides for the width and height of the newly drawn slices (see Figure 7-4).

> *Note that the top portion of the HTML template isn't shown. This is so because those images — the main graphic and the AIGA Cincinnati header — were going to take the complete width of the table. So, it's okay to bypass slicing those images in this step. Those images can be brought into the HTML table layout by exporting those images individually and adding two new table rows to the code.*

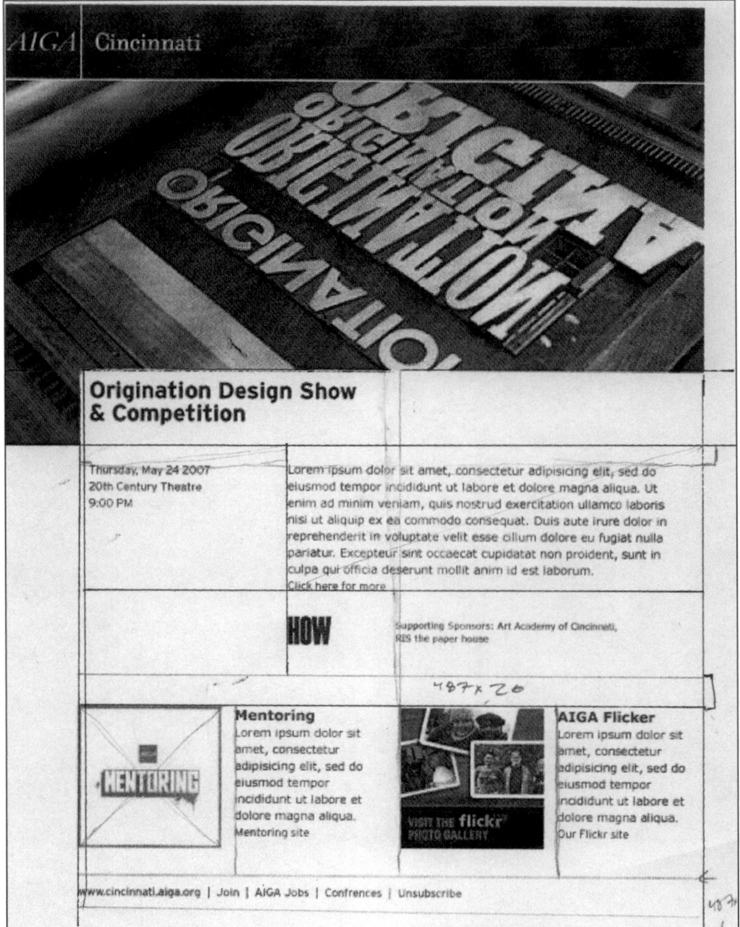


**Figure7-2: Determining the placement of the table cells.**

With the cells mapped out, go through each cell and make sure to map out the output for each slice, using the slice palette. In order to pick each slice, you need to use the Slice Select Tool. To get this tool in Photoshop, hold down the cursor over the Select tool, which makes the Slice menu appear. Choose the Slice Select Tool (distinguished from the Slice Tool by a small arrow cursor next to the blade). The Slice Select Tool takes the place of the original Slice Tool in the toolbar, as shown in Figure 7-5.

With the Slice Select Tool now being used, pick the first slice in the upper-left corner. To bring up the Slice options, as shown in Figure 7-6, click the right mouse button if you're using a PC or hold down the Control key while clicking if you're using a Macintosh.

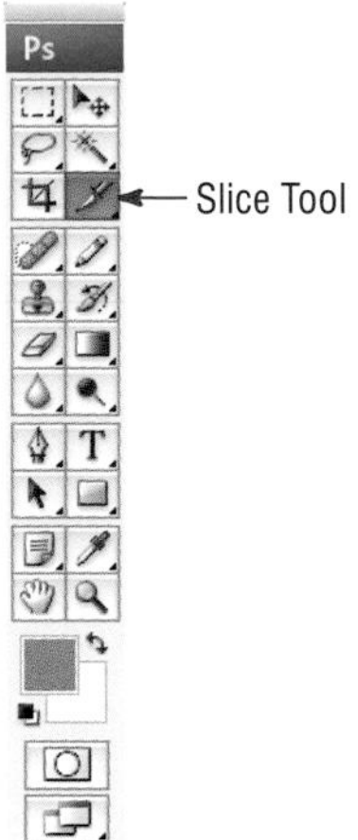


**Figure 7-3: The Slice Tool selected in the Photoshop toolbox.**

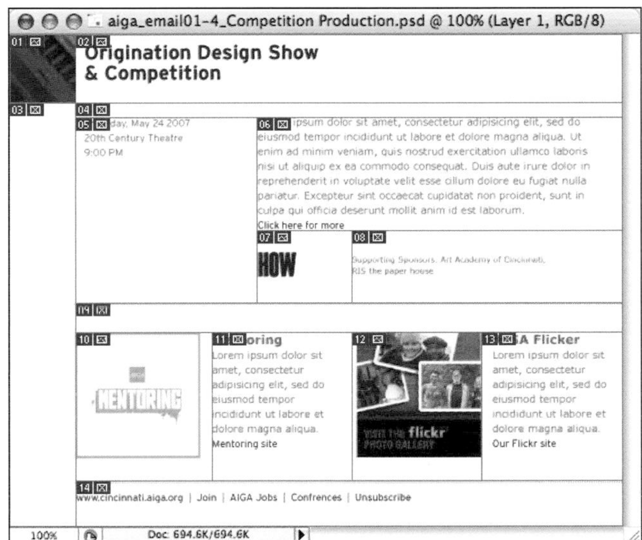


**Figure 7-4: Slices are made on the HTML template.**

I want the first slice to be exported as an image with a unique name. In this case, I am using the name `header_tidbit`, as shown in Figure 7-7.

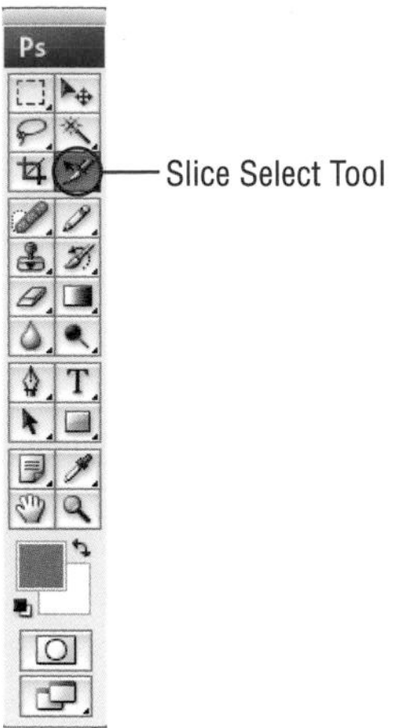


**Figure 7-5: The Slice Select Tool icon has a miniature arrow cursor in the upper-left corner.**

**Figure 7-6: Choose Edit Slice options.**

Continue setting slices you intend to use as images in this manner. However, for areas that should be filled with text, set the Slice Type to the No Image value, as shown in Figure 7-8.

With all the slices set, the next step is to select File ➪ Save for Web & Devices, which brings up the Save for Web & Devices dialog box, as shown in Figure 7-9.

Using the Slice Select tool in the upper-left corner, I go through each slice destined to be an image and fine-tune the image export settings.

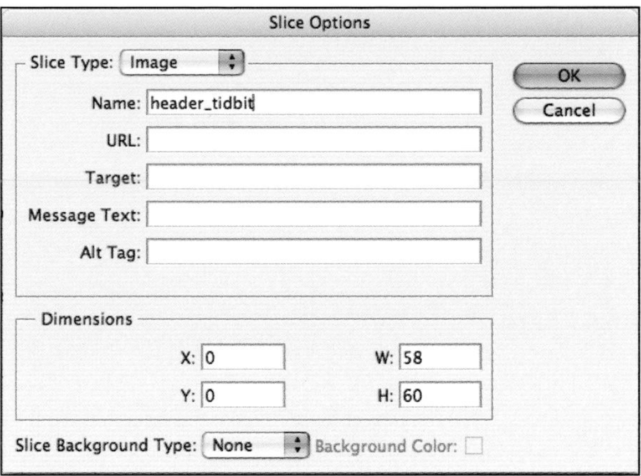


**Figure 7-7: The Slice Options dialog box.**

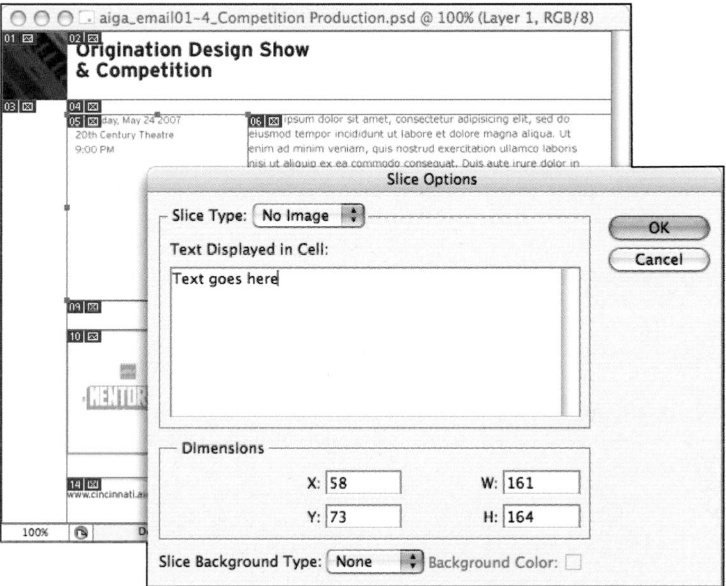


**Figure 7-8: Setting Photoshop to export text instead of an image.**

*As is typical for Web delivery, images with flat areas of color are set to be GIF files, and photorealistic images, such as the main image of the design, are exported as high-quality JPEGs.*

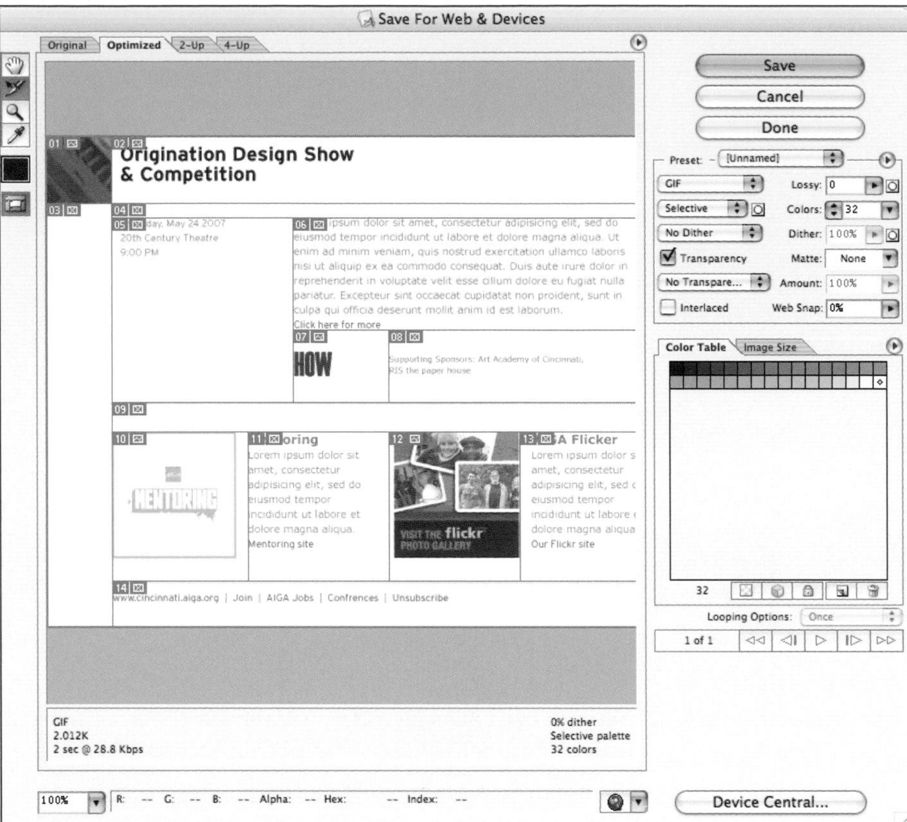


Figure 7-9: The Save for Web & Devices dialog box.

With all the images labeled, click the Save button in the Save for Web & Devices dialog box, which brings up the Save Optimized As dialog box, as shown in Figure 7-10.

For the format, select the drop-down menu option HTML and Images and click Save. This results in all the images being exported from Photoshop, auto-generating the HTML table that forms the basis of the HTML email template, as shown in Figure 7-11.

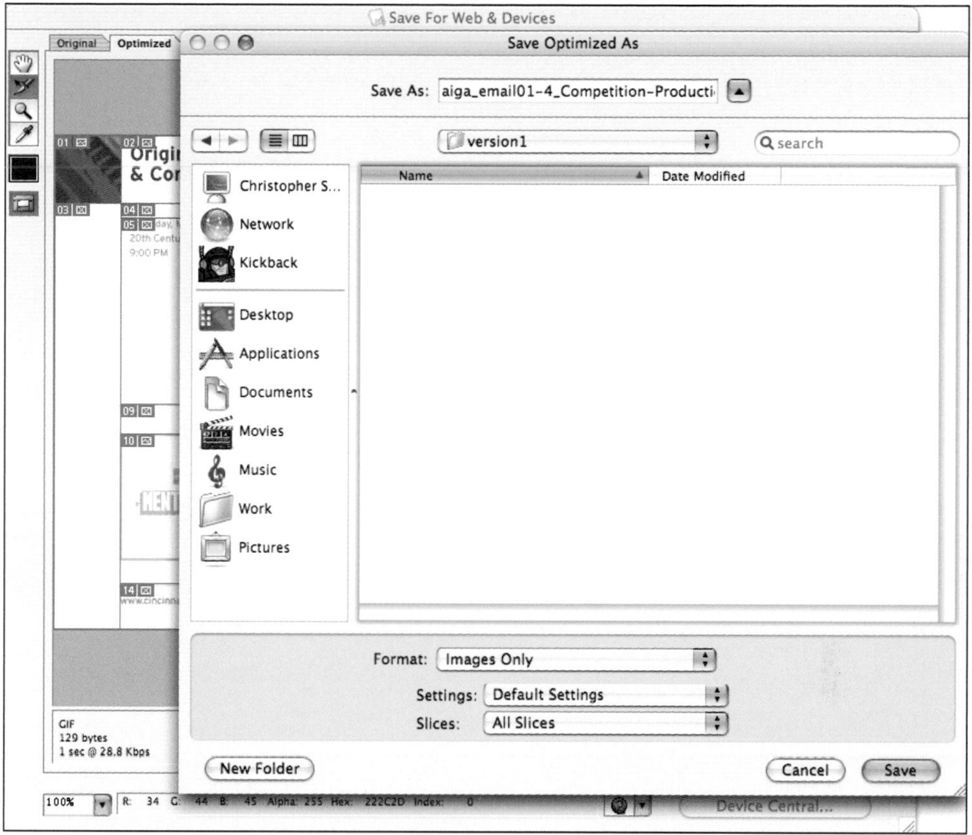


Figure 7-10: The Save Optimized As dialog box.

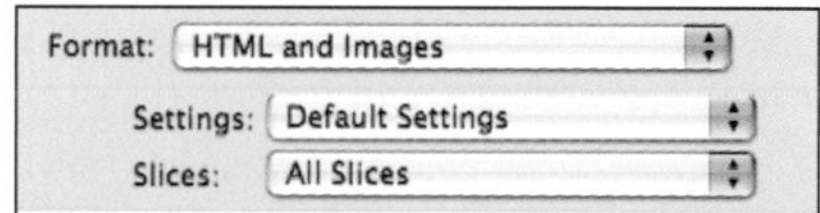


Figure 7-11: Setting the export format.

Here's the HTML that results in the output shown in Figure 7-12:

```
<body bgcolor="#FFFFFF" leftmargin="0" topmargin="0" marginwidth="0"
marginheight="0">
<!-- ImageReady Slices (aiga_email01-4_Competition Production.psd) -->
```

```
<table id="Table_01" width="545" height="436" border="0" cellpadding="0"
cellspacing="0">
 <tr>
  <td>
   <img src="images/header_tidbit.gif" width="58" height="60" alt=""></td>
  <td colspan="5">
   <img src="images/header_txt.gif" width="487" height="60" alt=""></td>
 </tr>
 <tr>
  <td width="58" height="375" rowspan="6" bgcolor="#FFFFFF">
   <img src="images/spacer.gif" width="58" height="375" alt=""></td>
  <td width="487" height="13" colspan="5">
   <img src="images/spacer.gif" width="487" height="13" alt=""></td>
 </tr>
 <tr>
  <td width="161" height="164" colspan="2" rowspan="2">Text goes here</td>
  <td width="326" height="100" colspan="3">Text goes here</td>
 </tr>
 <tr>
  <td>
   <img src="images/aiga_email01-4_Competition-Production_07.gif" width="85"
height="64" alt=""></td>
  <td width="241" height="64" colspan="2">Text goes here</td>
 </tr>
 <tr>
  <td width="487" height="26" colspan="5" bgcolor="#FFFFFF">
   <img src="images/spacer.gif" width="487" height="26" alt=""></td>
 </tr>
 <tr>
  <td>
   <img src="images/aiga_email01-4_Competition-Production_10.gif" width="121"
height="131" alt=""></td>
  <td width="125" height="131" colspan="2">Text goes here</td>
  <td>
   <img src="images/aiga_email01-4_Competition-Production_12.gif" width="116"
height="131" alt=""></td>
  <td width="125" height="131">Text goes here</td>
 </tr>
 <tr>
  <td width="487" height="41" colspan="5">Footer navigation goes here</td>
 </tr>
 <tr>
  <td>
   <img src="images/spacer.gif" width="58" height="1" alt=""></td>
  <td>
   <img src="images/spacer.gif" width="121" height="1" alt=""></td>
  <td>
   <img src="images/spacer.gif" width="40" height="1" alt=""></td>
  <td>
   <img src="images/spacer.gif" width="85" height="1" alt=""></td>
```

```
    <td>
     <img src="images/spacer.gif" width="116" height="1" alt=""></td>
    <td>
     <img src="images/spacer.gif" width="125" height="1" alt=""></td>
  </tr>
</table>
<!-- End ImageReady Slices -->
</body>
</html>
```

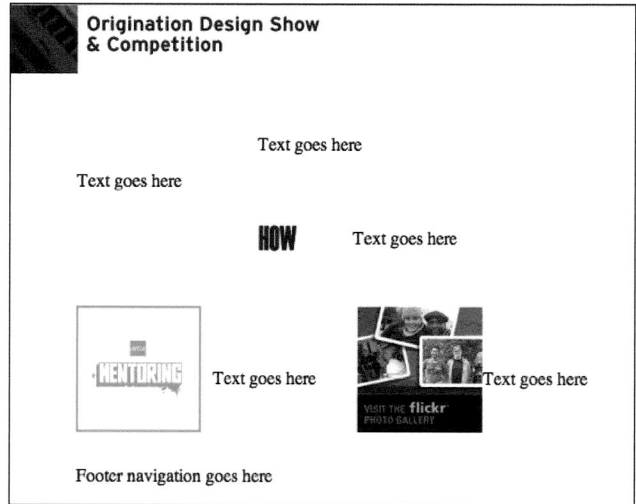


**Figure 7-12: The basic HTML table setup.**

If you recall, the original headers were left off from the slicing feature because they required the full width of the HTML table. With the basic table structure set in place, you can add two table rows containing those header graphics to the top of the table as shown in Figure 7-13.

```
<tr>
<td colspan="6">
<a href="http://cincinnati.aiga.org/" style="text-decoration: none; color:
#f030a2;"><img src="images/letterhead_agia.gif" border="0" height="61" alt="AIGA
Cincinnati" width="545" /></a></td>
</tr>
<tr>
<td colspan="6"><img src="images/header_designcomp_text.gif" border="0"
height="229" alt="" width="545" /></td>
</tr>
```

Next, I added the filler text, some of which was used by the designer in the original design, as shown in Figure 7-14. This new text fleshes out the design quite a bit.

**Figure 7-13: Header graphics added to the top of the page.**

## Adjusting the Design

With the major outline of the template set in place by the HTML table, it's a simple matter to apply a few basic CSS rules to get the Web document to look more like the original design (see Figure 7-15):

```
h2 {
 font-size: 12px;
 font-family:  Verdana, Arial, Helvetica, sans-serif;
 line-height: 1.3;
 color: #8a8b8c;
 font-weight: bold;
 padding: 0;
 margin: 0;
}
p {
 font-size: 10px;
 font-family:  Verdana, Arial, Helvetica, sans-serif;
 line-height: 1.4;
 color: #8a8b8c;
 margin: 0;
}
```

```
a {
 color: #f030a2;
 text-decoration: none;
}
#eventinfo p {
 margin-left: 8px;
}
#badge1 {
 padding-right: 28px;
}
```

**Figure 7-14:** Working with filler text gives a better view of the finished product.

**Figure 7-15: The HTML template massaged with a few CSS rules.**

*Note that the lack of shorthand CSS rules. This is intentional because email clients may not be robust enough to handle shorthand CSS values. So, to play it safe, expand the shorthand to separate declarations.*

## Exploring the Effects of CSS Rules on an HTML Email Template

Let's go through the CSS rules line by line to see the effect on the HTML email template.

For the two subheads — Mentoring and AIGA Flickr — the text is treated with sans-serif typefaces, 12 pixels font size, set to bold and a gray color as shown in Figure 7-16. Also, the margins and padding are set to zero.

*You may be wondering why the type is set to pixels. Lack of support for em or keyword sizes for the font-size property in the email clients, as stated in Jeffrey Zeldman's old article, Fear of Style Sheets (see* `http://alistapart.com/articles/fear`*), means that pixels are the only way to specify a font size on the Web with any degree of certainty.*

```
h2 {
 font-size: 12px;
 font-family:  Verdana, Arial, Helvetica, sans-serif;
 line-height: 1.3;
 color: #8a8b8c;
 font-weight: bold;
 padding: 0;
 margin: 0;
}
```

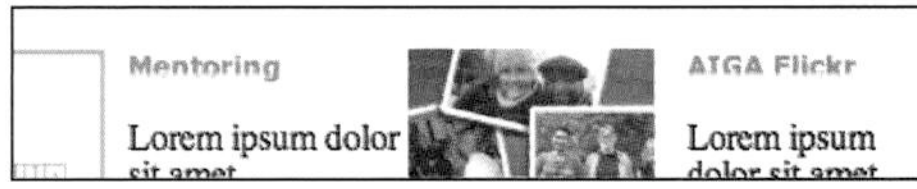

**Figure 7-16: Adjusting the subheadings.**

The paragraphs are treated next, as shown in Figure 7-17. A variation of the treatment for the subheads, but, of course, less bold and smaller size for legibility.

```
p {
 font-size: 10px;
 font-family:  Verdana, Arial, Helvetica, sans-serif;
 line-height: 1.4;
 color: #8a8b8c;
 margin: 0;
}
```

**Figure 7-17: The paragraphs are styled.**

The next step is to set the link colors. Instead of setting the links with pseudo-classes, such as link or hover, like those you see with numerous rollover effects, I want to make sure that all links are set to only one color, even if the recipient has already visited a page before and thus the links remain "fresh." (See Figure 7-18.)

```
a {
 color: #f030a2;
 text-decoration: none;
}
```

**Figure 7-18: Setting the link color.**

The next step is to maneuver the alignment of the text for a couple of paragraphs. The event information is flush left to the heading, and the paragraph for Mentoring has added padding set to the right, as shown in Figure 7-19.

```
#eventinfo p {
 margin-left: 8px;
}
#badge1 {
 padding-right: 28px;
}
```

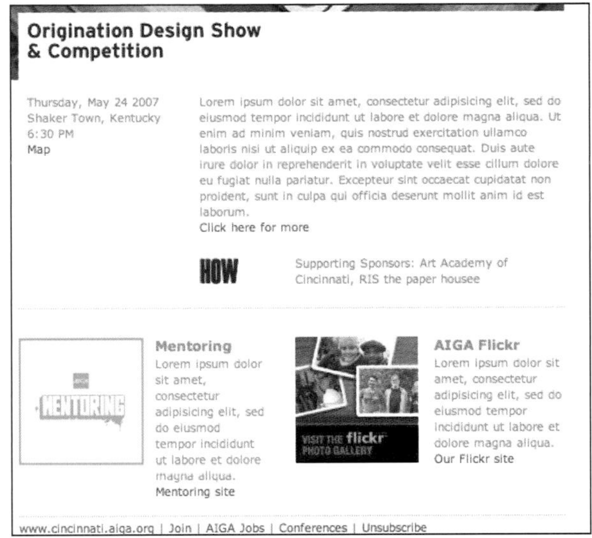


**Figure 7-19: Adjusting the margins and padding.**

# Embedding Styles

With Web pages, CSS is typically applied through the `link` element or `@import` method. This technique is used in order to separate the presentation code from the markup. This separation allows you to keep the content clean of presentation and allows you to modify the CSS be independently of the Web documents themselves.

However, when sending HTML email, separating the design and the content could be disastrous, since the HTML email clients might not know how to render inline or external CSS rules in your design.

One way to move the CSS rules from inline to embedded is to meticulously copy and paste the CSS rules into each HTML element. For example, the table cell for event information:

```
<td id="eventinfo" height="164" valign="top" rowspan="2" colspan="2" width="161"><p
style="font-size: 10px; margin: 0 0 0 8px; line-height: 1.4; font-family: Verdana,
Arial, Helvetica, sans-serif; color: #8a8b8c;">Thursday, May 24 2007 <br />
Shaker Town, Kentucky<br />
6:30 PM<br />
<a href="designcompetition.html#" style="text-decoration: none; color:
#f030a2;">Map</a></p></td>
```

While that gets the job done, manually embedding styles is very prone to error, not to mention very boring. Thankfully, there's an alternative that automates the process.

# Using Preflight for HTML Email

Out on the Web is a service, Premailer (see `http://code.dunae.ca/premailer.web`), written by Alex Dunae, that takes a typical Web page with inline or linked style sheets, relative image paths, and so on and creates an HTML email-friendly version.

Not only that, but the Premailer (as shown in Figure 7-20) performs the additional step of analyzing your CSS to determine whether it has support in some of the popular email clients.

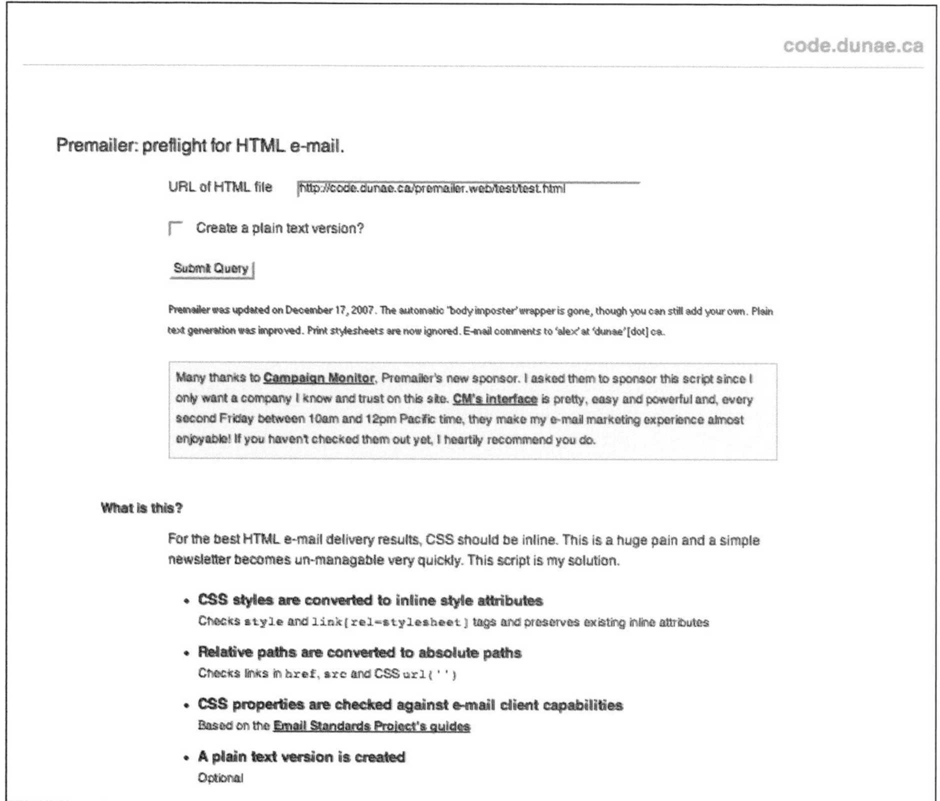


**Figure 7-20:** Premailer Web site.

After you upload the HTML email template to a local development server and press submit, the Web service does the job of converting the CSS rules to be embedded and gives you a report showing how your CSS rules are going to come out in various email clients, as shown in Figure 7-21.

| | |
|---|---|
| **text-decoration CSS property** | |
| Support level: SAFE | May not render properly in Eudora |
| **color CSS property** | |
| Support level: SAFE | May not render properly in Eudora, dotMac |
| **font-size CSS property** | |
| Support level: SAFE | May not render properly in Eudora, dotMac |
| **margin CSS property** | |
| Support level: RISKY | May not render properly in AOL, Live Mail, Hotmail, Notes 6, Eudora, dotMac |
| **line-height CSS property** | |
| Support level: POOR | May not render properly in Notes 6, Eudora, dotMac |
| **font-family CSS property** | |
| Support level: POOR | May not render properly in Gmail, Eudora, dotMac |
| **padding-right CSS property** | |
| Support level: POOR | May not render properly in Notes 6, Eudora, dotMac |
| **font-weight CSS property** | |
| Support level: SAFE | May not render properly in Eudora, dotMac |
| **padding CSS property** | |
| Support level: POOR | May not render properly in Notes 6, Eudora, dotMac |

**Figure 7-21: Results of the preflight check.**

The report shows that using the margin property is risky. Because this property is being used in this instance only to nudge the text ever so slightly to get the design to look as intended, it's okay to continue.

*To remove the margin property altogether to play it safe as the Premailer suggests, you could create a more complex HTML table with additional table cells to take the place of CSS padding and margins.*

# Summary

You looked at how to take a Web page layout and how to use Photoshop's Slice and Web tools to create an HTML email template that's ready to be used. Also, we touched on how to add delicate CSS rules so as not render your emails illegible in some of the more popular email clients.

The next chapter takes a look at how to use PNGs in Internet Explorer 6 and beyond.

# 8

# Professional CSS Book Site: Using Transparent PNGs

*What passes for woman's intuition is often nothing more than man's transparency.*
*— George Jean Nathan*

In this chapter you learn how to use Transparent PNGs while designing a Web site. As a practical example, the sample that will be used will be the home page of `www.procssbook.com`, shown in Figure 8-1. The page was designed with the use of Transparent PNGs.

Before learning *how* to use Transparent PNGs, it's important to discuss *why* Transparent PNGs can be useful when laying out a design for a Web site.

Like GIFs and JPEGs, PNG images are ideal for Web use. Like GIFs, the PNG is great for displaying small images with few colors, such as logos and icons. Also, PNGs sport a few advantages over GIF images. Most notably, they support alpha-transparency. What is alpha-transparency? GIF files are only capable of displaying a pixel as either completely transparent or completely opaque: this is known as binary transparency. When an image contains alpha layers, however, parts of an image can be partially transparent. You can specify a level of transparency from 0 to 255. Figure 8-2 shows a comparison of images with layers of varying transparency.

When working with most images and graphic files, you will find that a PNG is able to achieve greater compression than a GIF. PNGs provide for a much greater range of transparency options than GIFs. Alpha-channel transparency is the number one option available. A PNG can also provide for a much wider range of color depth in an image, far more than the standard GIF. You can use truecolor up to 48 bits instead of 8 bit (and 256 colors) with PNG. This gives you more color control, allowing you to produce smoother fades, for example. PNGs thus give you the potential to create some interesting effects on a Web page, such as translucent background images and drop shadows.

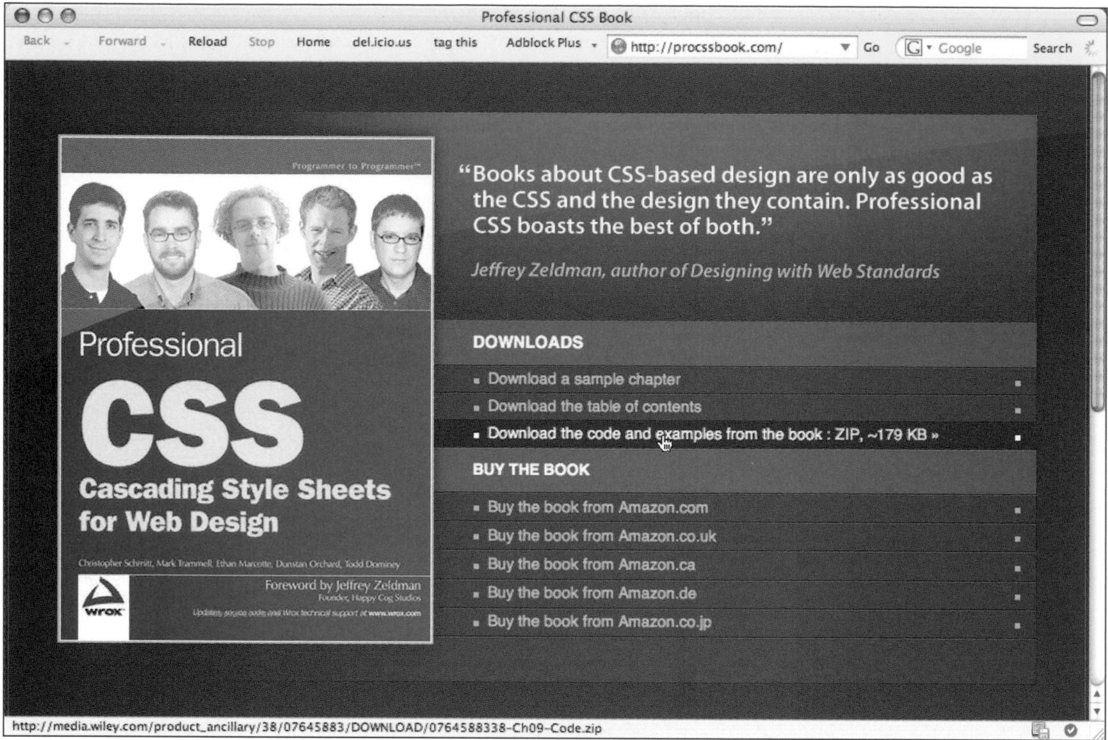


Figure 8-1: The Web site for *Professional CSS, First Edition* is located at procssbook.com.

Figure 8-2: Different levels of opacity set on the individual brackets.

PNGs are a great choice, but don't rule out two strengths of using GIFs: their ability to support animation, and the wide level of browser support. Despite their advantages over GIFS, PNGs aren't nearly as popular as GIFs in Web design, primarily because of the impression that PNGs don't enjoy wide browser support. This view of PNGs is a bit of a misconception.

# PNGs and Browser Support

While Internet Explorer for Windows 6 (IE6) and previous versions of IE don't support PNGs' alpha-transparency feature, all popular browsers — Safari, Opera, Firefox, and even the successor to IE6, Internet Explorer for Windows 7 (IE7) — can display PNGs.

*With all these modern browsers supporting PNG's alpha-transparency, is it necessary to still worry about IE6? The answer is "it depends." Check your site's log files and see how much of your audience still uses IE6. If the percentage is low to none, you might not have to worry about IE6.*

While IE6 doesn't explicitly support alpha-transparency out of the box, if you will, there is a workaround that ensures PNG's cross-browser compatibility.

## Image Filter Workaround for Using PNGs with IE6

Microsoft has a plethora of proprietary visual filters and transitions (see `http://msdn2.microsoft.com/en-us/library/ms532847.aspx`) that are available to IE4+. These filters are designed to apply various multimedia affects (transition wipes, light effects, and so on) to images in a Web page that are viewed with IE. One of these image filters — AlphaImageLoader — lets you display a PNG with alpha-transparency in IE6.

You can employ this filter within the HTML of your page by creating a `div` element and embedding into it a bit of CSS, as shown in Figure 8-3:

```
<div style="position:relative; height: 188px; width: 188px;
filter:progid:DXImageTransform.Microsoft.AlphaImageLoader
(src='images/image.png',sizingMethod='scale');"></div>
```

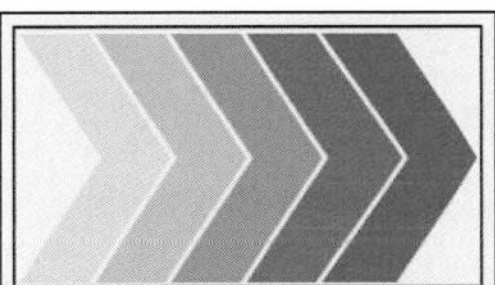

**Figure 8-3: Light purple color shines through transparent parts of PNG image.**

The key property here is the `filter` property. While `filter` is not valid CSS property, it does allow you to apply the AlphaImageLoader filter to the image specified in the parentheses. However, because code isn't standards-compliant, you may want to apply this property only as needed (that is, only when the page is being displayed in IE6).

Using this method, developers can build rich image-based designs with alpha-transparency as they would for modern browsers such as Safari, Firefox, and Internet Explorer 7, which all support PNG alpha-transparency natively.

## HTC Script Workaround for Using PNGs with IE6

Another available method for using PNGs with IE6 employs Angus Turnbull's `.htc` script.

First, download the `.htc` script at TwinHelix Designs (`www.twinhelix.com`). HTC is a scripting language only usable by Internet Explorer (because it was created by Microsoft), and this specific script contains (as well as) applies the AlphaImageLoader filter to all images within a Web page. It can run on both Microsoft's IIS (Internet Information Services) Web server, as well as Open Source–based Apache.

After downloading the script, upload the script to your Web server.

Next, create a blank GIF file. This image file is 1 × 1 pixel with the color set as transparent. (Back in the '90s, these gems were called "single-pixel GIFs.") You may want to also download this image from www.twinhelix.com/css/iepngfix.

Within the .htc script, change the line that references the blank.gif file so that it points to the GIF's location on the server.

Create a separate CSS file (named ie.css), and include within it the following single line, referencing the location of the .htc file:

```
img {
 behavior: url(iepngfix.htc);
}
```

The behavior property attaches a script to some selector (in this case, all img elements). So, this CSS file attaches the .htc file to all of your images, thus applying the desired filter effect to every image within a Web page.

But, you only want to load this CSS file when the page is viewed in IE6. To do this, just add the following conditional comment to your page's header:

```
<!--[if lte IE 6]>
<link rel="stylesheet" type="text/css" media="screen"
href="ie.css" />
<![endif]-->
```

Conditional comments like these are understood by IE. What the comment says is, "if the browser is IE6 or below, then read the lines within the comment tags. Otherwise, ignore them." Conditional comments provide a convenient way of applying IE-specific HTML or CSS. Here, the ie.css style sheet loads only if the page is displayed in IE6, letting you apply the noncompliant CSS only when it's absolutely necessary.

Common techniques for presenting inline images may not work:

- When placing images in the background of elements, normal behavior is for the image to tile out. With the solution, the PNG image doesn't because the filter property was designed to have this effect.
- Don't use this solution in combination with the CSS sprites technique. Make sure that you are using one image and only one image for the effect.
- If you're trying to run multiple versions of IE on one installation of the Windows operating system, using a method like that discussed at http://tredosoft.com/Multiple_IE, conditional comments may not work, and the work image may appear on your local system. However, the solution could be working okay. Try using a third-party testing solution such as BrowserCam (http://browsercam.com) to address this problem.

The IE6 script works by basically placing the image from the inline position to the background of an element.

## Color Issues with PNGs

Another issue is with color correction. Ever notice that colors on Mac tend to be lighter than those on a PC? That's because the people who built those respective systems made changes that created that situation. A PNG can contain gamma information that could be used to correct the problem.

The process goes something like this: Your digital authoring software records the gamma information along with the other data necessary to render the image in the PNG file. Then the PNG is distributed through the Internet and is displayed on numerous operating systems and browsers. Since the gamma information is included with the PNG file, the browser or whatever application is rendering the image displays the PNG with the appropriate color correction.

The problem is that the information is incomplete, and the rendering application can't recreate your original color profile in another person's system and doesn't have the right settings to display color properly. (When was the last time you calibrated your computer's monitor?)

Essentially, the systems are guessing at the best way to present the PNG image when the gamma information is contained in the images, and this attempt at trying to fix the problem actually makes the problem more severe.

> *This is, of course, a simplification of what happens. For more information on the problem, see* `http://hsivonen.iki.fi/png-gamma`.

The best approach is to get rid of the gamma information stored in PNGs. How do you do this? If you already use Photoshop's Save for Web feature, the PNG setting leaves out the gamma information. However, if you don't own this software and use a Mac, try Gammaslamma (see `www.plasticated.com/GammaSlamma-1.1.dmg`) from Shealan Forshaw to download the `.dmg` file.

# Using Alpha-Transparency

PNGs offer a number of advantages that may make their use worthwhile, despite the support problems with IE6."

## Better Shadows

Making drop shadows is easier with PNGs. With GIFs only having one color set to transparency, smooth gradients like those found in drop shadows would have be lined up perfectly to complete the effect. However, if the image is off by even one pixel, as shown in Figures 8-4 and 8-5, the effect can alter a design unintentionally.

In Figure 8-4 the book image's drop shadow aligns with the background. If positioning is exact with a GIF image containing a drop shadow, a misalignment may occur, as in Figure 8-5.

With PNGs that have shades of transparency, a drop shadow can be made once and not ruin an image even if elements aren't pixel perfect (and most things for the Web aren't pixel perfect!), as shown in Figure 8-6.

Figure 8-4: Image's drop shadow aligns with background.

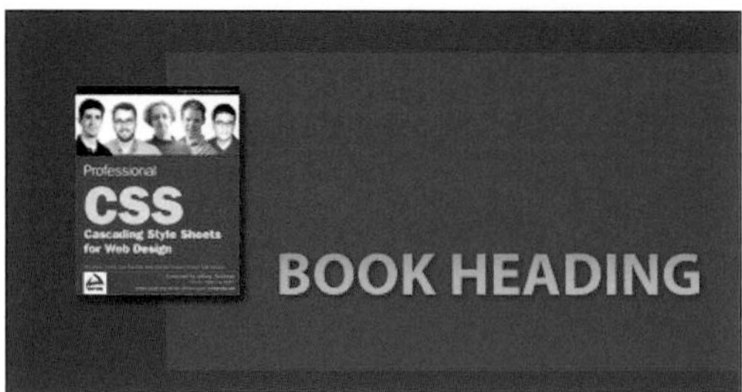


Figure 8-5: A misalignment.

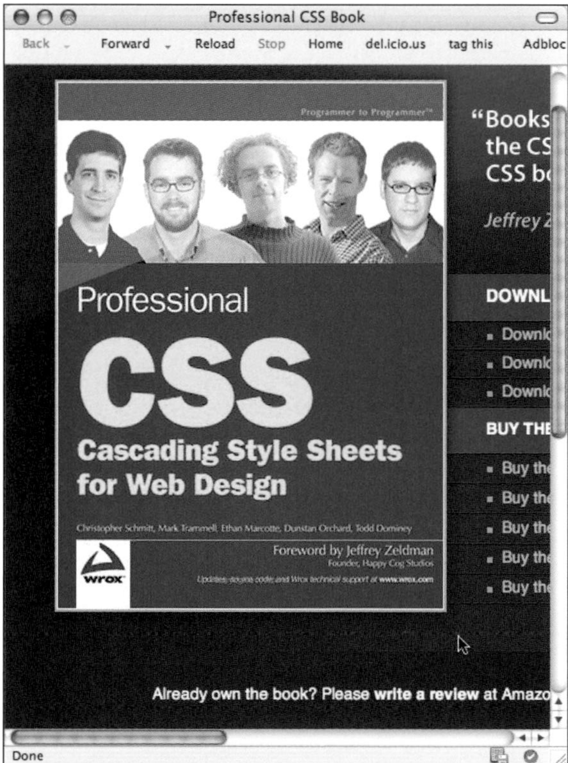


Figure 8-6: The book cover's drop shadow.

Figure 8-7 shows that even as the text is resized, the drop shadow in the PNG image does not interfere with the overall design.

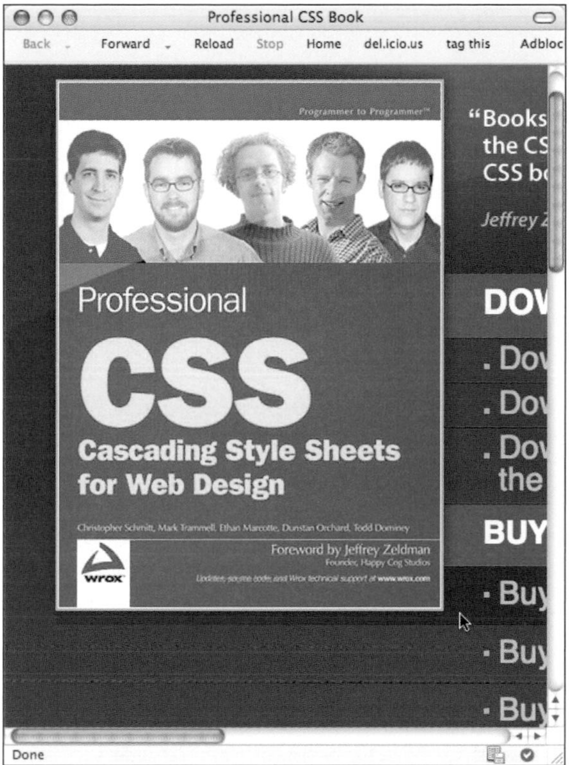


Figure 8-7: Drop shadow in PNG image does not interfere with the design.

## Using Color Shades

Color shades are small PNG images filled with a black or white color set to a certain opacity, which can be used for tinting background colors or images. You can download a set of color shades from `http://christopherschmitt.com/2007/03/16/color-shades/` or you can easily create your own.

To make your own color shades, set a 24 × 24 pixel image in Photoshop, and then adjust the Opacity, as shown in Figure 8-8.

The use the File ➪ Save for Web & Devices to export the image as PNG-24, as shown in Figure 8-9.

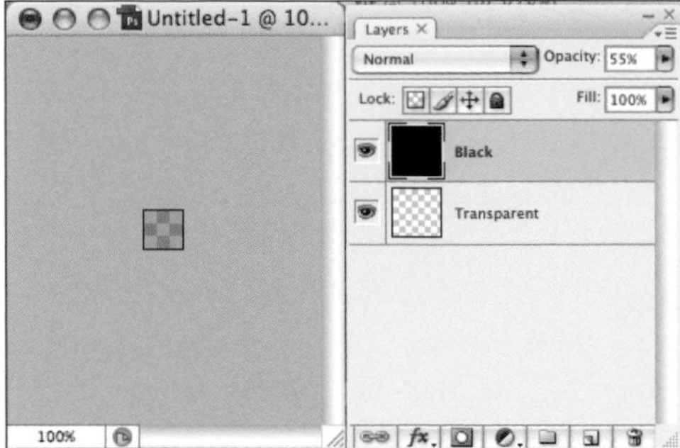


Figure 8-8: The opacity of top layer is set to 55%.

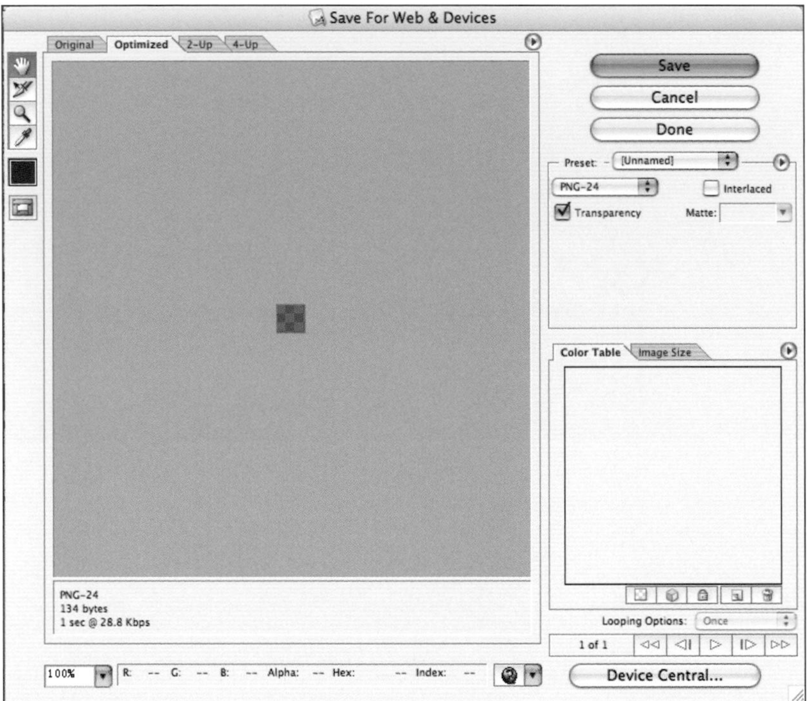


Figure 8-9: The Save for Web & Devices dialog box.

An interesting use of color shades uses a layered effect. Take these two images: The first uses the basic concept of color shade, but instead of solid area color, a vertical gradient of white color to transparency is used. In Figure 8-10, a duplicate image is placed below it with a dark red background to better highlight the faint gradient.

The second image, as shown in **Figure** 8-11, is an abstract color image from the *Professional CSS* book site used for the main background image.

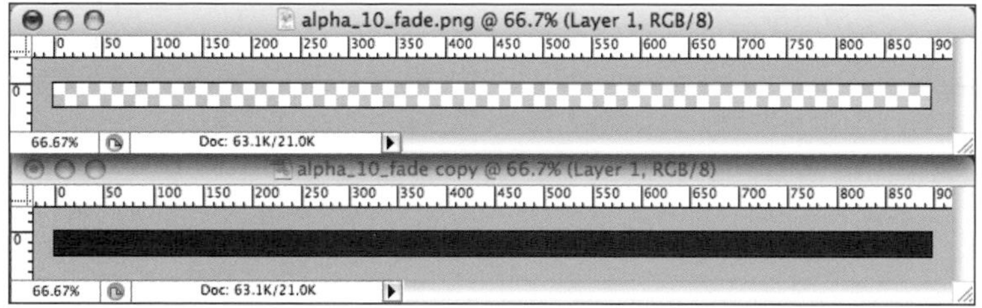


**Figure 8-10: The gradient goes from transparent to 10% white from left to right.**

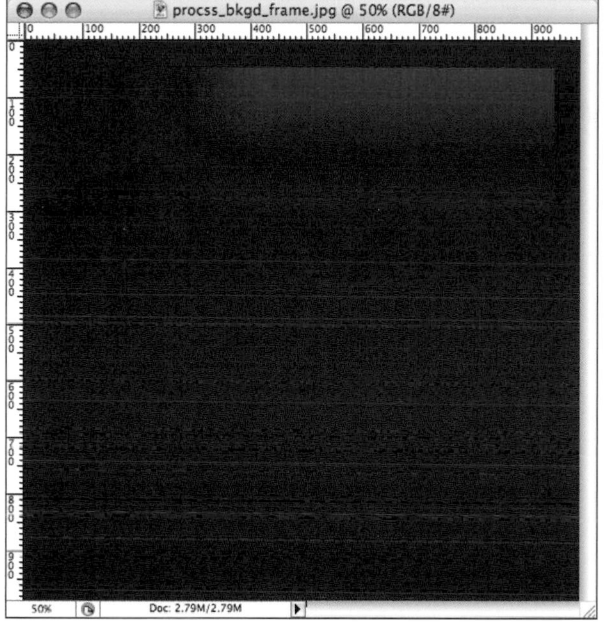


**Figure 8-11: Notice the color changes in the background image.**

These two images can be used to great effect when layered on top of a background image with a subtle color change, as shown in Figure 8-12.

PNGs can even be used for rollovers, as shown in Figure 8-13.

```
#buybook ul:hover {
 background-image: url(/_assets/img/alpha_90_fade_blck.png);
}
```

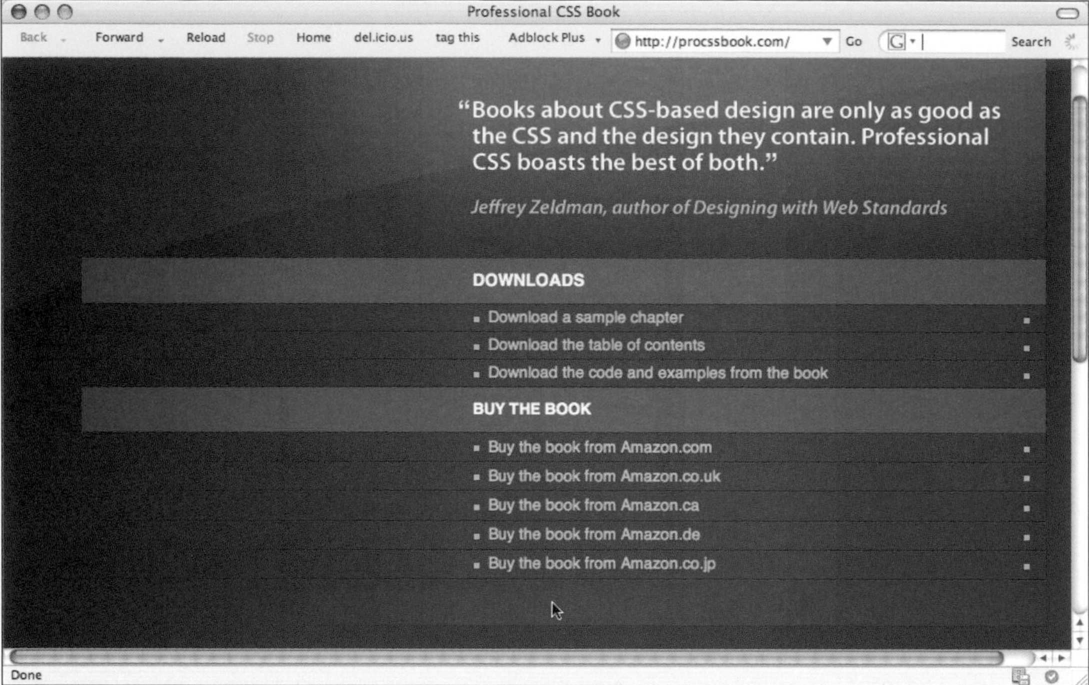


Figure 8-12: With a dark background image, the light gradient is seen.

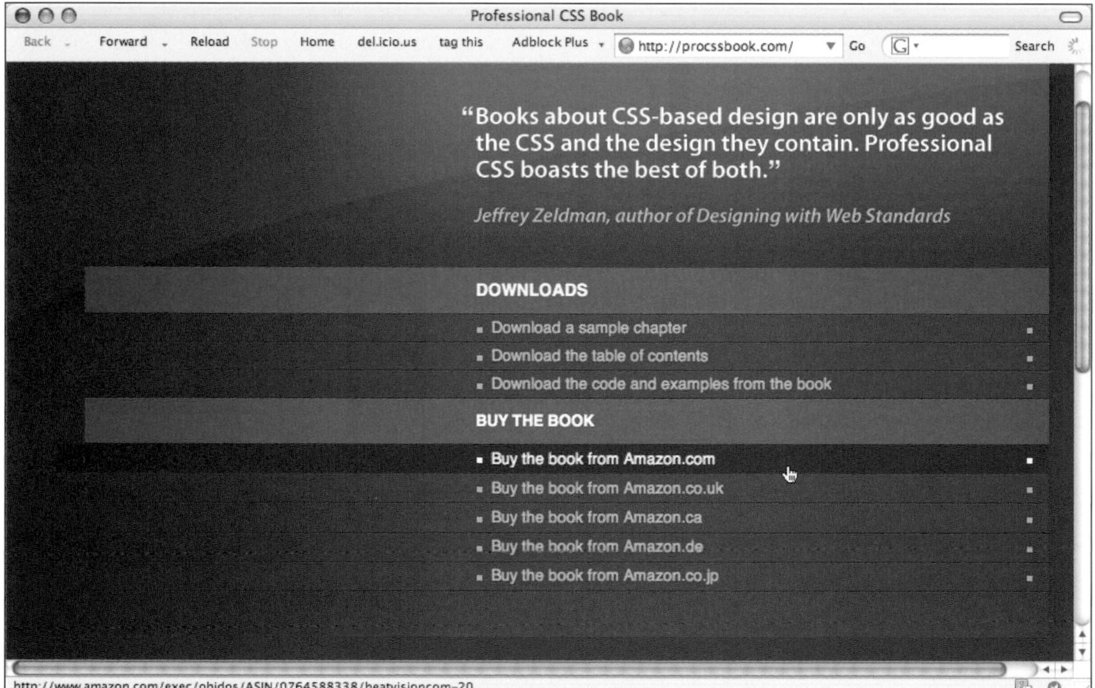


Figure 8-13: A color shade set to 90% black is used for the rollover effect.

# Summary

This chapter covered the use of transparent PNGs — their strengths (and weaknesses) as well as their practical application. You learned how to use transparent PNGs within a Web browser, even with IE6's lack of native support for the image format. The chapter also included a discussion of color issues and explained how to use alpha-transparency and color shades to make your work look better.

The next chapter looks at how to use CSS layouts in revising a site's design.

# 9

# Building CSS Layouts

*We adore chaos because we love to produce order.*
*— M. C. Escher*

By the time 2003 began in earnest, a rather sizable snowball was rolling. In October of 2002, *Wired News* abandoned traditional table-driven layout methods for a CSS-driven design. At that time, *Wired* wasn't the first redesign of its kind, but it was certainly the most highly trafficked. The site's chief designer, Douglas Bowman, took a highly visible and well-established brand and delivered a compelling new design — all with standard technologies such as CSS and XHTML that would, as Bowman put it, help "lift the Web out of the dark ages" (*Wired News*, "A Site for Your Eyes": `www.wired.com/news/culture/0,1284,55675,00.html`).

For the next few months, you could almost hear the crickets chirping. *Wired News* had lifted style sheets out of the realm of academics and saber-waving standards advocates and placed them squarely and confidently in the realm of mainstream.

## On Grids and Layouts

Layouts come from the practice of designing with grids. By dividing up a page into logical, repeating sections, you can bring order to chaos. With humans looking at the page and wanting to get on with their lives, content needs to be organized into a sane presentation. Grids and, by extension, the layouts they create allow you to create that presentation.

An excellent example of layouts in everyday usage is the newspaper. Every day the front page has to promote dozens of stories and elements covering a range of subject matter.

Take a look at a newspaper layout like the one shown in Figure 9-1. Notice the amount of text on that one page, the different types of stories and information.

UTAH'S INDEPENDENT VOICE SINCE 1871

# The Salt Lake Tribune

« WWW.SLTRIB.

LAKERS 123, JAZZ 109: UTAH DOESN'T GET MUCH OF A CHANCE, D1

BYU IN JERUSALEM

A quiet life in the heart of the biblical world, C1

TOP INVESTMENT SCAMS TO AVOID

If it looks too good, think again. E1

SATURDAY ✧ DECEMBER 29, 2007

Pakistan on fire

## A volatile goodbye to Bhutto

As unrest spreads across the nation, officials claim an extremist linked to al-Qaida is behind the assassination

LARKANA, Pakistan — Waving colorful party flags and venting rage at the government, tens of thousands of followers of Benazir Bhutto gave her a boisterous farewell at her funeral Friday. A day after the former prime minister's assassination, unrest spread to many parts of the country, and the government blamed the killing on an Islamic extremist linked to al-Qaida.

With a minimum of formal ritual, Bhutto's coffin was lowered into a grave dug in the floor of the Bhutto family's marble-domed mausoleum. Mourners crowded close to the coffin,

See BHUTTO DEATH, A10

Backers of slain opposition leader Benazir Bhutto chant slogans during a protest rally in Multan, Pakistan, on Friday. Rampaging protesters burned train stations and looted banks.

Farewell, friend – or beat it, blowhard?

## ROCKY'S WAY

**Looking back »** The outgoing mayor acknowledges there were mistakes, but says all major goals were "completed." A6

**What's ahead »** No public office and no leaving Utah for D.C. — grass-roots work on human rights and climate change. A6

## Life after Anderson: Love him, loathe him, but Salt Lake City will never be the same

By Derek P. Jensen

Brandishing a baritone that belies his body — and a muscular mind to match — Rocky Anderson wrestled a political revolution out of once-sedate Salt Lake City during a quixotic eight-year run defined by equal parts passion and polarity.

Yes, he launched after-school programs, removed freight trains from west-side neighborhoods, added center-of-the-street parking downtown, steered Utah's capital through a triumphant Olympics and trotted out life-saving pedestrian upgrades.

But by far the mayor's most memorable moments — as he prepares to exit the civic stage next week — sprang from big issues and sometimes bigger clashes: The Main Street Plaza. Legacy Highway. Global warming. President Bush. The Iraq war.

Anderson shouldered a global agenda that jolted the local landscape. As a consequence of his substance and his style, the capital's image and brand of governance were recast.

"He's created a major-league city," says Robert Newman, dean of University of Utah Humanities.

But Anderson's legacy forever may be misunderstood by his paradox. He strived tirelessly to fos

See ROCKY, A6

"Anderson's legacy is planting the seed of hope that Salt Lake City could actually become an interesting place to live."

DAVID KELLER
Downtown resident and director of the Center for the Study of Ethics at UVSC

ANDERSON'S LEGACY » From orange flags and Olympics to "Impeach Bush" rallies, A6

SLTRIB.COM » See a gallery of photos covering Rocky Anderson's eight-year tenure as mayor.

Deadly blaze

## Son dies trying to help father

Taylorsville man doesn't know his dad had jumped to safety, is killed as he re-enters the burning house

By Melinda Rogers

Panicked shouts jolted Keith Hafen from his Taylorsville home Thursday night. Seconds after running down his driveway, Hafen saw the house next door on fire and witnessed neighbor John Easterbrook leaping from a second-story window to escape the flames.

"I could see fire and smoke coming out of their house and heard yelling," said Hafen, who has lived next door to the Easterbrooks for more than 25 years. "It was scary. It was upsetting to see all this happen."

Easterbrook and his wife Connie escaped the blaze that gutted their two-story house at 3261 W. Bitter Root Place (4890 South) shortly

Slade Easterbrook
Died in the fire

See TAYLORSVILLE, A10

A surprise veto

## Bush rejects defense bill, says it may bring pricey lawsuits to Iraq

**Bush stops a defense bill** he had been pushing for because of an obscure provision that could expose Iraqi government to billions of dollars in legal claims dating to Saddam's rule. **NATION, A8**

Coming Sunday

*Tribune* honors Utahns of 2007

It was a year that saw three of Utah's most horrific events – the Trolley Square murders, the savage wildfires and the Crandall Canyon mine disaster. *The Salt Lake Tribune* honors as Utahns of the Year those who protect the innocent, tend to the battered and broken, fight the fires and claw through fallen coal in search of their vanished comrades.

Inside

Weather Page E8

Light snow north,

Samoan adoption scandal

## Affidavits: Parents knew they were giving up rights

High-ranking attorneys can prove we're right, say accused Utah couple

By Pamela Manson

A Utah couple accused in an international adoption scandal say four of Samoa's most prestigious attorneys can help prove their innocence.

But the lawyers will not travel to the United States to testify because they fear being charged themselves, according to Scott and Karen Banks of Wellsville.

So the couple are asking a federal judge to allow future jurors to read four sworn affidavits from the men describing how Samoan birth parents were repeatedly told they were giving up legal rights to their children and should not expect to see them again.

The affidavits take aim at one of the prosecution's key claims: that parents were duped into putting their children up for adoption in America.

"Not only are the affidavits highly probative, they may be the only truly probative evidence available to the defense on how the formal

See ADOPTION, A12

**Figure 9-1: A newspaper layout with numerous columns.**

*Photo by theogeo / http://tinyurl.com/3b3poy*

If the content were not placed into a multicolumn layout, as shown in Figure 9-2, the front page of the newspapers would be hard on the eyes. (Also, newspapers are able to provide more content on one page thanks to designers.)

UTAH'S INDEPENDENT VOICE SINCE 1871

The Salt Lake Tribune

« WWW.SLTRIB.

LAKERS 123, JAZZ 109: UTAH DOESN'T GET MUCH OF A CHANCE, D1

BYU IN JERUSALEM

A quiet life in the heart of the biblical world, C1

TOP INVESTMENT SCAMS TO AVOID

If it looks too good, think again. E1

SATURDAY ✦ DECEMBER 29, 2007

Pakistan on fire

A volatile goodbye to Bhutto

As unrest spreads across the nation, officials claim an extremist linked to al-Qaida is behind the assassination

Farewell, friend – or beat it, blowhard?

ROCKY'S WAY

Looking back »
The outgoing mayor acknowledges there were mistakes, but says all major goals were "completed." A6

What's ahead »
No public office and no leaving Utah for D.C. — grass-roots work on human rights and climate change. A6

Life after Anderson: Love him, loathe him, but Salt Lake City will never be the same

"Anderson's legacy is planting the seed of hope that Salt Lake City could actually become an interesting place to live."

DAVID KELLER

ANDERSON'S LEGACY » From orange flags and Olympics to "Impeach Bush" rallies, A6

SLTRIB.COM » See a gallery of photos covering Rocky Anderson's eight-year tenure as mayor.

Deadly blaze

Son dies trying to help father

Taylorsville man doesn't know his dad had jumped to safety, is killed as he re-enters the burning house

A surprise veto

Bush rejects defense bill, says it may bring pricey lawsuits to Iraq

Coming Sunday

Tribune honors Utahns of 2007

Inside

Weather

Samoan adoption scandal

Affidavits: Parents knew they were giving up rights

High-ranking attorneys can prove we're right, say accused Utah couple

Figure 9-2: The columns are highlighted.

While columns have been used in print for ages, they can do wonders for the Web as well. For example, the MidSouth Federal Credit Union went through a redesign of its site; the old version is shown in Figure 9-3.

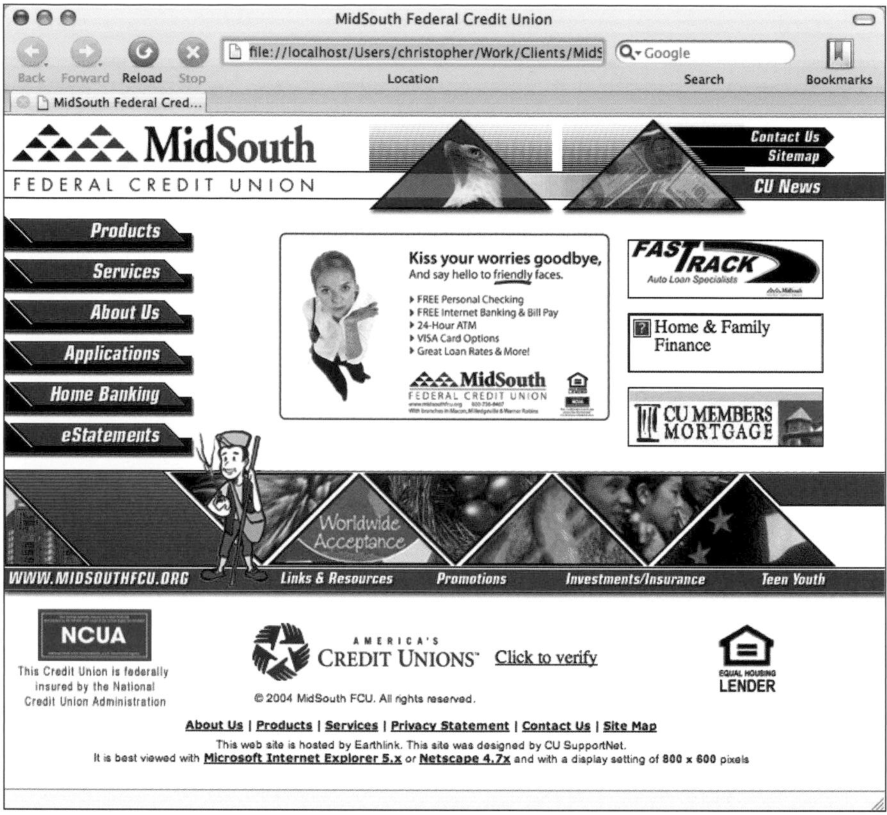


**Figure 9-3:** The previous design of the Web site for the MidSouth Federal Credit Union.

As you can see, the home page elements are arranged to avoid the use of white space. Elements are placed into almost any open spot. While triangular or 45-degree angle elements are repeated, this is being done at the expense of presenting the content in a coherent manner.

In the redesign, which introduced a two-column fixed-width layout, as shown in Figure 9-4, MidSouth's site presentation of the content is brought to order. The navigation menu is tamed and orderly, but not hidden, and the content is allowed to breathe.

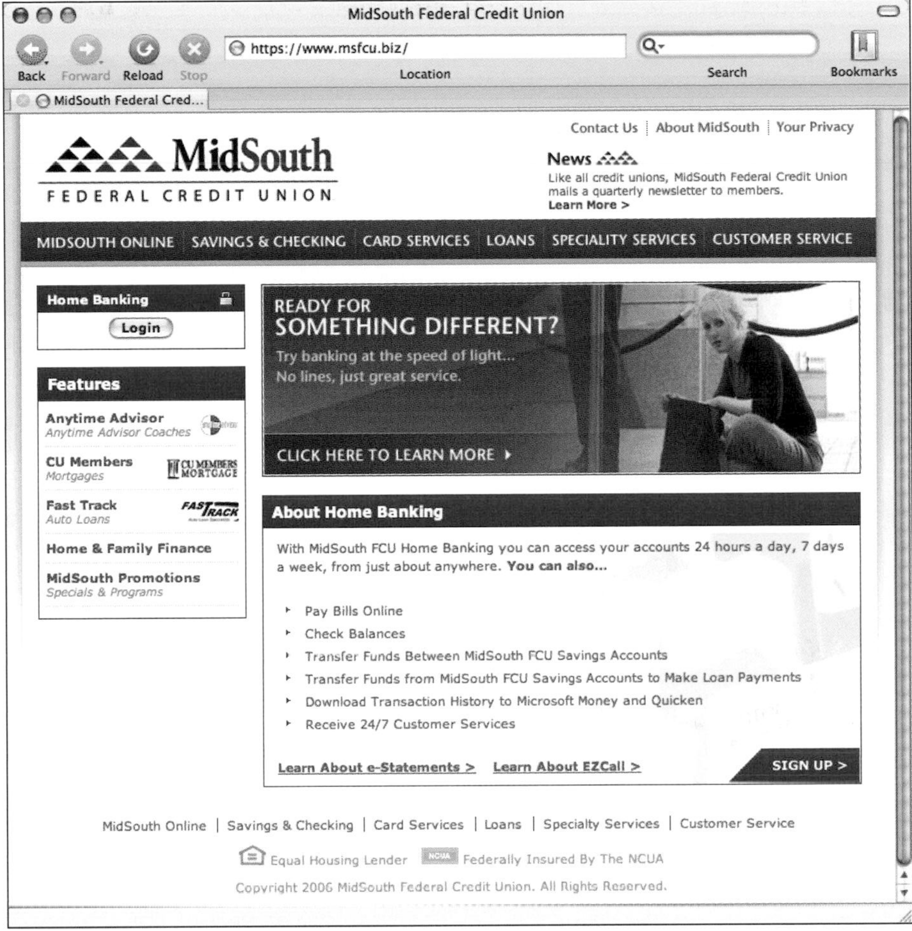


**Figure 9-4:** The redesign uses a two-column design solution.

# Doing What Print Can't

One thing that print design can't do, which the Web medium can, is allow for *fluid* layouts. Take a look at Molly E. Holzschlag's Web site (see molly.com), as shown in Figure 9-5.

Aside from the fresh color scheme, Molly's site design is eminently flexible. Rather than succumbing to the temptation of building a fixed-width design, Molly's built its site to accommodate the user's preferred window size. See Figure 9-6, which demonstrates how the main, middle column looks when it's stretched to the maximum width for a 1280×600 resolution.

Let's look at how a three-column layout like the one used on Molly's site can be created.

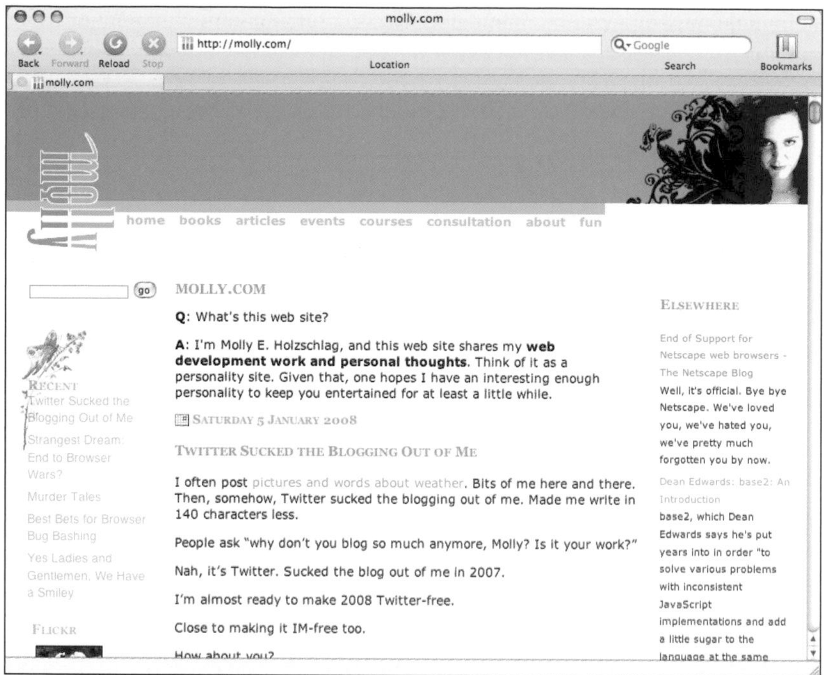


**Figure 9-5: Molly E. Holzshlag's Web site.**

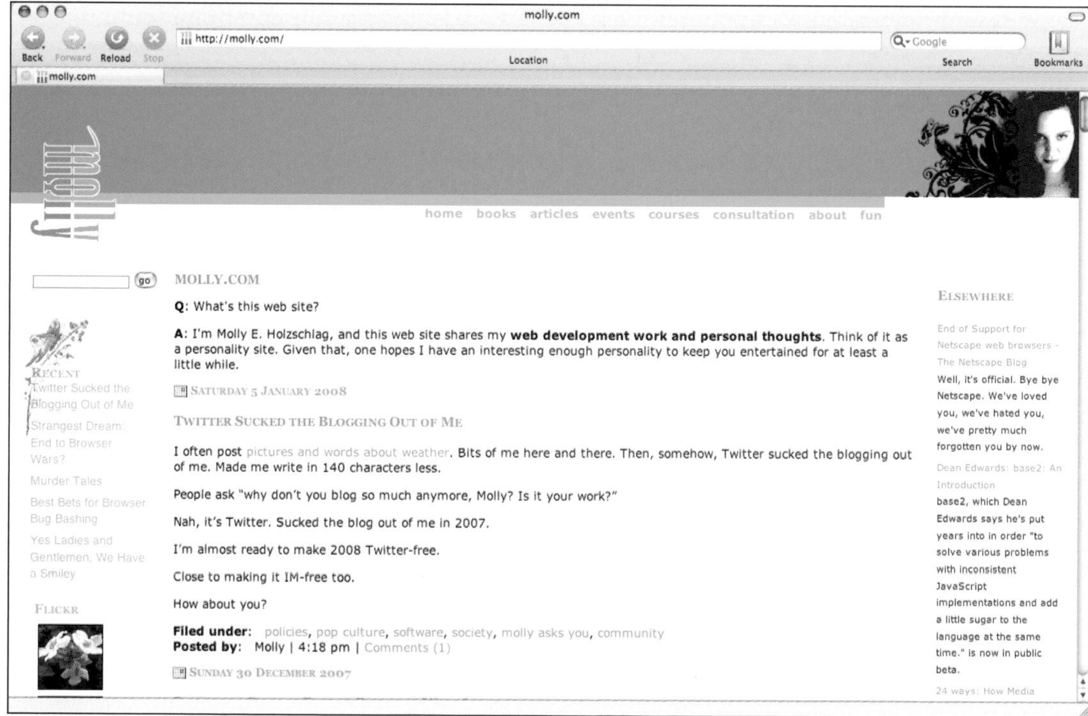


**Figure 9-6: The Web site's layout stretches to accommodate a larger resolution.**

# CSS Positioning: The Fundamentals

Before you begin replicating Molly's layout, you should first step back and examine some of the mechanics behind CSS positioning. As you've seen in previous chapters, every element in your markup occupies a position within the document's flow.

*Block-level elements* — such as headings, `div`s, lists, and paragraphs — are stacked like boxes atop each other, each expanding horizontally to occupy the full width of their containing element.

On the other hand, *inline elements* are laid out horizontally within a containing block-level element, one after another. Some examples of inline elements include links, images, and phrase elements such as `em` and `strong`.

Initially, each element in your unstyled document is considered to have a "static" position — in other words, its position has not been modified from its default. That's why that paragraph is placed directly beneath that `h2`, and why that image appears within that `div`.

The official term for this default positioning scheme is the "normal flow" of the document. If you look at an unstyled HTML document, you see that boxes elements (such as `p`, `h1`, or `div`) "flow" vertically within their containing block, each stacked immediately below the preceding one. However, inline boxes (such as `span`, `a`, or `img`) simply flow horizontally within their container. And without any additional style rules from you, this default flow remains intact.

But, of course, we're about to change all that. I'm nothing if not predictable.

What makes CSS such a compelling layout tool is its ability to override these default positioning rules and create incredibly complex layouts without opening a single `td`. An element can be removed from its normal, static position by writing a simple CSS selector that sets a new value for — you guessed it — the element's `position` property, like this:

```
p {
 position: absolute;
}
```

Besides `static`, there are three valid values for this `position` property:

- ❑ `fixed`
- ❑ `relative`
- ❑ `absolute`

Setting the property to any of the three non-`static` values gives you a different means of removing the element from its place in the normal document flow and positioning it in another section of the document.

Let's examine these two property values — relative and absolute positioning — and the relationship between them, and how you can better apply them to your own sites' designs.

## Absolutely Fabulous Positioning

When absolutely positioned, an element's position is specified through some combination of `top`, `right`, `bottom`, and `left` properties, as shown here:

```
div#content {
 position: absolute;
left: 10px;
top: 100px;
}
```

Here, the `left` and `top` properties specify offsets for the `div` with an `id` attribute of "content." Rather than appearing sandwiched between the block-level elements immediately before and after it in the markup, the content `div` is instead removed from the document flow. But *where* is it placed, you ask?

To find an answer, look at the following markup structure, which, for the sake of brevity, is placed within the `body` of a valid XHTML document:

```
<div id="outer">
 <p>This is a paragraph in the <cite>outer</cite> block.</p>
 <div id="inner">
  <p>This is a paragraph in the <cite>inner</cite> block.</p>
 </div>
</div>
```

These are two rather unassuming `div`s, one (with an `id` of "inner") nested inside the other (named, cleverly enough, "outer"). Each `div` contains one child paragraph — nothing award-winning here. Just to move this beyond the realm of angle brackets and into a screenshot or two, apply some basic style to this markup:

```
#outer {
 background: #DDF;
 border: 4px solid #006;
 height: 300px;
 margin: 120px 20px 0;
}

#inner {
 background: #FDC;
 border: 4px solid #930;
}
```

Again, these two selectors aren't designed to floor clients. The first rule applies to the `div` with an `id` of "outer." You're setting an oh-so-comely blue border and background to the `div`, setting its height to 300 pixels, and then increasing its margins to offset it from its normal position (120 pixels down, and 20 pixels on either horizontal side). The second rule simply applies a light red background color and matching border to the `inner div`.

Yes, that's right: red on blue. I never said I was discriminating when tossing together code examples.

But before you slam this book shut in a fit of palette-driven indignation, let's examine how these two elements appear on the page. As you can see in Figure 9-7, I've taken the liberty of applying some basic type information to the document as well (Times New Roman is *so* 1995). But with the (somewhat garish, I'll admit) colors and borders activated, you can see that the two `div`s are placed in the normal document flow — the `inner` block is a child of the `outer` block, and the page's current display reflects that.

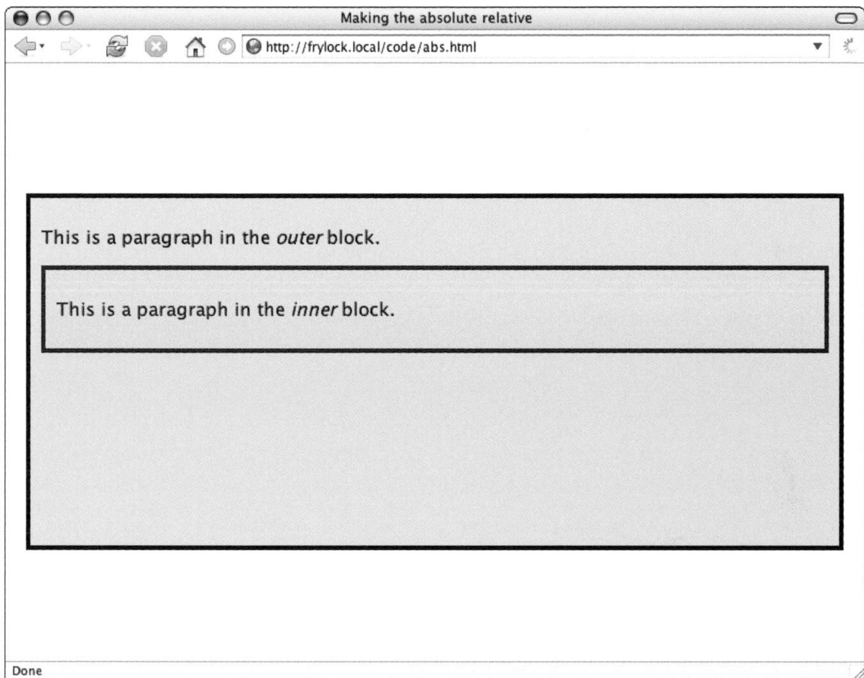


**Figure 9-7: The bland-looking elements in the normal document flow.**

However, by using CSS to change the value of the inner element's `position` property, the design doesn't *have* to reflect this parent-child relationship. You can add three brief lines to the `#inner` selector:

```
#inner {
 background: #FDC;
 border: 4px solid #930;
 position: absolute;
 right: 20px;
 top: 20px;
}
```

The difference is rather marked, as Figure 9-8 shows. You've visually broken the parent-child relationship between the two `div`s. While the inner block is still a child of the outer one in the markup, CSS is used to override the former's position in the normal document flow. Instead, it's positioned absolutely, offset 20 pixels from the topmost and rightmost edges of the `body` of the document.

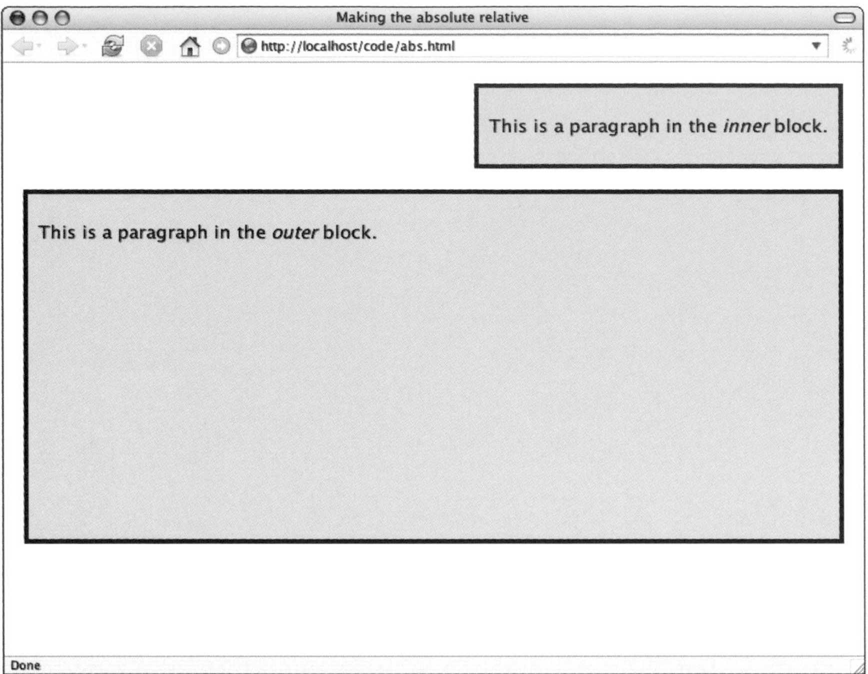


**Figure 9-8: In the markup, the topmost block is a child of the bottom one. However, using `position: absolute;` removes the block from the document flow and positions it relative to the viewport.**

The inner block typically appears in the normal flow of the document, in the context established by the other block-level elements that surround it in the markup. The rule has *redefined* that context and placed it in one that is relative to the boundaries of the browser window. This is why the `body` root of our document — the `html` element — is also known as the *initial containing block*, as it typically provides the positioning context for all elements contained within it.

Furthermore, this new positioning context for `#inner` has redefined that of its child elements — namely, the paragraph contained therein. In other words, you not only repositioned the `div` but also any and all elements contained therein. This becomes a bit more apparent if you add a few more paragraphs to the absolutely positioned block, as shown in Figure 9-9.

When two new paragraphs are added to `#inner` (the absolutely positioned block), they inherit their parent's positioning context — which is all a fancy way of saying that since their parent block is absolutely positioned, it will expand to contain its new children.

Another important thing to note in Figure 9-9 is that after increasing the height of the absolutely positioned block, the outer block is partially obscured. Remember that by applying `position` to the block, you removed it from the normal flow — and in the case of absolutely positioned elements, the browser doesn't reserve any space for it within the document. Because of this, absolutely positioned elements are designed to overlap other elements on the page, be they positioned or not. This is a very important issue to consider when building a layout with absolute positioning, and one I'll return to later in greater detail.

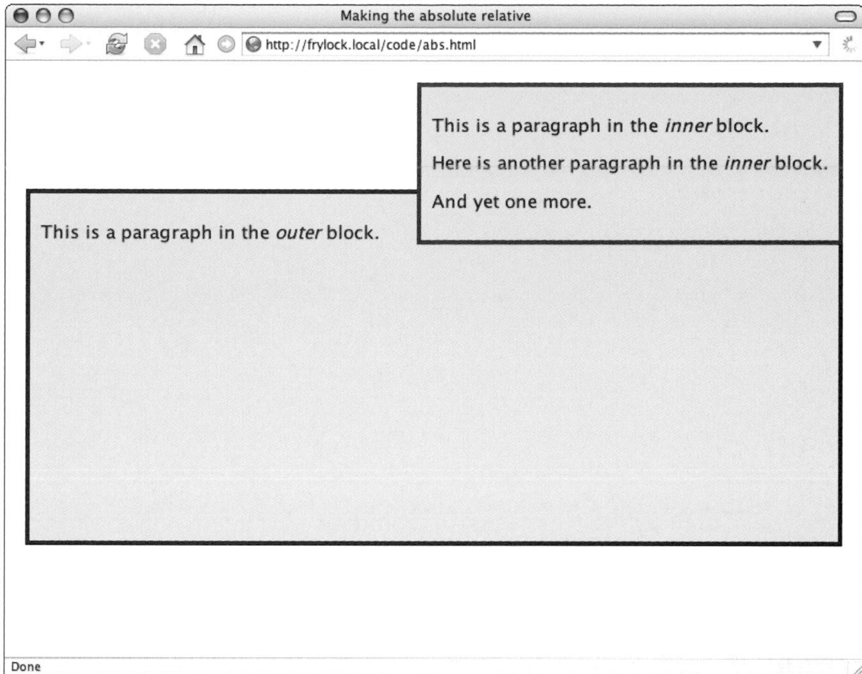


**Figure 9-9: Adding more content to the absolutely positioned block demonstrates just how far you've come.**

## Positioning That's Absolutely Relative

But what if you want to exercise a bit more control over the position of that inner block? What if you don't want to position it relative to the browser window, but to the outer `div`? As it turns out, the absolute positioning you've seen so far is only the *default* behavior. If an absolutely positioned element isn't placed within another positioned element — that is, if all of its ancestor elements are in their default, static position — then it will be placed as in Figure 9-4: relative to the boundaries established by the initial containing block, the `body` element.

If you noticed that the last sentence contained quite a few "if"s," I'm happy I haven't put everyone to sleep. So, if your absolutely positioned element *is* contained within another positioned element, what happens then? Let's see what happens when you apply this bit of logic to the outer `div`, which, as we determined previously, is the parent to your absolutely positioned element:

```
#outer {
 background: #DDF;
 border: 4px solid #006;
 height: 300px;
 margin: 120px 20px 0;
 position: relative;
}
```

As shown in Figure 9-10, the changes to inner `div` are quite striking. Because the outermost `div` is now a positioned element, it establishes a new positioning context for all absolutely positioned descendant elements — in this case, the `#inner` block. So, the offset of `right: 20px;` and `top: 20px;` no longer position the inner `div` in relation to the `root` of our markup, but to the container `div` to which you applied the `position: relative;` rule. Just to hammer the point home, let's change the `top: 20px;` in the `#inner` selector to `bottom: 20px;`, like this (see Figure 9-11):

```
#inner {
 background: #FDC;
 border: 4px solid #930;
 position: absolute;
 right: 20px;
 bottom: 20px;
}
```

Rather than creating a vertical offset between the inner box's top edge and that of its parent, you've positioned it 20 pixels from the bottom — all by changing one line in the selector. As you continue through this chapter, I'll discuss the benefits of this approach in more detail. For now, this relationship between absolutely positioned elements within relatively positioned containers will serve as the basis for your work creating a flexible, three-column layout in the style of Molly.com.

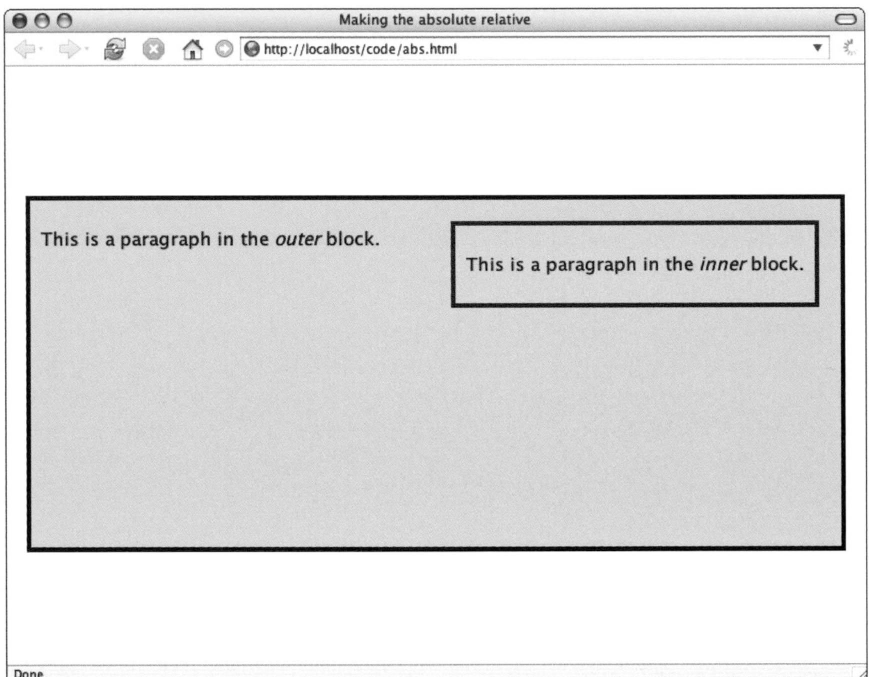


**Figure 9-10: By setting the outer block to `position: relative;` the inner block is now positioned in relation to its parent.**

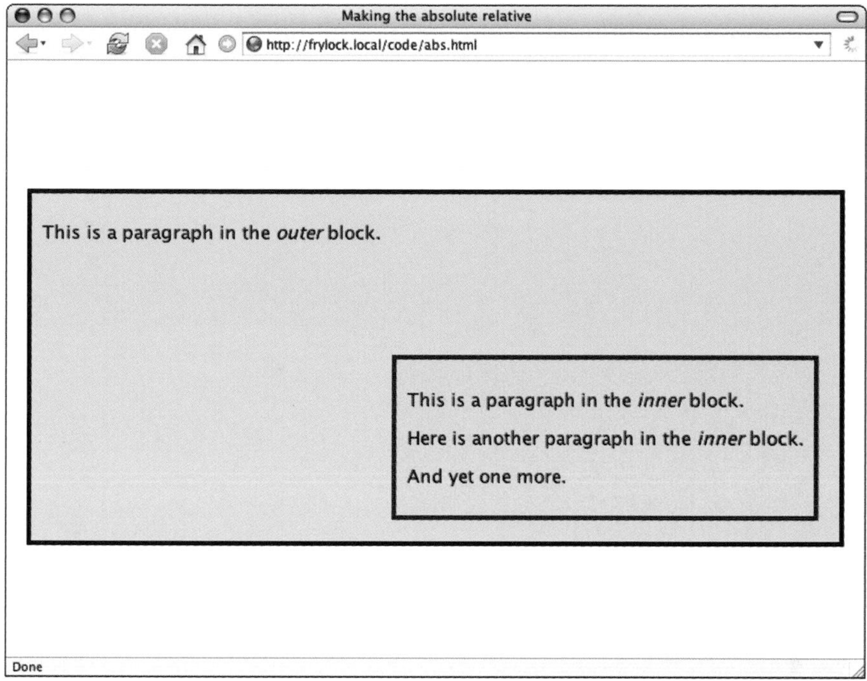


**Figure 9-11: Courtesy of CSS: bulletproof bottom-edge positioning. Ain't technology grand?**

# Building Three Columns: Laying the Foundation

Just as when you converted the Harvard University home page to an all-CSS/XHTML layout (see Chapter 1), the three-column layout must be founded upon lightweight, well-meaning markup. To do so, begin by taking a quick inventory of the content areas on the page (see Figure 9-12).

This chapter focuses on the following primary areas of the home page's layout:

- The horizontal header that spans the top of the page
- The primary center column, which contains high-priority content and other features of interest
- The left- and right-hand columns, which house such auxiliary content as subnavigation, advertising banners, and the like

Think of each of these top-level blocks as a container for other content. Within each block, you can store other discrete chunks of content, and apply CSS rules to precisely control the presentation of each.

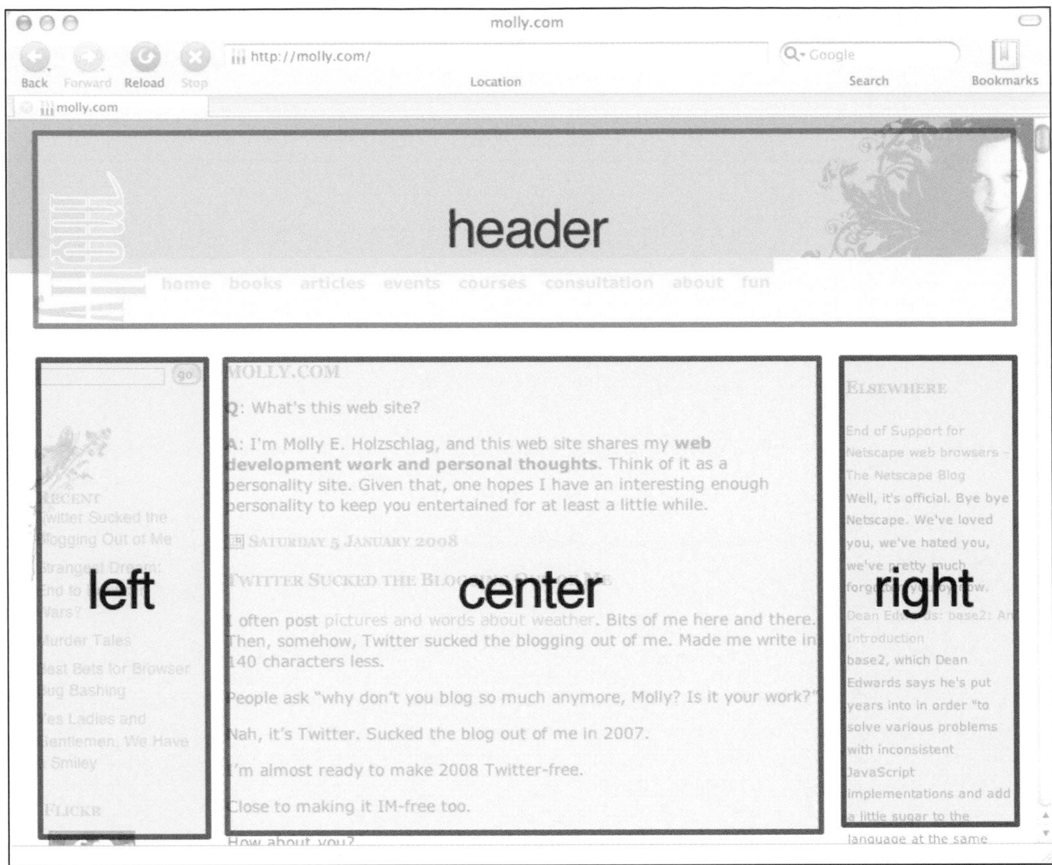


**Figure 9-12:** Identifying the areas of content you need to incorporate into markup. (The footer's not shown because of the length of the page.)

Establishing this flexible, three-column layout is the primary goal of this chapter. Once that has been established, you can style the finer points of the design to your heart's delight. Therefore, you focus on establishing this layout framework — of header, content, left- and right-hand columns — to prepare the page for a truly professional-looking design.

## Writing the XHTML: From Mockup to Markup

With this in mind, create a basic markup document to reflect this framework, as shown in Listing 9-1.

**Listing 9-1: Markup Foundation for Three-Column Layout**

```
<!DOCTYPE html PUBLIC "-//W3C//DTD XHTML 1.0 Transitional//EN"
    "http://www.w3.org/TR/xhtml1/DTD/xhtml1-transitional.dtd">
<html xmlns="http://www.w3.org/1999/xhtml">
<head>
```

```
<title>My 3-column layout</title>
<meta http-equiv="Content-Type" content="text/html; charset=utf-8" />
</head>
<body>
<div id="header">
  <p>How do you like them apples?</p>
  <hr />
</div>
<div id="left">
  <h2>This is the left column.</h2>
  <p>Some basic information goes here.</p>
  <!-- More content here -->
</div>
<div id="right">
  <h2>This is the right column.</h2>
  <ul>
    <li>Did you know that lists rock?</li>
    <li>They do.</li>
    <li>Quite a bit.</li>
  </ul>
  <!-- More content here -->
</div>
<div id="content">
  <h1>Welcome to my page layout.</h1>
  <p>Certe, inquam, pertinax non ero tibique, si mihi probabis ea...</p>
  <!-- More content here -->
</div>
<div id="footer">
  <hr />
  <p>Them apples were <em>tasty</em>.</p>
</div>
</body>
</html>
```

Reflecting the three areas of the content inventory in Figure 9-12, you simply marked up the four divisions in your page as such — that is to say, by using the `div` element. Each of those `div`s has been given a unique `id`, which in turn corresponds to the section of the document it represents: the first `div` is "header," the next "left," and so on. I've also taken the liberty of including a "footer" block at the bottom of the page.

> *The `id`s used in the sample markup here (and throughout the rest of the chapter) are used for demonstration purposes. By naming your elements according to how they might look, or where they might be positioned on-screen, you're effectively wedding your markup to one particular presentation. Should you ever redesign your site, what happens when your `#left div` suddenly is displayed on the right of the page? Or on the top?*
>
> *Instead, you should consider the meaning of the content contained in your elements, and name those elements accordingly. Perhaps `#right` would be better described as `#advertising`, or `#left` as `#subnav`. There are no right answers here; instead, you should make your names as descriptive as possible, ensuring an even cleaner separation of structure from style.*

Within each section of the page, you settled on some simple (and admittedly, pretty arbitrary) content to serve as placeholders. However, even when coding gibberish, you try to keep your code well meaning: The most important header on the page has been tagged with an `h1`, the titles of the left and right columns have been accorded a place next in line with `h2`, and the remainder of the page's text has been marked up with proper list and paragraph elements. Without any style rules, your markup looks pretty unimpressive indeed (see Figure 9-13).

How do you like them apples?

This is the left column.
Some basic information goes here.
This is the right column.
• Did you know that lists rock?
• They do.
• Quite a bit.
Welcome to my page layout.
Certe, inquam, pertinax non ero tibique, si mihi probabis ea...

Them apples were *tasty*.

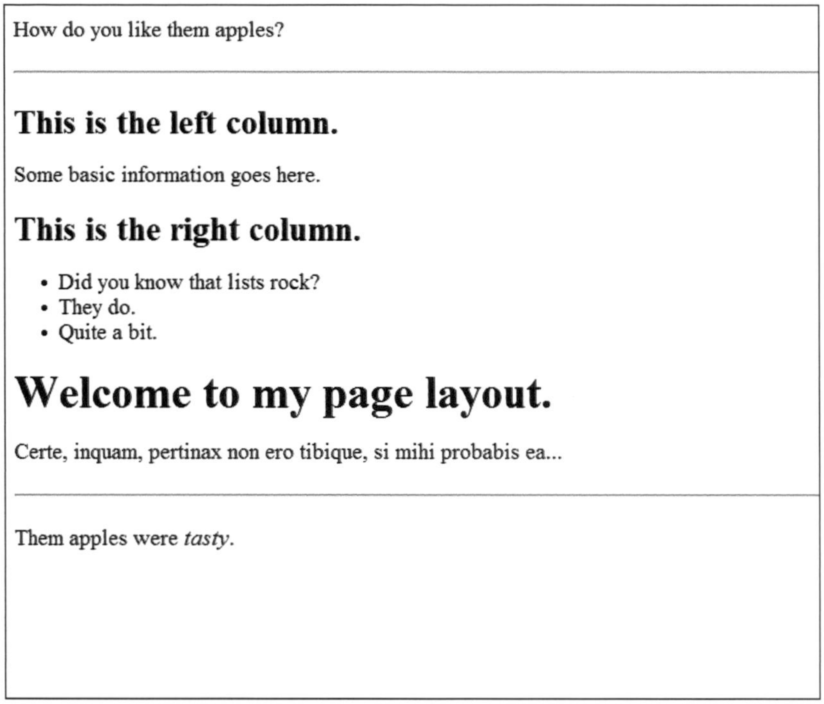

**Figure 9-13: The unstyled HTML document, replete with meaningful markup . . . and, well, meaningless text.**

It's at this stage that the need for well-meaning, semantically rich markup becomes a bit more evident. When using style sheets to control your site's presentation, it's important to consider exactly how users will access your content if they don't have a CSS-aware browser. When presented with a page that looks like the one in Figure 9-9, users might not see your meticulously planned design. However, they will *still be able to access your site's content*; hence the use of horizontal rules (`hr` elements) in the header and footer `div`s. While you use CSS later to hide these elements in your design, these elements can provide a nice break in the content for users on legacy, CSS-blind browsers.

For a bit more detail, take the two levels of heading elements you used in your markup. Sighted users surfing *sans* CSS will be able to quickly tell that "Welcome to my page layout" is weighted with more importance than the titles of our side columns. Screen readers will announce at what level the header has been marked up, which will enable nonsighted users to quickly orient themselves in the page's hierarchy. And, as accessibility advocates are quick to point out, the biggest blind user on the Web is Google — which is a trite way of saying that search engines don't care about presentation, only about content. Applying this kind of intelligent markup to your content not only helps human users navigate your pages but also helps search engines better understand how they should weight and index them.

# A Layer of Style

With that little digression out of the way, let's apply some basic presentational rules to your content, as shown in Listing 9-2.

**Listing 9-2: Applying Basic CSS Rules to a Document**

```
body {
 color: #000;
 font: 76%/1.5em "Lucida Grande", Verdana, Geneva, Helvetica, sans-serif;
 margin: 0;
 padding: 0;
}

h1, h2 {
 font-family: "Trebuchet MS", Verdana, Geneva, Helvetica, sans-serif;
 font-weight: normal;
 line-height: 1em;
 margin-top: 0;
}

#header {
 background-color: #DFD;
 border: 2px solid #060;
}

#footer {
 background-color: #FDD;
 border: 1px solid #C00;
}

#left, #right {
 background-color: #DDF;
 border: 2px solid #00C;
}

#header hr, #footer hr {
 display: none;
}
```

The first rule applies some basic color and type information to the `body` element, information that is inherited from each of its descendant elements in the document tree — that is, until we override it in the second rule. By applying a different `font-family` value to the header elements in our document (`h1` and `h2`), we can override the inheritance and apply a different style than the default. This should, we hope, give them a bit more visual prominence in our rough-cut design.

The next three rules apply borders and background colors to the main sections of your document: a bright green for your header, an eye-catching red for the footer block, and a striking blue for the left- and right-hand columns. You're going for contrast here, not panache — and as you can see from Figure 9-14, that's exactly what you have.

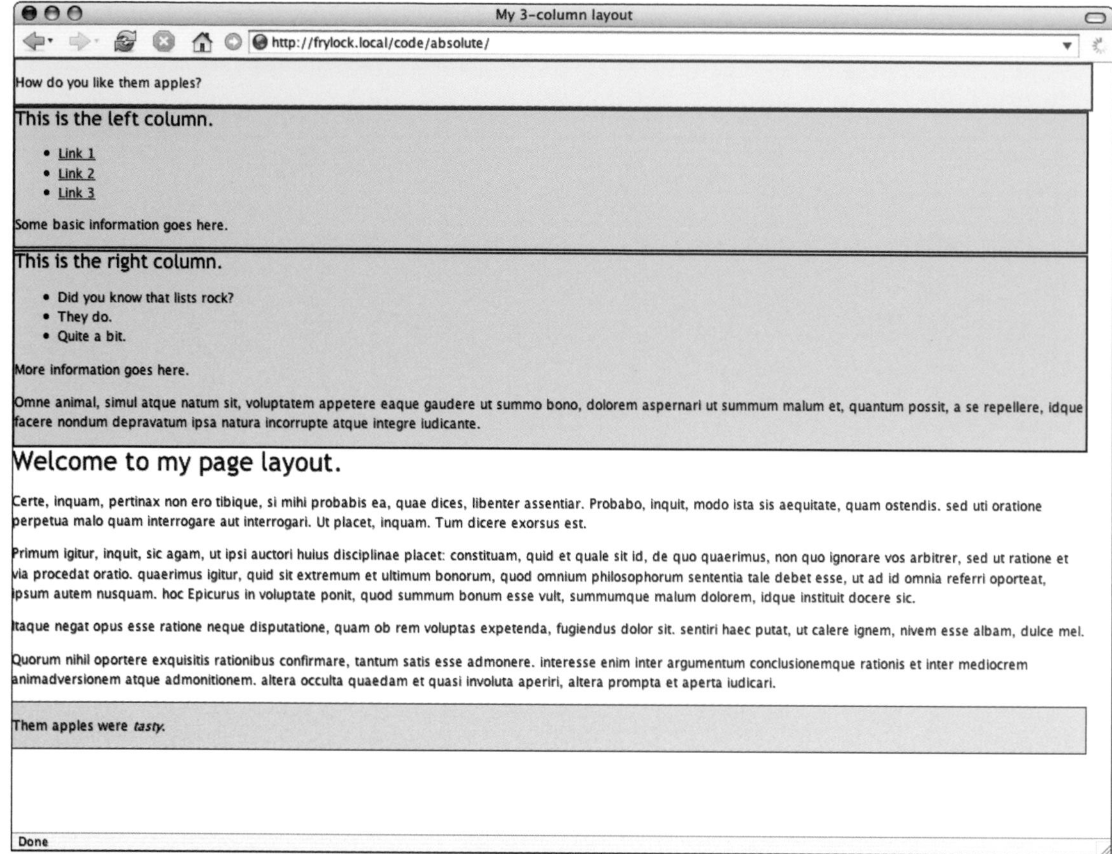


**Figure 9-14: You used CSS to apply some basic type and color information to your bare-bones HTML document.**

## *Get Your Offset On: Introducing the Positioning Rules*

With a clearer understanding of where the boundaries of your different content elements lie, you can now begin to flesh out the layout (see Figure 9-15):

```
#left {
 position: absolute;
 left: 0;
 top: 0;
 width: 175px;
}

#right {
 position: absolute;
 right: 0;
 top: 0;
 width: 175px;
}
```

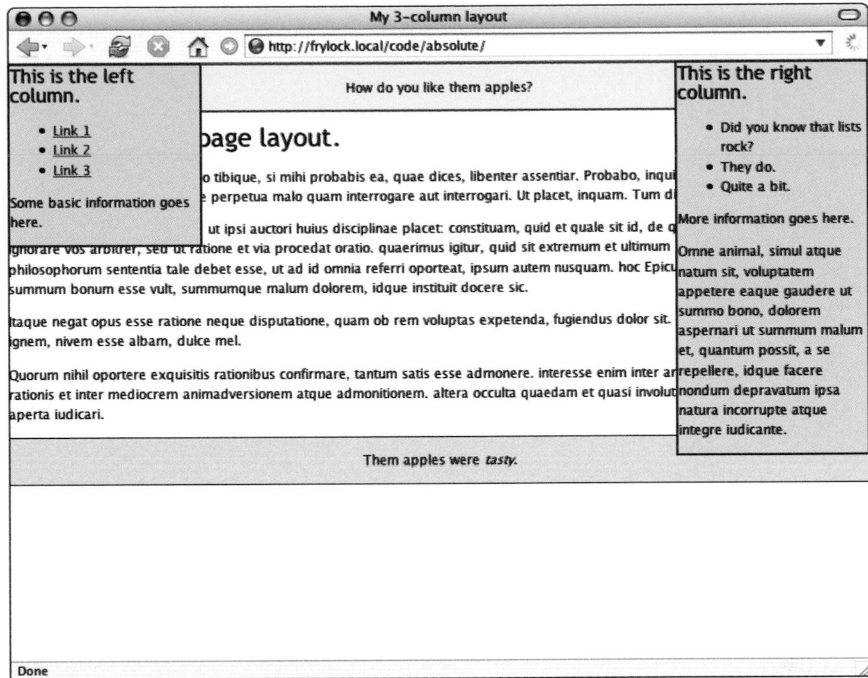


**Figure 9-15: Absolute positioning allows you to place the left and right columns — however, you're not out of the woods yet.**

These two selectors move the left and right blocks out of the normal document flow and position them absolutely. Each `div` has been given an explicit width of 175 pixels and is then catapulted to the top of the window (`top: 0;`). The horizontal offsets you've specified (`left: 0;` for `#left`, and `right: 0;` for — you guessed it — `#right`) further complete the effect and create the beginning of our three-column layout. The "left" and "right" blocks begin to live up to their names, and columns begin to take shape.

But, as you can see, the layout is far from complete. The left- and right-hand columns overlap the header, footer, and content `div`s. By applying absolute positioning to these two blocks, you've completely removed them from the normal document flow. This means that, while you are able to place them with pixel-perfect precision, the other elements in the document flow no longer need to reserve space for them. To get your layout up and running, you need to take a few extra steps.

## Remembering to Keep It Absolutely Relative

As you begin to puzzle through this issue, it's helpful to remember that the only reason the two blocks are positioned relative to the `html` element is that *they aren't descendants of a positioned element*. What happens if you change that?

In Listing 9-3, you wrap the three nonheader blocks in a `div` titled "`container`."

**Listing 9-3: Applying a Container to Your Markup**

```
<div id="header">
  <p>How do you like them apples?</p>
  <hr />
</div>
<div id="container">
  <div id="left">
    <h2>This is the left column.</h2>
    <!-- More content here -->
  </div>
  <div id="right">
    <h2>This is the right column.</h2>
    <!-- More content here -->
  </div>
  <div id="content">
    <h1>Welcome to my page layout.</h1>
    <!-- More content here -->
  </div>
</div>
<div id="footer">
  <hr />
  <p>Them apples were <em>tasty</em>.</p>
</div>
```

Granted, this container doesn't add much to the document's overall semantic worth — it's what markup purists might term a *presentational hack*, an element added for the sole and simple purpose of achieving some goal in your design. But with this container `div` in place, you can apply a three-line CSS selector upon it that will restore some measure of sanity to your site's layout (see Figure 9-16):

```
#container {
 position: relative;
}
```

Because the container `div` can now be considered a positioned element, it establishes a new context for all of the positioned elements that descend from it — you guessed it, the left and right column blocks. The left, top, and right offsets are no longer relative to the dimensions of the `html` element, but to those of the container `div`. This means that as the container element expands and grows horizontally, the left and right blocks will reposition themselves accordingly. If, say, the vertical size of the header block increases (see **Figure 9-17**), then the new horizontal position of the container `div` will be reflected in its absolutely positioned children.

But, while you made the header visible once again, the bulk of your page is still unreadable. The content and footer still must be "saved" from their absolutely positioned brethren. Given that the content area needs to be flexible, how exactly do you do that?

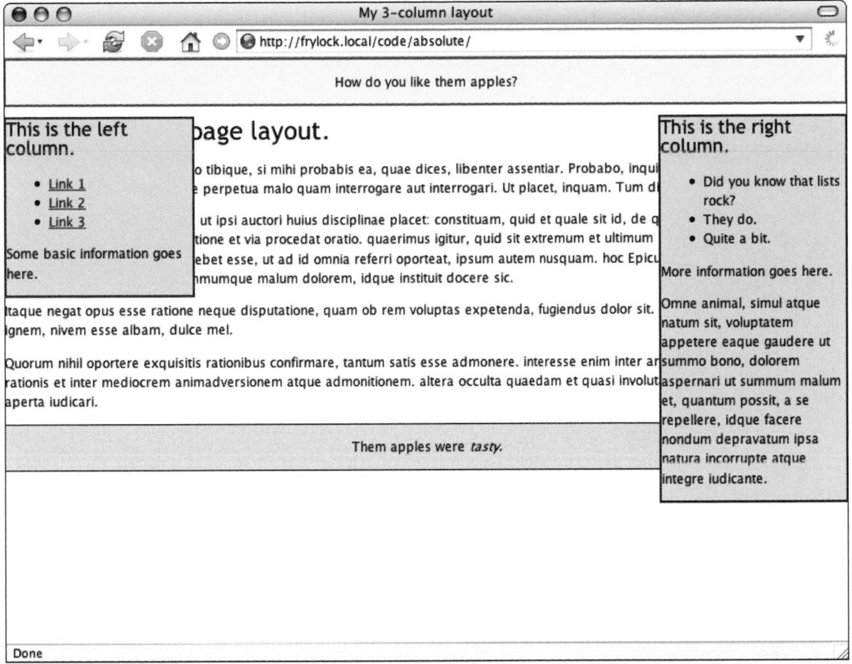


**Figure 9-16:** With `position: relative;` applied to your new container block, the left- and right-hand columns' top edges are now contained within their parent. But what about your page's content?

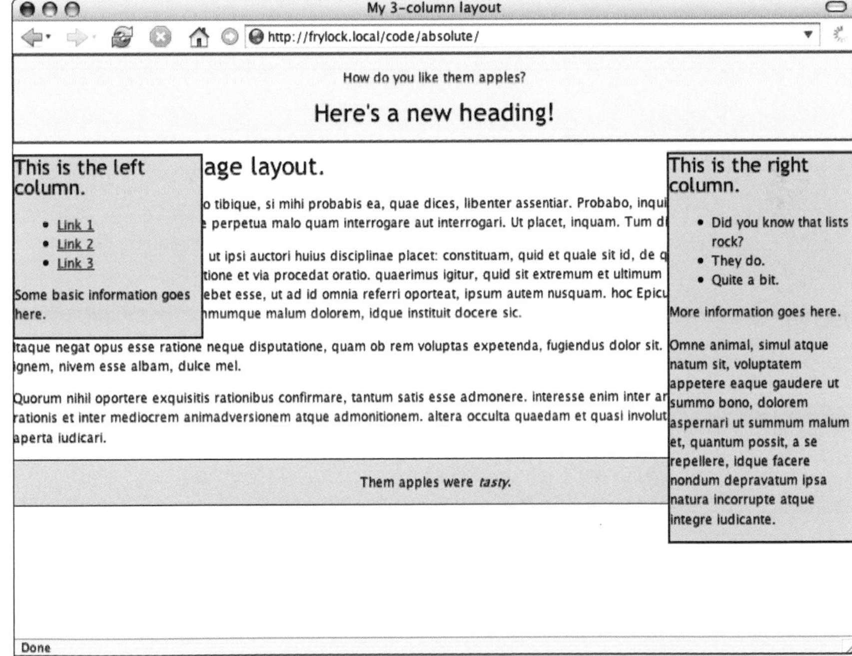


**Figure 9-17:** You can edit the content before the container without breaking your nascent layout.

Thankfully, you don't need to resort to any more fancy positioning footwork. Since you know that the width of each of the side columns is a fixed 175 pixels, you can use the box model to escape your content block, like this:

```
#content {
 margin: 0 190px;
}
```

Here, you settled upon 190 pixels for the two horizontal margin values: 175 pixels for the width of a side column, plus a healthy 15 pixels of white space. When you apply these margins to the left- and right-hand sides of the inner block, the calculated width of the block is compressed and fits nicely within the visible space between the two sidebar columns (see Figure 9-18).

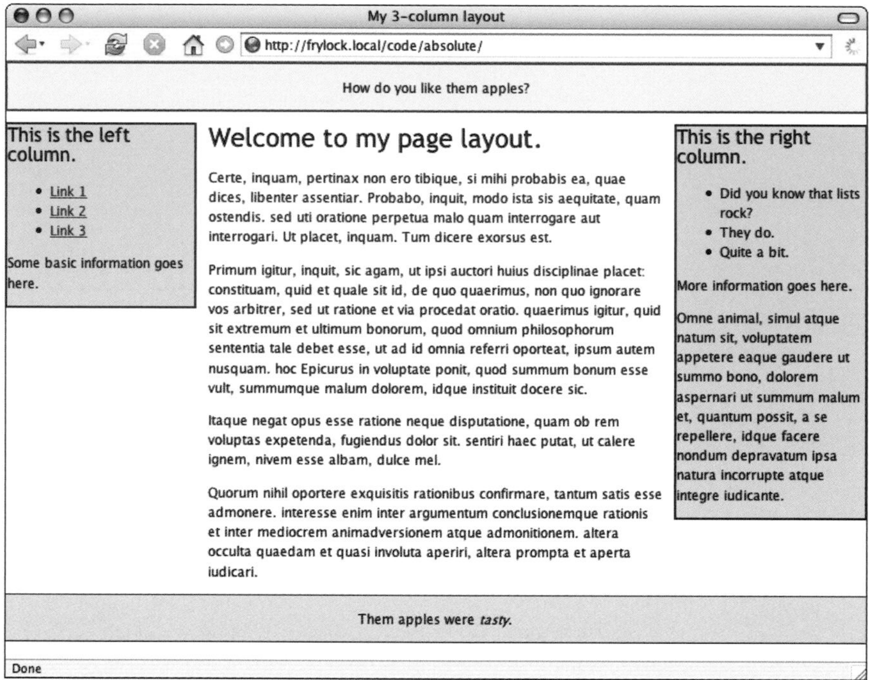


**Figure 9-18: By adding padding to the content `div` that corresponds to the width of the flanking side columns, you can create the illusion of a middle column distinct from those on either side.**

If you temporarily remove the columns from your markup (or hide them with CSS), you can better see what's at play here (see Figure 9-19). While the dimensions of the content block aren't affected by the two side `div`s (and vice versa), you used CSS to create the illusion that it does. Any changes to the width of the window will cause the entire page's contents to reposition themselves.

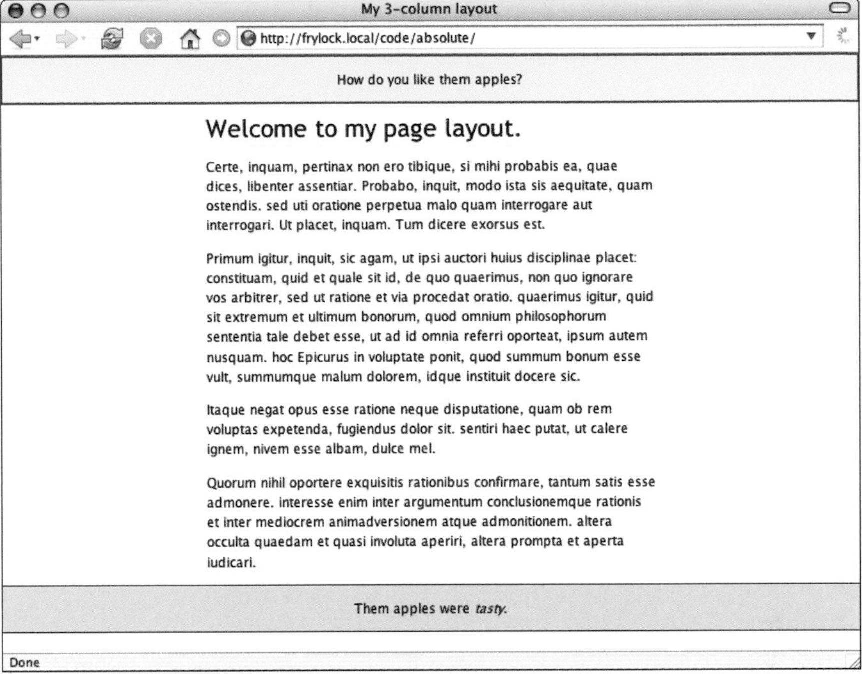


**Figure 9-19: Temporarily delete the left- and right-hand columns from your markup to see how the margins affect the content `div`.**

Sadly, you not nearly as done as **Figure 9-19** might lead you to believe. While you gained quite a bit of mastery over the top-edge and horizontal positioning of your page's layout, the footer you created is in a bit of a precarious spot. While your sidebar elements are *positioned* relative to the container `div`, they aren't *sized* relative to it. If their height exceeds that of their container, bad things can easily happen to elements that appear beneath them in the design. **Figure 9-20** shows this in action. Adding a few additional paragraphs to the right-hand block quickly obscures the footer again.

As you saw before, elements in the regular document flow (such as the header, content, and footer blocks) obey a different positioning context than absolutely positioned elements. This is what causes the overlap you first saw in the header and content blocks, and that you're faced with again on the footer. Thankfully, you can apply the same logic used on the content block. With your understanding of the box model, you can define margins around the footer `div`, once again creating the illusion that the middle "column" exists independently of those on either side of it.

So, in some fashion, you must apply the same 190-pixel-wide margins to both horizontal sides of the footer `div`. With the rest of your layout in place, you have two options:

- ❑ Write a new CSS selector that applies margins to the footer element.
- ❑ In the markup, move the footer `div` into the content block. This will then effectively contain the footer within its own calculated width.

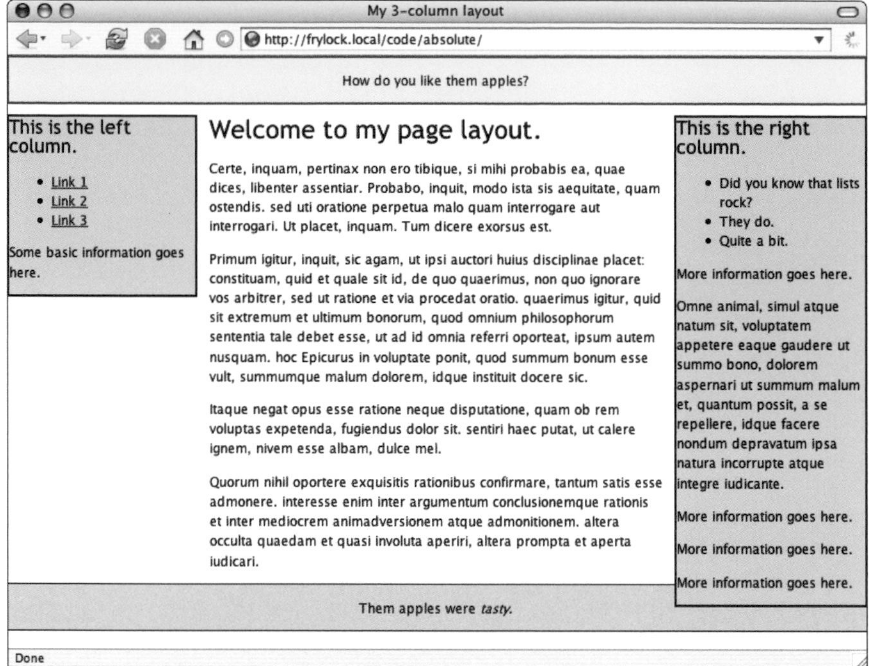


**Figure 9-20: Adding a few additional paragraphs causes an overlap between the absolutely positioned column and the static element that succeeds it.**

Either solution will have the same effect — whether the margins are applied to the footer `div` itself or a container, the effect will be the same (see Figure 9-21). The footer will always appear *between* the two sidebars, if not always below them.

To prevent any overlap from the absolutely positioned sidebars, you can place the footer `div` within the main content block. However, when the height of the sidebar columns exceeds the height of the central column, the footer will appear significantly higher than the bottom of the page.

This is a serious shortcoming of the absolute positioning model. An absolutely positioned element can be removed from the document flow and placed with uncanny position on the page, true — but what severely limits absolute positioning as a design tool is its blindness to the context of elements surrounding each positioned element. Absolutely positioned elements can overlap not only nonpositioned elements but also other `position: absolute;`–enabled blocks. This is why many CSS designers rely more heavily on the `float` model to control their layouts.

> *There are, in fact, non-CSS solutions to the "bottom blindness" of the absolute positioning model. Shaun Inman, a well-known Web designer and developer, wrote some rather elegant JavaScript (*`www.shauninman.com/mentary/past/absolutely_positive.php`*) to automatically clean up any overlap that resulted from absolute positioning.*
>
> *Of course, you should thoroughly test any workarounds (CSS, markup, or otherwise) before you apply them to your sites. While they may address the issue at hand, they add an additional layer of support and maintenance to which you should be prepared to commit.*

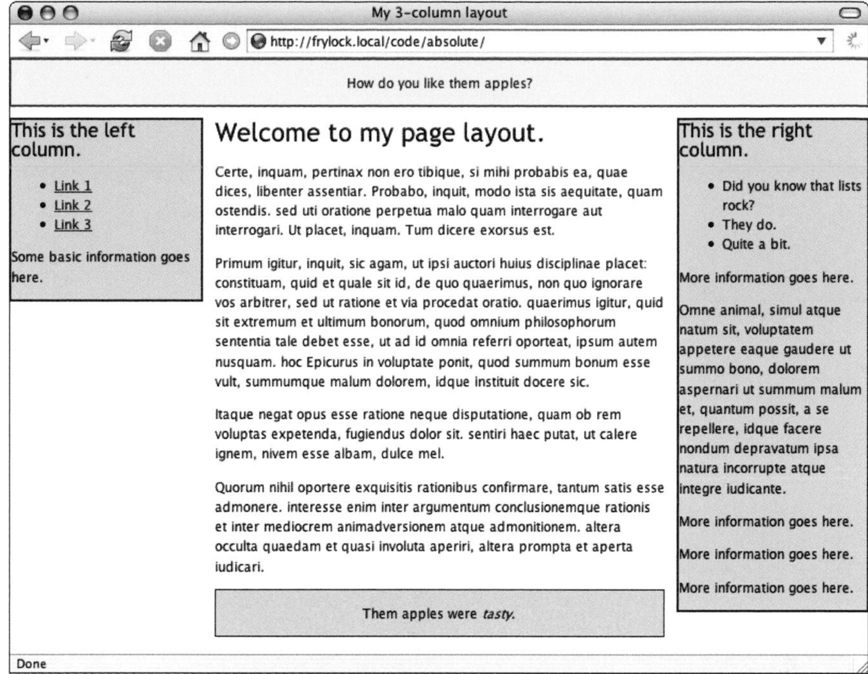


**Figure 9-21:** By applying the same margins to the footer `div`, you create the illusion of "escaping" it from the absolutely positioned elements that overlap it.

# Battling Browser Bugs

Where are you now? Well, your layout is looking sharp in your browser of choice, the markup is valid, and your style sheet is selecting with ninja-like precision. So, naturally, your design is looking perfect in all browsers known to humanity, right? Right?

If you honestly believed that, you'd be riding the slow boat to Depressionville more than you care to think about. While contemporary browsers *do* enjoy rich support for cascading style sheets, the level of support between them varies quite drastically — as I like to say, all browsers are created unequal. Unfortunately, valid code does not equal a perfect display across today's browser landscape. Because of the small army of bugs each browser brings to the table, you must thoroughly test your code across the board. And, more often than not, you must introduce browser-specific hacks to ensure that your design displays as intended for all members of your audience.

Let's take a look at two bugs in your layout and investigate some workarounds.

## Macintosh Internet Explorer 5

Upon opening your three-column layout in Internet Explorer 5 for the Macintosh, all seems to be displaying just fine — that is, until you notice the very bottom of the browser window (see Figure 9-22). To fix this little hiccup, let's see if you can't *isolate* the bug. Because you validated your style sheet and your markup, you can eliminate invalid code as the issue. From there, you triage your troubleshooting approach: First, try editing parts of the markup to see if you can restrict the issue to one particular section. From there, see if editing style rules applied to that section of the document resolves the bug. Once you establish *what* is causing the bug, you can better create and apply a patch to fix it.

> *Appendix D has some other great tips for working through browser-related issues.*

With this process firmly in mind, let's see if you can't isolate the bug in the markup. Since the issue is occurring on the right-hand side of the page, perhaps that's a good place to start. If you temporarily remove the entire "right" `div` from the markup and reload the page, your suspicions are confirmed: the horizontal scroll bar is gone! Removing the rightmost column establishes that it was at the heart of your scroll bar bug (see **Figure 9-23**). But now that you know the *where* of the bug, how do you determine exactly *what* is causing it? And more important, how do you fix it?

What follows is an occasionally frustrating goulash of coding, deleting, Web searching, and testing. Because each browser has its own set of idiosyncrasies, it can be frustrating to encounter each for the first time. Once you gain more experience with these bugs and how to work around them, the debugging process becomes much less time-intensive — and less frustrating as well. Until browsers have more uniform support for Web standards, however, such testing phases are going to be a fixture in any design project for some time to come. My guess is that you'll be waiting for that until a certain place freezes over, but the eternal optimist must press on.

After a bit of experimentation, you hit on a small breakthrough. Changing the value of the `right` property can make the scroll bar disappear. Specifically, anything greater than or equal to 15 pixels will fix the bug; anything less, and you're scrolling until the cows come home. But applying this fix isn't an ideal one, as your layout doesn't exactly look perfect (see **Figure 9-24**).

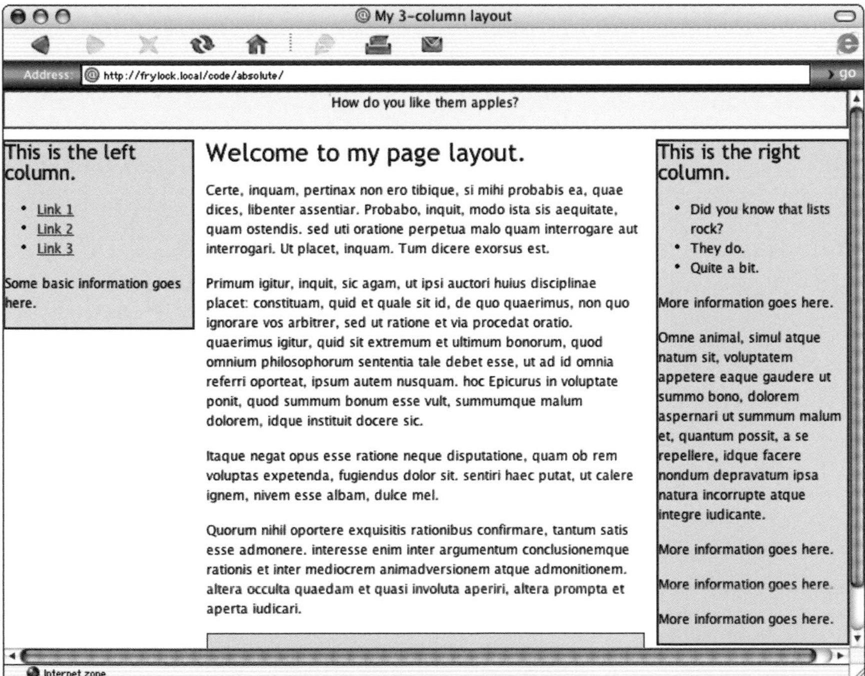


**Figure 9-22:** How did that horizontal scroll bar get there?

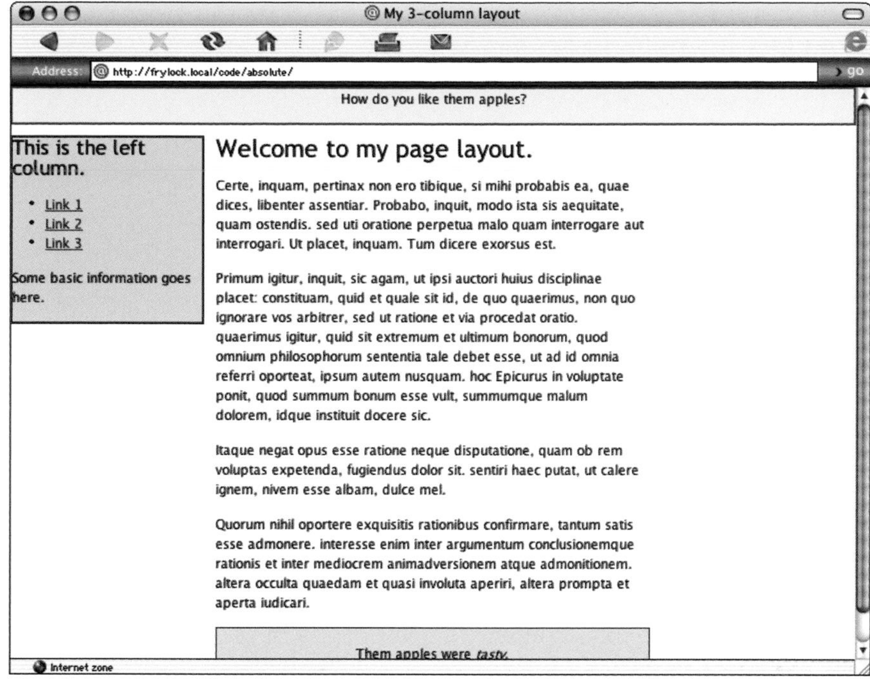


**Figure 9-23:** When in doubt, delete.

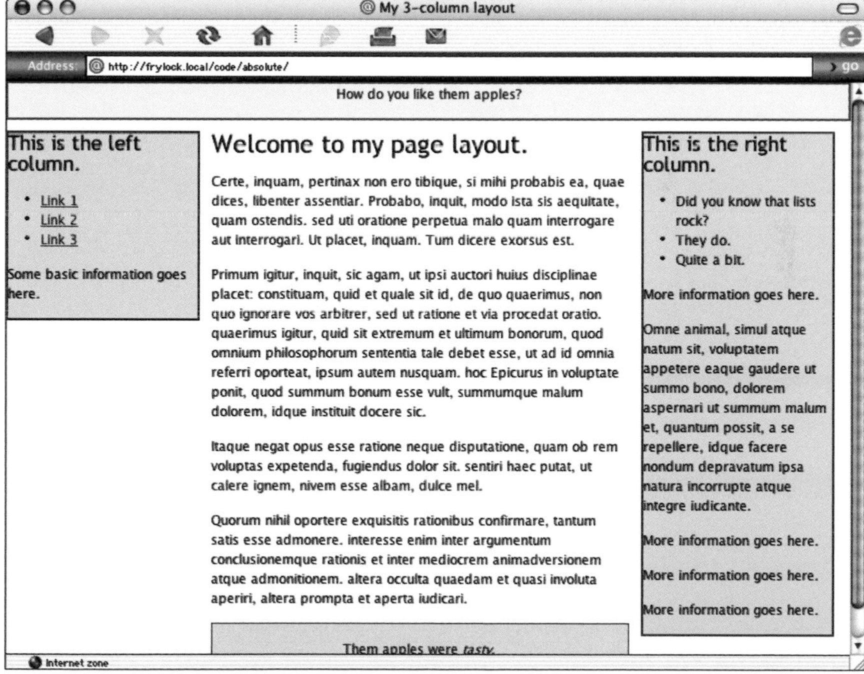


**Figure 9-24:** Changing the right property of our `#right` selector to 15 pixels removes the scroll bar, but the positioning is a bit off.

So, while you removed the scroll bar, the right-hand column is no longer flush against the edge of the window. If possible, you should fix this. Let's take a look at what you established so far:

1. Even though you have no margin set on the right `div`, IE5/Macintosh seems compelled to supply a "hidden" margin of 15 pixels.
2. Therefore, IE5/Macintosh sees `margin-right: 0;` as `margin-right: 15px;`.

From this, wouldn't `margin-right: 15px;` translate to `margin-right: 0;` in IE5/Macintosh-speak? Try editing the `#right` selector:

```
#right {
 position: absolute;
 right: 0;
 top: 0;
 width: 175px;
}
```

Now, see if you can't apply some IE-friendly fuzzy math:

```
#right {
 position: absolute;
 margin-right: -15px;
 right: 15px;
 top: 0;
 width: 175px;
}
```

Reload and see what happens (see Figure 9-25).

*Voilà!* With a workaround in place, things are looking sexy once again. By catering to IE5/Macintosh's rendering quirk, you restored order to that browser.

Furthermore, initial tests seem to indicate that these two new lines don't have any adverse effects on more well-behaved browsers. However, just to be safe, you can easily isolate the "hack" from the real rule:

```
#right {
 position: absolute;
 top: 0;
 right: 0;
 width: 175px;
}

/*\*//*/
#right {
 margin-right: -15px;
 right: 15px;
}
/**/
```

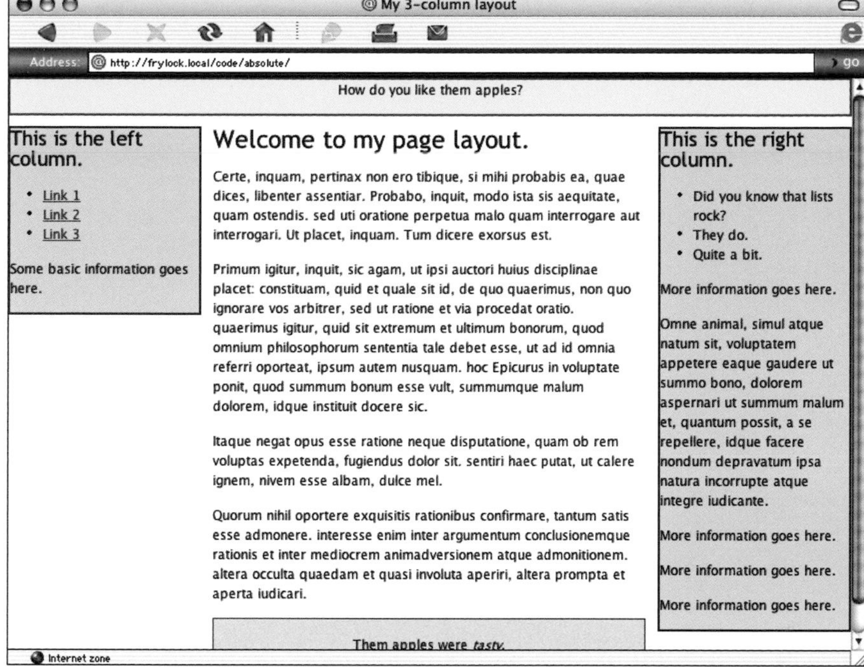


**Figure 9-25: With the hack applied, the horizontal scroll bar has been removed in IE5/Macintosh.**

The first rule is the original `#right` selector that you've been using throughout the chapter; the second rule contains the one-two property values that iron out the display issue in IE5/Macintosh. Surrounding that second rule, however, is the IE5/Macintosh Band Pass Filter (see Chapter 2 for more information). This odd-looking sequence of characters makes the second rule invisible to all user agents *but* IE5/Macintosh, ensuring that all of the browsers that get the math right won't be affected by a browser-specific hack.

One bug down, one to go — let's move on.

*As mentioned in Chapter 2, you can create separate browser-specific style sheets, each containing a host of hacks for that browser's idiosyncrasies. The benefit to (and details of) this approach is discussed in that chapter, but suffice it to say that it leaves your core CSS files free of hacks — and as a result, easier to maintain.*

## Windows Internet Explorer 5.x+

As Figure 9-26 shows, opening our test page in any of the Windows versions of Internet Explorer — 5.0, 5.5, or 6.0 — left much to be desired.

Having just fixed a bug with the `#right` block, you're now faced with the exact opposite problem! Well, almost. Rather than being flush to the leftmost edge of the window, the left-hand column seems to be stuck inside the content block. After going through some of the steps outlined in our IE5/Macintosh debugging session — delete/revise the markup, tweak the CSS — nothing seems to work.

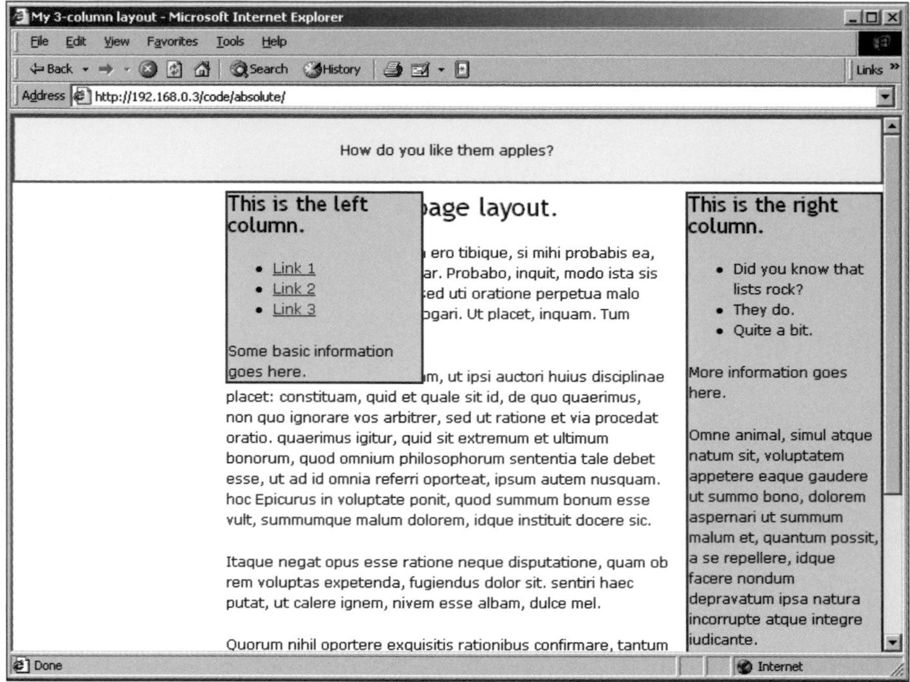


**Figure 9-26: Now that ain't right — or more specifically, that ain't *left*.**

Thankfully, a quick search online yields some information about a known IE/Windows bug. When dealing with a box without stated dimension (as you are with the container `div`), IE/Windows has some trouble initially drawing the box in such a way to sufficiently contain its descendant elements. To work around the issue, you must tell IE/Windows that, "Yes, the box does indeed have a stated dimension — and if it isn't too much trouble, you'd like it to draw it *properly*."

To that end, an IE-specific workaround known as *The Holly Hack* (`www.communitymx.com/abstract.cfm?cid=AAA7C45E7CD65D33` or `http://positioniseverything.net/articles.html`) comes to the rescue:

```
/* hide from Mac IE5 \*/
* html #container {
 height: 1%;
}
/* END hide from Mac IE5 */
```

Named after its creator, Holly Bergevin, the Holly Hack is in fact two hacks in one. The backslash at the end of the first comment is a hack that causes IE5/Macintosh to ignore everything up to the second closing comment line. The selector in the second begins with a universal selector (`*`), followed by `html`, which is in turn followed by a selector for the problematic element — here, the container `div`. As it turns out, IE browsers on both the Windows and Macintosh operating systems recognize an invisible element wrapped around the `<html>` element. Known as the *Star HTML Hack*, the use of the universal selector before the `html` selector will work only in IE browsers. Therefore, because IE5/Macintosh isn't affected by this particular layout bug, you used the comment hack in the first line to hide the rule from that browser.

With a height of 1 percent applied, see how your layout looks now (see **Figure 9-27**).

The 1 percent height rule managed to kickstart IE's buggy rendering engine. By supplying it with an initial (if microscopic) height for the container block, IE knows to expand that block to surround its descendants (which, honestly, it should anyway — but you don't have to wait for that browser to make your life easier).

After this bout of debugging, you determined that your three-column framework is holding up admirably in all the browsers you tested. However, what you built so far is missing one crucial component. Let's turn to the last component needed to round out your imitation of the Molly.com layout and put this three-column layout to bed.

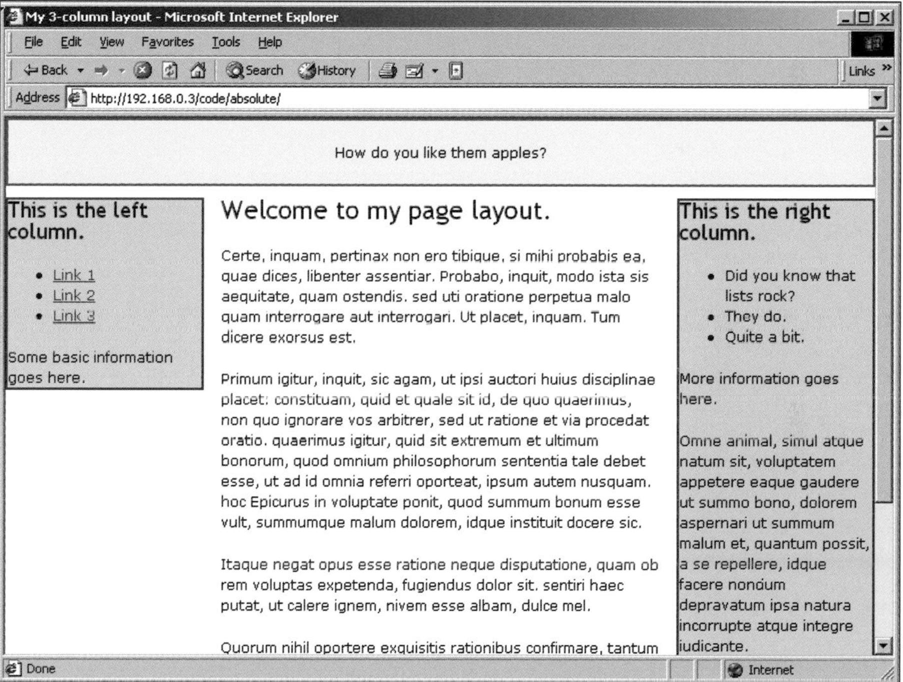


**Figure 9-27: One quick hack later, and you're cooking with gas once more.**

# Setting Some Boundaries: The max-width Property

The final piece is the flexible nature of the design. Currently, your layout expands to fill the entire width of the browser window, no matter how small (or wide) it may be. In larger windows, the lines of text in the fluid design can become almost unmanageably long, making it difficult to read.

`max-width` is a handy CSS property that does exactly what it says: It establishes the *maximum width* for a given element. Let's apply this property to your design and see what comes of it. Set the value upon a `max-width` of 1,000 pixels:

```
#header, #container {
 max-width: 1000px;
}
```

After refreshing, the difference might not be evident. However, once you begin to increase the width of your browser window, the property's effects are readily apparent (see Figure 9-28).

As the browser window expands or contracts, the design remains flexible enough to follow suit. However, once the width of the window exceeds 1,000 pixels (the value set in the `max-width` property), the page's layout stops scaling. With the `max-width` property, you place an implicit cap on the horizontal width of your page, ensuring a level of flexibility in your design that doesn't impede the ability of users to easily scan your content.

Unfortunately, `max-width` is a part of the style sheet specification that doesn't enjoy widespread browser support. Or, to be more specific, it enjoys incredibly robust support in your browser — unless, of course, your browser happens to be Internet Explorer. As of the writing of this book, the most prevalent browser on the planet turns a blind eye to this handy property, as well as other related properties such as `min-width`, `min-height`, and `max-height`. Given IE's inability to interpret them, each of these properties is relegated to the realm of the theoretical, or the best ideas you can't currently rely upon.

Thankfully, this lack of support doesn't prevent you from *using* these techniques. Instead, your design will fill the entire horizontal space of browsers that don't support the `max-width` property (see Figure 9-29).

*A number of workarounds are available online to force Internet Explorer to support useful CSS properties such as* `max-width` *(one example is* `http://svendtofte.com/code/max_width_in_ie`*). However, many of these solutions involve introducing IE-only properties into your CSS — be wary of this, as proprietary code will invalidate your style sheet and could adversely affect other, more compliant browsers.*

*Additionally, Dean Edwards has written "IE7"* (`http://dean.edwards.name/IE7`)*, a library of JavaScript modules that improve Internet Explorer 5+'s support for the CSS specification. As a JavaScript-only solution, Edwards' work has no chance of invalidating your style sheets. However, be sure to test and evaluate it fully before using it in a production environment.*

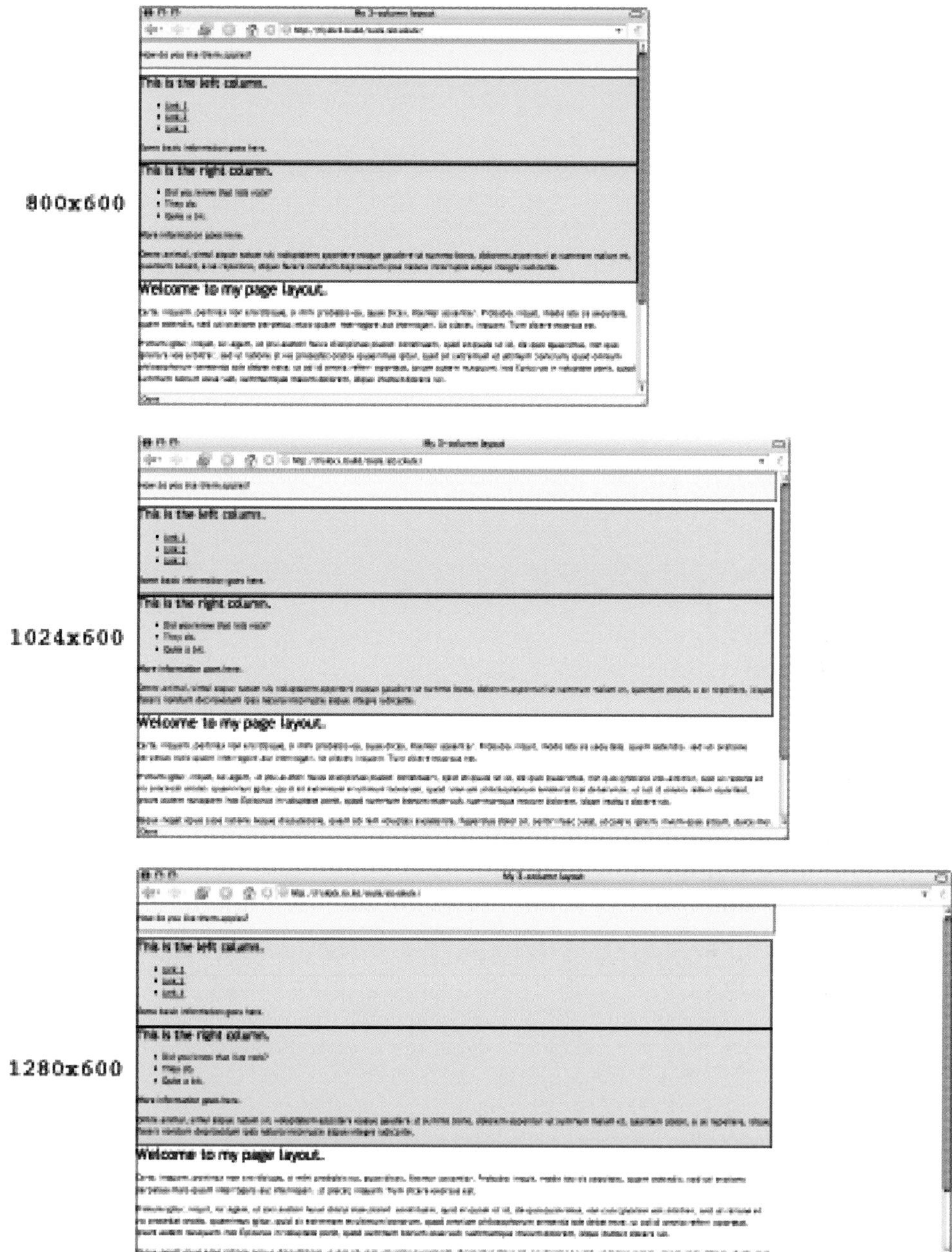


**Figure 9-28:** The `max-width` property places a cap on the width of the content area — do not pass "Go," do not collect $200.

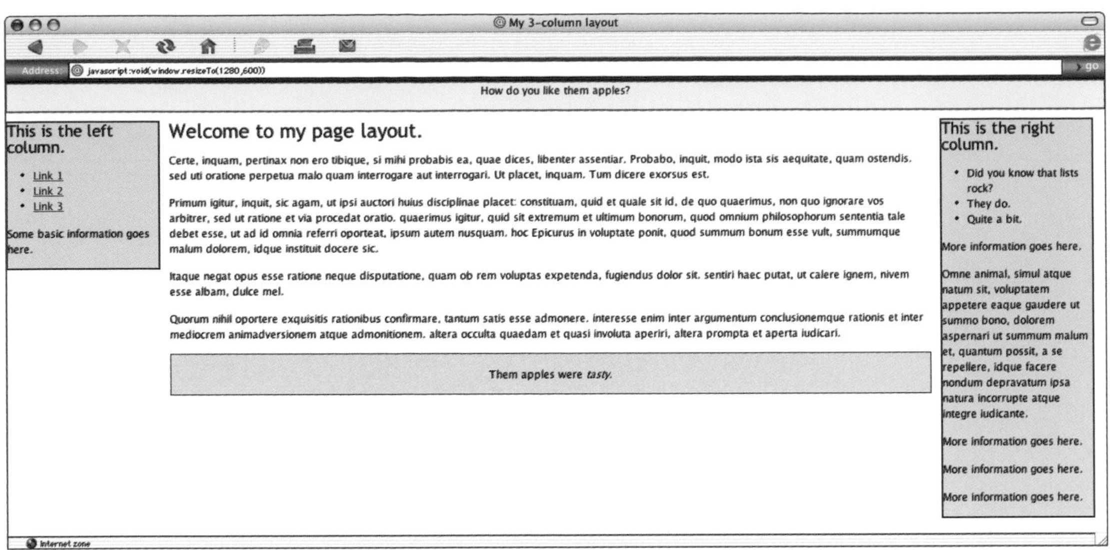


**Figure 9-29:** In browsers that don't respect the max-width CSS property (such as Internet Explorer on the Mac, shown here), the page layout will simply expand to the width of the window.

# Summary

Your whirlwind tour of the three-column layout began with a blank slate: the default, normal flow of an unstyled document. From there, you examined how CSS positioning could be used to override this default scheme and allow you to remove elements from their normal place in the document flow.

This understanding of absolute and relative positioning provided you with the building blocks for reconstructing a three-column layout. By using a combination of absolutely positioned blocks contained within a relatively positioned parent, you could create a flexible, three-column layout. And with a minimal amount of CSS hacking, you established a style foundation that's looking quite smart across all modern browsers, one that you can flesh out with additional content and information.

# HTML 4.01 Elements

Before you design with CSS, the content in a Web document must be marked up with HTML elements. To efficiently make use of CSS, those HTML elements must be used properly by placing the correct HTML element around the appropriate content.

The following table provides a listing of all the HTML elements in the 4.01 specification provided by the World Wide Web Consortium (W3C), the governing body that determines Web-related standards. The far-left column shows the name of the element. The next column indicates whether the element has a start tag. The next three columns describe the element in more detail. If the column has an "O," it means the part of the element is optional. "F" means forbidden, "E" means empty, and "D" means deprecated. The DTD column provides information on which Document Type Definition an element belongs in. If the element is found only in one kind of DTD, the key will either be "L" for Loose DTD or "F" for Frameset DTD. The final column provides a text description of the element.

| Name | Start Tag | End Tag | Empty | Deprecated | DTD | Description |
|---|---|---|---|---|---|---|
| A | | | | | | Anchor |
| ABBR | | | | | | Abbreviated form (for example, WWW, HTTP, and so on) |
| ACRONYM | | | | | | Indicates an acronym |
| ADDRESS | | | | | | Information on author |

*Continued*

| Name | Start Tag | End Tag | Empty | Deprecated | DTD | Description |
|---|---|---|---|---|---|---|
| APPLET | | | | D | L | Java applet |
| AREA | | F | E | | | Client-side image map area |
| B | | | | | | Bold text style |
| BASE | | F | E | | | Document base URI |
| BASEFONT | | F | E | D | L | Base font size |
| BDO | | | | | | I18N BiDi override |
| BIG | | | | | | Large text style |
| BLOCKQUOTE | | | | | | Long quotation |
| BODY | O | O | | | | Document body |
| BR | | F | E | | | Forced line break |
| BUTTON | | | | | | Push button |
| CAPTION | | | | | | Table caption |
| CENTER | | | | D | L | Centers content |
| CITE | | | | | | Citation |
| CODE | | | | | | Computer code fragment |
| COL | | F | E | | | Table column |
| COLGROUP | | O | | | | Table column group |
| DD | | O | | | | Definition description |
| DEL | | | | | | Deleted text |
| DFN | | | | | | Instance definition |
| DIR | | | | D | L | Directory list |
| DIV | | | | | | A division |
| DL | | | | | | Definition list |

| Name | Start Tag | End Tag | Empty | Deprecated | DTD | Description |
|---|---|---|---|---|---|---|
| DT | | O | | | | Definition term |
| EM | | | | | | Emphasis |
| FIELDSET | | | | | | Form control group |
| FONT | | | | D | L | Local change to font |
| FORM | | | | | | Interactive form |
| FRAME | | F | E | | F | Subwindow |
| FRAMESET | | | | | F | Frame container; replacement of body for frames |
| H1 | | | | | | Heading level 1 |
| H2 | | | | | | Heading level 2 |
| H3 | | | | | | Heading level 3 |
| H4 | | | | | | Heading level 4 |
| H5 | | | | | | Heading level 5 |
| H6 | | | | | | Heading level 6 |
| HEAD | O | O | | | | Document head |
| HR | | F | E | | | Horizontal rule |
| HTML | O | O | | | | Document root element |
| I | | | | | | Italic text style |
| IFRAME | | | | | L | Inline subwindow |
| IMG | | F | E | | | Embedded image |
| INPUT | | F | E | | | Form control |
| INS | | | | | | Inserted text |
| IFRAME | | | | | L | Inline subwindow |
| IMG | | F | E | | | Embedded image |

*Continued*

| Name | Start Tag | End Tag | Empty | Deprecated | DTD | Description |
|---|---|---|---|---|---|---|
| INPUT | | F | E | | | Form control |
| INS | | | | | | Inserted text |
| ISINDEX | | F | E | D | L | Single-line prompt |
| KBD | | | | | | Text to be entered by the user |
| LABEL | | | | | | Form field label text |
| LEGEND | | | | | | Fieldset legend |
| LI | | O | | | | List item |
| LINK | | F | E | | | A media-independent link |
| MAP | | | | | | Client-side image map |
| MENU | | | | D | L | Menu list |
| META | | F | E | | | Generic meta-information |
| NOFRAMES | | | | | F | Alternate content container for nonframe-based rendering |
| NOSCRIPT | | | | | | Alternate content container for nonscript-based rendering |
| OBJECT | | | | | | Generic embedded object |
| OL | | | | | | Ordered list |
| OPTGROUP | | | | | | Option group |
| OPTION | | O | | | | Selectable choice |
| P | | O | | | | Paragraph |
| PARAM | | F | E | | | Named property value |

| Name | Start Tag | End Tag | Empty | Deprecated | DTD | Description |
|---|---|---|---|---|---|---|
| PRE | | | | | | Preformatted text |
| Q | | | | | | Short inline quotation |
| S | | | | D | L | Strikethrough text style |
| SAMP | | | | | | Sample program output, scripts, and so on |
| SCRIPT | | | | | | Script statements |
| SELECT | | | | | | Option selector |
| SMALL | | | | | | Small text style |
| SPAN | | | | | | Generic language/ an inline style container |
| STRIKE | | | | D | L | Strikethrough text |
| STRONG | | | | | | Strong emphasis |
| STYLE | | | | | | Style info |
| SUB | | | | | | Subscript |
| SUP | | | | | | Superscript |
| TABLE | | | | | | Table container |
| TBODY | O | O | | | | Table body |
| TD | | O | | | | Table data cell |
| TEXTAREA | | | | | | Multiline text field |
| TFOOT | | O | | | | Table footer |
| TH | | O | | | | Table header cell |
| THEAD | | O | | | | Table header |
| TITLE | | | | | | Document title |

*Continued*

| Name | Start Tag | End Tag | Empty | Deprecated | DTD | Description |
|---|---|---|---|---|---|---|
| TR | | O | | | | Table row |
| TT | | | | | | Teletype or monospaced text style |
| U | | | | D | L | Underlined text style |
| UL | | | | | | Unordered list |
| VAR | | | | | | Instance of a variable or program argument |

# B

# Rules for HTML-to-XHTML Conversion

Hypertext Markup Language (HTML) is a simple language that led to the boom of the Web in the 1990s. However, its simplicity was also a roadblock to progress. The early success of HTML attracted a larger Web developer audience and spawned a desire to push the medium. HTML outgrew its simple upbringing.

For example, while placing images in a Web page is easy to do with HTML, placing the images in a specific location on a Web page is impossible without violating the intent of the `table` tag. Another example is placing the multimedia content in a Web page, which usually results in the use of invalid, proprietary elements and attributes.

In addition, HTML contains a limited set of elements and attributes. Other industries such as engineering or chemical companies couldn't mark up their formulas. Instead of writing an all-encompassing version of HTML, the W3C worked on Extensible Markup Language (XML), which is a flexible meta-language.

XML provides the framework for other markup languages to be created. Other industries can create their own markup languages rather than face a restrictive environment such as HTML.

However, for most Web developers who are familiar primarily with HTML, the major benefits of XML (creating new elements and specifying their treatment) are not important. Instead, the elements found in HTML will be of the most use.

The W3C reformulated HTML from the XML standard to create backward compatibility while making the language embrace the structure found in XML. XHTML is the essence of HTML defined in the XML syntax. In other words, XHTML is a set of rigid guidelines written to allow Web developers familiar with HTML to write valid XML documents without getting completely lost.

Yet, reworking content from HTML into XHTML creates headaches when developers move into a stricter coding environment. The XHTML syntax (or rules for coding) is less forgiving of coding mistakes than old-school HTML and browsers.

To help you achieve more solid understanding of coding XHTML correctly, this appendix serves as a guide to transition the Web developer from an old-school HTML developer to a proper XHTML user.

# The XML Declaration

No doubt as a Web developer you know the importance of having the `html` element at the top of your Web document. With XHTML you may place the following line above the `html` element:

```
<?xml version="1.0" encoding="iso-8859-1"?>
```

That line simply states that you are using `version 1.0` of XHML with the character set of `iso-8859-1`.

The XML declaration is recommended but not required. Because it's a simple line that goes at the top of your Web document, why wouldn't you include it? Well, here are some potential problems when using the XTML declaration:

- Some browsers might render the markup as it appears when you "view source" a Web page instead of rendering the document.
- Other browsers might parse the Web document as an XML tree instead of rendering the document.
- In Internet Explorer for Windows 6.0, the browser will display the Web document in quirks mode, even if the Web document is valid.
- If you use PHP to create dynamic pages, you might notice that the start of that line with the left bracket and question mark is how you begin writing PHP code. This code, if left as is in your PHP document, confuses your server, and it will not successfully parse your page. The workaround for this situation is to use the `echo` function in PHP at the start of the document to write out the first line:

  ```
  <?php echo "<?xml version=\"1.0\" encoding=\"iso-8859-1\"?>\n"; ?>
  ```

# Picking Your Comfort Level

XHTML comes in three different flavors: *strict*, *transitional*, and *frameset*. These varieties are based on three Document Type Definitions (DTDs). DTDs define XHTML and determine which elements and attributes are allowed and how they should be used. Think of a DTD as a dictionary of allowable terms for a certain document.

To create a valid XHTML document, you must include a `DOCTYPE` declaration, which makes up a line or two at the top of your document below the XML declaration (should you decide to use one). The line of code indicates what kind of DTD you are using and sets the groundwork for how the browser and validators should handle your content.

To define your Web document as *strict* means that you will follow the letter of the law as well as the spirit. You are a true believer in XHTML and no longer want to use any HTML elements that were used for presentation. With the *strict* DTD, you are using XHTML elements to mark up content and not to format the presentation of the page. Place the following line below the XML declaration but before the `html` element:

```
<!DOCTYPE html
 PUBLIC "-//W3C//DTD XHTML 1.0 Strict//EN"
 "http://www.w3.org/TR/xhtml1/DTD/xhtml1-strict.dtd">
```

*It may be difficult to read in lowercase, but in capital letters that's XHTML1, not XHTM11.*

The *transitional* DTD is best if you want to dive into XHTML but want some more freedom to use deprecated elements and attributes along the way, or to use certain classic HTML tags:

```
<!DOCTYPE html
 PUBLIC "-//W3C//DTD XHTML 1.0 Transitional//EN"
 "http://www.w3.org/TR/xhtml1/DTD/xhtml1-transitional.dtd">
```

The *frameset* DTD is for the Web documents that require you to use frames in your Web pages:

```
<!DOCTYPE html
 PUBLIC "-//W3C//DTD XHTML 1.0 Frameset//EN"
 "http://www.w3.org/TR/xhtml1/DTD/xhtml1-frameset.dtd">
```

The frameset DTD is to be used only in Web documents that contain the frameset . You do not need to use the frameset DTD for each Web document that composes a "frame" in a frameset. For those documents, you should use either a strict or transitional DTD.

# Rules for XHTML

Now that you have set up the XML declaration and the DTD, the next step is to properly format your Web document. The following sections cover how to properly mark up your content and use XHTML correctly.

## Don't Forget the Namespace Attribute

Stating what type of document type you're using at the top of the document indicates which elements and attributes are allowed in the document. Along with the `DOCTYPE` declaration, the namespace is an additional means of identifying your document's markup, in this case XHTML.

To identify the namespace, place what's called a *namespace attribute,* `xmlns`, in the `html` element, in the opening `html` tag:

```
<html xmlns="http://www.w3.org/1999/xhtml" lang="en">
```

## Quoting Attribute Values

All values for attributes in an element are required to be wrapped in quotation marks. So, you would not use this example:

```
<img src=file.gif width=133 height=133 />
```

Instead, follow this correct example:

```
<img src="file.gif" width="133" height="133" />
```

## No Attribute Minimization

For some elements in HTML (such as the horizontal rules tag, `hr`), attributes can be minimized, and simply listing the attribute name is valid:

```
<hr noshade />
```

In XHTML, however, there is no attribute minimization. When you are faced with an attribute that typically has never needed a value, set the value of the attribute to the name. In this example using the `hr` element, the value for the attribute `noshade` is `noshade`:

```
<hr noshade="noshade" />
```

## Terminating Empty Elements

Empty elements are elements that do not come in pairs (such as `img`, `br`, or `hr`).

Non-empty elements (such as `p` or `h2`) are fairly common in HTML. They are used for marking the starting and ending of content in a Web page. `p` tags indicate paragraphs, as this example shows:

```
<p>That's when I thought I should decline a second helping of her infamous
spaghetti and meatball salad.</p>
```

With XHTML, all elements — including empty ones — must be terminated.

To keep using empty elements in XHTML, empty elements must be modified slightly. Add a space and a forward slash at the end of the element:

```
<img src="file.gif" alt="Company logo" width="125" height="36" />
```

Note that including the space before the trailing slash isn't a requirement for the code to be valid but a technique to keep older browsers, such as Netscape Navigator 4, from failing to render the element.

## Cleaning Nests

Nesting elements properly is simple and should already be a part of any Web developer's practices. In the following line, the ending tag for the `strong` element is outside of the closing `p` element.

```
<p>That's when I thought I should <strong>decline a second helping of her infamous
spaghetti and meatball salad.</p></strong>
```

Whereas, this is the correct method for marking up the content:

```
<p>That's when I thought I should <strong>decline</strong> a second helping of her
infamous spaghetti and meatball salad.</p>
```

## XHTML with CSS and JavaScript Files

Associating CSS and JavaScript files is the preferred method by which you incorporate presentation and behaviors to your Web pages:

```
<script src="/js/validator.js" type="text/javascript"></script>
<link rel="stylesheet" href="/css/layout.css" type="text/css" />
```

If you must use internal JavaScript, wrap the code with the starting marker `<![CDATA[` and ending marker `]]>`.

```
<script type="text/javascript">
/* <![CDATA[ */
// Javascript goes here
/* ]]> */
</script>
```

## Lowercase Element and Attribute Names

All elements and attribute names in XHTML must be set in lowercase. This means you should not use all uppercase or mix uppercase and lowercase. The following are examples of incorrect usage:

```
<HTML> </HTML>
<Strong></Strong>
```

Following is an example of correct usage:

```
<body></body>
```

Using a mixture of lowercase and uppercase for the values of attributes is, of course, still valid:

```
<a href="IWantToBelieve.html">Photos of Aliens</a>
```

## Introduce ID When Using `name`

In XHTML the `name` attribute is deprecated and will be removed from the specification altogether in the future. In its place, you must use the `id` attribute. Until the `name` attribute is no longer a valid attribute, use `id` in addition to the `name` attribute:

```
<a name="admin" id="admin">Administration at CLC</a>
```

## Encode Ampersands

When you are using an ampersand (&) for the value of an attribute, be sure to use the character entity, `&`.

When encoding ampersands, and when working with dynamic pages, pass parameters through the URL string in the browser like this:

```
<a href="add-cart.html?isbn=9780470177082&amp;id=023">Add this item to your cart</a>
```

## When in Doubt, Validate

All of us are human, and all of us make mistakes with coding. To help point out troubles with XHTML or just to make sure what has been created is coded correctly, take your page to a validator such as `http://validator.w3.org` and test often.

Also, most WYSIWYG and some non-WYSIWYG Web authoring tools have built-in validators. Read the documentation that came with the software to learn more about them.

# C

# CSS 2.1 Properties

When marking up content with HTML, you must be aware of the elements that are at your disposal. The same goes for designing with CSS — you must be fully aware of the properties and their values to effectively design for the Web.

In this vein, the following table lists all the CSS 2.1 properties that are at your disposal. In the far left column is the name of the CSS property. Next are the values associated with that property and then the initial value. The next column states what HTML element that CSS property applies to. The Inherited column states whether the property can be inherited by other elements. The far right column indicates the applicable media group.

<table>
<tr><th>Name</th><th>Values</th><th>Initial Value</th><th>Applies to (Default: All)</th><th>Inherited</th><th>Media Groups</th></tr>
<tr><td>'azimuth'</td><td><angle> | [[ left-side | far-left | left | center-left | center | center-right | right | far-right | right-side ] || behind ] | leftwards | rightwards | inherit</td><td>center</td><td>All</td><td>Yes</td><td>Aural</td></tr>
<tr><td>'background-attachment'</td><td>scroll | fixed | inherit</td><td>scroll</td><td>All</td><td>No</td><td>Visual</td></tr>
<tr><td>'background-color'</td><td><color> | transparent | inherit</td><td>transparent</td><td>All</td><td>No</td><td>Visual</td></tr>
<tr><td>'background-image'</td><td><uri> | none | inherit</td><td>none</td><td>All</td><td>No</td><td>Visual</td></tr>
<tr><td>'background-position'</td><td>[ [ <percentage> | <length> | left | center | right ] [ <percentage> | <length> | top | center | bottom ]? ] | [ [ left | center | right ] || [ top | center | bottom ] ] | inherit</td><td>0% 0%</td><td>All</td><td>No</td><td>Visual</td></tr>
<tr><td>'background-repeat'</td><td>repeat | repeat-x | repeat-y | no-repeat | inherit</td><td>repeat</td><td>All</td><td>No</td><td>Visual</td></tr>
<tr><td>'background'</td><td>['background-color' || 'background-image' || 'background-repeat' || 'background-attachment' || 'background-position'] | inherit</td><td>Shorthand property; see individual properties</td><td>All</td><td>No</td><td>Visual</td></tr>
<tr><td>'border-collapse'</td><td>collapse | separate | inherit</td><td>separate</td><td>'table' and 'inline-table' elements</td><td>Yes</td><td>Visual</td></tr>
<tr><td>'border-color'</td><td>[ <color> | transparent ]{1,4} | inherit</td><td>Shorthand property; see individual properties</td><td>All</td><td>No</td><td>Visual</td></tr>
</table>

<table>
<tr><th>Name</th><th>Values</th><th>Initial Value</th><th>Applies to (Default: All)</th><th>Inherited</th><th>Media Groups</th></tr>
<tr><td>'border-spacing'</td><td><length> <length>? | inherit</td><td>0</td><td>'table' and 'inline-table' elements</td><td>Yes</td><td>Visual</td></tr>
<tr><td>'border-style'</td><td><border-style>{1,4} | inherit</td><td>Shorthand property; see individual properties</td><td>All</td><td>No</td><td>Visual</td></tr>
<tr><td>'border-top' 'border-right''border-bottom' 'border-left'</td><td>[ <border-width> || <border-style> || 'border-top-color' ] | inherit</td><td>Shorthand property; see individual properties</td><td>All</td><td>No</td><td>Visual</td></tr>
<tr><td>'border-top-color'<br>'border-right-color'<br>'border-bottom-color'<br>'border-left-color'</td><td><color> | transparent | inherit</td><td>The value of the 'color' property</td><td>All</td><td>No</td><td>Visual</td></tr>
<tr><td>'border-top-style'<br>'border-right-style'<br>'border-bottom-style'<br>'border-left-style'</td><td><border-style> | inherit</td><td>none</td><td>All</td><td>No</td><td>Visual</td></tr>
<tr><td>'border-top-width'<br>'border-right-width'<br>'border-bottom-width'<br>'border-left-width'</td><td><border-width> | inherit</td><td>medium</td><td>All</td><td>No</td><td>Visual</td></tr>
<tr><td>'border-width'</td><td><border-width>{1,4} | inherit</td><td>Shorthand property; see individual properties</td><td>All</td><td>No</td><td>Visual</td></tr>
</table>

<table>
<tr><th>Name</th><th>Values</th><th>Initial Value</th><th>Applies to (Default: All)</th><th>Inherited</th><th>Media Groups</th></tr>
<tr><td>'border'</td><td>[ <border-width> || <border-style> || 'border-top-color' ] | inherit</td><td>Shorthand property; see individual properties</td><td>All</td><td>No</td><td>Visual</td></tr>
<tr><td>'bottom'</td><td><length> | <percentage> | auto | inherit</td><td>auto</td><td>Positioned elements</td><td>No</td><td>Visual</td></tr>
<tr><td>'caption-side'</td><td>top | bottom | inherit</td><td>top</td><td>'table-caption' elements</td><td>Yes</td><td>Visual</td></tr>
<tr><td>'clear'</td><td>none | left | right | both | inherit</td><td>none</td><td>Block-level elements</td><td>No</td><td>Visual</td></tr>
<tr><td>'clip'</td><td><shape> | auto | inherit</td><td>auto</td><td>Absolutely positioned elements</td><td>No</td><td>Visual</td></tr>
<tr><td>'color'</td><td><color> | inherit</td><td>Depends on user agent</td><td>All</td><td>Yes</td><td>Visual</td></tr>
<tr><td>'content'</td><td>normal | [ <string> | <uri> | <counter> | attr(<identifier>) | open-quote | close-quote | no-open-quote | no-close-quote ]+ | inherit</td><td>normal</td><td>:before and :after pseudo-elements</td><td>No</td><td>All</td></tr>
<tr><td>'counter-increment'</td><td>[ <identifier> <integer>? ]+ | none | inherit</td><td>none</td><td>All</td><td>No</td><td>All</td></tr>
<tr><td>'counter-reset'</td><td>[ <identifier> <integer>? ]+ | none | inherit</td><td>none</td><td>All</td><td>No</td><td>All</td></tr>
<tr><td>'cue-after'</td><td><uri> | none | inherit</td><td>none</td><td>All</td><td>No</td><td>Aural</td></tr>
<tr><td>'cue-before'</td><td><uri> | none | inherit</td><td>none</td><td>All</td><td>No</td><td>Aural</td></tr>
</table>

<table>
<tr><th>Name</th><th>Values</th><th>Initial Value</th><th>Applies to (Default: All)</th><th>Inherited</th><th>Media Groups</th></tr>
<tr><td>'cue'</td><td>[ 'cue-before' || 'cue-after' ] | inherit</td><td>Shorthand property; see individual properties</td><td>All</td><td>No</td><td>Aural</td></tr>
<tr><td>'cursor'</td><td>[ [<uri> ,]* [ auto | crosshair | default | pointer | move | e-resize | ne-resize | nw-resize | n-resize | se-resize | sw-resize | s-resize | w-resize | text | wait | help | progress ] ] | inherit</td><td>auto</td><td>All</td><td>Yes</td><td>Visual, Inter-active</td></tr>
<tr><td>'direction'</td><td>ltr | rtl | inherit</td><td>ltr</td><td>All</td><td>Yes</td><td>Visual</td></tr>
<tr><td>'display'</td><td>inline | block | list-item | run-in | inline-block | table | inline-table | table-row-group | table-header-group | table-footer-group | table-row | table-column-group | table-column | table-cell | table-caption | none | inherit</td><td>inline</td><td>All</td><td>No</td><td>All</td></tr>
<tr><td>'elevation'</td><td><angle> | below | level | above | higher | lower | inherit</td><td>level</td><td>All</td><td>Yes</td><td>Aural</td></tr>
<tr><td>'empty-cells'</td><td>show | hide | inherit</td><td>show</td><td>'table-cell' elements</td><td>Yes</td><td>Visual</td></tr>
<tr><td>'float'</td><td>left | right | none | inherit</td><td>none</td><td>All but positioned elements and generated content</td><td>No</td><td>Visual</td></tr>
<tr><td>'font-family'</td><td>[[ <family-name> | <generic-family> ] [, <family-name>| <generic-family>]* ] | inherit</td><td>Depends on user agent</td><td>All</td><td>Yes</td><td>Visual</td></tr>
</table>

<table>
<tr><th>Name</th><th>Values</th><th>Initial Value</th><th>Applies to (Default: All)</th><th>Inherited</th><th>Media Groups</th></tr>
<tr><td>'font-size'</td><td><absolute-size> | <relative-size> | <length> | <percentage> | inherit</td><td>medium</td><td>All</td><td>Yes</td><td>Visual</td></tr>
<tr><td>'font-style'</td><td>normal | italic | oblique | inherit</td><td>normal</td><td>All</td><td>Yes</td><td>Visual</td></tr>
<tr><td>'font-variant'</td><td>normal | small-caps | inherit</td><td>normal</td><td>All</td><td>Yes</td><td>Visual</td></tr>
<tr><td>'font-weight'</td><td>normal | bold | bolder | lighter | 100 | 200 | 300 | 400 | 500 | 600 | 700 | 800 | 900 | inherit</td><td>normal</td><td>All</td><td>Yes</td><td>Visual</td></tr>
<tr><td>'font'</td><td>[ [ 'font-style' || 'font-variant' || 'font-weight' ]? 'font-size' [ / 'line-height' ]? 'font-family' ] | caption | icon | menu | message-box | small-caption | status-bar | inherit</td><td>Shorthand property; see individual properties</td><td>All</td><td>Yes</td><td>Visual</td></tr>
<tr><td>'height'</td><td><length> | <percentage> | auto | inherit</td><td>auto</td><td>All elements but non-replaced inline elements, table columns, and column groups</td><td>No</td><td>Visual</td></tr>
<tr><td>'left'</td><td><length> | <percentage> | auto | inherit</td><td>auto</td><td>Positioned elements</td><td>No</td><td>Visual</td></tr>
<tr><td>'letter-spacing'</td><td>normal | <length> | inherit</td><td>normal</td><td>All</td><td>Yes</td><td>Visual</td></tr>
<tr><td>'line-height'</td><td>normal | <number> | <length> | <percentage> | inherit</td><td>normal</td><td>All</td><td>Yes</td><td>Visual</td></tr>
<tr><td>'list-style-image'</td><td><uri> | none | inherit</td><td>none</td><td>Elements with 'display: list-item'</td><td>Yes</td><td>Visual</td></tr>
</table>

<table>
<tr><th>Name</th><th>Values</th><th>Initial Value</th><th>Applies to (Default: All)</th><th>Inherited</th><th>Media Groups</th></tr>
<tr><td>'list-style-position'</td><td>inside | outside | inherit</td><td>outside</td><td>Elements with 'display: list-item'</td><td>Yes</td><td>Visual</td></tr>
<tr><td>'list-style-type'</td><td>disc | circle | square | decimal | decimal-leading-zero | lower-roman | upper-roman | lower-greek | lower-latin | upper-latin | armenian | georgian | none | inherit</td><td>disc</td><td>Elements with 'display: list-item'</td><td>Yes</td><td>Visual</td></tr>
<tr><td>'list-style'</td><td>[ 'list-style-type' || 'list-style-position' || 'list-style-image' ] | inherit</td><td>Shorthand property; see individual properties</td><td>Elements with 'display: list-item'</td><td>Yes</td><td>Visual</td></tr>
<tr><td>'margin-right'<br>'margin-left'</td><td><margin-width> | inherit</td><td>0</td><td>All elements except elements with table display types other than table and inline-table</td><td>No</td><td>Visual</td></tr>
<tr><td>'margin-top'<br>'margin-bottom'</td><td><margin-width> | inherit</td><td>0</td><td>All elements except elements with table display types other than table and inline-table</td><td>No</td><td>Visual</td></tr>
<tr><td>'margin'</td><td><margin-width>{1,4} | inherit</td><td>Shorthand property; see individual properties</td><td>All elements except elements with table display types other than table and inline-table</td><td>No</td><td>Visual</td></tr>
</table>

| Name | Values | Initial Value | Applies to (Default: All) | Inherited | Media Groups |
|---|---|---|---|---|---|
| 'max-height' | <length> \| <percentage> \| none \| inherit | none | All elements except non-replaced inline elements and table elements | No | Visual |
| 'max-width' | <length> \| <percentage> \| none \| inherit | none | All elements except non-replaced inline elements and table elements | No | Visual |
| 'min-height' | <length> \| <percentage> \| inherit | 0 | All elements except non-replaced inline elements and table elements | No | Visual |
| 'min-width' | <length> \| <percentage> \| inherit | 0 | All elements except non-replaced inline elements and table elements | No | Visual |
| 'orphans' | <integer> \| inherit | 2 | Block-level elements | Yes | Visual, Paged |
| 'outline-color' | <color> \| invert \| inherit | invert | All | No | Visual, Interactive |
| 'outline-style' | <border-style> \| inherit | none | All | No | Visual, Interactive |

<table>
<tr><th>Name</th><th>Values</th><th>Initial Value</th><th>Applies to (Default: All)</th><th>Inherited</th><th>Media Groups</th></tr>
<tr><td>'outline-width'</td><td><border-width> | inherit</td><td>medium</td><td>All</td><td>No</td><td>Visual, Interactive</td></tr>
<tr><td>'outline'</td><td>[ 'outline-color' || 'outline-style' || 'outline-width' ] | inherit</td><td>Shorthand property; see individual properties</td><td>All</td><td>No</td><td>Visual, Interactive</td></tr>
<tr><td>'overflow'</td><td>visible | hidden | scroll | auto | inherit</td><td>visible</td><td>Block-level and replaced elements, table cells, inline blocks</td><td>No</td><td>Visual</td></tr>
<tr><td>'padding-top'<br>'padding-right'<br>'padding-bottom'<br>'padding-left'</td><td><padding-width> | inherit</td><td>0</td><td>All elements except elements with table display types other than table, inline-table, and table-cell</td><td>No</td><td>Visual</td></tr>
<tr><td>'padding'</td><td><padding-width>{1,4} | inherit</td><td>Shorthand property; see individual properties</td><td>All elements except elements with table display types other than table, inline-table, and table-cell</td><td>No</td><td>Visual</td></tr>
<tr><td>'page-break-after'</td><td>auto | always | avoid | left | right | inherit</td><td>auto</td><td>Block-level elements</td><td>No</td><td>Visual, Paged</td></tr>
<tr><td>'page-break-before'</td><td>auto | always | avoid | left | right | inherit</td><td>auto</td><td>Block-level elements</td><td>No</td><td>Visual, Paged</td></tr>
</table>

<table>
<tr><th>Name</th><th>Values</th><th>Initial Value</th><th>Applies to (Default: All)</th><th>Inherited</th><th>Media Groups</th></tr>
<tr><td>'page-break-inside'</td><td>avoid | auto | inherit</td><td>auto</td><td>Block-level elements</td><td>Yes</td><td>Visual, Paged</td></tr>
<tr><td>'pause-after'</td><td><time> | <percentage> | inherit</td><td>0</td><td>All</td><td>No</td><td>Aural</td></tr>
<tr><td>'pause-before'</td><td><time> | <percentage> | inherit</td><td>0</td><td>All</td><td>No</td><td>Aural</td></tr>
<tr><td>'pause'</td><td>[ [<time> | <percentage>]{1,2} ] | inherit</td><td>Shorthand property; see individual properties</td><td>All</td><td>No</td><td>Aural</td></tr>
<tr><td>'pitch-range'</td><td><number> | inherit</td><td>50</td><td>All</td><td>Yes</td><td>Aural</td></tr>
<tr><td>'pitch'</td><td><frequency> | x-low | low | medium | high | x-high | inherit</td><td>medium</td><td>All</td><td>Yes</td><td>Aural</td></tr>
<tr><td>'play-during'</td><td><uri> [ mix || repeat ]? | auto | none | inherit</td><td>auto</td><td>All</td><td>No</td><td>Aural</td></tr>
<tr><td>'position'</td><td>static | relative | absolute | fixed | inherit</td><td>static</td><td>All</td><td>No</td><td>Visual</td></tr>
<tr><td>'quotes'</td><td>[<string> <string>]+ | none | inherit</td><td>Depends on user agent</td><td>All</td><td>Yes</td><td>Visual</td></tr>
<tr><td>'richness'</td><td><number> | inherit</td><td>50</td><td>All</td><td>Yes</td><td>Aural</td></tr>
<tr><td>'right'</td><td><length> | <percentage> | auto | inherit</td><td>auto</td><td>Positioned elements</td><td>No</td><td>Visual</td></tr>
<tr><td>'speak-header'</td><td>once | always | inherit</td><td>once</td><td>Elements that have table header information</td><td>Yes</td><td>Aural</td></tr>
</table>

<table>
<tr><th>Name</th><th>Values</th><th>Initial Value</th><th>Applies to (Default: All)</th><th>Inherited</th><th>Media Groups</th></tr>
<tr><td>'speak-numeral'</td><td>digits | continuous | inherit</td><td>continuous</td><td>All</td><td>Yes</td><td>Aural</td></tr>
<tr><td>'speak-punctuation'</td><td>code | none | inherit</td><td>none</td><td>All</td><td>Yes</td><td>Aural</td></tr>
<tr><td>'speak'</td><td>normal | none | spell-out | inherit</td><td>normal</td><td>All</td><td>Yes</td><td>Aural</td></tr>
<tr><td>'speech-rate'</td><td><number> | x-slow | slow | medium | fast | x-fast | faster | slower | inherit</td><td>medium</td><td>All</td><td>Yes</td><td>Aural</td></tr>
<tr><td>'stress'</td><td><number> | inherit</td><td>50</td><td>All</td><td>Yes</td><td>Aural</td></tr>
<tr><td>'table-layout'</td><td>auto | fixed | inherit</td><td>auto</td><td>'table' and 'inline-table' elements</td><td>No</td><td>Visual</td></tr>
<tr><td>'text-align'</td><td>left | right | center | justify | inherit</td><td>'left' if 'direction' is 'ltr'; 'right' if 'direction' is 'rtl'</td><td>Block-level elements, table cells, and inline blocks</td><td>Yes</td><td>Visual</td></tr>
<tr><td>'text-decoration'</td><td>none | [ underline || overline || line-through || blink ] | inherit</td><td>none</td><td>All</td><td>No</td><td>Visual</td></tr>
<tr><td>'text-indent'</td><td><length> | <percentage> | inherit</td><td>0</td><td>Block-level elements, table cells, and inline blocks</td><td>Yes</td><td>Visual</td></tr>
<tr><td>'text-transform'</td><td>capitalize | uppercase | lowercase | none | inherit</td><td>none</td><td>All</td><td>Yes</td><td>Visual</td></tr>
<tr><td>'top'</td><td><length> | <percentage> | auto | inherit</td><td>auto</td><td>Positioned elements</td><td>No</td><td>Visual</td></tr>
</table>

<table>
<tr><th>Name</th><th>Values</th><th>Initial Value</th><th>Applies to (Default: All)</th><th>Inherited</th><th>Media Groups</th></tr>
<tr><td>'unicode-bidi'</td><td>normal | embed | bidi-override | inherit</td><td>normal</td><td>All elements, but see prose</td><td>No</td><td>Visual</td></tr>
<tr><td>'vertical-align'</td><td>baseline | sub | super | top | text-top | middle | bottom | text-bottom | <percentage> | <length> | inherit</td><td>baseline</td><td>Inline-level and 'table-cell' elements</td><td>No</td><td>Visual</td></tr>
<tr><td>'visibility'</td><td>visible | hidden | collapse | inherit</td><td>visible</td><td>All</td><td>Yes</td><td>Visual</td></tr>
<tr><td>'voice-family'</td><td>[[<specific-voice> | <generic-voice> ],]* [<specific-voice> | <generic-voice> ] | inherit</td><td>Depends on user agent</td><td>All</td><td>Yes</td><td>Aural</td></tr>
<tr><td>'volume'</td><td><number> | <percentage> | silent | x-soft | soft | medium | loud | x-loud | inherit</td><td>medium</td><td>All</td><td>Yes</td><td>Aural</td></tr>
<tr><td>'white-space'</td><td>normal | pre | nowrap | pre-wrap | pre-line | inherit</td><td>normal</td><td>All</td><td>Yes</td><td>Visual</td></tr>
<tr><td>'widows'</td><td><integer> | inherit</td><td>2</td><td>Block-level elements</td><td>Yes</td><td>Visual, Paged</td></tr>
<tr><td>'width'</td><td><length> | <percentage> | auto | inherit</td><td>auto</td><td>All elements but non-replaced inline elements, table rows, and row groups</td><td>No</td><td>Visual</td></tr>
<tr><td>'word-spacing'</td><td>normal | <length> | inherit</td><td>normal</td><td>All</td><td>Yes</td><td>Visual</td></tr>
<tr><td>'z-index'</td><td>auto | <integer> | inherit</td><td>auto</td><td>Positioned elements</td><td>No</td><td>Visual</td></tr>
</table>

# CSS Troubleshooting Guide

Even after staring at the monitor for what seems like hours, does everything appear fine in the code, but not when you press the Refresh button?

Relax.

CSS beginners and gurus alike have all been through this. Use this troubleshooting guide to save you from Refresh frustrations.

## Validation

When you run into a problem, the first thing that must be done is ensure that your HTML and CSS syntax are correct. The syntax that Adobe Dreamweaver or Microsoft Expression generates can hide code while your design still needs to be checked.

If your Web development software does not come with its own validators (check your software's documentation for details), be sure to set the preferences so the Web development software excludes proprietary elements, such as `center`, so that the validator is checking the standard DTD.

This section describes Web sites for HTML and CSS validation.

### HTML

For HTML validation service as shown in Figure D-1, see `http://validator.w3.org`.

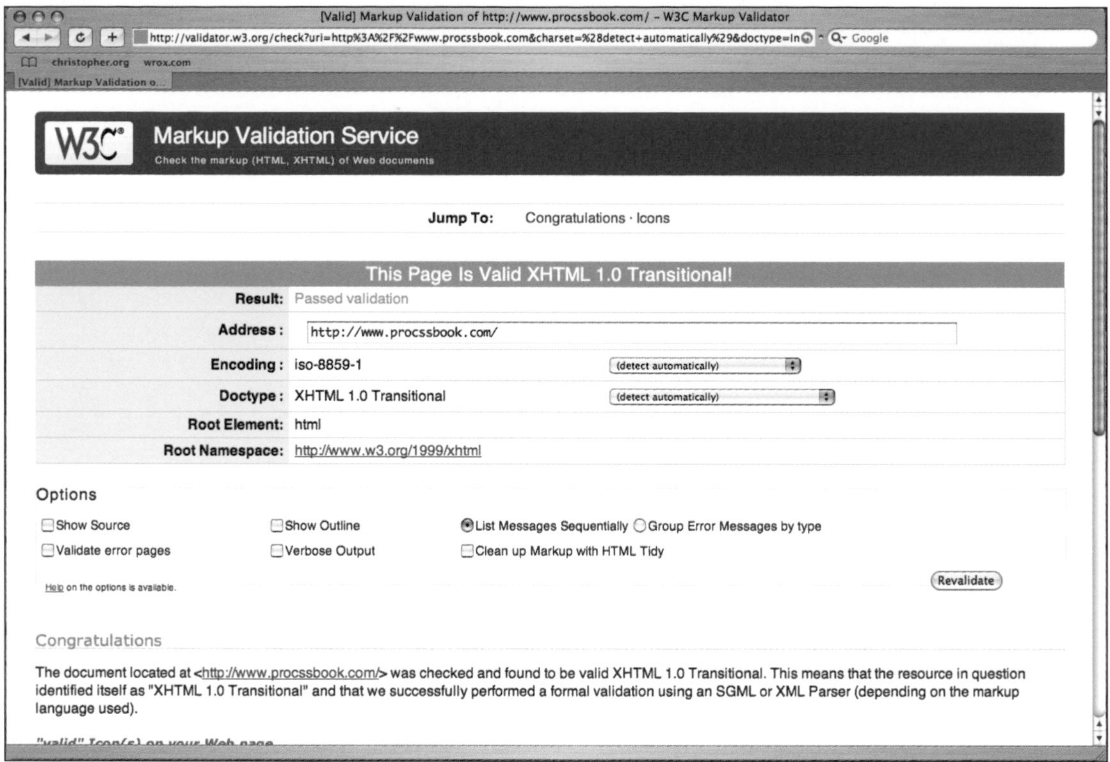


**Figure D-1: The HTML validator from W3C.**

Once at this site, enter into the form the URL of the page that is causing you trouble. If you use the URL, make sure that the Web address is actually visible on the Web, meaning that the file is not behind a firewall or a password-protected zone such as an intranet. If your HTML file falls into one of those categories, use the upload feature provided by the validation service.

*For information about HTML elements, see Appendix A. If you need information about how to convert HTML to XHTML, see Appendix B.*

# CSS

For a CSS validation service as shown in Figure D-2, see `http://jigsaw.w3.org/css-validator`.

Like the HTML validator, validation can be conducted through the submission of a URL or uploading a style sheet file. Be sure not to submit a file that includes both CSS and HTML because that confuses the validator, which is reason enough for automatic validation failure.

Another option to test CSS syntax is to copy and paste the code in the direct input form located at the bottom of the page. This option might be best suited for your needs — and might be a bit faster too — if your CSS is not accessible on the Web or if your file is actually an HTML file with some CSS code.

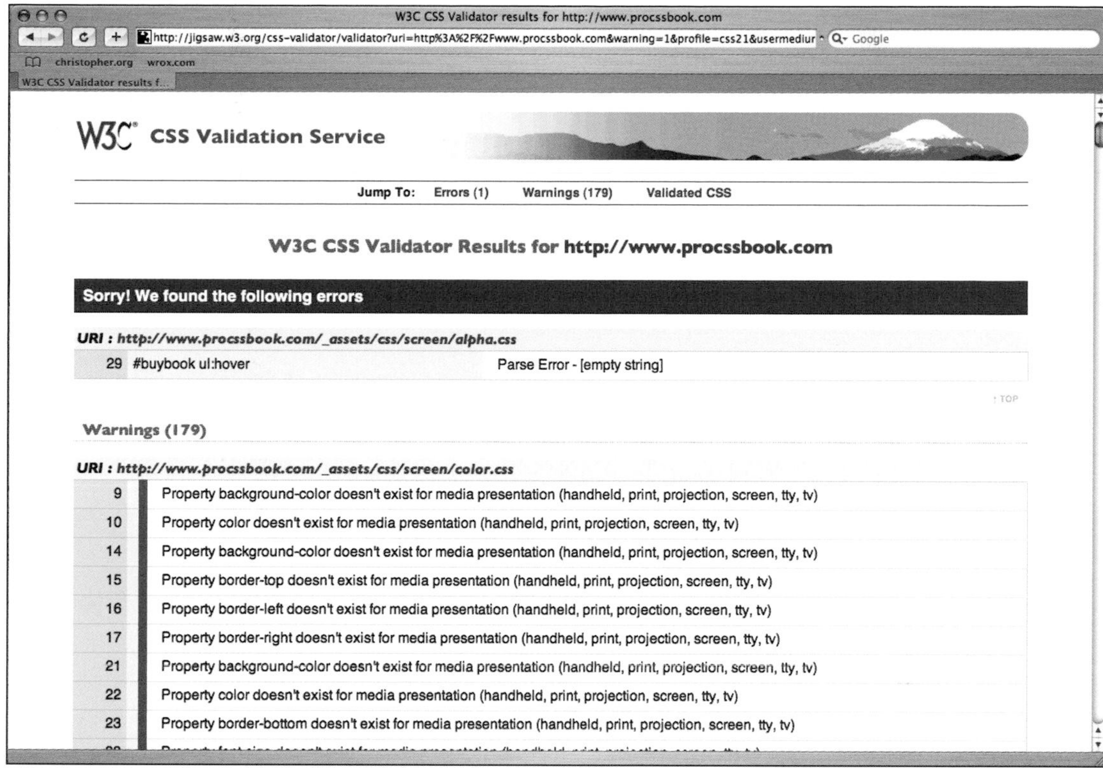


**Figure D-2: The CSS validator from W3C.**

# Manipulating the Elements

At this stage, the syntax is accurate, but that doesn't mean much. Even if your French is spot on, you could still find yourself *accurately* ordering your aunt's handbag for lunch to the bewilderment of your waiter at an outdoor café near the Louvre: *Je voudrais le sac à main de ma tante pour le déjeuner.*

The next move is direct manipulation of the CSS itself. Use one or a combination of the following techniques to help isolate your CSS problems.

## Zeroing Out the Padding and Margins

The default style sheet used by browsers places default values for margins and paddings on block-level elements. To ensure that those default values are not interfering with your design, set the margin and padding for the block-level elements to zero.

A fast, easy way to zero out the padding and margins is to use the universal selector like this:

```
* {
 margin: 0;
 padding: 0;
}
```

Then, place that CSS rule at the start of the style sheet. This allows other CSS rules that have values for padding, margin, or both in the style sheet to override the effects of zeroing out the padding or margins.

*For a more robust set of CSS rules for zeroing out the default styles set by browsers, try Eric Meyer's style sheet for resetting (see* `http://meyerweb.com/eric/thoughts/2007/05/01/reset-reloaded`*). In fact, try to include CSS resetting as part of your normal workflow process.*

Look for any changes in your page design and make any required adjustments.

## Applying Color to Borders and Backgrounds

Highlight the CSS rules you are working on to see if they are indeed the design elements of the Web page that are causing the problems. Once you have identified the right problematic element, you can move on to fixing the problem. You can highlight them by applying color to a border or background.

Here's an example:

```
#content #navigation {
 border: 1px solid red;
}
```

This CSS rule creates a red border around the specified block-level element to better see it in the page design. If you have too much red in the design to notice a red outline, try blue or green, or simply change the background color instead, as shown here:

```
#content #navigation {
 background-color: green;
}
```

## Placing Variations in Property Values

After finding the CSS that is causing problems, the next step is to adjust the values of the properties. Is the problem that the padding is too much in one browser? Is the font size too small in another browser?

When placing different values than the ones you are using, start with cartoonish large amounts. For example, change 25px for padding to 2500px to see if the design breaks as you know it should.

Then the next moves should be small. Use tiny increments, for example, in adjusting font sizes from 0.8 em to .81 em.

## Playing Hide and Seek

The way in which you write CSS rules can also cause problems. CSS is set up to allow certain properties and their values to become inherited by their children. For example, if you set the font properties for the `body` element, child elements within that body will take up those characteristics as well.

While CSS has built-in conflict resolution with cascade, inheritance, and specificity, the rules you write may inherit values you don't want. If you think this is the case, simply comment out unnecessary property and value pairs from problematic CSS rules and refresh the page design to look for changes. In the following snippet, placing the letter "x" in front of the font-size declaration block keeps it from being displayed.

```
#downloads h2 {
 font-family: "Myriad Pro", "Myriad Web", sans-serif;
 xfont-size: 1.4em;
 text-transform: uppercase;
}
```

## Validating Again

At this stage, the CSS might have been rewritten, revised, or completely mangled during the troubleshooting process. Check the validation again, just to be sure nothing was missed.

# Bringing in Outside Help

If you haven't found the cause of the CSS problem, it's time to seek outside help. Use the following resources to investigate the problem or ask for help.

## Web Site Resources

This section provides information on some key resources.

### positioniseverything.net

Maybe the problem isn't the CSS, but instead it is the browser. For a list and explanation of modern browser bugs, check out www.positioniseverything.net.

### Web Developer Toolbar

If you use Netscape 7+, Mozilla, or Firefox browsers for development, run (don't walk) to Chris Pederick's browser extension called Web Developer at www.chrispederick.com/work/firefox/webdeveloper.

Offering numerous features that benefit the Web designer and CSS wrangler, this an indispensable tool when troubleshooting CSS. Some of the tips mentioned in this troubleshooting guide can be implemented with the click of the button on the Web Developer's toolbar, rather than editing code by hand.

### Firebug

Another Firefox extension, Firebug allows users to inspect HTML, CSS, and JavaScript components of a Web document (see http://getfirebug.com). In addition to inspecting the code, Firebug allows you to make on-the-fly edits and see how they affect the document in real time.

## Mailing Lists

This section provides information on some key mailing list resources.

## css-discuss

If everything else has not worked to your satisfaction, try the kind folks at css-discuss. This is a mailing list dedicated to practical discussions of CSS-enabled design. The people on the mailing list range from professionals to beginners, so chances are they have seen every problem you might encounter.

For more information on the list and instructions on how to join, see `www.css-discuss.org`.

## Babble List

Geared to advanced Web design issues, the Babble List community offers a lively exchange of information, resources, theories, and practices of designers and developers, including CSS development. The overall goal is to hone skills and share visions of where this new medium is going.

For more information on the list and instructions on how to join, see `www.babblelist.com`.

# Index

## SYMBOLS AND NUMBERS



## A



## B

# C

# I